THE YALE-HOOVER SERIES ON STALIN, STALINISM, AND THE COLD WAR

GULAG TOWN, COMPANY TOWN

FORCED LABOR AND ITS LEGACY IN VORKUTA

ALAN BARENBERG

Hoover Institution
Stanford University
Stanford, California

Yale UNIVERSITY PRESS
New Haven and London

Yale University Press books may be purchased in quantity for educational, business, or promotional use. For information, please e-mail sales.press@yale.edu (U.S. office) or sales@yaleup.co.uk (U.K. office).

Set in Sabon type by Newgen North America.
Printed in the United States of America.

ISBN: 978-0-300-17944-6 (cloth)

Library of Congress Control Number: 2014934005

A catalogue record for this book is available from the British Library.

This paper meets the requirements of ANSI/NISO Z39.48–1992 (Permanence of Paper).

10 9 8 7 6 5 4 3 2 1

For Abby

The shape of contemporary man and the world in which he lives takes on other features when seen from Vorkuta.
—Bernhard Roeder, *Katorga*

Contents

Acknowledgments

During the decade in which I have been working on this project, I have amassed a considerable number of personal, professional, and intellectual debts. The research and writing of this book were generously funded by a number of fellowships and institutions, including the Council on Library and Information Resources, the Eurasia Program of the Social Science Research Council with funds provided by the State Department under the Program for Research and Training on Eastern Europe and the Independent States of the Former Soviet Union (Title VIII), the University of Chicago, Auburn University, and Columbus State University. I wish to express my special thanks to the Office of the Provost, the College of Arts and Sciences, and the Department of History at Texas Tech University, which funded and supported the final stages of research and manuscript preparation. I, and not the organizations listed above, am solely responsible for the opinions and content expressed herein.

During my undergraduate and graduate studies I had the good fortune of working with exceptional teachers and mentors. At Carleton College, Adeeb Khalid and Diane Nemec Ignashev provided me with a strong foundation in Russian history and language, respectively. Both saw me through my first attempts to examine the history of the Soviet Gulag. At the University of Chicago, I was privileged to work with a remarkable group of PhD advisors, each of whom had a profound effect on my development as a scholar. Ron Suny provided valuable advice in framing this project. Michael Geyer provided a steady stream of off-the-wall ideas, encouraging me to stretch conceptual limits. The late, great Richard Hellie taught me the value of quantitative methods and the (University of) *Chicago Manual of Style*. He was a constant source of encouragement throughout my graduate career. Sheila Fitzpatrick was an incomparable teacher and PhD advisor. From her I learned not only the ins and outs of Soviet history, but also the craft of research. Her advice, probing questions, and good humor helped shepherd me through my time at the University of Chicago and beyond.

The research for this project was carried out at numerous libraries and archives in Chicago, IL, Cambridge, MA, San Marino and Stanford, CA, USA; London, England; and Moscow, Syktyvkar, and Vorkuta, Russia. Although they are too numerous to mention here, I wish to express my gratitude to all the librarians and archivists who assisted my research. June Pachuta Ferris, the Slavic bibliographer at the University of Chicago, facilitated my research by acquiring large amounts of print and microfilm materials, in addition to supporting my fellowship applications. Dina Nikolaevna Nokhotovich at the State Archive of the Russian Federation patiently answered my many queries. The staff at the Vorkuta Museum-Exhibition Center plied me with manuscripts, photographs, and tea during my visit there, for which I will be eternally grateful. Thanks especially to Galina Vasil'evna Trukhina and Galina Vasil'evna Spitsyna for their assistance and hospitality. I owe a special debt of gratitude to the staff at the Hoover Institution Library and Archives at Stanford University, who facilitated the completion of critical research in the book's late stages.

Many friends and colleagues in Russia gave freely of their time and expertise to help shepherd me through life and research in Moscow and the Komi Republic. In particular, I wish to thank Al'bert Efimovich Bernshtein, Olesya Aksenovskaia, Evgeniia Alekseevna Khaidarova, Andrei Kustyshev, Vladimir Nikolaevich Mastrakov, Kostia Meshcherikov, Nikolai Alekseevich Morozov, Khristina Petkova, Anatolii Aleksandrovich Popov, and Mikhail Borisovich Rogachev. I owe a particular debt to the anonymous interview subjects who patiently discussed difficult chapters of their past with me. Semyon Samuilovich Vilensky and Liudmila Sergeevna Novikova in Moscow played a particularly important role in helping this project see the light of day. They shared with me not only their considerable expertise, but also their friendship and hospitality.

This book has benefited greatly from feedback that I received at various conferences and workshops at the University of Chicago, the University of California-Berkeley, the University of Birmingham, the University of Manchester, the Davis Center for Russian and Eurasian studies at Harvard University, the Havighurst Center of Russian and Post-Soviet Studies at Miami University Ohio, The Hoover Archives China-Russia Summer Workshop, and various meetings of the International Council for Central and East European Studies, the Midwest Russian History Workshop, and the Association for Slavic and East European and Eurasian Studies. Special thanks are due to Klaus Gestwa, Yoram Gorlizki, Mark Harrison, Michael Jakobson, and Amir Weiner for providing key feedback at important stages of this project. Paul Josephson read and gave helpful advice on the epilogue. Marc Elie gave freely of his considerable knowledge on all things relating to ex-prisoners and the Gulag under Khrushchev. Tim Johnston, Rosa Magnusdottir, Jenny Smith, and Ben Tromly helped make a long stint in Moscow bearable. Wilson Bell has proven to be a good friend and a generous colleague ever since we met and discovered how much our work overlapped. Lynne Viola has been a constant source of sensible advice and a tireless champion of this project. The anonymous readers for Yale University Press read the manuscript carefully and offered useful criticism and advice. Whatever flaws remain, their insights have resulted in a stronger, more readable book.

The University of Chicago served as an incomparable environment in which to develop my ideas and present my research. Comments and criticism received at the Russian Studies and Modern European History Workshops profoundly influenced this book's development. In particular, I wish to thank Josh Arthurs, Edward Cohn, John Deak, Mark Edele, Emma Gilligan, Rachel Green, Charles Hachten, Cameron Hawkins, Steve Harris, Brian LaPierre, Tania Maync, Mie Nakachi, Chris Raffensperger, Oscar Sanchez, Andrew Sloin, and Ben Zajicek. The history department at Auburn University gave me a temporary home after leaving Chicago. At Columbus State University, I was welcomed by faculty, staff, and students alike. Special thanks are due to Patty Chappel, Alice Pate (now of Kennesaw State University), and John

Ellisor for their friendship and support during my time there. Numerous friends and colleagues at Texas Tech University have helped make West Texas my home (in a real and a scholarly sense) since I arrived in 2009. I wish to thank all my remarkable colleagues in the history department for making Texas Tech an exceptional place to work. In particular, Aliza Wong provided excellent advice on reframing my dissertation as a book, and Randy McBee ensured that I had the time and resources to complete this project. Peggy Ariaz, Nina Pruitt, Mayela Guardiola, and Debbie Shelfer in the department office were patient with my many requests. My Russian Studies colleagues Erin Collopy, Tony Qualin, and Frank Thames provided stimulating discussions over Wednesday night margaritas.

Parts of chapter 1 first appeared in the articles "Tiede ja asuttaminen varhairsessa Gulagissa," *Idäntutkimus* (Finnish Review of East European Studies) 4 (2010): 33–45, and "'Discovering' Vorkuta: Science and Colonization in the Early Gulag," *Gulag Studies* 4 (2011): 21–40. Parts of chapters 1, 2, and 4 first appeared in the article "Prisoners without Borders: *Zazonniki* and the Transformation of Vorkuta after Stalin," *Jahrbücher für Geschichte Osteuropas* 57, no. 4 (2009): 513–34. Parts of chapter 6 first appeared in the article "From Prisoners to Citizens? Ex-Prisoners in Vorkuta during the Thaw" in *The Thaw: Soviet Society and Culture in the 1950s and 1960s* (University of Toronto Press, 2013), 143–75. I am grateful to the publishers for their kind permission to reprint parts of these articles here.

The process of transforming the manuscript into a published book has been a smooth one thanks to the staff at Yale University Press. Vadim Staklo, now of George Mason University, guided the project from proposal to manuscript. William Frucht, Jaya Chaterjee, and Margaret Otzel took up the reins and made sure the book proceeded quickly through final submission and production. Mary Petrusewicz copyedited the manuscript with great care. I am especially thankful to Paul Gregory, the editor of the Yale-Hoover Series on Stalin, Stalinism, and the Cold War, for his encouragement, support, and timely advice. Thanks to Bill Nelson for preparing the map.

Finally, I wish to thank my family for their patience, love, and support during the long journey this book has taken. My mother, Judy Cole, and my brother, Michael Barenberg, provided love, support, and advice throughout the process. My wife, Abby Swingen, has shared every step of the process with me. She has gone far beyond the call of duty, not only supporting me through ups and downs, but also reading many successive drafts of all parts of this book with care. Her insights and advice helped bring a fresh perspective to the many questions and problems that arose. This book is dedicated to her. Ruby, our daughter, has also played a key role in helping this book see the light of day. Ever since she arrived on the scene, she has been a sustaining source of laughter, love, and inspiration.

Abbreviations and Glossary

Counterrevolutionary	Prisoner convicted under Article 58 of the Soviet Criminal Code.
Gorispolkom	City Council.
Gorkom	City Committee of the Communist Party.
ITR	Engineering and technical workers.
Katorga	Hard-labor regime.
Katorzhnik	Prisoner subject to a hard-labor regime.
Komi ASSR/Republic	Komi Autonomous Soviet Socialist Republic. After the collapse of the Soviet Union, known as the Komi Republic.
Komsomol	Communist Youth League
Kulak	"Fist." Term for so-called rich peasants targeted for expropriation, arrest, and/or exile during collectivization.
KVU	Vorkutaugol', Vorkuta Coal Mining Trust.
KGB	Committee on State Security.
MinIust	Ministry of Justice.
MUP	Ministry of Coal Industry.
MVD	Ministry of Internal Affairs. Succeeded NKVD.

NKVD	People's Commissariat of Internal Affairs. Succeeded OGPU.
Northern Pechora main line	Rail line connecting Kotlas and Vorkuta.
Obkom	Oblast' Committee of the Communist Party.
OGPU	Unified State Political Administration.
Okruzhentsy	The "encircled." Refers to Red Army soldiers captured by the enemy during the Second World War.
Orgnabor	Organized recruitment.
Pechora krai	Territory in the area of the Pechora River and its basin.
Politotdel	Political Department. Communist Party organization in a Soviet corrective labor camp.
Rechlag	River Camp. "Special" camp located in Vorkuta, 1948–1954.
RSFSR	Russian Soviet Federated Socialist Republic
Severnyi krai	Northern Territory, 1929–1937.
Sevpechlag	Northern Pechora Camp, 1940–1950. Camp dedicated to building the northern portion of the Northern Pechora main line.
Sovmin	Council of Ministers of the Soviet Union. Succeeded Sovnarkom.
Sovnarkom	Council of People's Commissars of the Soviet Union.
Ukhtpechlag	Ukhta-Pechora Camp. Created from Ukhta Expedition in 1931. Reorganized into smaller camps in 1938.
Vorkutlag	Vorkuta Camp. Created as Vorkutpechlag (Vorkuta Pechora Camp) in 1938. Became a "corrective labor colony" in 1960.

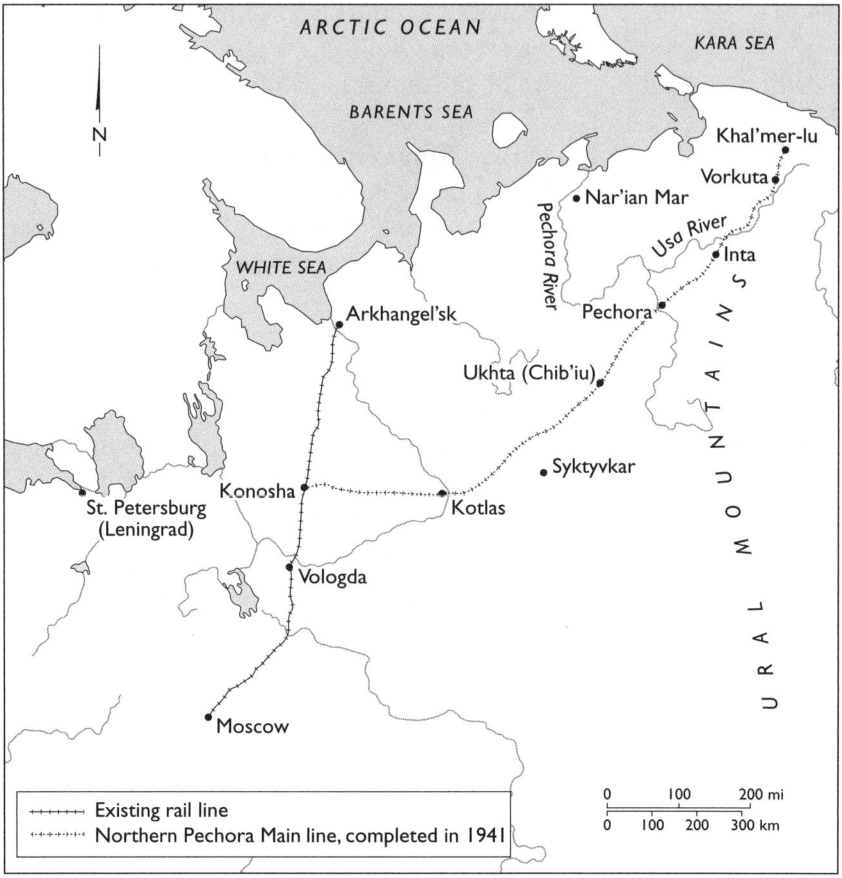

Map of Northwestern USSR with Transportation Routes to Vorkuta. Copyright © 2014 by Bill Nelson.

Introduction

A mine is an iceberg. Scholars maintain that an iceberg shows only one-fifth of its mass, whereas four-fifths are insidiously hidden underwater.
—*Unnamed Soviet writer, as quoted in Valentin Griner,* Poslednye dni bab'ego leto

ON 21 DECEMBER 1961, the Vorkuta city council (*Gorispolkom*) made a decision that starkly changed the landscape of one of the Soviet Union's largest Arctic cities. On that day, the council passed a resolution calling for the removal of a monument to Stalin from its pedestal in Moscow square, one of the city's central public spaces (figure 0.1). After the bronze statue was carted away, it was replaced by a monument dedicated to former Leningrad party chief Sergei Kirov, which had been located in a square a few blocks away.[1] Now Kirov would stand on the square at the intersection of Moscow and Miner streets, at the very heart of the city, surrounded by its architectural jewels, examples of Stalinist neoclassical style. After presiding over the square for nearly two decades, Stalin disappeared from public sight, presumably to be stored at the city's metalworking factory before being melted down at a later date.

The decision to remove the Stalin monument did not come out of the blue, nor was it the result of local initiative. It was part of the process of de-Stalinization that marked the reign of Stalin's successor, Nikita Khrushchev. The removal followed the decisions of the Twenty-second Party Congress that had taken place in Moscow in October 1961. At the Congress, Khrushchev renewed the criticism of Stalin that he had begun five years earlier in his so-called secret speech at the Twentieth

Figure 0.1. Stalin Monument, Moscow Square, Vorkuta, 1958. Photograph courtesy of Vorkuta Museum-Exhibition Center.

Party Congress.[2] Stalin's body was soon removed from the mausoleum on Red Square, where it had been lying in state with Lenin since 1953, and buried beside the Kremlin wall nearby. Although the new burial site was public, it was a clear ritual demotion. In the following months, streets, factories, even entire cities that had been named after Stalin were renamed. Monuments to the leader around the country were removed. Thus, swapping Stalin for Kirov in Vorkuta was a local manifestation of a national campaign.

Just as Khrushchev's renewed criticism of Stalin during the Twenty-second Party Congress was meant to establish a new, stable, post-Stalinist order, Stalin's removal from his place in Vorkuta's main square was intended to mark a new beginning.[3] Indeed, the event appears to be an important dividing point between two very different incarnations of the city. Vorkuta's first life was as one of the deadliest parts of the Soviet Gulag, a network of prisons, camps, colonies, and exile settlements that was an integral part of the Soviet system.[4] The camp in Vorkuta was established at the beginning of the 1930s as a tiny, remote outpost on the banks of the Vorkuta River, the first attempt to systematically exploit the extensive reserves of the Pechora coal basin, the largest coalfield in European Russia. By the late 1930s and early 1940s it had become one of the fastest-growing and deadliest prison camp complexes in the Soviet Union. Driven by a seemingly limitless supply of prisoners and a boundless hunger for coal during wartime and postwar reconstruction, the *Vorkutinskii lager'* ("Vorkuta camp," better known as Vorkutlag) and its twin *Rechnoi lager'* ("river camp," better known as Rechlag) saw approximately half a million prisoners pass through their gates by the middle of the 1950s. The Vorkuta camp complex held those considered to be the Soviet Union's most dangerous criminals in some of the most brutal conditions in the Gulag. Even according to the Gulag's own records, which tended to underestimate mortality, at least twenty thousand prisoners died there between 1942 and 1954.[5]

But Vorkuta was not just a prison camp complex. It was also a Soviet company town. Officially incorporated in 1943, by the time of Stalin's death ten years later there were roughly as many people living in the city as in the camp complex. When Stalin's monument was removed in December 1961, the city already had over 183,000 residents, making it the largest city in the Komi ASSR.[6] The citizenry, which consisted not only of former prisoners and exiles but also of young recruits from all over the Soviet Union, worked to support what had become a significant source of coal for northwestern Russia. By 1965, the area's mines were producing just over 12 million tons of bituminous coal per year.[7] In 1975, the largest coal mine in Europe, *Vorgashor,* with a projected annual output of 4.5 million tons of coal per year, was completed.[8] By this time, Vorkuta had become a desirable place for those seeking social mobility, as various subsidies and bonuses made it possible to secure a comfortable retirement after a relatively short working career. The city itself became something of a Soviet showpiece: as a thriving industrial city in the tundra, Vorkuta came to embody the Soviet Union's stunning achievements in settling the Far North.

These two incarnations of Vorkuta are often treated as separate entities. Take, for example, the 2001 *Encyclopedia of the Komi Republic,* where "Vorkuta" and the "Vorkuta camp of the NKVD-MVD SSSR" are given separate entries whose content does not overlap whatsoever.[9] On some levels, such an approach makes a great deal of sense, since the city of Vorkuta and the camp complex were, on paper at least, completely separate, with different "residents" and institutions, and occupying different geographical spaces.[10] Further, the two periods of Vorkuta's history were separated by momentous political, social, and economic changes. Such changes included the renunciation of mass terror, the release of millions of prisoners from the Gulag, and the fundamental transformation of the Soviet Union's prison camp system. The removal of Stalin's monument in December 1961 was indicative of a series of upheavals and reforms after Stalin's death in 1953 that transformed Vorkuta in significant ways. The Vorkuta of 1961 hardly resembled the city even a decade earlier.

Yet there were significant continuities between the two incarnations of Vorkuta as well. People, institutions, and practices all provide connections between these two periods, reaching across seemingly impermeable boundaries. Although tens of thousands of prisoners left Vorkuta after their release from the camps in the 1950s, never to return, thousands of others remained as workers in the new company town. Many became long-term city residents. Indeed, by the turn of the twenty-first century there remained a small but significant group of former prisoners living in the city. There were institutional continuities as well. The coal mining trust that was responsible for the management of Vorkuta's mines from the 1950s until the 1990s was created in the 1940s to operate alongside the prison camp complex. Although its organization, personnel, and place within national bureaucratic structures changed significantly in the 1950s, much nevertheless remained the same in the way that it operated on the ground. There were also significant continuities in social practices that bridged the chasm of post-

Stalin-era reforms. The structure of families, neighborhoods, and labor collectives retained influences from the camp complex for decades. Thus, both continuity and change marked Vorkuta and the experiences of its residents from the 1930s until the late Soviet era.

This book examines the social and economic history of Vorkuta from the founding of the first prison camp outpost on the banks of the Vorkuta River in the early 1930s until the first decade of the twenty-first century. In doing so, it attempts to reassemble its fragmented history. It examines the experiences of various groups that made up the population of the city over its eighty-odd years of existence, including prisoners, exiles, former prisoners, Gulag officials, Komsomol volunteers, demobilized soldiers, and free migrants. Whenever possible, the stories of these groups are told through the lives of individuals. The narrative of Vorkuta in the twentieth and twenty-first centuries is also one of how the Soviet Union (and post-Soviet Russia) sought to exploit natural resources of its vast hinterlands. The project of turning the Pechora coal basin into a major mining center began as an exercise in internal colonization, with prisoners and exiles serving as involuntary settlers.[11] Although development strategies shifted significantly over the ensuing decades, enthusiasm and commitment for transforming one of the most extreme natural environments in all of Russia into a modern Soviet city did not wane. It was not until the collapse of the Soviet Union in 1991 and subsequent economic reforms that the city's continued growth and very existence came into question.

By examining Soviet history through the story of one particular camp complex and city, this book provides a ground-level perspective of many of the most significant processes and transformations that took place during the Soviet era. Such an approach has both advantages and disadvantages. Focusing on a relatively small geographic area allows one to be more ambitious chronologically, so that Vorkuta can be examined in the broad sweep of Soviet and post-Soviet history. While scholarly monographs often put the year 1953 near the beginning or end of a narrative about the Stalin or post-Stalin eras, here the death of Stalin is placed in the middle. This allows one to closely examine threads of continuity and change across the Stalinist and post-Stalin divide. In so doing, this study offers new insights into the grand, subtle, and often unexpected ways that Stalin's death changed, or did not change, the lives of Soviet citizens. Further, the local focus allows one to discern phenomena and processes that are easily overlooked when examining national or regional histories. This is particularly true, for example, when analyzing the fate of ex-prisoners after Stalin's death. It is difficult to understand how they adapted to civilian life in the Soviet Union without understanding locally embedded social networks and a broad range of informal social practices. As local studies by historians such as Stephen Kotkin and Kate Brown have shown, examining the history of a single city or place can lead to profound insights about the nature of the Soviet experience.[12]

There are, of course, serious limitations to what one can learn from a local study. Vorkuta, after all, was only one of tens of thousands of Soviet cities. Further, there are elements of its history that make it exceptional, including its remote location and extreme natural environment, the fact that its settlement began in the Stalin era, and the close ties of its history to the rise of a vast system of forced labor. Clearly, Vorkuta cannot be considered a typical Soviet city. Nevertheless, some of the very characteristics that make it exceptional also make it very useful to study, as they make certain phenomena easier to recognize and understand. For example, Vorkuta was built in the remote tundra that had never been settled, part of a large area where Nenets reindeer herders brought their stock during summer migration.[13] Thus, the location makes it a good case for examining how Soviet leaders sought to transform space through colonization and forced labor, but also reveals the limitations in what the state could accomplish toward this end. The story of Vorkuta is, on the one hand, the story of a particular place. Yet, when properly placed in the broader context of Soviet history, it can reveal a great deal about the nature of the Soviet Union that is easily overlooked in larger-scale studies.

SPACE AND IDENTITY IN THE GULAG TOWN

In addition to problematizing the temporal boundaries between the Stalin and post-Stalin eras, this book reexamines the nature of space and identity in the Soviet Union, particularly in the many parts of the Soviet Union where the Gulag played an important role. As such, it is part of the new wave of scholarship arguing that the Gulag was more closely connected to Soviet society than was previously thought. Until the 1990s, most scholars of the Soviet Gulag tended to follow the approach advanced by Aleksandr Solzhenitsyn in his landmark work *The Gulag Archipelago*. For him, the Gulag was another world, separated from the rest of the Soviet Union by "all kinds of walls and fences made of rotting wood, rammed earth, bricks, concrete, iron railings."[14] Once someone passed from freedom to imprisonment, from one world into the other, there was no opportunity to cross back to the other side, at least not until one was released once and for all. They were, in a sense, two different realities that did not overlap. As is clear from the title of his grandiose work on the Gulag, if not always from the details related within its pages, Solzhenitsyn defined the relationship between the Gulag and Soviet society using the metaphor of the archipelago: Soviet prison camps and exile colonies were islands separated from the mainland of Soviet society. This metaphor of the Gulag as an "archipelago" has had a remarkably long life, and has been a fundamental assumption of many works on Soviet terror and imprisonment ever since.[15]

However, over the past two decades new approaches and new sources have led scholars to reexamine the nature of the Gulag and its place in Soviet society. Once access to the Soviet archives improved significantly in the late 1980s and early 1990s, researchers began to discover details about life in the Gulag that had not been so apparent previously. For example, access to official statistical data from the Gulag revealed that 20–40 percent of the total population of camps and colonies were released every year, even at the height of Stalinist terror.[16] This led historian Golfo Alexopoulos to conclude that the Gulag operated on a "revolving door" system of frequent arrests and frequent releases.[17] The discovery of the enormous scale of the system of "special settlements" for de-kulakized peasants has led historians like Lynne Viola to expand the conceptual boundaries of the system, demonstrating that such settlements (what Viola calls "the other archipelago") made up one of the key institutions of the system.[18] Making extensive use of new kinds of sources, such as individual prisoner files and the records of the "cultural-educational department," Steven Barnes has argued that the Gulag was an institution thoroughly imbued with Soviet ideology that was seen to play a fundamental role in the construction of a Soviet civilization. Rather than simply serving to isolate perceived enemies and provide slave labor, he argues that the overarching purpose of the Gulag was to reclaim society's margins whenever possible, and to exclude and destroy those determined to be irredeemable.[19] Wilson Bell and I have both noted the presence in camp records and memoirs of frequent contacts between prisoners and non-prisoners, leading to arguments that the borders between the inside and the outside of the Gulag were far more permeable than previously thought.[20]

This book argues that the Gulag was closely connected to Soviet society at large. In fact, it demonstrates that it was an integral part of that society. Rather than treat the camp and the city as separate entities, this work examines the Gulag town as a whole, emphasizing economic connections and social relationships in particular. Whereas much work on the Gulag emphasizes the clear distinction between the world of the "zone" (*zona*) and the outside, this book problematizes the notion that barbed wire and other barriers made the world of the city and the world of the camp spatially distinct.[21] The territories occupied by Soviet prison camps were not always enclosed. Particularly in the early life of camp complexes, there were few physical barriers between the zone and the outside. Borders were frequently moved, and spaces could be easily redesignated. Even well-established and clearly delineated borders were regularly crossed by both prisoners and non-prisoners, both as a result of everyday practices in the Gulag and extraordinary privileges given to certain prisoners. Thus, spatial relationships in the Gulag town were far more complex and unstable than previously thought.[22]

The same can be said about social relationships, status, and identity. Permeable borders allowed personal relationships to span the barbed wire, whether between coworkers, friends, family members, or sexual partners. Despite the existence and enforcement of regulations designed to limit such relationships, they were in fact a systemic and integral part of the Gulag. Following the work of Russian sociologist Vladimir Il'in, this book argues that the population of the Gulag town was part of a complex social hierarchy where one's place was determined by a wide range of factors.[23] As was the case throughout Soviet society, social status was to a large degree ascribed by the state.[24] But other factors, including informal social relationships and local authorities' willingness to sidestep or ignore official regulations, meant that official hierarchies were subverted in significant ways. In practice, the majority of non-prisoners living in Vorkuta occupied a position in the social hierarchy that was in many ways indistinguishable from most prisoners. It was even possible, though rare, for prisoners to occupy a significantly higher position in the social hierarchy than most non-prisoners. Hierarchies of political, economic, and social status certainly existed in the Gulag town, and the gap between how those on the top of the hierarchy and those on the bottom lived was enormous. Nevertheless, social status was far more complex and nuanced than a simple division between city residents on the one hand and prisoners on the other. Thus, this book seeks to reconceptualize the nature of identity and status within the Gulag and in the communities that surrounded camp complexes.

One of the implications of this approach to status and identity is that the straightforward distinction between "free" workers (*vol'nonaemnye*) and prisoners (*zakliuchennye*) that one often encounters in archival documents and memoirs, and in much of the historiography of the Gulag, falls short of being able to describe the social intricacy of camp complexes and their surrounding communities. Rather than divide the population of the Gulag town into "free" people and prisoners, this book seeks to place individuals and groups along a continuum of status ranging from those on the one end who had the most freedom of movement and access to goods and services to those on the other who had the least.[25] This method follows the conclusions of historians Sheila Fitzpatrick and Donald Filtzer, who separately argued that "free" labor could hardly have existed under Stalin, particularly from 1940 until 1953.[26] Thus, rather than distinguish between "free" and "unfree" people I use the terms "prisoners" and "non-prisoners" throughout this book. Even these categories oversimplify an incredibly complex social structure, as individuals and groups within these categories were ascribed a wide spectrum of political, social, and economic statuses. However, the primary fault line running through the population of Vorkuta city was between those who were incarcerated and those who were not.

FROM GULAG TOWN TO COMPANY TOWN

In 1943, at the height of the Second World War, Vorkutlag director Mikhail Mal'tsev initiated the process of having the small settlement of non-prisoners that grew beside the camp officially designated as a city. While at first the community existed more on paper than it did in physical space, it grew steadily while remaining closely intertwined with, and heavily dependent on, the camp complex. But over the course of the 1950s, the city began to acquire its own political and economic institutions, housing, and public spaces. At the same time, the camp complex shrank considerably, as mass prisoner releases and a radical shift in Soviet penal policy left Vorkutlag only a fraction of its former size. Thus, the company town rose where the Gulag town had once stood. The second half of this book examines this transformation that began in the 1950s, extended into the heyday of the company town during late socialism, and concluded with its near collapse in the first two decades of post-Soviet Russia.

What defined Vorkuta as a Soviet company town? Like its counterparts in other parts of the Soviet Union and even in the United States, it was shaped by a utopian vision bent on creating a rationally planned environment that would alleviate many urban ills and result in a happy, productive community.[27] Thus, in the 1950s, copious attention was paid to rebuilding the city along a rational plan, with broad boulevards, comfortable parks, and functional, modern buildings. Yet, as in the case of other Soviet company towns, the realization of the ambitious vision of planners was complicated by chaos, shortages, and the usual inefficiencies of the Soviet command economy.[28] Further, the new city was built alongside remnants of the camps, including barbed wire, watchtowers, and the ubiquitous low-slung, dilapidated barracks. Although the plan was to replace camp construction with new buildings erected using the most advanced methods and technologies, the reality was that camp barracks built in the 1940s remained in use until the 1990s. The physical legacy of the camps was difficult to escape.

The same was true for the institutional framework of the Gulag town. Camp chiefs and managers from the top to the bottom of the political hierarchy in Vorkutlag had spent decades exercising virtually unlimited authority over prisoners and exiles. Arbitrariness, cruelty, and violence were a reality of daily life in the city. Personnel and practices did not change overnight, and much of the way that the company town was run, and the way that citizens were treated, was strongly influenced by precedents set in the 1930s and 1940s. Former camp officials retained a significant presence in all major city institutions well into the 1960s. This continuity of personnel reinforced and magnified many tendencies of the typical Soviet company town that were observed by William Taubman.[29] In cities dominated by a powerful industry, factory management played an outsized role in local politics, often wielding authority over the city party committee (*Gorkom*) that usually ran local affairs. Such was the case in Vorkuta, where the coal mining trust *Vorkutaugol'* (KVU), which had been created in the 1940s as an arm of the camp complex, would dominate local politics well into the 1990s. As Pavel Grebeniuk has demonstrated in the case of Magadan, the capital of the Kolyma region in northeastern Siberia, the legacy of forced labor weighed heavily on the evolution of cities and regions dominated by the Gulag long after Stalin's death.[30]

The fact that Vorkuta remained a company town also played a key role in determining the fate of the city's large population of ex-prisoners. Because the needs of production tended to be considered a first-order priority, this had a significant effect on ex-prisoners' prospects for successful reintegration into Soviet society after release. Former prisoners in Vorkuta faced legal obstacles, discrimination, and prejudice just as they did elsewhere in the Soviet Union.[31] Some had adopted oppositional worldviews that significantly hindered their prospects of reintegration. Indeed, it is difficult to deny Miriam Dobson's conclusion that "although all former prisoners were expected to become law-abiding, hard-working citizens, many of them were under constraints that made this almost impossible."[32] Yet former prisoners starting new lives for themselves in Vorkuta in the 1950s had advantages that could work against official discrimination and ambivalence. After release they were able to continue making use of social networks they had built while prisoners, networks that helped them secure scarce resources such as good jobs and housing. In fact, because of changes in penal policy after Stalin's death, thousands of prisoners had actually obtained jobs and housing before they were even released. Further, the shortage of skilled labor created by the release of tens of thousands of prisoners in the shift of Vorkuta's mines and industries to non-prisoner labor meant that many former prisoners were actually in high demand, so much so that managers were willing to sidestep and subvert official policies of discrimination in order to maintain their workforce. This study suggests that company towns like Vorkuta were in fact places where many former prisoners successfully reintegrated themselves into Soviet society. Thus, this book serves as a corrective to the historiography on the reintegration of former prisoners into Soviet society, which overwhelmingly argues that former prisoners remained on the margins of Soviet society after Stalin.

SOURCES AND OVERVIEW

In reconstructing the history of Vorkuta as a Gulag town and a company town, this book relies on a wide variety of published and unpublished sources. Foremost among them are materials from the former archives of the Communist Party and Soviet state at the local, regional, and national levels. By utilizing material produced by a wide range of individuals and institutions, this book attempts to reconstruct the complex relationships among the various actors who played a role in Vorkuta's history. The Vorkuta local history museum proved to be a valuable resource containing unique artifacts, photographs, and manuscript sources that help illuminate a variety of issues. Local newspapers, particularly *Zapoliar'e* (The polar north), the city newspaper founded in 1952, were useful for following the construction of the city and the everyday concerns of citizens. Wherever possible, I have made use of personal narratives in order to fill gaps in the archival record and to provide balance for the state-centric view that archives often provide. Thus, this book makes extensive use of published and unpublished memoirs written by prisoners and non-prisoners at various stages in the Soviet and post-Soviet era. Finally, I had the good fortune to be able to collect oral histories of former prisoners, family members, and other residents of Vorkuta. This material has been particularly valuable in humanizing the overall story that this book tells.

The first three chapters of this book explain the rise of Vorkuta as a Gulag town. Chapter 1 examines the growth of the Vorkuta camp complex from the first discovery of coal in the summer of 1930 until 1942, when the nominal completion of a rail line linking Vorkuta to Moscow made it an important part of the Soviet home front in the Second World War. It examines how Vorkuta was transformed over the course of the 1930s from a project of internal colonization into a camp for the Soviet Union's most dangerous prisoners. By the beginning of the war, Vorkutlag had become one of the Soviet Union's largest camp complexes, yet was threatened by mass starvation. Chapter 2 examines the development of the Gulag town during its period of most rapid expansion, from 1943 to 1947. At this time, the camp was a place of mass death, with the highest mortality rates in its history, but also a place of privilege, as the camp director doled out patronage to prisoners whose skills were particularly valuable. In the midst of a desperate war effort, the city of Vorkuta was founded, its first public spaces were created, and architectural showpieces were built. Thus, as the Gulag town expanded, many of the foundations for the future company town were put into place. Chapter 3 follows the transformation of Vorkuta during late Stalinism from 1947 to 1953. With the most intense period of expansion over, now local authorities attempted to establish a degree of "normalcy" among both the prisoner and non-prisoner populations. Such "normalcy" meant not only increasing the size of the non-prisoner population, but also isolating the camp complex's most dangerous inmates. Yet rising tensions between camp and city populations meant that instability continued, and seemed to be growing on the eve of Stalin's death.

Chapters 4–6 address Vorkuta's rapid transition from a Gulag town into a company town. Chapter 4 explores the crisis created by Stalin's death and the reforms that followed from 1953 to 1955. In particular, it focuses on two manifestations of this crisis: a large-scale prisoner strike that broke out in the summer of 1953, and an administrative struggle for control of Vorkuta and its mines precipitated by attempts to transform the Gulag. As local authorities waited for the future of the Gulag to be decided in Moscow, they took advantage of new opportunities to allow tens of thousands of prisoners to live outside the camp zone, thereby alleviating administrative gridlock and setting the stage for the recruitment of prisoners once they were released from the camps. After it was determined in August 1955 that Vorkuta's mines would rely primarily on non-prisoner labor, the process of transforming Vorkuta into a company town, which is the subject of chapter 5, began in earnest. This transformation involved recruiting thousands of new workers to replace departing prisoners, building urban infrastructure and housing, and rebuilding many of the area's mines. Although this "second birth" of the city dragged on for much longer than envisioned by planners, by the middle of the 1960s a new social and economic equilibrium had been established. But it was not only new recruits who became city residents, as tens of thousands of prisoners remained after their release. Chapter 6 examines the fate of these ex-prisoners in Vorkuta. Using individual stories and employment data, it argues that Vorkuta was a place of successful reintegration for many former prisoners. Despite the many obstacles that they faced, local conditions allowed ex-prisoners to establish new lives for themselves.

The epilogue examines how the new equilibrium established during late socialism was severely disrupted by perestroika and the Soviet collapse, when Vorkuta became one of the centers of a strike movement pushing for economic and political reforms. Reforms and neglect in the 1990s quickly transformed Vorkuta from a showcase of Soviet success into a cautionary tale of Soviet failures. Public memorialization of the Gulag, which finally became possible during perestroika, also became entangled in the Soviet collapse and post-Soviet crisis. As the epilogue demonstrates, Vorkuta has a tenuous existence in the post-Soviet era, and the legacy of the Gulag continues to shape the city in the twenty-first century.

Overall, this book aims to free the Gulag from Solzhenitsyn's metaphorical "archipelago." The study of the Soviet system of forced labor is important in its own right, not least of which because it helps honor the memory of those who suffered and died in it. Yet it is also important to recognize that the Gulag did not exist in isolation from the rest of Soviet society. As much recent scholarship has shown, it was a fundamental part of the Soviet system, linked politically, socially, economically, and ideologically. Examining Vorkuta as a Gulag town and as a company town facilitates the exploration of such linkages. In so doing, this book aims to produce new insights about the place of forced labor in the Soviet system under Stalin, and its legacies in the post-Stalin and post-Soviet eras.

1 From the Margins to the Home Front
Vorkuta as an Outpost

IN AUGUST 1930, Georgii Aleksandrovich Chernov, a geology student who had recently graduated from Moscow University, made a remarkable discovery. As part of a summer expedition to hunt for coal in the Russian Far North, he and a small group had struggled their way up the Vorkuta River for two weeks. At the end of a long day Chernov climbed up one of the banks of the river. There, literally under his feet, he found a large seam of coal. By the time he left that summer, he had found a total of five thick, easily accessible seams of what appeared to be extremely high-quality coal.[1] Following up on his discovery, Chernov returned the following summer with a group of thirty-nine "mining engineers of Ukhta." In 1931, these men began building the first permanent settlement and the first coal mine in what would later become the city of Vorkuta, above the Arctic Circle in one of the most remote areas of European Russia.[2]

This narrative of discovery, which was told in a series of early 1930s publications and further elaborated by Chernov himself in a 1968 memoir, failed to acknowledge the most important detail of the discovery of coal in Vorkuta: beginning in the summer of 1931, the development of coal mining and the construction of settlements was part of the emerging system of prisons, camps, colonies, and settlements that would come to be known as the Gulag. The thirty-nine "mining engineers of Ukhta" who arrived in Vorkuta were in fact prisoners sent from the Ukhta Expedition, a prison camp that had been established in 1929 to colonize and exploit the resources near the town of Chib'iu (later Ukhta). This camp, which would be renamed Ukhto-pechorskii lager' (Ukhtpechlag), soon became a massive prison camp complex that stretched throughout an enormous hinterland in the northeastern corner of European Russia.[3] The area surrounding the coal discovery on the banks of the Vorkuta River became a place of hard labor, suffering, and death for thousands of prisoners and exiles.

This chapter examines Vorkuta during the first decade after the discovery of coal and the initial attempts to establish a prison camp complex. It is the story of an outpost, a far-flung settlement separated from cities and transportation networks by hundreds of miles. Over the course of the 1930s development of the area and its coal mines would proceed in fits and starts with a varying degree of attention and oversight from Moscow. In the early 1930s especially, Vorkuta, like many sparsely settled areas of the Soviet Union, was seen as a potential site of colonization by the Soviet state. The colonizers, by and large, would be prisoners sent from points south and west. Under the leadership of police chief Genrikh Iagoda, which lasted throughout the first half of the decade, there were plans for these colonists to remain on site after the expiration of their sentences, reformed and reforged, the new permanent settlers of a Soviet hinterland.

Yet after an initial flurry of activity and investment in the early 1930s, the prison camp expanded little until the fall of 1936, when a large wave of prisoners arrived. As more and more former members of opposition movements within the Communist Party were arrested in the wake of the murder of Sergei Kirov in 1934, Vorkuta was flooded with prisoners convicted of "counterrevolutionary" crimes. Dramatic increases in the prisoner population continued in 1937 and 1938 as prison camps across the Soviet Union were overwhelmed by arrests made under the auspices of the "mass operations" of the Great Terror. The small but growing camp complex in Vorkuta was subject to all of the other major effects of the terror: overcrowding and worsening living conditions, mass executions intended to permanently eliminate alleged enemies of the Soviet state, and administrative reorganization as a result of bloody purging of the Gulag and NKVD bureaucracies. By 1940 Vorkutlag was not only an independent camp complex with nearly thirty thousand prisoners; it was considered to be a strategic priority, as Stalin and NKVD chief Lavrentii Beriia imagined that the camp would soon supply virtually all of the coal for the north of European Russia. With the outbreak of hostilities with Germany in June 1941, the camp would be thrust into the desperate struggle of total war, with terrible consequences for its prisoners.

COLONIZING THE "USA SECTION"—VORKUTA IN THE EARLY 1930S

Georgii Chernov's fateful expedition that discovered coal on the banks of the Vorkuta River in August 1930 was not a fluke. It was, in fact, only one highlight in a decades-long effort to hunt for precious natural resources in a region known as Pechora krai. After 1936 this area was located mostly within Komi ASSR (today, Komi Republic), but at the time it was contained within the sprawling administrative unit known as *Severnyi krai* (Northern Territory). Pechora krai takes its name from the Pechora River, a major river system that dominates an area of taiga and tundra. Until the 1940s, it was one of the most sparsely populated parts of European Russia. The native peoples who lived there, the Komi-Izhemtsy and Nentsy, hunted, farmed, and herded reindeer. Expeditions by Russians to study the geography and geology of the region, as well as to characterize and categorize the native peoples, began in the nineteenth century, and the first known map was published in 1846.[4] Russian interest in exploration and settlement increased somewhat with the discovery of coal deposits in the nineteenth century, although regular expeditions did not begin in earnest until the decade before the revolution. The first group of Russians to come to Vorkuta itself predated the Russian Revolution, when an expedition from Moscow University traveled some 90 kilometers up the Vorkuta River to map its upper reaches in the summer of 1913. They did not report discovering anything of note, however.[5]

The systematic exploration of Pechora krai did not begin until the 1920s. It is closely associated with a geologist who taught at Moscow University, Aleksandr Aleksandrovich Chernov, Georgii's father. Aleksandr Chernov had visited the area in 1902, 1904, 1917–18, and was convinced by what he and others had found that the Pechora River basin contained massive coal deposits.[6] Beginning in 1921, and continuing throughout the 1920s and early 1930s, Aleksandr Chernov led yearly expeditions to the region. At first these expeditions were modest, including only a handful of geologists and local guides.[7] But in 1924 they became considerably larger due to funding from both the Geological Committee, a major state agency responsible for geological exploration operating under the auspices of the Supreme Economic Council, and by the regional Executive Committee. For the rest of the 1920s, small groups fanned out across the tributaries of the Pechora River during the summer to hunt for coal. Each year the expeditions went farther afield, to areas that were increasingly remote and difficult to access. They found significant coal deposits in several places, but nothing of the quality and quantity to justify major development. That is, until the summer of 1930, when Aleksandr Chernov's son Georgii, who had begun participating in his father's expeditions in 1923, made his promising coal discovery on the banks of the Vorkuta River. This river, which flowed west and south into the Usa River, was barely navigable along its entire length by rowboats even during the brief summer months of high water. Yet it was on its banks, after nearly a century of speculation and a decade of systematic exploration, that a large source of high quality coal had finally been located in Pechora krai.[8]

The discovery of a promising coal deposit in Vorkuta came in the midst of the first five-year plan, in an atmosphere of extraordinarily aggressive industrial expansion and brutal war in the countryside. As other historians have noted, the creation and rapid expansion of the Gulag system was intimately connected to industrialization and collectivization, twin processes that created both an insatiable demand for labor and a simultaneous pool of potential forced laborers.[9] It was within this context that high-level state and party officials had begun discussing the possibility of using forced labor to colonize remote regions of the Soviet Union like Pechora krai. In July 1929 the Sovnarkom had passed a resolution calling for the creation of corrective labor camps to hold prisoners with sentences of over three years, under the supervision of the OGPU. This resolution is notable for at least three reasons. First, it specifically mentioned Ukhta, an area not far from Vorkuta, as the site for a new "corrective labor" camp. This would lead to the creation of the so-called Ukhta Expedition, soon renamed Ukhtpechlag, the camp that Vorkuta would become a part of for most of the 1930s. Second, the resolution explicitly stated that the new camps would be created "in order to colonize" remote regions. Last, the goal of colonization was connected to the exploitation of natural resources.[10] The idea of using forced laborers as colonists to exploit natural resources was given another boost in April 1930, when Genrikh Iagoda, who was then deputy chief of the OGPU (and later went on to run it and the NKVD), wrote a memo arguing that prisoners and "kulaks" should be used to colonize the North.[11] Thus, Chernov's discovery of coal in Vorkuta came at a particularly fortuitous moment when colonization for the purposes of exploiting natural resources was on the mind of top Soviet officials.

By the spring of 1931, the idea of using prisoners to colonize Pechora krai had landed on the agenda of the Politburo. On 20 March 1931 Stalin ordered the Supreme Economic Council to investigate the idea of extracting coal in the Pechora basin.[12] On 15 April the Politburo followed up, passing a resolution calling for the systematic exploitation of coal to begin that year under the supervision of the Party Committee for Northern Region and the OGPU.[13] This Politburo resolution represents a key turning point in the history of Vorkuta. Now, significant resources would be devoted to creating a permanent settlement on the banks of the Vorkuta River in order to mine its coal. The fact that the OGPU was given joint authority and responsibility for this colonization project would fundamentally shape the future of this new outpost. It meant that the vast majority of the "colonists" who would settle the region would be prisoners and exiles. Thus, this resolution not only set in motion the establishment of what would one day become the company town of Vorkuta, but it also led to the creation of one of the most infamous prison camps in the Soviet Gulag.

The first 39 prisoners, sent from the Ukhta Expedition, arrived that summer from Chib'iu (Ukhta), after an arduous journey on river and land that took several weeks to complete.[14] Prisoners and supplies continued to arrive in a steady stream during the short summer season, so that by November there were already 2,009 prisoners.[15] Exploration, scientific study, and initial mine construction continued frantically during the brief Arctic summer.[16] Construction of a permanent settlement on the banks of the Vorkuta River proceeded, although it was greatly delayed by a lack of construction supplies, which had to be brought in from a great distance. By September, the end of the first summer season, prisoners had built a bread bakery, a bathhouse/laundry, and a storehouse.[17] They had also begun work on a brick factory. On paper, the new colony on the banks of the Vorkuta River now had a sizable prisoner population, an official geographical designation, the "Usa section of the Ukhta Expedition," and an administrative center, known as Rudnik. In practice, however, the colonists were now completely cut off from the Soviet "mainland," engaged in a struggle for survival that would claim thousands of lives.

During this first winter Vorkuta was plunged into a state of crisis that would last throughout much of the next decade. With virtually no supplies to build barracks or any other kind of permanent shelter, the prisoners spent the winter living in dugouts cut into the steep riverbanks that they covered in sod. The winter was an extremely cold one, with temperatures regularly falling below −50° C. Food supplies lasted only until April.[18] No official records of mortality seem to have been preserved in the Soviet archives, but there is little question that hundreds of prisoners succumbed to sickness, exposure, and starvation during that first winter. Here, at one of the geographic margins of the Soviet Union's vast territory, the yawning chasm between the utopian visions of Soviet leaders and the actual capacity of the state to carry out these visions became apparent, with tragic consequences.[19]

Uninterested or unaware of the tragedy unfolding on the banks of the Vorkuta River, Stalin and the Politburo remained enthusiastic about the prospects of mining the region's coal. In March 1932 the Politburo once again considered the issue of coal mining in the Pechora basin, "in view of the necessity of creating our own coal center in the Soviet north."[20] After hearing the report of a commission charged with investigating the possibilities of further development, the Politburo passed another resolution that allocated resources and set targets for coal production. Acknowledging the significance of the coal discoveries, the resolution called for coal mining to be carried out "in complex with the development of the industrial strength of the Pechora region. . . ." Surveying work was to be completed by 1 October 1932 and three mines were to be sunk that year. By 1933, the Pechora region as a whole (including two other mines) was expected to produce 300,000 tons of coal. The resolution also called for a rail link to be built between Vorkuta and the Usa River, which would allow coal to be shipped by boat down the Pechora River system and eventually to Arkhangel'sk. Work in Vorkuta was to proceed apace regardless of desperate straits in which the colonists found themselves.

By the summer of 1933, it was abundantly clear to local and regional authorities that the extremely difficult conditions that had existed during that first winter of 1931–32 had not improved. An unforgiving natural environment, chronic shortages of food and building materials, and poor planning all contributed to making prisoners' chances of survival marginal at best. A particularly damning analysis of the situation was provided by Usa section head Danilovskii to Iakov Moroz, the chief of Ukhtpechlag. Of a total of 2,852 prisoners, "colonists," non-prisoners, and exiles in the section, Danilovskii estimated that as many as two-thirds were too ill to work. Even though only one-third of the prisoners were officially recuperating from illnesses in medical facilities, this was simply because there was insufficient room to house them. Conditions in the medical barracks were so poor that hundreds of prisoners chose to continue working rather than "recuperate" there. Scurvy, what Danilovskii referred to as the "scourge of the Usa section," wreaked havoc on a population left almost entirely at the mercy of the elements. Living in tents and dugouts in Arctic conditions with an inadequate diet, it was difficult to see how any prisoner could survive long. In 1933 alone, 686 prisoners died, nearly one out of every five in the section.[21] This figure undoubtedly underestimates the total number of deaths, since prisoners who died during transportation in and out of the camp would not have been counted, nor would prisoners who were released but did not survive long afterward.

The same report reveals that even those prisoners who survived went through a cycle of working for brief periods, falling ill, and then being sent elsewhere to "recuperate." Prisoners declared healthy enough to work in the mines would arrive in Vorkuta and last perhaps two to three weeks of hard labor underground before being evacuated to points south. Factoring in the twelve- to sixteen-day journey (one way) that it took to get from the nearest settlement to Vorkuta, prisoners were typically away for three to five months before returning to Vorkuta for another few weeks of work. Prisoners were sent to two different sites to recuperate: Ad'zva (400 kilometers away) and Vorkuta-Vom (200 kilometers away), and the journey itself, by boat or on foot, took a terrible toll. Prisoners frequently arrived in Vorkuta already in a weakened state, without adequate clothing or footwear to survive the extreme Arctic conditions. One group sent from Chib'iu (Ukhta) in May 1933 serves as an example. Of the 141 prisoners sent in a convoy, five froze to death in the early part of the journey, and 26 were left at another camp section because of their weakened state. Of the 105 prisoners who finally arrived, only 20 were fit for physical labor.[22] Over the course of a typical two-month period, the entire prisoner population of Vorkuta turned over, whether because of death or transfer. Such high rates of turnover had a devastating effect on productivity. Over the course of 1933, Vorkuta's mines produced a total of only 6,000 tons of coal, some 2 percent of the 300,000-ton quota set by the Politburo the previous year. This was less than 10 tons of coal per prisoner who lost his life that year. The contrast between the paltry production figures and the number of lives destroyed in order to produce the coal is sobering.

The appalling conditions in Vorkuta in the early 1930s led Usa section chief Danilovskii to conclude that the majority of prisoners were being treated as expendable human "refuse."[23] Such an observation clashed directly with official Soviet penal policy in the early 1930s, which called for prisoners to be "reforged" through corrective labor. Indeed, in the early 1930s Soviet public discourse often trumpeted not only the achievements made through Gulag labor, such as the construction of new factories or infrastructure, but also the potential of such projects to reform criminals and reclaim them as "new Soviet men." The quintessential example of this was the White Sea Canal project, which was celebrated by a team of writers in a lavish volume edited by the writer Maksim Gorky, among others.[24] As Steven Barnes has demonstrated, the notion that the Gulag was a place to "reclaim the margins" of Soviet society is important to understanding both the theory and practice of the camps.[25] But as the conditions in Vorkuta in the early 1930s suggest, shortages of food and other essential supplies, brutal working conditions, and extreme natural settings often rendered notions of reforming prisoners moot.

Alongside the high mortality rate among the majority of prisoners, a hierarchy of privilege emerged within the camp. In keeping with the policy of "colonization," specialists whose talents were particularly valuable for the exploitation of natural resources formed the core of a group of "colonists" (*kolonizovannye*). The status of this group resembled that of permanent exiles, in that they were not guarded like regular prisoners, even though they were not allowed to leave the area. Colonists were given the opportunity to build their own houses in areas that were located separately from prisoners. They were strongly encouraged to summon their families to live with them, and the camp paid their families' travel costs, which would be deducted over time from the colonists' wages.[26] Colonists made up only a small proportion of the population of the Usa section, typically under 5 percent. On 1 January 1933, 79 belonged to the category; a year later, there were 201; by 1 January 1935, they numbered 122.[27] Much of the elite of the Usa section belonged to this status group, including engineer A. E. Nekrasov, who was section chief.[28] Thus, colonists came to represent a distinct, elite status group within the prisoner population.

In addition to the colonists, the Usa section had other categories of residents that enjoyed relative privilege. A small number of "special settlers," likely "de-kulakized" peasants who were swept up by the repressive apparatus during collectivization, were attached to the camp. At the beginning of 1934 there were 72 of them, whereas by the beginning of the following year, there were 119. Non-prisoner camp employees, who occupied the highest rung in the local hierarchy, numbered only 76 in 1934. The everyday lives of such employees were undoubtedly more comfortable than the majority of prisoners, given the fact that they were accorded priority for food and were not required to carry out backbreaking and dangerous physical labor in the mines. Nevertheless, the lines between the status categories of those present in Vorkuta in the middle of the 1930s were fluid and ill defined. Although prisoners lived in separate housing from the other categories of residents, there were no borders or barriers between prisoner and non-prisoner spaces. There were few guards in the camp to regulate prisoner movement, let alone prevent escape. Over the course of 1934, 472 prisoners attempted escape from the camp, well over 10 percent of the prisoner population. Although the majority of the escapees were later detained (419), security was clearly not a particular concern of the section administration.[29] Rudnik was so remote and isolated that it made little sense to waste precious resources and manpower on guarding prisoners who had nowhere to run.

Malnutrition, disease, overwork, a lack of suitable housing, escapes, and constant transfers in and out of the section meant that the prisoner population of this outpost grew little in the middle part of the 1930s. According to official camp records, there were 2,009 prisoners in this section on 1 November 1931.[30] Fourteen months later, on 1 January 1933, there were 2,936 prisoners in the section. A year later, on 1 January 1934, this figure had risen to 4,408. But the population dipped again over the course of the following year, falling to 3,309 on 1 January 1935, not far above what it had been just after the first significant wave of prisoners had arrived in November 1931.[31] Clearly, the camp section was struggling to maintain a stable prisoner population and would not see any sustained increase until 1936.

The extreme remoteness of the Usa section presented a huge challenge for the officials charged with keeping it supplied with food, construction materials, equipment, and healthy prisoners. There were only two routes to the camp, both of which could be completed only during the summer when rivers were thawed and had sufficiently high water. There was a river route from Chib'iu (Ukhta) that was rarely used because the journey was particularly arduous and time consuming.[32] The preferred route involved travel by water from Arkhangel'sk, a major city that was well integrated into the national transportation network. First, goods (and people) were shipped from Arkhangel'sk to Nar'ian-Mar across the White and Barents seas. At Nar'ian-Mar, they were transferred to barges that traveled up the Pechora River to the mouth of the Usa River. Because the Usa was not as deep, goods were transferred again to smaller barges. The final 65 kilometers from the mouth of the Vorkuta River (Vorkuta-Vom) to the Usa section headquarters in Rudnik had to be completed over land because the Vorkuta River was too shallow for anything more than a rowboat to navigate. From July 1933 to August 1934 prisoners worked to build a narrow gauge railroad to connect Vorkuta-Vom to Rudnik, significantly shortening the overall journey. However, even after the completion of the railroad the journey was time consuming and unreliable because it relied on the rivers being navigable and ice free, and on the railroad being cleared of snow and ice.[33] Fyodor Mochulsky, a non-prisoner official who completed a journey in 1940 from Moscow to Abez', the administrative center of the nearby Sevpechlag (Northern Pechora camp), relates in his memoirs that it took him forty-five days to complete the journey, which did not include the final leg from the Usa River to Vorkuta.[34] Transportation would remain the most significant bottleneck in Vorkuta's "colonization" well into the 1940s.

Despite the attention that had been devoted in the Politburo to colonizing the area around Rudnik and to establishing productive coal mines there, little progress had been made by 1935. The Usa section remained the most remote and inaccessible outpost in the peripheral and sprawling Ukhtpechlag system. Mine construction proceeded at a snail's pace, and precious little coal had made its way to points south. The population of the camp hovered near the three thousand prisoner mark, not far above where it had stood before the first winter of 1931–32. Although new prisoners were sent to the camp each summer, they were hardly enough to replace the hundreds of prisoners who became severely ill or died each winter. In short, by all appearances the Usa section was well on its way to becoming another forgotten and abandoned Gulag project of the 1930s and 1940s.[35]

"POLITICIZATION," TERROR, AND REORGANIZATION, 1936–1940

Mikhail Davidovich Baital'skii was only fourteen years old when the Russian Revolution broke out. This did not prevent him, however, from fighting in the Civil War as a volunteer near Odessa. A true believer in the Bolshevik cause, he joined the Komsomol in 1920 and became a party member in 1923.[36] As a journalist in the small town of Artemovsk in Ukraine, he became increasingly disenchanted with the rise of Stalin, joining the anti-Stalin opposition within the party. He was arrested for the first time in 1929 for his oppositional activities. After a short term in prison in Kharkov, he was released after signing a statement renouncing his support of the opposition.[37] Baital'skii then returned to work as a journalist, first in Astrakhan and then in Moscow. In 1936, however, he was arrested once again and imprisoned in Moscow's Butyrka prison.[38] After his case was investigated, he was convicted to five years' imprisonment in a labor camp for "counterrevolutionary Trotskyite activity." That summer, he was transferred to Vorkuta, where he would serve the first of two long periods of incarceration.[39]

Mikhail Baital'skii was one of thousands of prisoners who were sent to Ukhtpechlag in the summer and fall of 1936. Whereas Ukhtpechlag as a whole had held 21,750 prisoners on 1 January 1936, by 1 January 1937 this number had already increased to 31,035; by the following year, it would rise again to 54,792 prisoners.[40] In Moscow, the show trials of 1936 were the leading edge of a new wave of repression against suspected members of the former opposition.[41] Tens of thousands were arrested, many of them sentenced, like Baital'skii, to five years for "counterrevolutionary Trotskyite activities." Most were sent to one of two camps, Ukhtpechlag in Komi ASSR and Sevvostlag ("Northeastern camp") in Kolyma.[42] The result was the increasing "politicization" of Ukhtpechlag—that is, an increasing percentage of its prisoners had been convicted of "counterrevolutionary" rather than conventional crimes. In the first half of the 1930s the camp had held a fairly small number of "counterrevolutionary" prisoners, but by the end of 1937 they made up nearly half (48.2 percent) of the prisoner population. This was nearly three times the average in Gulag camps as a whole.[43] The Usa section held a particularly large proportion of such prisoners since its geographical isolation made it a logical destination for those considered to be the Soviet Union's most dangerous criminals. This change in the prisoner population of Vorkuta would turn out to be a lasting one: although the prisoner population would change in many other important respects in the next twenty years, the presence of a large proportion (if not a majority) of "counterrevolutionary" prisoners would be a constant, setting it apart from all but a handful of camps that were designated for the most dangerous "counterrevolutionaries."

Among the thousands of new prisoners sent to Vorkuta beginning in 1936, there were hundreds of avowed Trotskyite prisoners like Baital'skii who shared a common ideological orientation and opposition to the Stalinist order. Many thought of themselves as "political" prisoners, a category that had been recognized in imperial and early Soviet prisons, but had been abolished by the adoption of a new criminal code in 1926.[44] These prisoners, who were generally concentrated in only three camp points (including Rudnik), immediately began to organize opposition to the conditions to which they were subjected. In early October 1936, a group of prisoners presented the administration with a formal statement of protest (*zaiavlenie*). Signed by seventy-three prisoners, it described in detail the conditions to which the self-avowed "political prisoners" (*politzakliuchennye*) had been subjected, including starvation rations, overcrowded and filthy housing, and the insistence that all be subjected to heavy physical labor rather than be allowed to work in their specialty. Combined with the fact that they had been sent to Vorkuta, a "deadly place even for genuinely healthy people," it was clear to them that their prospects for survival were practically nil.[45] The statement concluded by making a number of demands, including adequate rations, permission to work in one's specialty, an eight-hour working day and regular days off, the establishment of "normal" living conditions including the isolation of "political prisoners" from the rest of the prisoner population, reasonable medical care, and permission to subscribe to central publications. If such conditions were not established, the prisoners threatened to begin a hunger strike at 10:00 a.m. on 18 October.[46] What the prisoners were demanding, in essence, was that the camp administration acknowledge their status as "political" prisoners and extend to them a special regime that political prisoners had often enjoyed in imperial and early Soviet prisons.[47]

However, the administration in Vorkuta categorically refused to recognize the special status of the Trotskyites. Refusing to back down, the prisoners began a hunger strike on 18 October that would last nearly four months. Although it is not known how many prisoners participated in the strike, it was a coordinated effort that involved prisoners in at least three different parts of the Usa section of Ukhtpechlag.[48] Initially there were 128 participants, but by 28 October the number had grown to 231. Three months later, on 1 February 1937, there were still 148 prisoners refusing food. Then, in the first two weeks of February the number of strikers declined rapidly, from 95 on 6 February to 19 on 9 February. By 13 February 1937, the administration considered the hunger strike to be over.[49] As can be deduced by the overall length of the strike, none of the prisoners refused food for its entire length. Rather, they would refuse food for two to three weeks at a time, apparently adhering to a coordinated schedule.[50] The camp administration periodically transferred the prisoners to camp clinics to recover, force-feeding them through tubes if necessary. Given the length of the hunger strike, the poor health of many of the participants, and the extremely difficult living conditions in which the strike took place, there were fatalities, although the exact number is not known. At least three deaths can be confirmed based on archival documentation and memoirs, although the actual number of deaths was probably considerably higher.[51]

Despite the heroism of its participants, such a strike had little hope of accomplishing any of the goals set out in the declaration that the Trotskyites had presented to the camp administration in October 1936. Given the rapidly expanding size of the population of the Usa section, the fact that two hundred to three hundred prisoners were not working had little effect on overall economic plans. Further, since 1926 prison and police officials had consistently refused to recognize that the category of "political prisoners" actually existed, and no longer bestowed special privileges vis-à-vis other prisoners. Thus, the strike appears to have ended in February not because the administration agreed to the prisoners' demands, but because the "fighting spirit" of the strikers had begun to wane after such a long and grueling ordeal.[52] It is possible that some small-scale, temporary concessions were made to appease them.[53] In the end, the hunger strike did not result in a major disruption of the operation of the camp, and in the aftermath of the strike camp authorities noted only minor infractions of the camp regime by the Trotskyites.[54]

Major changes in the lives of prisoners did take place in 1937, but they did not come as a result of the hunger strike. Instead, they came as a result of the launch of one of the largest police operations in the history of the Soviet Union. The so-called mass operations of 1937–1938, as they came to be called, began with the dissemination of order no. 00447 on 30 July 1937. Authorized personally by Stalin, and signed by People's Commissar of Internal Affairs Nikolai Ezhov, the order called for a vast operation to arrest various "anti-Soviet elements" living in the midst of Soviet society, including former kulaks, former prisoners and exiles, members of oppositional political parties, and common criminals. The order established quotas for the number of arrests to be made in each region of the Soviet Union, including the number to be sentenced to long terms of incarceration and those to be shot. As historians studying the "mass operations" have pointed out, a distinguishing characteristic of this operation was that regional and local authorities were granted greater autonomy to investigate, convict, and punish those swept up in the operation than was the usual practice before and after the Great Terror.[55] Although the initial order specified that the operation was to be completed within four months, it lasted over a year, ending only in November 1938. As provinces and localities, with the blessing and encouragement of the center, "overfulfilled" the quotas established in order no. 00447, the number of victims expanded far beyond what was specified in the initial order. These "kulak operations," in addition to the "national operations" against Poles, Koreans, ethnic Germans and other national minorities, would later come to be known as the Great Terror.[56]

The "mass operations" launched by order no. 00447 caused an enormous increase in the population of the camps and colonies. Of the approximately 1.6 million people who were arrested over the course of 1937–1938, approximately one half were executed and one half were given long sentences in prison camps.[57] According to official data, the population of all Gulag camps increased from 832,881 at the beginning of 1937 to 1,317,195 at the beginning of 1939, an overall increase of nearly 40 percent in only two years.[58] The Usa section of Ukhtpechlag was no exception, and its population continued the rapid increase that had begun in 1936. While there were only 3,866 prisoners on average throughout the first quarter of 1937, by 1 October 1937 there were already 6,549 prisoners in the section.[59] By the beginning of April 1939, six months after the "mass operations" had been wrapped up, there were 16,096 prisoners in the entire Vorkuta camp complex.[60] While some of this increase is no doubt attributable to the reorganization of Ukhtpechlag into a number of smaller entities (see below), it is clear nevertheless that the Great Terror caused the prisoner population held in Vorkuta and its environs to increase three- or fourfold.

The rapid growth of the prisoner population caused a corresponding deterioration of living conditions in the camps. As the infrastructure of existing camps strained to accommodate the rapid influx of new prisoners, high rates of sickness and mortality became all too commonplace.[61] Ukhtpechlag was singled out for having some of the worst conditions. Because the construction of barracks could not keep pace with the influx of new prisoners, 40 percent of the prisoner population lived in tents. There were not enough shoes and warm clothing to go around, and the camp had only half of its needed supply of each. Inspectors sent to the camp in the winter of 1937–38 described conditions there as "exceptionally appalling." According to their report, sanitary conditions had become so bad that some sections had become "havens of infectious disease and mass death. . . ."[62] Following so quickly on the heels of a significant increase in the camp population in 1936, the influx of prisoners due to the "mass operations" of 1937–1938 brought living conditions throughout Ukhtpechlag to their worst levels since the early 1930s.

The Great Terror also led to arrests and executions throughout Ukhtpechlag because prisoners themselves were a target of the "mass operations." The Gulag was assigned its own quotas for arrests and executions, 10,000, which was divided among individual camps.[63] In Ukhtpechlag, the "mass operations" began after a coded telegram was received on 8 August 1937 that established the number of prisoners to be arrested and investigated, as well as the procedure for carrying this out.[64] Although the initial quota for Vorkuta and Ukhtpechlag is unknown, reasonable estimates suggest that it may have been as high as 2,000 prisoners.[65] In any case, the quota was far exceeded in operations that lasted until late 1938. In all, 2,614 prisoners were convicted (in absentia) by the "troika" that met in Arkhangel'sk to decide the fate of suspect prisoners.[66] The operations in Ukhtpechlag were not aimed solely at "counterrevolutionary" prisoners, as they made up only half of those convicted under order no. 00447.[67] In fact, of the first group of 597 prisoners whose cases were referred to the "troika" on 4 November 1937, only 105 were charged with "counterrevolutionary" crimes.[68] As the operation continued, however, charges were increasingly made against "counterrevolutionary" prisoners. In particular, it seems that local authorities used the opportunity presented by the "mass operations" to eliminate those suspected of connections to the hunger strike that had ended earlier that year.[69]

Once convicted by the "troika," prisoners were transferred to a special punishment subsection at the "brick factory" camp point located on the banks of the Iun'-Iaga River, some 30 kilometers from Rudnik. In order to accommodate the sudden influx of prisoners, they were held in tents.[70] Most of the killing was carried out on only two dates, 1 and 30 March 1938, when 524 prisoners were shot.[71] These particular executions were overseen by E. I. Kashketin, an NKVD officer who had been sent to Vorkuta in January 1938 with the apparent task of uncovering and eliminating Trotskyites in the Vorkuta prisoner population.[72] Indeed, many (though not all) of the prisoners executed on those dates were associated with the Trotskyite opposition, including Trotsky's former personal secretary, I. Poznanskii.[73] As Kashketin later reported, prisoners were led out in groups of up to 60 to the designated execution location, where they were then shot by camp guards. Afterward, "all useful camp property" recovered from the victims was inventoried, packed up, and held in the "brick factory" camp point for later use.[74] It is unclear what was done with the victims' bodies, and they have never been found.[75] In all, approximately 2,500 prisoners were executed throughout Ukhtpechlag under the "mass operations," 604 of them in Vorkuta.[76] Despite the fact that virtually all of those arrested under order no. 00447 were shot in isolated locations, rumors of what took place at the brick factory and other execution sites spread among the rest of the prisoner population, rumors that would have significant consequences in the early 1940s.

Against the backdrop of the "mass operations," Ukhtpechlag was reorganized, a process that would have a significant long-term effect on the development of Vorkuta and of Komi ASSR as a whole. At the same time that it was expanding during 1937–1938, Ukhtpechlag was broken into more discrete geographic chunks. Ostensibly this was carried out at the request of Ukhtepchlag's longtime director, Iakov Moroz. In a report to his superiors in the Gulag dated 2 November 1937, Moroz argued that the camp needed to be broken into smaller, independent units. Now that it held nearly sixty thousand prisoners and occupied a territory greater than 700,000 square kilometers, it had become too complex to be managed by a single administration. Further, the camp was engaged in a diverse array of economic activities, including the extraction of coal, oil, radium, asphalt, gas, and also railroad construction, not to mention agriculture in auxiliary farms. For Moroz, who had been under fire for some months, this was likely a last-ditch effort to save his job, even if it meant becoming the chief of a somewhat smaller camp.[77]

In the midst of the considerable expansion of the prisoner population and while the "mass operations" were still under way, the NKVD began to explore Moroz's proposal. On 10 December 1937 the NKVD ordered that the process of splitting the camps into smaller entities get under way by sending inspectors to Ukhtpechlag.[78] After six months of work, Ukhtpechlag was split into four independent camps on 10 May 1938. One of these was the Vorkuta-Pechora camp (known by its acronym Vorkutpechlag, later Vorkutlag), which was centered in what had once been the Usa section. The new camp was to fulfill the functions of "mine construction, coal extraction, and the construction of barges on the Pechora River."[79] Rudnik, the settlement on the banks of the Vorkuta River, was now the administrative center of a sizeable prison camp complex that occupied the northeastern corner of Komi ASSR. Like the thousands of prisoners who died in Ukhtpechlag during the Great Terror, Iakov Moroz did not live to see the results of the reorganization. The inspectors who were sent to the camp in January 1938 in connection with the reorganization "uncovered" illegalities and irregularities in the camp's operation, which were used as a pretext for his removal.[80] Moroz was arrested on 4 September 1938 and executed on 20 or 21 January 1940.[81] He was one of many camp directors to fall victim to the Great Terror.[82]

Despite the significant changes that took place in 1936–1938, much about Vorkutlag remained in the same state as it had been in the first half of the 1930s. When Vorkutlag's first director, Leonid Aleksandrovich Tarkhanov, and his deputy, Vasilii Petrovich Sokolov, arrived in the fall of 1938, they were struck by just how little had actually been built there. Sokolov described the camp in the following manner just after his arrival in October 1938: "We lived in quasi-summer tents. . . . The administration was housed in a single-story, dilapidated building. The other half of the building was occupied by the bathhouse and laundry, so the building was damp and cold—we worked without taking off our coats. The entrance to mine no. 1–2 (later mine no. 8) and the electrical station, a small building with repair shops, another building occupied by geologists, and a pump house were located within an area of 200 meters. This was all that had been built on the left bank [actually the right bank of the Vorkuta River]. On the right bank [actually, left] stood a two-story building, wooden barracks, two tents, and a primitive pile driver hung over the 'kapital'naia' mine."[83] These few buildings were all that existed of what would soon become the center of one of the largest and most notorious prison camp complexes in the Soviet Union (see figures 1.1 and 1.2). Although there were some sixteen thousand prisoners being held in Vorkutpechlag when Sokolov arrived, they were spread out over a large geographic area and engaged in a wide range of economic activities. Only a few thousand prisoners were mining coal.

Although it was no longer part of the camp complex that had covered some 700,000 square kilometers, the geography of newly separate Vorkutlag was still vast and sprawling. Most camp sections were located along rivers: the Usa (which is over 500 kilometers from its mouth at the Pechora River to the mouth of the Vorkuta River) and on parts of the Pechora River, an enormous area stretching hundreds of kilometers. The continued reliance on river transportation meant that Vorkutlag was organized on an east-west axis, with Arkhangel'sk serving as the "mainland" city through which goods and people flowed in and out of the camp.[84] Not only were permanent camp sections established all along the route, but whenever the entire route was navigable

Figure 1.1. A street in Rudnik, ca. 1936. Photograph courtesy of Vorkuta Museum-Exhibition Center.

thousands of prisoners were transferred from other work (including coal mining) in order to move goods. Communications between sections had to be done by radio or courier, neither of which was reliable considering the frequency of bad weather.[85] Vorkutlag was so geographically dispersed, and communications between camp sections so slow and unreliable, that during this period it was divided into regional units (*railag*).[86] The result was that Vorkutlag remained a vast, sparsely populated camp at the end of the 1930s, with little regional or national economic significance.

Not only did Vorkutlag remain geographically dispersed, but also little effort had been made to separate camp sections from the surrounding non-prisoner settlements. Many of the camp divisions had not been surrounded by barriers to prevent escape and to limit interactions between prisoners and non-prisoners. To put it in the official language of the time, many parts of Vorkutlag had not been "zonified" (*zonirovano*), thereby separating the inside of the camp, or zone, from

Figure 1.2. A view of Rudnik from across the Vorkuta River, ca. 1936–1937. Photograph courtesy of Vorkuta Museum-Exhibition Center.

the outside. According to Gulag regulations, camp sections were to be rectangular in shape and isolated from the surrounding area by some type of fence.[87] However, this particular rule was honored in the breach in Vorkutlag. In the summer of 1939, even the camp section in Rudnik, the administrative center of Vorkutlag, had not yet been enclosed with barbed wire, although there were guard towers surrounding the zone.[88] In 1940, only half of the forty camp sections that made up the sprawling Vorkutlag system had been enclosed and therefore "zonified."[89] Although the slow pace of "zonification" was partly due to a severe shortage of barbed wire and other material, separating prisoners from non-prisoners was clearly not a high priority for the camp administration.[90] Further, the camp's remoteness made the possibility of a successful escape unlikely.

The lack of divisions between camp sections and non-prisoner settlements was further underscored by the continued lack of a separate "civilian" administration to govern the non-prisoner population. Unlike the usual Soviet practice of governing the populations through institutions of party and state, in Vorkuta camp officials wielded authority over the entire local population, regardless of one's status as a prisoner or non-prisoner, party member or non-member. Party members were guided and disciplined by the camp's "political section" (*politotdel*) rather than by a city or district-level party committee. Municipal and district authorities, weak as they often were in the Stalin-era Soviet Union, were wholly absent in Vorkuta. Although a civilian construction trust called *Vorkutstroi* had been established when the Vorkuta camps were spun off into Vorkutlag in May 1938, at this time it was little more than a euphemism for the camp administration itself.[91] Although the relationship between camp and civilian institutions would become more complicated in the coming years, by the end of the 1930s local authority was concentrated in the hands of the new Vorkutlag administration, which answered directly to Moscow, rather than Ukhta, the old center of Ukhtpechlag.

PREPARING FOR WAR

In the spring of 1940 Leonid Aleksandrovich Tarkhanov, the director of Vorkutlag, was summoned to Moscow. There he met personally with Stalin, Beriia, and Viacheslav Molotov to discuss the future of Vorkuta. Upon his return, he announced to his subordinates, "Vorkuta is now going to be a construction project like Belomor, Noril'sk, and others. . . . This task was assigned by Comrade Stalin himself."[92] As Stalin and Beriia had made clear to Tarkhanov, Vorkuta was soon going to be a massive coal-mining center that would serve the entire Russian Northwest, including the city of Leningrad and the Northern Fleet. Two joint Politburo and Sovnarkom decrees in May and July called for vastly increased investment in Vorkutlag and correspondingly fantastical production targets. By 1948, Vorkuta was expected to produce 25 million tons of bituminous coal.[93] This would amount to one hundred times the amount of coal that Vorkuta produced in 1940, and over 5 percent of all of the bituminous coal produced by mines across the Soviet Union in 1940. Vorkuta would never come close to meeting this fantastical figure in the 1940s, nor even by the 1980s when coal production reached its apex.[94] Nevertheless, these targets demonstrate that Stalin and his inner circle intended Vorkuta to become the largest coal-producing area in European Russia. This attention from Moscow was indicative of a renewed emphasis on maximizing the industrial output of the Gulag, a trend that was further reinforced in February 1941 when responsibility for the economic management of many camps was spun off from the central Gulag administration itself into specialized subunits.[95] As a mining camp, Vorkutlag was subordinated to the Department of Fuel Industry, an entity that was itself soon absorbed into the Chief Administration of Camps for Railroad Construction (GULZhDS).[96]

The focus on extracting coal to supply the Russian Northwest led to further geographic concentration of the complex and continued reorientation of its regional connections. In May 1940 barge construction on the Pechora River, located several hundred kilometers away from Rudnik, was spun off into Sevpechlag, a new camp whose primary function was railroad construction.[97] On 17 November 1941 construction and mining activities in Inta, a smaller mining region to the south, were split away into yet another independent camp (Intlag), further narrowing the focus of Vorkutlag's mining activities to the area surrounding Rudnik.[98] In order to simplify its structure, the various regional divisions of Vorkutlag were eliminated as well.[99] The Vorkutlag complex still sprawled across hundreds of kilometers, but its economic and geographic boundaries were now better defined. Further, in October the "worker's settlement" of Vorkuta, the official designation for the non-prisoner spaces in and around Rudnik, was annexed by Komi ASSR from the Arkhangel'sk region.[100] This decision was an important step in the reorientation of Vorkuta toward Moscow to the southwest rather than Arkhangel'sk to the west, and was likely connected with planned transportation links. This change also created the first administrative links between Vorkuta and the Komi capital of Syktyvkar, although these were weak throughout much of the 1940s.

The tenuousness of the transportation links between Vorkutlag and Arkhangel'sk remained a significant bottleneck to the expansion of coal production. The sea/river/narrow-gauge railroad route from Arkhangel'sk remained an extremely unreliable way to transport prisoners and supplies into the camp, and coal out of it. Work on the Northern Pechora main line, which was intended to connect Vorkuta to the national rail network via Kotlas, began in 1938.[101] However, the prison camps that had been set up to build the 1,560-kilometer line had made little progress by 1940. But in connection with the planned expansion of Vorkuta, in May 1940 N. A. Frenkel was put in charge of an accelerated construction program. Frenkel, one of the most experienced (and infamous) officials in the Gulag, had been deeply involved in running a number of Gulag camps and projects, including the construction of the White Sea Canal and the "Baikal-Amur main line."[102] The NKVD ordered that 135,000 able-bodied prisoners be transferred to the two camps that were building the Kotlas-Vorkuta portion of the rail line, Sevpechlag and Sevzheldorlag. Although the main line was set to officially open along its entire length in July 1944, the short-term goal was to "open temporary movement of trains along the whole length of the main line in December 1941 in order to deliver no less than 2 million tons of bituminous coal from Vorkuta to the Northwest and central regions of the USSR in 1942."[103] In fact, the Northern Pechora main line did open temporary service on time, although large coal shipments were not possible until 1943.[104]

In order to meet the fantastical goals set by Stalin and Beriia, Vorkutlag would need many more prisoners. Whereas the camp population had grown considerably in the years 1936–1939, in 1939–1940 the population leveled off somewhat, reaching a level of 16,509 prisoners as of the beginning of 1940. Thereafter the population began to increase fairly swiftly: at the beginning of 1941, there were 19,080 prisoners; on 1 July, there were 27,393 prisoners; and by 1 January 1942, 28,588 prisoners.[105] Thus, the prisoner population nearly doubled in two years. Most of the increase came during the first six months of 1941, and most of the new prisoners were Polish citizens who were arrested after Soviet forces occupied eastern Poland in 1939.[106] Although 7,805 Polish citizens would be amnestied from Vorkutlag on 12 August 1941, just after the German attack on the Soviet Union, the overall population of Vorkutlag did not decline from year to year, suggesting that the amnestied prisoners were quickly replaced by others.[107]

A snapshot of the prisoner population on 1 January 1942 demonstrates that it was somewhat different from the average for Gulag camps and colonies. Continuing the trend that began in 1936, prisoners in Vorkutlag were much more likely to be serving time for "counterrevolutionary crimes," 50.3 percent versus 29.6 percent for the system as a whole.[108] As had been the case since 1936, Vorkutlag would continue to be among the camps where those considered to be the state's most dangerous criminals would be sent. Aside from a handful of prisoners who were serving sentences of under three years and a few who were serving sentences of over ten years, the prisoner population was evenly split between those serving sentences of between three to five years and those serving five to ten years.[109] Although the percentage of Russian prisoners in Vorkutlag was close to 60 percent, which was nearly identical to the Gulag average, a few national groups were overrepresented in the camp population, including Jews and Poles.[110] This was likely the legacy of the thousands of prisoners who had been sent from eastern Poland in 1940. Although many had been amnestied in 1941 in order to join a new Polish national army being formed to fight the Germans (the so-called Anders' Army), many remained in the camp.

The number of non-prisoners in Vorkuta also increased rapidly beginning in 1940. Whereas Vorkuta had a non-prisoner population of approximately two thousand on 1 January 1940, by 1 January 1943, this had grown to 6,500 people.[111] Because there was virtually no settled indigenous population in the area, all of these non-prisoners were connected to the camp complex in one way or another. Some of them were camp officials who had been sent by the USSR NKVD from other parts of the country or who came from within Komi ASSR. There were now several hundred members of the camp militarized guards, who were frequently transferred from other camps or recruited from urban centers in central Russia.[112] But as had been the case in the 1930s, the majority of the non-prisoner population in the early 1940s came from the ranks of ex-prisoners.

More than half of the non-prisoners living in Vorkuta in the early 1940s had at some point been imprisoned in Vorkutlag or a nearby camp.[113] One such former prisoner living in Vorkuta after release was Vladimir Vasil'evich Zubchaninov. Arrested in March 1936, he was sent to Vorkuta later that year to serve out a three-year sentence for "counterrevolutionary activity."[114] While a prisoner, he worked in the planning section of Vorkutlag, then located in Vorkuta-Vom. In March 1939 his sentence ended, but he remained in Vorkuta as a "free" worker. Describing his decision to remain in Vorkuta, he wrote, "In March 1939 I was to be released. There was no great joy in that. I could not go home [to Moscow because of passport restrictions]. Further, I did not know what had been going on there for the last two years, and whether home still existed. I could not count on finding work in other places. It was clear that for at least a year I would have to remain in Vorkuta. Which is what I did." Although he continued to work in the same position he had occupied as a prisoner, he moved to barracks for non-prisoners and ate in a separate cafeteria.[115] Over the course of the next six years he worked as the deputy head of the planning department for Vorkutlag in Vorkuta-Vom, as an economist in the Ust'-Usa regional subdivision of Vorkutlag, and as an economist in the main camp administration in Rudnik. In 1945 he was arrested again and sentenced to ten years for allegedly preparing an uprising against Soviet power.[116]

Another former prisoner who remained in Vorkuta was I. A. Duritskii, who arrived in Vorkuta on a prisoner transport on 13 August 1938.[117] After working for two and a half years in mine no. 1 ("kapital'naia"), mostly as a demolitions man, he was released on 13 May 1941.[118] After his release, he continued to work in the mine as a member of a tunneling brigade. Not only did Duritskii remain in Vorkuta until his retirement in the 1960s, but he actually joined the Communist Party in 1942. As he recalled in a letter addressed to the Vorkuta Regional Museum in 1968, a member of the party bureau from mine no. 1 asked him and two other former prisoners to join the party in December 1942. He responded with a reminder that they were former prisoners, certain that this would be the end of the conversation. However, he was told that they had nevertheless earned the honor of joining the party through their hard work and self-discipline. Duritskii remained in the Communist Party until long after he had retired and left Vorkuta.[119]

Although some prisoners were indeed able to leave after release to resettle elsewhere, the experiences of Duritskii and Zubchaninov were common.[120] In the late 1930s and early 1940s Vorkutlag actively recruited former prisoners to stay on after their release, particularly those who had valuable skills. For example, on 25 March 1942 camp director Tarkhanov signed an order releasing seventeen prisoners from imprisonment who belonged to "production and engineering-technical personnel" who had distinguished themselves as "enterprising workers." The very same order spelled out that each of the former prisoners had decided to remain as "free workers."[121] This was a common strategy throughout the Gulag, and one that Tarkhanov's successors would continue. Prison camps such as Vorkutlag were constantly short of qualified specialists, and so they took any opportunity to retain valuable prisoners after they were released.

With increasing geographic concentration, more barbed wire surrounding camp sections, and an increase in the non-prisoner population,

Vorkutlag became more clearly divided from surrounding settlements in the early 1940s than it had been in the 1930s. But although "zonification" had progressed since the late 1930s, it still had not reached all camp sections by the beginning of 1942. As the deputy head of the Komi ASSR NKVD wrote in a report in February 1942, "a whole series of camp subdivisions completely lack a zone. [There are] the farms *Medvezhka, Khar'iaga* with its subsections, *Sivaia Maska,* the subsections of the farm *Novyi Bor* and others, where prisoners are never under guard."[122] The result was that a significant proportion of the prison population, 2,743 prisoners, were living outside a camp zone, nearly 10 percent of the 28,588 total prisoners in Vorkutlag.[123] While most of these prisoners were held in agricultural sections hundreds of kilometers south of Rudnik, the presence of so many prisoners outside the barbed wire clearly troubled officials in Syktyvkar and Moscow.

Gulag regulations at this time did allow for some exceptions to an overall policy of strict isolation between prisoners and non-prisoners. Prisoners could be granted passes to leave the area of the camp zone and move outside it without a guard convoy. This category of prisoners was often referred to as *bezkonvoinye*, or "de-convoyed," in camp jargon.[124] Other prisoners were granted permission not only to move unguarded outside the zone, but to also live outside it. Such prisoners were in later decades called *zazonniki,* or "de-zoned."[125] Strict regulations had been in place since August 1939 to limit the use of both categories. Both were only allowed in cases where it was necessitated by the needs of production, and only if a range of security measures were properly followed. For example, de-convoyed prisoners were only allowed to travel on specific routes to and from work, and de-zoned prisoners were not allowed to live near populated areas. No prisoners convicted of "counterrevolutionary" crimes were allowed to be de-zoned, and only a few specific categories could be de-convoyed.[126] The regulations made it clear that exceptions were to be made only in extraordinary circumstances.

The situation on the ground in Vorkutlag in the early 1940s tells a different story. By early 1942, nearly 10,000 prisoners, approximately one-third of the prisoner population, had been de-convoyed or de-zoned, often in direct contradiction of the regulations. Clearly, the granting of such privileges was far more routine than intended. Further, many of these prisoners belonged to the groups that were categorically excluded from being granted passes or being allowed to live outside the zone. Over 4,500 de-convoyed prisoners, nearly half of the total in Vorkutlag, had been convicted of "counterrevolutionary" crimes.[127] The clear flouting of regulations took place even in Rudnik, the administrative center of the camp complex, where the division between prisoners and non-prisoners should have been the strictest. There were 116 prisoners living outside the zone, which represented just under 3 percent of the 4,286 prisoners in the section. Of these de-zoned prisoners, nearly half (57) had been convicted of "counterrevolutionary" crimes, including espionage and terrorism. The vast majority of them had been granted this status not for reasons of "production necessity," but instead as a privilege that went along with working in the camp administration. Of the de-zoned prisoners in Rudnik, there were "only 3–4 production workers, [including] two TsES [electricity-generating station] workers who live in the zone of the TsES, and one mine worker."[128] Thus, Vorkutlag under Tarkhanov not only violated Gulag regulations requiring the enclosure of camp sections, but it also flouted regulations meant to strictly limit the number of prisoners moving unguarded or living outside the zone.

Such lax security and lack of attention paid to the isolation of prisoners meant that interactions between prisoners and non-prisoners remained common in the early 1940s. One oft-cited example of intimacy between camp officials and prisoners was the phenomenon of prisoner domestics. The practice of using prisoners as domestic workers was officially forbidden by the central Gulag administration, at least as early as July 1939.[129] Although a few cases of particularly intimate relations between non-prisoners and their domestics were condemned by the Vorkuta camp administration, the practice remained widespread.[130] In fact, it was so common that camp director Tarkhanov issued instructions in February 1942 to regulate which prisoners could be used as domestics, and how much they were to be paid.[131] Most of the top officials in the camp administration not only employed female prisoners in their homes, but they also frequently chose prisoners who were highly suspect in the eyes of the Soviet regime. One camp section head, for example, employed a prisoner who had been convicted of spying for Germany and sentenced to eight years' imprisonment. The official in charge of guarding the camp's food supply employed a Hungarian refugee convicted of illegally crossing state borders. The deputy head of the camp's party organization, or politotdel, employed a German prisoner convicted of counterrevolutionary Trotskyite activity. All were following the example of camp director Tarkhanov, who himself employed a prisoner sentenced to eight years' imprisonment as a "family member of a traitor of the motherland." Overall, of 139 prisoners working as domestics in February 1942, 88 had been convicted of "counterrevolutionary" crimes.[132] Thus, the buildings in Rudnik where elite members of the camp administration lived also housed prisoners considered to be among the state's most dangerous criminals.

The widespread use of counterrevolutionary prisoners as domestic employees of the elite of the Vorkutlag administration was only the most extreme example of the frequent interactions between the prisoner and non-prisoner populations. As a letter sent from the acting director of the Vorkutlag administration to all camp section chiefs on 9 March 1940 stated, "The proper revolutionary vigilance does not exist. Cohabitation [sexual relationships] of the free staff with prisoners, [and] everyday interactions, group drunkenness [between these two groups], and other violations have been noted."[133] Illicit interactions between the prisoner and non-prisoner populations were frequently noted and criticized, and the extreme cases could result in the firing or prosecution of camp officials. Yet they continued to be a common feature of life in the camp complex and surrounding area. With escape unlikely, given the harsh climate, the remoteness of Vorkutlag, and the lack of a reliable transportation link to the "mainland," relatively little attention was paid to maintain constant surveillance of prisoners. Further, the slow pace of "zonification," which owed perhaps as much to the inertia of the camp administration as it did to shortages of barbed wire, wood, and other supplies, indicated a lax attitude overall on the part of the camp administration toward rules for prisoner isolation, particularly those intended to keep counterrevolutionary prisoners away from the civilian population and camp staff. Although the camp administration periodically criticized the lax security in the camp, little was done to actually improve it.

The decision in 1940 to greatly expand coal production in Vorkuta and to accelerate the construction of a railroad to the camp placed an enormous amount of pressure on both the prisoner and non-prisoner populations of Vorkutlag. In order to meet the fantastically high goals set by Stalin and Beriia, thousands of new prisoners were sent to the camp. Those who were lucky enough to have their sentences expire in the early 1940s were likely to remain in the area as non-prisoner employees of the complex. As Vorkutlag became more geographically focused and greater attention was paid to isolating prisoners from non-prisoners, barbed wire fences went up around many of the camp sections. However, none of this prevented the continued practice of allowing thousands of prisoners to live or move freely outside the zone. Prisoners and non-prisoners continued to interact on a daily basis in ways that were officially forbidden and that caused some consternation among both local officials and those in the central Gulag administration who were responsible for ensuring that the camp followed all regulations. The culture and practices of the camp were changing, but much of the everyday existence of prisoners and non-prisoners remained as it had been in the second half of the 1930s.

WAR AND REBELLION

The outbreak of war with Germany on 21 June 1941 continued to transform Vorkutlag. The pressures that had been building on the camp administration and the prisoners to dramatically increase production began to take on a more desperate edge almost immediately after news of the German invasion reached the camp. According to Nikolai Petrovich Volkov, a prisoner who had arrived with the wave of alleged "Trotskyites" in 1936, life immediately became much more difficult for prisoners. As he wrote, "With the beginning of the war the camp regime tightened sharply. If previously brigades had gone to the mine without convoy, then with the beginning of the war they were brought by convoy. Among the free population a corresponding [propaganda] program was carried out, extremely crudely, to increase vigilance, where the camp population, excluding the ordinary criminals, were portrayed as the 'hot' enemy reserve."[134] Although security would remain surprisingly lax during the first six months of the war, by the beginning of 1942 an armed uprising in a remote section of Vorkutlag would put increased pressure on the camp administration to guard prisoners more closely and increase their isolation from non-prisoners.

Although the development of the Pechora coal basin had been considered a military priority since Tarkhanov's meeting with Stalin and Beriia in the spring of 1940, it was not until the beginning of actual conflict that the need for Vorkuta's coal became acute. The rapid loss of the Soviet Union's western territories to the German army in the first months of the war meant that Vorkuta's coal was desperately needed. By the end of 1941, the German army had occupied virtually all of Ukraine, thereby depriving the Soviet Union of approximately half of its total coal production capacity.[135] Coal production in the first six months of 1942 was only one-third of what it had been during the same period in 1941. Absolute shortages of coal were made worse by the fact that the volume of rail freight also fell to one-third of its prewar levels.[136] After the fall of the Donbas in Ukraine and the Moscow coal basin, Vorkuta was by far the closest coal supply to Leningrad, which faced an almost complete blockade from September 1941 to January 1944. Further, Vorkuta's coal was needed to supply the Allied ships landing in Murmansk to deliver aid under the "lend-lease" program.[137] The general shortage of coal throughout the Soviet Union, and in particular its desperate need in Leningrad, added a real sense of urgency to plans for the expansion of the Vorkuta coal complex.

At the same time that the demand for coal suddenly increased, supplies of food and other essential items began to decline sharply. The food supply remained fairly steady throughout the first year of the war, probably a result of the fact that the camp was a military priority. In 1942, forty-seven prisoners per thousand died, which was approximately twice the mortality rate in the general Soviet population in noncombat areas, but only about one-fifth of the mortality rate throughout the Gulag.[138] But by the winter of 1942–43, Vorkutlag's food supply was already running critically short. Between October and December 1942, Vorkutlag received only one-quarter of the food it was allotted by central plan. This brought about what camp director Tarkhanov described as a "nearly catastrophic situation with the food for prisoners." As he wrote in his yearly report to his superiors, "Already in November 1942 . . . such essential foodstuffs as fish and sugar had disappeared, by the end of the year there were no more groats, and because it was used in place of groats, the use of flour increased, even given low supplies of flour and grain. Already in January 1943 all the stores of flour and grain had been used up and the camp was under threat of ceasing to give bread rations to the entire population. Only by grinding fodder and barley into flour . . . were we able to bake bread."[139] These shortages affected the health of prisoners almost immediately: nearly as many prisoners died in the last three months of 1942 as had during the first nine.[140] But the worst effects were not felt until the following year. Three times as many prisoners would die over the course of 1943 as had in 1942, nearly 15 percent of the entire prisoner population.

The growing sense of desperation in the camp that was created by the wartime atmosphere, the increased pressure to produce coal, and the decreasing food supply, was further intensified by orders to stop releasing certain categories of prisoners. Although several thousand Polish soldiers and officers were released from Vorkutlag in order to join the Anders' Army in 1941, for the remaining prisoners, the majority of whom were "counterrevolutionaries," the prospects of release became much worse. On the day after the Nazi invasion, 22 June 1941, an NKVD circular was sent via telegraph to all camp directors that ordered them to "cease the release of counterrevolutionaries, bandits, recidivists, and other dangerous criminals from camps, prisons, and colonies."[141] On 29 April 1942 the group of prisoners not to be released was expanded to include citizens and residents of countries at war with the USSR (independent of crime), "members of anti-Soviet political parties and participants in bourgeois-nationalist counterrevolutionary organizations," citizens of the USSR belonging to nationalities of countries at war with the USSR (including Lithuania, Latvia, and Estonia), and immigrants from Bessarabia convicted of counterrevolutionary crimes.[142] The most "dangerous" of the prisoners whose sentences expired during the war continued to be imprisoned as before.[143] In this manner, approximately one thousand prisoners in Vorkutlag remained in the camp after the expiration of their sentences over the course of the war.[144] The less "dangerous" of the prisoners slated for release could leave the zone upon the expiration of their sentences, but were forced to remain in the surrounding area as exiles, which had not previously been the case.[145] By the end of the war there would be nearly three thousand such exiles in Vorkuta.[146] This policy not only prevented the return of suspect elements to the Soviet "mainland," it also prevented the departure of a significant proportion of Vorkutlag's workforce at a time when labor was desperately needed to meet the lofty goals set by the central government.

Rising tensions among prisoners and non-prisoners came to a head in unprecedented and unexpected fashion on 24 January 1942 when an armed uprising broke out in a remote part of the camp. At 4 in the afternoon, Mark Andreevich Retiunin, head of Lesoreid, a small lumber-sorting outpost located hundreds of kilometers from the center of Vorkutlag near the confluence of the Usa and Pechora rivers, ordered the guards to bathe at the section bathhouse. Taking advantage of their absence, Retiunin and a small group of prisoners attacked and disarmed the remaining four guards on duty, killing one and wounding another in the process. After seizing the weapons in the guards' small armory, the rebels captured the remaining guards in the bathhouse and locked them in a vegetable storehouse.[147] Retiunin and his co-conspirators now opened the gates to the camp zone and invited the rest of the prisoners to join them. Approximately half of the two hundred or so prisoners in the camp section agreed, and the rebels proceeded to open the camp storehouses to take food, equipment, and warm clothing that had been stockpiled there.[148] One of the most remarkable acts of mass resistance in the history of the Gulag, an elaborately planned armed rebellion, had begun.[149]

The rebels proceeded immediately to the town of Ust'-Usa, which was the district center and an important stop on the river transportation route to both Vorkutlag and Sevpechlag. The group, which now numbered somewhere around eighty men, attempted to capture the city.[150] After cutting off the town's outside telephone lines, they split into smaller groups to attack several parts of the city. Although the rebels successfully captured the jail, port, and communications office, they were soon bogged down in a firefight with the locals. The battle turned decisively against the rebels when fifteen militarized guards from the nearby Polia-Kur'ia camp section of Sevpechlag arrived with hand-held machine guns and forced the rebels to retreat from Ust'-Usa altogether.[151] After their first major engagement with government forces, the rebels sustained significant casualties: nine were killed, one was wounded, forty were captured, and an additional twenty-one turned themselves in. Among the residents of Ust'-Usa and camp guards who had fought the rebels, fourteen had been killed and eleven wounded, including a five-year-old child hit by a stray bullet.[152] Their numbers significantly diminished, the remaining forty-one members of the rebellion fled from Ust'-Usa on sleds.

The rebels headed south up the Pechora River, apparently hoping to reach Kozhva, the nearest station on the Northern Pechora main line. They stopped along the way to obtain supplies at the *Kyzrasdi* satellite section of Vorkutlag, whose chief, Murmillo, himself a former prisoner like Retiunin, agreed to help the rebels even though he declined to join them.[153] Next they stopped in the village of Akis' to ambush a guard convoy that was transporting arms to Vorkutlag, netting themselves a considerable quantity of firearms and ammunition.[154] The rebels then proceeded to the village of Ust'-Lyzha, some 40 kilometers from Ust'-Usa, where they obtained more supplies after disarming the local militia officer, leaving a receipt for the food and supplies that they took from the local depot.[155] By listening to phone conversations at the local post office, the rebels learned that they were being pursued by government forces and that their attempts to reach the railroad at Kozhva were futile.[156] Thus, the rebels set off to the west on reindeer paths near the Lyzha River, hoping to elude capture.[157]

By this time the rebels were indeed being pursued by a large force mobilized from nearby camp sections. During the attack on Ust'-Usa on 24 January, the port radio office had managed to inform the Komi ASSR NKVD in Syktyvkar about the uprising. Republican authorities had warned all camp sections and state reindeer farms in the area of the rebellion and ordered them to assist in putting it down, and high-level officials were sent to take control of the operation. By 27 January Beriia had sent a telegram to all camp directors in the Soviet Union warning them of the uprising, and sent orders to Syktyvkar for the rebellion to be put down immediately.[158] One hundred twenty-five camp guards mobilized from nearby camp sections were dispatched to intercept the rebels, and on 28 January the two sides fought a pitched battle on the Lyzha River, some 70 kilometers west of Ust'-Lyzha. The battle resulted in a victory for the rebels. Although casualties were more or less equal on both sides, the guards were forced to withdraw after nearly half of them began suffering from frostbite.[159] The rebels then split into several small groups that headed in different directions.

With the arrival of authorities from Syktyvkar to take control of the operation against the rebels on 28 January, the tide turned in favor of the government, although it would take them some time to capture the scattered groups of rebels.[160] The main group of eleven rebels, led by Retiunin, was overtaken by government forces on the evening of 1 February, 175 kilometers from Ust'-Lyzha on the Malaia Terekhovaia River, a tributary of the Lyzha. The battle between the rebels and government forces raged for nearly twenty-four hours, and it was not until the afternoon of 2 February that the government forces claimed victory. In the end, three rebels were killed and two were captured. Six of the rebels, including Retiunin, took their own lives rather than be captured.[161] With the death and capture of most of the rebels, including their leaders, the rebellion was considered "liquidated." Indeed, deputy Narkom NKVD Komi ASSR Simakov sent a report to Beriia on 12 February 1942 claiming that the armed uprising had been put down and all the rebels captured.[162] However, on 3–4 March 1942, the NKVD received word of the existence of two additional bands of armed rebels, both of which were soon apprehended. With the capture of these last groups the Lesoreid uprising was declared over. During the previous six weeks, nearly fifty prisoners had been killed, as well as over thirty members of the militarized guard that the rebels had encountered.[163]

What is remarkable about this uprising is not only that it was armed, but also that it was a rebellion *of* a camp section, not *in* a camp section. The rebellion was in fact led by the administrative elite of Lesoreid. Subsection chief Mark Andreevich Retiunin, himself a former prisoner, was the apparent leader. Convicted of banditry in 1929 and sentenced to ten years' confinement for participation in a bank robbery, he had been recruited to run a camp section after his sentence expired.[164] It was not unusual for former prisoners to occupy important positions of authority in the Vorkutlag administration because of a shortage of qualified personnel, and fact Retiunin was one of four former prisoners in charge of camp sections at this time.[165] He enjoyed an excellent reputation as an able and loyal employee who had done his time working in Vorkuta's mines.[166] Even during the rebellion, Vorkutlag chief Tarkhanov expressed disbelief that this man had chosen to lead a rebellion and continued to describe Retiunin in a complimentary fashion.[167] Retiunin was not the only former prisoner to participate in the rebellion, as his deputy, Afanasii Ivanovich Iashkin, was also a recently released prisoner who had done time for banditry.

The rebellion's other leaders were prisoners working in the administration of Lesoreid. One was Aleksei Trofimovich Makeev, the former director of a major timber conglomerate in Komi who had been arrested in 1938 as part of a case that brought down virtually the entire political elite of Komi ASSR.[168] Two others, Ivan Matveevich Zverev and Mikhail Vasil'evich Dunaev, were former military men.[169] I. S. Rykov, who apparently was in charge of supplies for the rebellion, had been convicted of "counterrevolutionary activity" in 1938 and was serving an eight-year sentence.[170] Aside from Retiunin and Iashkin, all of the leaders had been convicted of "counterrevolutionary" crimes, and all were between the ages of thirty and forty. At least half had been members of the Communist Party, and all came from relatively elite positions in Stalinist society. Although a few still had long sentences to serve, most were expecting to be released within the year or had been set free but remained in the camp because of the wartime regulations noted above.[171] According to the subsequent NKVD investigation of the rebellion, it had been planned and led by the camp section leadership, with no dissenting voices among them.

The plotters maintained secrecy as they planned their uprising, rendering it unlikely that many of the remaining two hundred prisoners in the section had any prior knowledge of what was to take place. However, once the rebel leaders disarmed the guards and threw open the camp gates on 24 January, they were joined by as many as half of the rank-and-file prisoners. According to the subsequent NKVD investigation, approximately half of these participants were *bytoviki* (convicted of "ordinary" crimes), whereas the other half had been convicted of "counterrevolutionary" crimes. Yet the size of the rebellion shrank swiftly as many rank-and-file prisoners abandoned it after the failure to capture Ust'-Usa. By the time the rebels retreated from Ust'-Usa toward Kozhva, only forty-one men remained in the rebel force, thirty-five of whom were "counterrevolutionaries." In addition to those injured, killed, or captured in the failed raid, many chose to abandon it, particularly from among the bytoviki. Such prisoners tended to serve shorter sentences and therefore had much more to lose by continuing to participate.

Although a fair amount is known about the rebel leaders and participants, it is far more difficult to determine what motivated them to take up arms. The government case against the rebels, which was largely based on the confession of the only rebel leader who was captured alive, Afanasii Ivanovich Iashkin, stated that the rebellion was motivated by a desire to start a prisoner uprising in the Russian Far North to aid the German side in the war.[172] This testimony is hardly reliable, given both the circumstances of his confession (which was likely fabricated or coerced) and the fantastical things to which Iashkin "confessed." For example, the confession stated that among the rebels' primary goals were "the immediate development of private property in all sectors of the economy, in industry and in agriculture" and the unification of captured rebel territory with Germany or Finland.[173] While the Germans did apparently land paratroopers in northeastern Komi ASSR in 1943 in an attempt to create a prisoner rebellion to disrupt the flow of coal on the Northern Pechora main line, the idea that they somehow infiltrated the leadership of a remote camp subsection to foment revolt during the first winter of the war stretches the limits of credulity.[174] The supposed plan to aid the German war effort was typical of the kinds of plots "uncovered" by the NKVD during wartime.

On the other hand, the explanations offered in prisoner memoirs are equally unbelievable. Because no prisoner eyewitnesses survived, descriptions of the revolt from memoir sources are based largely on the rumors of the uprising that spread throughout the camps in the area. L. Gorodin, a prisoner who was transferred from Lesoreid to Kozhva just before the rebellion broke out, claimed that the rebels intended to commandeer a train and head for the front in order to fight the Germans.[175] This explanation, it should be noted, represents the mirror image of the one provided in the government case. Zubchaninov, a former prisoner working in the Vorkutlag planning department in Rudnik who was also well acquainted with some of the principal actors in the revolt, wrote that the rebels intended to raise an army of prisoners and "special settlers" to free everyone held in captivity or exile.[176] Both of these explanations suggest that the actions of Retiunin and the other rebels quickly became romanticized as word of the rebellion spread throughout Vorkutlag and beyond. It is little wonder that the story of the rebellion spread among the prisoners as a tale of tragic heroism—while the vast majority of prisoners and non-prisoners could only look at the worsening conditions in the camps with quiet desperation, a small group of men had taken direct action, no matter how futile.[177]

It is most likely that the rebels were motivated primarily by a growing sense of desperation. Just as it was apparent that living conditions were likely to worsen rapidly during the war for all prisoners, those running Lesoreid had particular reason to be concerned. Retiunin and his co-conspirators undoubtedly knew of plans to eliminate the Lesoreid camp division entirely and transfer the prisoners and personnel to Kozhva or elsewhere in Vorkutlag. Once the railroad was completed, sections that had existed along the river routes would be eliminated in favor of those along the new rail link. The prisoners and non-prisoners who led the rebellion had lived in positions of relative privilege in the context of wartime Vorkutlag, including special barracks, improved rations, and according to the subsequent NKVD investigation of the uprising, frequent drinking and cardplaying.[178] If the camp section were eliminated, it was unlikely that any of the administrative group, including Retiunin, would have found themselves in such positions of relative privilege, authority, and autonomy. The rebellion's leaders apparently also believed that the camp was in for another round of mass shootings along the lines of those that had taken place during 1937–1938, executions that they had heard about through the camp rumor mill.[179] Fearing a general worsening of conditions in Vorkutlag, the end of their relatively privileged existence in Lesoreid, and perhaps mass executions, Retiunin and his co-conspirators decided to fight for their own freedom and likely die in the process, rather than wait to be shot, starved, or worked to death. In many respects, the rebels were acting as bandits often do, they were acting to resist the expansion of central state power, in this case more direct control from the central camp administration in Rudnik.[180]

The effects of the armed rebellion by the Lesoreid subdivision reverberated throughout the wartime Gulag. Upon learning of the rebellion on 27 January 1942, Beriia sent a telegram to all prison camp directors and republican, regional, and local NKVD departments giving a brief account of the uprising and ordering that security be increased significantly.[181] A criminal investigation into the conspiracy behind the uprising was immediately launched. By the time it had concluded on 16 September 1942, sixty-eight prisoners had been convicted of various crimes, fifty of whom were sentenced to death.[182] In addition to the criminal investigation, the Komi ASSR NKVD was charged with determining the circumstances that had made the uprising possible. This investigation revealed the systematic violation of a whole series of Gulag regulations, particularly those calling for the strict separation of prisoners from non-prisoners, and steps were immediately taken to rectify this. The camp guards were put on a state of "full battle readiness" and extra care was taken to guard weaponry. Camp section and subsection chiefs who were ex-prisoners convicted of counterrevolutionary crimes or banditry were removed from their posts. Orders were given for all of the camp sections that had not yet been "zonified" to be enclosed by the end of February 1942. In April, several officials in Vorkutlag and surrounding camps were fired for their negligence and incompetence, including no less a figure than A. I. Zakhmalin, the head of the Vorkutlag politotdel. It appears that only one Vorkutlag official was criminally charged in connection with the revolt, an NKVD operative who had worked in Lesoreid until only a few months before the uprising and who had allegedly ignored information from informants of what was being planned.[183]

Vorkutlag director Tarkhanov received a surprisingly light punishment, a "placing in view" (*postanovka na vid*), little more than a slap on the wrist.[184] Yet it was clear that his days as Vorkutlag director were numbered. The fact that the rebellion had taken place under his watch and had been led by a subsection chief that he had personally appointed was yet another black mark against a man whose stock was rapidly declining in Moscow. Although coal production would more than double between 1941 and 1942, Vorkutlag would fall short of its plan for 1942.[185] Given Vorkuta's perceived importance to the war effort, failure to meet plan targets would not be tolerated for long. Indeed, in early 1943 Tarkhanov would be replaced as director of the camp complex.

CONCLUSION: FROM COLONY TO HOME FRONT

Around the same time that the Lesoreid uprising was being put down with brutal force, another version of the story of Vorkuta's foundation was being formulated. This alternative narrative went as follows: Vorkuta's coal had not been discovered in 1930 by Georgii Chernov, a geologist from Moscow, but had in fact been uncovered nearly a decade earlier by a local Komi hunter named Viktor Iakovlevich Popov. As Popov himself had related in a letter sent to Politburo member Lazar Kaganovich in August 1940, he had found a black rock on the banks of the Vorkuta River in 1921, long before Chernov or anyone else had arrived from Moscow. After noting how well it burned in a fire, he sent an entire sack of the stuff to the Kremlin in Moscow. Although his letter to Kaganovich does not appear to have reached its intended recipient, Popov's story did catch the attention of Gulag officials. After determining that Popov's claim had merit (on what basis is not known), it was passed on to the Komi Sovnarkom, which awarded the hunter

1,000 rubles.[186] Further, Popov's version of events was adopted as the official story of Vorkuta's foundation. When an article about the history of Vorkuta appeared on the front page of *Pravda* in 1946, entitled "Northern Lights," it was Popov's sack of coal, which was received by Stalin in the Kremlin in 1919 (not 1921, as Popov's letter had stated) that marked the opening of the Pechora coal basin.[187]

While there is no document clearly explaining why Popov's story was suddenly thought to be more compelling than Chernov's, it is not difficult to suppose why the authorities seized on it. If coal had been discovered in 1921 (or 1919) rather than 1930, it placed an additional decade, and another layer of myth, between the discovery of coal and the construction of the prison camp on the banks of the Vorkuta River. Gone were the days of the early 1930s when the Soviet press spoke openly about its prison camps and even bragged about them as international models, as had been the case with the White Sea Canal, which had been immortalized in the book *Belomor.*[188] Camps were now shrouded in official secrecy, especially once war broke out with Germany. The Popov story was also appealing in that it rendered the discovery of coal as a local, national discovery of the Komi people. In this regard, it fit well with the anti-imperialist rhetoric of the Soviet empire, the idea that the Bolsheviks did not oppress the non-Russian peoples, but allowed them true national self-realization within the Soviet system.[189] Chernov's version of the events may simply have smacked too much of colonialism, especially given the fact that his expedition had been part of an effort to explore the region that had begun before 1917, in the bad old imperialist days of the Russian Empire.

In many important respects, the substitution of one myth of discovery for another symbolizes the transformation that Vorkuta underwent from 1930 until 1942. The decision to send prisoners there to begin building a coal-mining settlement in 1931 had been explicitly conceived as a colonial project by many officials in the upper echelons of the Soviet party-state, especially Genrikh Iagoda. In the early 1930s, Vorkuta had been discussed publicly and privately as a colony, with some of its prisoners officially classified as "colonists."[190] Yet this changed dramatically in 1936. Not only did discussions of Vorkuta disappear for a time from the public record, but the idea of using the Gulag as an explicit tool of colonization also fell by the wayside. Vorkuta now became an important part of the regime's battle against its perceived political enemies, the destination for thousands of "counterrevolutionary" prisoners who began to flood the Gulag system in the middle of the decade. After the bloodletting of the Great Terror, which saw hundreds of prisoners in Vorkuta killed in mass executions, the camp was spun off into its own administrative entity. In 1940 Stalin and Beriia decided that the area's coal was of great strategic importance, so another wave of expansion began as coal production began to ramp up. With the outbreak of war with Germany in June 1941, Vorkuta became an integral part of the war effort. It was no longer considered a colony, but rather an important part of the Soviet home front, soon to be connected to the national rail network by the Northern Pechora main line, at the cost of thousands of lives.

In the process, Vorkutlag had undergone an enormous transformation. The first small group of prisoners had been brought there in the summer of 1931, but within a decade it had become a sprawling camp complex with nearly thirty thousand prisoners. While it had been part of the massive Ukhtpechlag complex for most of the 1930s, it was now a separate camp with its own administration. Over time, the Vorkuta camp complex had become increasingly geographically concentrated in the area surrounding coal mines in Rudnik. By the early 1940s, many subsidiary enterprises, such as farms and transportation waypoints, had been spun off into other camps. Perhaps most important, the divisions between the camp complex and the surrounding settlements had become increasingly better defined over time. Whereas in the first half of the 1930s there had been virtually no defined borders between the territory of the camp and areas inhabited by non-prisoners, by the early 1940s virtually all of the sections in Vorkutlag had been enclosed in barbed wire, creating what appeared to be a clear separation of space between the "inside" and the "outside." As we shall see in the following chapters, such borders were by no means impermeable, but the fact that they existed at all represented a remarkable change from the situation in the early 1930s.

The armed rebellion of the Lesoreid subdivision in early 1942 was, in many respects, the last gasp of Vorkuta's existence as an outpost. Whatever goals have been ascribed to the rebels by police officials, memoirists, and historians, it is clear that they were reacting against changes that were transforming the camp and, as a result, their everyday lives. The fact that the rebellion broke out in a remote satellite section and that it was led by the elite of that section, including both prisoners and non-prisoners, suggests that it was a reaction against the increased tensions of wartime and to the changes that many feared were on the horizon. Tightened security, increased geographic concentration, and more clearly defined borders would put an end to many aspects of the relatively privileged existence that some prisoners and non-prisoners had enjoyed during the 1930s and early 1940s. In this respect, the rebellion was an attempt by those on the margins of the camp to resist the extension of greater control by its center. But as war with Germany continued to rage, conditions would continue to deteriorate in Vorkutlag, intensifying the suffering of Vorkuta's growing prisoner population.

2 Saving Leningrad, Defining Vorkuta

A Camp and City at War

ON 7 AUGUST 1943, "a demonstration of the workers of Vorkuta" took place in honor of an extraordinary event. Vorkuta was sending a train laden with coal to blockaded Leningrad, "as a gift to the workers of the city of Lenin." After speeches by various mine personnel, deputy politotdel chief Sukhin read a letter "from the miners of the polar region . . . that had been unanimously approved and signed by delegations from all parts of Vorkutstroi."[1] By August 1943, the people of Leningrad were about to begin their third year of a horrible siege, virtually cut off from the rest of the Soviet Union by the German army. But since the Leningrad blockade had been partially relieved by the Red Army in January 1943, some supplies were now able to reach the city by rail.[2] Vorkutlag now played a key role in supplying the city, because the Pechora coal basin was the closest source of coal that had not been occupied or destroyed by the Germans. The description of this August demonstration, which appeared in the newspaper of the Vorkutlag politotdel, *Zapoliarnaia kochegarka* (The polar stoker), was filled with obvious euphemism. Although the speechmakers were nonprisoners, most of the "miners" whom they claimed to represent were prisoners extracting coal under compulsion. Vorkutstroi, the name of the nominally separate entity responsible for building the area's coal mines, was used instead of Vorkutlag, suggesting somehow that the coal was being mined by a civilian entity rather than by a Gulag enterprise. The "gift" of coal was hardly a gift at all, since those who were "giving" it had little choice in the matter.[3] In fact, the prisoners of Vorkutlag were suffering and dying in unprecedented numbers in order to send fuel to Leningrad.

The public demonstration and the shipment of coal to Leningrad carried important symbolic weight. As was the practice throughout the Soviet Union, public demonstrations and descriptions of them in the press were important for defining the proper place of individuals, groups, and places in the Soviet universe of meaning.[4] When a short news item appeared two weeks later in *Pravda* describing the arrival of the shipment, this signaled that something important was taking place.[5] On a symbolic level, Vorkuta would not be a far-flung outpost tenuously connected to the Soviet mainland much longer. Its link with Leningrad gave it a location in the public understanding of Soviet geography. But Vorkuta's contribution to Leningrad and the war effort did more than begin to define the city symbolically—it also led to concrete transformations of Vorkutlag that would have significant impact on the lives of tens of thousands of people, both in the short and long term. The Second World War, and Vorkuta's participation in the effort to win it, would prove transformative for the camp complex.

This chapter examines Vorkutlag from 1943, when the Pechora coal basin became an integral part of the Soviet war effort, to 1947, a year that represented the divide between immediate postwar reconstruction and attempts at a "return to normalcy" across the Soviet Union.[6] It examines the important changes that followed Vorkuta's integration into the wartime economy. It explores how the prisoner population, and what this population experienced, was altered by the war. Not only did the numbers of prisoners rapidly grow, but who the prisoners were also changed. A massive construction boom, the likes of which the city would not see again until the 1960s and 1970s, combined with wartime shortages of food and supplies to create some of the most brutal conditions in the history of Soviet forced labor. For the tens of thousands of new prisoners who were shipped to Vorkuta from 1943 to 1947, overwork, disease, and starvation made survival increasingly difficult.

The war brought with it not just a massive expansion of population, construction, and industry, but also the beginning of a fundamental shift in the configuration of both space and identity in Vorkuta. Just a few months after the triumphant shipment of coal from Vorkutlag to Leningrad, a separate city of Vorkuta was officially created. A new camp director, Mikhail Mitrofanovich Mal'tsev, who replaced Tarkhanov in March 1943, oversaw the beginnings of a nominally separate civilian settlement. Although Mal'tsev ruled Vorkutlag and Vorkuta using military discipline, he was also a quintessential Soviet patron. Cultivating patron-client relations with members of the artistic and technical intelligentsia from among the prisoner and non-prisoner populations, he oversaw the construction of public spaces and a monumental architectural ensemble for the new city. At a time of desperate shortages and deprivation, valuable resources were expended on the pet projects of the new director. The war also delivered a population for the new city, as thousands of released prisoners, exiles, and members of suspect populations became the new residents of Vorkuta.

In theory, at least, there were now two Vorkutas. There was the world of the camp, where prisoners experienced profound deprivation and brutality. There was now the world of the city as well, which boasted a park, boulevards, and striking neoclassical architecture. Barbed wire and guard towers separated these two worlds from each other. Nevertheless, divisions between camp and city, and prisoners and non-prisoners, remained contested and ambiguous. Borders between the zone and the outside remained porous. The social hierarchy, which in theory placed all non-prisoners above prisoners, remained complex and at times contradictory. Nowhere was this uncertainty surrounding space and status divisions more apparent than in the case of the Vorkuta Musical Drama Theater, which will be examined in the final section of this chapter. Founded in 1943 by Mal'tsev to provide escapist entertainment for non-prisoner elites, the nature of the theater, its company, and its performances challenged the strict divisions between the inside and the outside of the camp.

LIFE, DEATH, AND WORK IN WARTIME VORKUTLAG

Edward Buca arrived in Vorkutlag in late 1945. A Pole who had resisted both the Nazis and the Soviets during the war, he had been sentenced to twenty years' hard labor for the attempted assassination of a Polish communist. After a thirty-three-day train journey from L'vov, he arrived on the outskirts of Vorkutlag. He described the scene he witnessed in memoirs, stating, "When we stopped that morning the scene I could see through our tiny window reminded me a little of the coal mining district in Poland's Silesia: the wooden towers at the pit heads, piles of coal or slag between them, administration buildings, and stacks of timber. Farther away there were hills, and it was only the wooden towers that showed there were mines there too. The snow covered all the roofs."[7] What Buca saw that first morning was a vast and rapidly expanding coal-mining complex. What he did not yet see, but would soon become all too familiar with, was the barbed wire, the guard towers, the barracks, and the guards. Buca, like tens of thousands of other prisoners who arrived in Vorkuta by train from 1943 to 1947, would pay the price for Vorkuta's contribution to the efforts of total war.

The massive expansion of Vorkutlag and its prisoner population was driven both by a fierce demand for coal and an increased supply of prisoners. The camp, now subordinated to the GULGMP (Chief Administration of Camps for Metallurgical Plants and Mines), was charged with meeting the Soviet economy's, and in particular Leningrad's, desperate need for coal, which resulted in a massive expansion of mining operations.[8] In 1943 there were six mines in operation in the Vorkutlag, but soon there would be many more. According to plans made by the State Defense Committee, ten additional mines would be built beginning in 1944.[9] By early 1948, the frenzied construction effort had begun to bear fruit: there were twelve mines operating at full capacity, and eleven additional mines in various phases of construction.[10] Over that same period of time, coal production had tripled, from 1.5 million tons to 4.6 million tons per year.[11] Vorkutlag's coal output was indeed of vital importance to Leningrad. In 1943–1944 Vorkuta supplied the majority of Leningrad's coal, and it would continue to be a major supplier after the war.[12] The fast pace of growth in coal production also meant that Vorkutlag had become a nationally significant source of coal. Whereas in 1940 it had produced less than 0.2 percent of the Soviet Union's yearly output of bituminous coal, by 1945 its share of national production had increased to nearly 3 percent.[13]

As demand for coal increased, so did the supply of prisoners allocated to work in the mines. After the victory at Stalingrad in February 1943, the Red Army began to reconquer territory and march west, in the process subjecting new populations to the system of exile and imprisonment. Many former Soviet POWs, civilians suspected of collaborating with the Germans, and rebels accused of resisting the Soviet takeover of the western borderlands were swept into the Gulag.[14] It was largely members of these new categories of prisoners, convicted most often of offenses like treason and war crimes, who made up the new, much larger population of Vorkutlag.[15] In fact, the expansion of the prisoner population in Vorkuta from 1943 to 1947 was nothing short of breathtaking. Whereas there had been just over 25,000 prisoners at the end of 1943, by the beginning of 1947 this number had more than doubled, to just over 60,000 prisoners.[16] The rate of growth is all the more impressive when one considers that at the same time that tens of thousands of prisoners were being brought to Vorkuta, there was also a high rate of mortality, release, and transfer. In fact, more than 75,000 prisoners arrived in Vorkuta over these three years, at the same time that nearly 42,000 departed (table 2.1). This means that not only did the size of the prisoner population more than double, but it turned over completely as well.

Of course, neither the increased demand for coal nor the expanded supply of prisoners could have touched off such explosive growth in Vorkutlag without a reliable transportation link with the Soviet Union's major urban centers. The Northern Pechora main line, which had been completed early in the war at the cost of many thousands of lives, finally made it possible for people, coal, and supplies to be shipped in and out of the camp year round. In 1943, the traffic in goods and people reached new milestones, with over thirty thousand prisoners traveling by train in and out of the camp, and over 1 million tons of coal shipped to customers.[17]

Table 2.1. Net change in the prisoner population of Vorkutlag, 1943–1947

	Year				
	1943	1944	1945	1946	1947
Arrived	10,107	22,630	28,784	25,924	11,094
Departed	12,461	9,468	17,024	16,184	8,925
Net Change	−2,354	13,162	11,760	9,740	2,169

Source: GARF, f. R-9414, op. 1 ch. 2, d. 400, l. 6; GARF, f. R-9414, op. 1 ch. 2, d. 416, ll. 5–6; GARF, f. R-9414, op. 1 ch. 2, d. 434, ll. 5–5a; GARF, f. R-9414, op. 1 ch. 2, d. 450, ll. 5–6; GARF, f. R-9414, op. 1, d. 1280, ll. 5–6.

The new prisoners who arrived by railroad were different from their predecessors. In a striking change from the 1930s, most were not Russians. The majority of the new prisoners, like Edward Buca, came from the western borderlands of the Soviet Union: Ukraine, the Baltics, Belarus, and Poland. In 1944 alone, the number of Ukrainians held in Vorkutlag increased by nearly 10,000, from just over 11 percent to 27 percent of the population. Also noteworthy was the increase in the number of Lithuanian prisoners, which went from just 167 (0.4 percent) on 1 January 1945 to nearly 6,000 (11.6 percent) a year later.[18] By the beginning of 1946, Russian prisoners made up less than half of the prisoner population, a situation that would remain for the next decade. The overwhelming majority of the new prisoners had been convicted of treason, and so by the beginning of 1948 there were over 35,000 prisoners in Vorkutlag (56.96 percent of the total) serving time for this crime.[19] They were also serving longer sentences than their predecessors. It was now increasingly common for prisoners to be serving sentences of ten and fifteen years in length.[20] If the statistically average prisoner in 1942 had been a Russian serving a five-year sentence for "anti-Soviet agitation," by 1946, he was a Ukrainian serving a fifteen-year sentence for treason.

Ramped up demand for coal and an expanded supply of prisoners combined to make the lives of prisoners held in Vorkutlag incredibly "cheap." With trainloads of prisoners arriving almost daily, and demand from Moscow to produce more and more coal, there was little incentive to ensure that prisoners maintained their ability to work, let alone survive. Even the new camp director, Mal'tsev, apparently confided as much to Leonid Agranovich, a screenwriter who visited Vorkuta in 1946 to research a screenplay he was writing. According to Agranovich's description of his first meeting with Mal'tsev, the following conversation took place: "[Mal'tsev began] 'So, you're going to write—pause—about *perekovka* [reforging]?' (On that day the radio had played a program about the construction of the Belomor canal.) In response I muttered something incomprehensible. [Mal'tsev replied] 'That's right,' the general snorted and added measuredly. 'This is a camp. Our task is the slow murder of people.'"[21] If Mal'tsev truly said this, it was a remarkably accurate assessment of the camp, although the destruction of human life was hardly "slow." In 1943, 147 prisoners per thousand died, more than one out of every ten. This was nearly triple the rate of the previous year, a startling reflection of the tragically poor living and working conditions. Mortality remained high throughout the rest of the war, falling to 97 deaths per thousand in 1944 and 86 deaths per thousand in 1945. By 1946 mortality had stabilized, falling to 28 deaths per thousand. Prisoners in Vorkutlag were still twice as likely to die as the general Soviet population, but the worst conditions of war had passed.[22]

What caused such high rates of mortality? Working conditions were certainly one element that made Vorkutlag so deadly. Edward Buca, who worked in a brigade in 1945 digging a mine shaft, relates just how tough the conditions were. Six men working in a pit used crowbars and sledgehammers to extend a shaft that was 4 meters square down to a depth of approximately 50 meters. While a demolition specialist was called in to blast through layers of rock, the six men had to dig their way through permanently frozen soil, sand, and slate. According to Buca, after a ten-hour shift it was typical to have made only eighteen holes in the frozen soil. At this rate, it took months to dig a shaft for a mine that was relatively shallow.[23] It was not uncommon for prisoners like Buca to work outside in the winter without proper clothing for several hours on end, at risk of exposure and frostbite.[24] Those working underground in the mines, like Elena Markova, who began serving her term in Vorkuta in the summer of 1944, had to contend with different risks. As she wrote,

> I will never forget my first descent into a mine . . . the guards stopped us in front of a black hole. We put a miner's kerosene lamp over a padded jacket, a lamp whose twinkling yellowish light still illuminated nothing. With a push in the spine each of us was shoved underground. We literally groped our way down a narrow inclined tunnel . . . finally we reached the mine gallery. The men were sent to the coal face, the women to the chutes and conveyors. My first job in the mine was to push the coal on the conveyors . . . with a shovel. I, as a rule, did not have the strength to cope with this task, and piles of coal quickly grew which threatened to fill the passageway and bury me. The brigadier (a criminal) ran to me and began to beat me. But because this action could not stop the piles of coal growing to frightening heights, he was forced to shovel them himself.[25]

Brutal work environments such as these quickly led to the physical and mental exhaustion of the prisoners.

Wartime food shortages also greatly contributed to the rise in mortality in Vorkutlag. As was the case across the Soviet Union, official food norms and rations were cut during the war, with agricultural production down and much food being diverted to feed the Red Army.[26] Food supplies in Vorkutlag reached their lowest point in the winter of 1942–43, when incoming food shipments were drastically reduced. Even though Vorkutlag began to receive more food in 1943 and 1944, most prisoners continued to live on the cusp of starvation.[27] In 1944 director Mal'tsev wrote in his yearly report to his superiors, "There were days when Vorkuta had enough flour literally for one day, several times for five or six days the entire population was given bread on a reduced norm . . . this bread was baked by substituting oats and corn flour, for several weeks the prisoner population received no fat [or] meat."[28] Even for prisoners who were used to receiving just enough food to survive, the results of the shortages were palpable. Markova describes a typical meal from the summer of 1944, after the food situation had already improved somewhat: mushy kasha, *balanda* (a watery soup) with turnips and fish heads, a few pieces of cooked capelin (an Arctic fish related to smelt), and bread. She does not recall seeing meat, fats, or milk products until at least 1947.[29]

One of the main reasons why the food situation was so catastrophic in Vorkutlag was that the camp, like everywhere else on the Soviet home front, was not supplied with adequate food by the central distribution network.[30] Throughout the Soviet Union, Soviet citizens relied on local supplies to make up the difference between official rations and dietary needs, including subsidiary farms attached to enterprises, urban garden plots, and the private plots of collective farmers.[31] In the Arctic, poor soil, lack of rainfall, and an extraordinarily short growing season all combined to make it quite unlikely that Vorkutlag could rely on local food supplies to make up the difference for the prisoner and non-prisoner populations. Even though nearly 9,000 tons of vegetables and tubers were grown locally in 1943, nearly three times the previous year's harvest, this was not enough to prevent hunger, starvation, and a sharp increase of disease in Vorkutlag.[32] Both infectious diseases, such as typhus, and diseases caused by vitamin deficiencies, such as scurvy, flourished among the permanently weakened prisoner population.

It bears remembering that certain groups in the prisoner population faced additional risks that threatened their chances of survival. Female prisoners, who made up between 5 and 15 percent of the camp population during these years, were often victims of sexual violence at the hands of camp officials.[33] Given the extraordinary verticality of power relations in Vorkutlag, refusing the advances of officials lowered prisoners' chances of survival. Elena Markova describes a case from 1946, when a camp administrator picked her out of a group of newly arrived female prisoners, calling her forward out of a column of prisoners. Soon after, a guard brought her to this official's office. The conversation began innocently enough, with the young official remarking on how both of them came from the same city (Kiev), and that he had decided on this basis to spare her a job assignment in the mine. Then, the official invited her into the adjoining room for "dinner." The exchange turned sour when he told her to undress and Markova first hesitated and then began to retreat. As she writes, "Not even a trace remained of his good will. His face took on an evil look and broke out in red splotches. . . . I moved toward the exit . . . he suddenly burst out into evil laughter. [He said,] 'And I am supposed to prostrate myself in front of this creature of hard labor! You haven't yet understood, perhaps, that you are a complete nonentity, worse than a slave, that whatever I want, I can do to you! I could shoot you right now like a wild dog. Nothing would happen to me, do you hear, I wouldn't have to answer for it . . . but I'm not going to soil my hands with you! I'm going to send you to do such a job that you'll die within a few days!'" In fact, Markova was immediately transferred to the most difficult job in the mine: to carry beams meant for tunnel supports to the coal face.[34] This vivid example illustrates the violent way in which camp officials preyed on female prisoners.[35]

The sharp increase in prisoner mortality was not just caused by food shortages, overwork, sexual predation, and general neglect. It was also the result of a deliberate effort to increase the punishment for prisoners considered to be guilty of the most heinous crimes. In April 1943, a new toughened regime was introduced in the Soviet justice system for "German-Fascist criminals, spies, traitors, and their accomplices." In cases where prisoners were found guilty of crimes normally subject to the death penalty, they could instead be sentenced to ten to twenty years of imprisonment in the new enhanced regime.[36] Such prisoners were to be housed in separate barracks that had barred windows, were locked at night, and were located in spaces physically divided from the rest of the camp zone. Strict limits were placed on their ability to correspond with the outside world. They were assigned only the most difficult jobs, with a working day one hour longer than that of other prisoners. Most infamously, they were required to wear numbers on their clothing.[37] The name that was chosen for this new prisoner regime, *katorga*, had special significance, as it was the name for an especially hated regime of hard labor practiced in the Tsarist era to which Stalin himself had been subject.[38]

Katorga was not widely introduced throughout the Gulag.[39] Rather, those sentenced to the regime were sent to only four camps, of which Vorkutlag was one. Initially, 10,000 *katorzhane* (as prisoners subject to katorga were called) were to be sent there to work in the construction of new coal mines and other underground work, but actual numbers soon surpassed this quota, reaching 18,158 in 1946, 24,663 in 1947, and 27,402 in 1950.[40] This last figure accounts for over a third of all prisoners held in the Vorkuta camp complex, meaning that the katorga experience was a common one among Vorkuta's prisoners. This was fairly unusual for the Gulag as a whole, and according to one historian's estimate, nearly half of all katorga prisoners in the Soviet Union were held in Vorkuta.[41] The high preponderance of katorga prisoners in Vorkuta lasted into the early 1950s, confirming the camp complex's status as a holding place for those considered to be the most dangerous criminals in the Soviet Union.

Given that they were more harshly treated than other prisoners, katorzhane were much more likely to die. In 1944, more than one out of every three prisoners subject to this regime did not survive, an absolutely staggering death rate. In such conditions, many prisoners suffered from absolute desperation. In her memoirs, Elena Markova summed up her existence in katorga, writing, "My reality was so frightening, that it seemed impossible for me to survive even one day. And I was looking at a fifteen-year term."[42] Camp administrators who were responsible for enforcing the new regime understood this as well. Even one of the highest-ranking officials in the Gulag, Deputy Commissar of the NKVD Chernyshev, admitted in 1945 that "the experience of work with katorzhane in the Vorkuta coal camp shows that those sentenced to katorga labor for fifteen to twenty years, in the conditions of the special regime for katorzhane, lose the perspective needed to endure until the end of their sentence."[43] In the social hierarchy of wartime

Vorkutlag, these prisoners occupied the lowest position, and thus they were the most vulnerable and least likely to survive this period of rapid expansion and widespread shortages.

PATRONAGE AND PRIVILEGE IN WARTIME VORKUTLAG

The brutality of life in Vorkutlag during wartime was undoubtedly increased by the strict policies of its director, Mikhail Mitrofanovich Mal'tsev, who was personally chosen by NKVD chief Lavrentii Beriia to run Vorkuta after distinguishing himself for commanding sapper forces during the battle of Stalingrad.[44] Mal'tsev's military experience commended him to his superiors in the NKVD, who saw Vorkuta's coal as vital to the war effort. Further, his skills as an engineer gave him practical expertise that his predecessors had clearly lacked. From March 1943 he sat atop the administrative hierarchy in Vorkuta, serving both as the director of Vorkutlag and the chief of the area's industrial trust, Vorkutstroi, and its successor organization, *Vorkutaugol'* (KVU).[45] For nearly four years, he played a central role in the lives of tens of thousands of prisoners and non-prisoners. In fact, Mal'tsev put a personal stamp on virtually every aspect of life for prisoners and non-prisoners alike.

There is little doubt that Mal'tsev brought with him an increasing emphasis on discipline consistent with his military background and the context in which he found himself, running a camp complex at a time of total war. Upon his arrival in April, Mal'tsev wasted little time enacting changes to make Vorkutlag a more effective part of the Soviet war machine.[46] One of the very first orders he signed as camp director, on 3 May 1943, forbade any department head or deputy head from leaving work during working hours without his explicit permission.[47] This relatively minor change was soon followed by other, more substantive orders. As Vladimir Vasil'evich Zubchaninov, a former prisoner who worked closely with Mal'tsev, wrote, "[After Mal'tsev arrived] a twelve-hour working day was established for prisoners and a ten-hour day for non-prisoners. As far as his closest circle, it had to 'conduct battle' both day and night. At the end of each day Mal'tsev conducted a dispatcher's report. Each mine manager had to report, via radio, how the day had gone, what was needed, and how they had prepared for the next day. This continued until two or three in the morning, sometimes four. The mine managers feared the dispatcher's reports like schoolchildren were afraid of tests."[48] Military discipline was extended to the prisoner population as well. Prisoners who performed above expectations were rewarded, whereas those who shirked responsibility were punished. Rewards and punishments ran the gamut, from early release to execution. In all cases, Mal'tsev's decisions were read over the camp radio as examples for all.[49] By all reports, Mal'tsev widely commanded the respect of the prisoner and non-prisoner populations alike.

Yet not everything was run "by the book." While Mal'tsev indeed expended a great deal of time and effort instilling military discipline in the camp, emphasizing formal, vertical power relations both within the hierarchy of the camp administration and between non-prisoners and prisoners, he engaged in other kinds of relationships with prisoners and non-prisoners that were qualitatively different. In fact, for a small minority of prisoners this was a time when privilege flourished, making their experiences radically different from the majority who lived on the razor's edge between survival and death. On the basis of informal exchanges between Mal'tsev and his subordinates, a well-developed system of patronage emerged. While it might seem contradictory that a director so focused on establishing military discipline would rely on informal relations in his management of the camp, Mal'tsev used patronage effectively to accomplish goals that would have been much more difficult to realize using the formal hierarchy. For the most part, privilege and discipline coexisted quite comfortably in Vorkutlag during Mal'tsev's tenure.

Aleksei Iakovlevich Kapler, who was imprisoned in Vorkutlag from 1943 to 1948, lived in a manner far different from the life described by prisoners like Edward Buca and Elena Markova. Undoubtedly the most famous prisoner in Vorkutlag, Kapler had been a fixture of the Soviet film industry, a screenwriter who had written two enormously successful films at the end of the 1930s, "Lenin in October" and "Lenin in 1918."[50] How he came to be imprisoned in Vorkutlag is an unusual story. In the early 1940s, he began courting Stalin's teenage daughter, Svetlana Allilueva. Although the Soviet leader voiced his disapproval of the much older (and Jewish) Kapler seeing his daughter, the relationship continued. Responding to his personal problems in much the same way that he dealt with issues of national importance, Stalin had Kapler arrested in early 1943, and he was sent to Vorkutlag to serve out a five-year term.[51] Mal'tsev, however, decided that Kapler should not spend his term working in the coal mines. Instead, he was made the official photographer of the city and camp complex, during which time he lived in the back room of a photo hut in the center of the non-prisoner settlement.[52] Kapler was charged with documenting the day-to-day construction of camp and city, as well as putting together official publications about Vorkuta for Malt'sev's superiors.[53] He also served the everyday photographic needs of the non-prisoner population, taking portraits by request. In exchange, he lived in a manner that appeared comfortable compared to what was going on within the barbed wire. Although he could not leave Vorkuta, he was not guarded and was free to come and go as he pleased. Protected by a powerful patron, his ability to survive his term of imprisonment was no longer called into question.

Mal'tsev was not simply the patron of individual prisoner-celebrities like Kapler. He also played the role of patron to entire institutions. For example, he actively supported the Vorkuta Musical Drama Theater, which Mal'tsev himself founded soon after his arrival in August 1943. The camp director established a special relationship with Boris Arkad'evich Mordvinov, who had been chief director of the Bolshoi Theater before his arrest in 1940. Mordvinov wrote a letter to Mal'tsev suggesting the idea of creating a camp theater company, a notion that the camp director strongly supported.[54] Mordvinov became the company's first artistic director, and like Kapler parlayed his celebrity status into a relatively privileged existence. But the privileges bestowed by Mal'tsev extended far beyond Mordvinov to the company as a whole. The company, which by November 1947 numbered at least 150 people, was a mix of about two-thirds prisoners and one-third non-prisoners, most of whom came from the artistic intelligentsia of Moscow and Leningrad.[55] Utilizing the talents of these prisoners, Mal'tsev made escapist entertainment available to the camp and city elites at a time and place where distractions were especially welcome. It gave him the opportunity to compete with rival camp directors, many of whom had established their own camp theaters.[56] The theater also represented one of the few locations for cultured leisure activities available in the city, and so was a central part of Mal'tsev's drive to create a city with public spaces. In exchange, prisoners in the theater company were released from manual labor. Most were given passes allowing them to travel unguarded between the camp zones where they lived and the theater. In other words, becoming part of the camp theater company allowed some prisoners the opportunity to escape the harsh brutality and discipline of life in Vorkutlag and experience an existence of relative privilege.

Partners in patron-client relationships are by definition unequal. Mal'tsev's relations with Aleksei Kapler, Boris Mordvinov, and the members of the camp theater company were extremely vertical, even by Soviet standards. In fact, the gulf between the social, political, economic status of the two parties makes it seem, on the surface at least, that it would be difficult to characterize what was going on as a two-way exchange between patrons and clients. Nevertheless, they did involve mutually beneficial reciprocal exchanges. It is easy to see how Mal'tsev's clients benefitted from their relationship with the director. As prisoners and non-prisoners in Vorkutlag during wartime, they were extremely vulnerable.[57] At a time when thousands were dying from starvation, disease, exposure, and overwork, patronage by the camp director all but ensured survival. Clients avoided backbreaking and potentially deadly manual labor in the mines.[58] Instead, many had the opportunity to look beyond day-to-day survival and engage in potentially meaningful work. They often gained access to scarce goods, such as money, food, or clothing, which Mal'tsev liked to give out as reward for a job well done.[59] Rewards were just as often given in kind, such as when "American gifts," including coats, suits, dresses, and footwear received through lend-lease, were distributed to members of the Vorkutlag planning department on Mal'tsev's orders in December 1946.[60] Other material benefits handed out included better housing and extended vacations.

Another privilege frequently given by Mal'tsev as part of the reciprocal exchange was greater freedom of movement. For prisoners and non-prisoners whose movements were strictly controlled, this was a very valuable asset. Many prisoner clients were given passes that allowed them to be de-convoyed, that is, to travel from inside the camp zone to the city without guard.[61] While most de-convoyed prisoners were only allowed to travel along a specific route, the fact that they were not guarded represented an important exception to the normal camp routine. The most privileged were de-zoned as well, allowing them to live and work entirely outside the zone. Kapler was one of the latter, allowed to live and work in a three-room photo hut on Victory

Boulevard in the center of the new city. Special housing was also a frequent benefit, as was the case for clients in the theater company, who had permission to live in special barracks, which were less crowded and had a greater degree of privacy.[62]

Whereas it is readily apparent how clients benefited from their relationships with the patron, it is more difficult to discern what the patron gained.[63] There were multiple benefits for Mal'tsev. Patronage allowed him to make use of his clients' specialized talents, knowledge, and expertise that were in short supply in Vorkutlag. The official organization of labor in the Gulag, which assigned work to prisoners based on their physical condition and criminal classification, made little allowance for the utilization of specialized knowledge and talent. Patronage facilitated Mal'tsev's drive to contribute to the war effort because it allowed him to make more constructive use of prisoners' expertise. Further, the talents of his illustrious clients were essential for Mal'tsev to bring the Soviet "civilizing mission" to the remote corner of the North where he had been sent.[64] Finally, Mal'tsev's clients provided "intangibles" that were difficult to otherwise obtain as a camp director. As Sheila Fitzpatrick has pointed out about patron-client relations between Soviet officials and members of the "creative intelligentsia," patrons received "prestige and status associated with the ability to act as a patron; a sense of *noblesse oblige* or a desire to play the great man as it was traditionally played; a desire to see themselves as good, generous people; a desire to receive flattery and gratitude from clients."[65] In this regard, Mal'tsev was simply following the customs of Soviet bureaucrats and acting the part of a powerful and benevolent Soviet administrator, albeit in the unlikely context of a prison camp complex.

There is indeed evidence that Mal'tsev, despite his military bearing, was keenly interested in how he was perceived by others. If we return to the conversation recalled by Leonid Agranovich, where Mal'tsev allegedly stated that he was presiding over "the slow murder of people," this suggests that the camp director was intensely aware that others might be inclined to see him in a negative light. And when one reviews memoirs of this time written by people who knew Mal'tsev, one is certainly struck by the overwhelmingly positive characterization that he received. Even Alexander Solzhenitsyn, who for obvious reasons had little positive to say about any camp officials, singles out Mal'tsev as one of the few potentially "good men" in the camp administration. As Solzhenitsyn recounted,

> And Arnold Rappaport assures me that Colonel of Engineers Mikhail Mitrofanovich Maltsev [sic], an army field engineer, who from 1943 to 1947 was the chief of Vorkutlag—both the construction project and the camp—was, supposedly, a good man. In the presence of Chekists he shook the hands of zek engineers and addressed them politely. He could not stand career Chekists, and he held in contempt the chief of the Political Branch, Colonel Kukhtikov. . . . During the years of his administration, Rappaport assures me, not one single camp *case* was ever set in motion in Vorkuta. . . . This is a very important piece of evidence, if only A. Rappaport is not exaggerating involuntarily because of his own privileged position as an engineer at that time. Somehow I find it hard to really believe it; why, then, did they not get rid of this Maltsev[sic]? After all, he must have been *in everyone's way* [emphasis in original].[66]

Solzhenitsyn clearly had good reason to be skeptical, because if we look at Mal'tsev's tenure as camp director overall, the only reasonable way to explain positive remembrances of him is that they come from people whose loyalty was secured through patronage. In fact, Solzhenitsyn's comments confirm that Mal'tsev's use of patron-client relationships was highly effective overall. Not only did they allow him to realize his vision for the city, but they also validated his activities as a camp director in the eyes of those members of the technical and artistic intelligentsia whose approval he undoubtedly craved.

There were tensions, of course, between the official hierarchies and military discipline that Mal'tsev maintained and the informal world of patronage and privilege. We can see this clearly in the case of a denunciation of Mal'tsev sent to his superiors by an anonymous subordinate. In 1946, someone working in Vorkutlag complained to the GULGMP about the illegal privileges enjoyed by prisoners. The denunciation described the case of a prisoner named Bondar', who was living with his family in a separate apartment outside the camp. Despite the fact that he was serving a twenty-year sentence, he employed a non-prisoner domestic, had use of a camp horse, and frequently gathered non-prisoner specialists at his home for social events. Another prisoner named Shibaev, who was serving a fifteen-year sentence, lived with his family outside the zone, frequently visited the camp theater, and shopped at stores set aside for non-prisoner personnel.[67] What was troubling about such cases, both for the unidentified author of the denunciation and the GULGMP officials to whom it was sent, was not simply that prisoners were being given privileges that were in clear violation of Gulag regulations. Rather, it was the fact that these prisoners were enjoying privileges that were not only beyond the reach of most prisoners, but most non-prisoners in Vorkuta as well. They were living outside the zone in separate apartments at a time when the vast majority of Vorkuta's non-prisoners were living in squalid barracks. They socialized with non-prisoners as if they were equals. Worst of all, one prisoner employed a non-prisoner as a domestic. In such cases, privileges given to prisoners in Mal'tsev's patronage network blurred the line between prisoner and non-prisoner and actually appeared to invert the social hierarchy.

Yet there was no explicit contradiction between these types of formal and informal relationships and, in fact, they often complemented one another. As in the rest of Soviet society, skilled officials like Mal'tsev mixed their official roles with patronage in order to get things done. In fact, both were necessary for officials to effectively carry out their duties. Of course, when patronage appeared to step over the boundaries of what was acceptable, it might be denounced as corrupt behavior, as was the case with the 1946 denunciation referred to above. On the whole, Mal'tsev's management techniques suggest that directors of prison camps behaved largely in the same manner as officials did throughout the Soviet Union, combining official authority with less formal activities like patronage in order to accomplish their goals. In so doing, they might undermine social hierarchies or spatial boundaries, but as long as it did not appear to be systemic in the eyes of their superiors, camp directors like Mal'tsev were given fairly free rein to bestow privilege on prisoners who could provide valuable services in return.

A CITY IS BORN

The Second World War resulted in more than just the expansion of the camp complex and increase in the prisoner population. It was also the occasion for the creation of the city of Vorkuta, a nominally distinct civilian settlement. While there had always been non-camp spaces around Vorkutlag where non-prisoners lived, by the early 1940s the idea, let alone the reality, of a separate settlement scarcely existed. In the 1930s, the settlement of Rudnik, on the right bank of the Vorkuta River, had served as little more than the administrative center of the complex. By the early 1940s, most construction had moved across the river to the left bank, to the small "workers' settlement" of Vorkuta. By 1943, the area was essentially a giant construction site, filled with camp zones and the occasional collection of derelict barracks that housed non-prisoners. At the time, the area had a non-prisoner population of only about 5,500.[68] But on 26 November 1943, Vorkuta was officially designated a city by the USSR Supreme Soviet. By 1947, the city could boast boulevards, parks, a central square, several major "public" buildings based on Stalinist neoclassical architectural styles, and a population of just over 35,000 people.

The foundation, construction, and peopling of Vorkuta at a time when Vorkutlag was ostensibly devoted to contributing as much as possible to the effort of total war requires some explanation. If Vorkutlag was truly part of the Soviet effort of total war, why were resources being devoted to a project that would seem to bear little on the bottom line, how much coal was being extracted and shipped to customers? One reason, surely, had to do with Vorkutlag's symbolic role in the war effort, as described at the beginning of this chapter. Creating a city of Vorkuta, at least on a rhetorical level, meant that the source of Leningrad's coal could be publicly discussed and lauded. Although there had been a time when the media had trumpeted the existence and exploits of Soviet camps, as was the case with the Belomor canal and other early Gulag projects, by the Second World War the world of the Gulag constituted a conspicuous silence in Soviet public discourse. If the significant achievements of Vorkutlag's coal mines were to be paraded, a city provided a suitable vehicle for this. Thus, we see the emergence of a place called Vorkuta on the pages of *Pravda* beginning in 1943 and continuing into the postwar period.

The creation of the city also owed a great deal to the initiative of the camp director Mal'tsev. In fact, Mal'tsev did more than patronize individuals like Aleksei Kapler and institutions like the Vorkuta Musical Drama Theater. During his tenure he also established himself as patron of Vorkuta itself. While he may have simply been following the orders of his superiors when he directed the Vorkutlag planning department to begin drawing up the paperwork for the city's official creation in August 1943, Vorkuta's foundation bore the stamp of Mal'tsev's patronage activities.[69] He assigned a group of three prisoners and three non-prisoners the task of drawing up the paperwork.[70] By 26 November 1943 the efforts of the planning brigade had borne fruit, and Vorkuta was officially designated a city.[71] But Mal'tsev did not just create a city on paper. He saw to it that Vorkuta acquired many of the trappings of a typical Soviet city, such as parks, public squares, and imposing neoclassical edifices. In order to do this, Mal'tsev did more than simply follow the chain of command. He also used his network of patron-client relationships with prisoners and non-prisoners who could help him realize his vision for the city.

Mal'tsev quickly moved beyond the formal creation of the city. First on the director's agenda was the creation of public spaces. As one former prisoner living in Vorkuta at the time late reported, "[Mal'tsev] said—soon Vorkuta will be a city, and what is a city without a boulevard?"[72] Victory Boulevard, a public park and boulevard, was built in 1943–1945 to commemorate the expected Soviet victory in the Second World War. The site for the boulevard was a marsh between Mine Street and the railroad branch to mine no. 1.[73] Not surprisingly, most of the labor to build the boulevard was done by prisoners, although some was done by the non-prisoner population on a "volunteer" basis after working hours. The close proximity of a railroad made it relatively easy to bring sand, dirt, and sod (from the tundra) to transform the space. Birch and pine trees were also planted. Although the boulevard and park would eventually feature numerous pavilions, arches, a band shell, and even a fountain, the first structures built in the boulevard were for the children's play area (figure 2.1).[74] While this may seem an incongruous choice to build in the center of a giant labor camp, the choice emphasized the sense of urban normalcy that Mal'tsev intended to create. Indeed, photo albums of major camp complexes produced by the NKVD during the war (for internal government consumption only, of course) suggest that parks and boulevards were considered to be standard features of prison camp cities.[75]

After the boulevard's completion, work began on a central square for the new city. The design was once again drafted by the planning department of Vorkutlag. The plans that they authored called not only for the construction of a square, but also for the casting of a monument to the

Figure 2.1. Children's play area in Victory Boulevard, ca. 1945. Photograph courtesy of Vorkuta Museum-Exhibition Center.

late Leningrad party boss, Sergei Kirov, after whom the square would be named. Kirov Square would play an important symbolic role for Vorkuta, confirming the importance of the ties between the two cities. This monument, which was presumably designed and cast in Leningrad, was completed and delivered to Vorkuta in February 1946.[76] By the summer of 1946, a year after construction had begun, the square itself was completed.

The task of designing this public space, as well as several important buildings, was given to a man who became one of Mal'tsev's most important clients, Vsevolod Lunev, a graduate of the Moscow Architectural Institute. Captured by the Germans during combat in 1941, Lunev managed to escape in 1942 and rejoined the Red Army. Like many other captured POWs, he ended up in a "verification and filtration camp" near Podol'sk. He arrived in Vorkuta in 1943 as part of a group of one thousand former POWs (the so-called *okruzhentsy*) that Mal'tsev requested be sent to Vorkuta (see below). Like the rest of his cohort, he had an ambiguous social status. Although he was not technically a prisoner, he was at first guarded and lived inside a zone. Although Lunev began his time in Vorkuta performing manual labor in mine construction of mine no. 7, his architectural skills were soon recognized and in 1944 he began working for the camp planning department.[77] Until he left Vorkuta in 1960, Lunev would design some of the most important buildings in the city and would play a central role in urban planning.

In addition to assisting with the design of Victory Boulevard and Kirov Square, Lunev was the chief architect responsible for realizing Mal'tsev's vision for the city center. His first major building project was the party education building (*dom partprosveshchenie*), which was completed in fifty-six days during the winter of 1945–46. However, Lunev would subsequently write that he was most proud of his second major building project, the Musical Drama Theater. Completed in 1946, its façade featured fourteen white columns, simulating a brick or stone design, despite the fact it was made entirely of wood (see figure 2.2).[78] This would be the home of the Vorkuta theater company for just over ten years, until the building burned down in 1957.[79] Although

Figure 2.2. Vorkuta Musical Drama Theater, ca. 1946. Photograph courtesy of Vorkuta Museum-Exhibition Center.

the architectural ensemble of Vorkuta's early city center would not be completed until the early 1950s, the buildings that were the neoclassical fruit of Mal'tsev's patronage and Lunev's designs dominated the symbolic center of Vorkuta for decades to come.

Yet the design and execution of monumental structures and new public spaces tells only part of the story of Vorkuta's creation. The parks, squares, and ornate buildings made up only a small fraction of the non-prisoner spaces in the city. Further, they were largely the habitat of the camp elite. The everyday spaces in which ordinary non-prisoners spent the majority of their time had far more humble and practical origins. The primary means of creating city spaces, in fact, was to convert parts of Vorkutlag for civilian use. This was particularly the case with residential housing. For instance, on 20 September 1945 Mal'tsev decreed that camp section 1, which served the construction and operation of mine no. 1, "kapital'naia," was to be entirely converted for the use of non-prisoners. Prisoner barracks were converted into apartments, and more often, dormitories. While some new construction would take place, most of the buildings that would serve the needs of the community, such as the movie theater, medical clinic, laundry, cafeteria, and stores, were converted from camp stock that had been used for other functions. Despite the ambitious program of building ornate and sophisticated architectural showpieces, the reality is that the first residential centers of Vorkuta came directly out of Vorkutlag.[80] This trend of converting camp to civilian housing would in fact continue throughout the next two decades, reaching its peak during the massive reorganization of Vorkutlag and Vorkuta in the middle of the 1950s. This had the ironic consequence that the housing for many non-prisoners was in much worse condition than camp barracks, since older and derelict camp barracks were most likely to be converted for civilian use.[81]

Vorkuta also lacked much of the institutional framework of most cities. Typically, local government was split between a city council (*Gorispolkom*) and a city party committee (*Gorkom*). As the former was a state institution and the latter a party institution, the Gorkom tended to be the real center of power in local government, where officials worked to implement decisions passed down to them from the regional capital by a regional party committee, or *Obkom*. Yet Vorkuta had an unusual institutional arrangement. While it had a city council that met regularly, its authority was even more severely circumscribed than normal, since the camp director wielded so much direct power. The city lacked a city party committee entirely, as responsibility for the management of local party members was left to the Vorkutlag political section. Finally, Vorkuta had only the most tenuous of relationships with the capital of Komi ASSR, Syktyvkar, which was several hundred kilometers away and not directly linked by rail. Thus, even from an institutional perspective the city operated as the fiefdom of the camp director, who was in most matters answerable only to his superiors at the NKVD in Moscow. It would not be until the early 1950s that the city would begin to acquire a typical Soviet city government.

It was clear that there was a certain socialist realist quality to the city, its public spaces, and the monumental buildings that Mal'tsev and his clients worked so hard to establish. On one level, these spaces, and the elites that lived and interacted in them, occupied the world of privilege and comfort that was far removed from the world of the prisoners with its barbed wire and brutal labor. Yet the vast majority of Vorkuta's ordinary citizens lived in a world that probably shared more in common with that of the prisoners. As we shall see, most had until recently lived in a way that was virtually indistinguishable from how those prisoners lived, and they continued to live in the same barracks on the same streets. The barbed wire might have moved, but it was still within sight, underscoring the ambiguous and uncertain place that the citizens occupied in the rapidly growing universe of Vorkuta. Mal'tsev had accomplished a great deal in creating Vorkuta, but the process was so raw, chaotic, and ultimately new that it would be a long time before the streets of Vorkuta would be imbued with the sort of everyday comings and goings of a typical Soviet city.

VORKUTIANE FOR VORKUTA

Cities need more than buildings, streets, and spaces. They also need people to inhabit them. When Vorkuta was officially founded in November 1943, residents, or Vorkutiane as they would come to be called, were in short supply. At the time, there were only about 5,500 men, women, and children living outside the barbed wire. Although no detailed analysis exists of who these people were, the majority likely consisted of camp guards and officials, exiles, released prisoners, and their families. But over the next few years the city population would expand rapidly. Already by the beginning of 1945, there were nearly 25,000 non-prisoner city residents, and by 1947 this number had grown to just over 35,000 people.[82] In other words, the non-prisoner population grew by seven times over less than four years, a rate even more rapid than the prisoner population. What made such a rapid expansion possible? Who were these new residents of Vorkuta?

Once again, it was the war that drove the rapid population growth. Just as the march of the Soviet army westward provided tens of thousands of new prisoners for the expansion of Vorkutlag, Soviet activities and policies in the second half of the war would bring tens of thousands of non-prisoners to Vorkuta. These men and women would make up the bulk of the Vorkutiane, the first residents of the new city. Most had not chosen to come to the city. Most, in fact, were not actually new residents of the area when they became "citizens." The overwhelming majority of the thirty-thousand-odd people who became "citizens" came from the population of Vorkutlag. In the same way that the spaces that made up the city came from the camp, so did most of the people who inhabited them. And although most non-prisoners did eventually enjoy a higher social status and better living conditions than most prisoners, at first most were largely indistinguishable from them.

There were several large groups of people who followed similar trajectories in becoming city residents. First, there were "mobilized" ethnic Germans, who began to arrive in Vorkuta in May 1943.[83] These were Soviet ethnic Germans who, having already been deported to Kazakhstan and Siberia in 1941, were now sent to work in various industries throughout the Soviet Union.[84] By the beginning of 1944, nearly seven thousand had been sent to Vorkuta as labor conscripts. The German exiles lived in conditions that differed little from those to which prisoners were subjected. Although they lived in areas technically isolated from prisoner zones, their living quarters were the same dilapidated barracks surrounded by barbed wire fences. The work that was required of them was also virtually indistinguishable from that of prisoners, as most worked in mines. The fact that nearly four hundred of these labor conscripts died in 1944 confirms that conditions made survival difficult.[85] But the status of the "mobilized" Germans changed considerably in November 1945, when the NKVD ordered that they no longer be held in zones. This freed them from some of the most draconian terms of their existence, such as living and working under armed guard. In

Vorkuta and elsewhere, their status changed from pseudo-prisoners to exiles without the right to leave their places of residence.[86] Now they were no longer part of the vast army of unfree laborers—instead, they were residents of Mal'tsev's new city. This status was shared by over eight hundred "kulak" exiles who were "mobilized" and transferred to Vorkuta during the war, only to become part of the non-prisoner population after its conclusion.[87]

Another group of exiles, the so-called okruzhentsy (literally, those who had been encircled), followed a similar trajectory. These were former Red Army soldiers who had been captured by the Germans but recently liberated by the Soviet army as it marched west. In June 1943, one thousand of these former POWs were sent to Vorkuta, likely at the personal request of Mal'tsev.[88] Like the "mobilized" Germans, they were subjected to living and working conditions on par with prisoners, even though they were supposed to live and work in strict isolation from them. In July 1944, however, the "special camp" in which they were held was liquidated and the POWs became "permanent cadres" of KVU.[89] Although this did mean an improvement in their living conditions, it essentially meant that imprisonment had been commuted to exile.

Throughout the war former Soviet POWs, as well as Soviet citizens suspected of actively collaborating with the Germans, were subject to a process of "verification and filtration" to determine whether or not they should be allowed to rejoin Soviet society.[90] In the first half of 1945, over ten thousand "repatriates" were sent to Vorkuta to undergo this process.[91] The treatment of those being "verified" was in line with the precedent established in the case of ethnic Germans and okruzhentsy. While they lived and worked separately from prisoners, they were kept under strict guard in zones while their cases were reviewed. By the end of 1946, the fates of these men and women were determined, after having their labor exploited to help the rapidly expanding coal complex. Only about three hundred were arrested and sentenced to terms in Vorkutlag proper.[92] Approximately half were released outright after investigations that determined their innocence. Most of the remaining "repatriates" were determined to be suspect, and so were designated for exile to far-flung parts of the Soviet Union. Of these, approximately two thousand were ordered to settle in Vorkuta. Now living outside the zone, they joined the ranks of Vorkuta's non-prisoner residents.[93] Even among those who were released after filtration, there were additional inducements to stay in Vorkuta, as former Red Army soldiers who had been cleared of wrongdoing were actively recruited to serve as camp guards in Vorkutlag.[94]

Taken together, these exile populations added nearly sixteen thousand to the non-prisoner population of Vorkuta from 1943 to 1947. Yet, as mentioned above, the total population of Vorkuta grew by nearly thirty thousand people during this interval. Who were the rest of the residents of Vorkuta? Most of them, in fact, were former prisoners of the camp itself. As was the case throughout the Gulag, Vorkutlag had a "revolving door" of prisoners, with releases and transfers nearly as common as the intake of new prisoners, particularly after the war.[95] Between 1943 and 1947, over thirty-four thousand prisoners were released from Vorkutlag, a number that far exceeds expectations. Nearly a third of the total came in 1945, when an amnesty was declared in honor of the Soviet victory in the Second World War.[96] As was standard practice in the Gulag, those with short sentences were most likely to be released, as were women, the elderly, juveniles, and invalids.[97] Some prisoners with longer sentences who had been convicted of counterrevolutionary crimes were released simply because their regular sentences expired. Yet being released from the camp did not always include the opportunity to leave Vorkuta. In the last year of the war, for example, Mal'tsev was given the explicit authority to keep all released prisoners in the city, even if they were subject to conscription into the Red Army, just one of many potential limitations on the geographical mobility of former prisoners.[98] Thus, released prisoners made up a substantial part of the city population.

That the overwhelming majority of the population of Vorkuta had its origins *within* the barbed wire speaks volumes about the fluidity of social categories and hierarchies in Vorkuta and Vorkutlag. While we are accustomed to think of the world of the Gulag as one where individuals were assigned specific places in an immutable social hierarchy, the reality of social relations in the Gulag camps and the larger communities in which they were embedded was not so neat and simple. As in the case of the bulk of Vorkuta's residents, one's social status, and the corresponding space to which one was attached (camp or city), could be changed with the stroke of a pen in Moscow. But it was not only official orders that could affect one's place in the social hierarchy.

Informal relationships also played an important role in determining social status. Patronage networks operated both among the prisoner and non-prisoner populations, bestowing privileges that did not necessarily correspond to one's official place in the social hierarchy. The result was that the social universe of the city and camp complex together was fluid and filled with many seeming contradictions.

The existence and experience of many of Vorkuta's residents constantly tested both social hierarchies and the fragile borders between camp and city. For example, after the Second World War an increasing number of non-prisoners made their way to Vorkuta in order to live near relatives who were imprisoned in the camp, creating mixed families of prisoners and non-prisoners. Such situations were a challenge to both the spatial divisions and the social hierarchy. Twelve-year-old Irina Skakovskaia accompanied her aunt to Vorkuta in August 1946 in order to live closer to her mother, one of the many prisoners who had served out her entire sentence in Vorkutlag but nevertheless continued to be held in the camp because of wartime regulations forbidding the release of certain categories of prisoners.[99] Although Skakovskaia's mother had received a pass allowing her to move freely in the city, she was still a prisoner and had to return to the zone each night. Mother and daughter did not get to see each other very often, even though they were practically neighbors. As Skakovskaia relates in her memoirs, "our path to school went by the camp zone, and Mama occasionally saw us in the mornings through the barbed wire."[100] Because the family was split on either side of the zone, her mother's friends, themselves former prisoners, expressed anxiety and skepticism about where Irina should fit into the social hierarchy. "What will she do here?" they had asked her mother, "Become the lover of some camp chief?"[101] But despite her separation from her mother, her proximity to the camp, and her ambiguous social status, her life in Vorkuta appears to have been a relatively happy one. She excelled in school, and once her mother was released in 1947, the family was reunited and lived outside the zone. But before her mother's release, the family did not fit into a clear place in the social hierarchy.

The variable and contradictory social and spatial relationships of the city were most clearly on display during the many performances on the stage of the Vorkuta Musical Drama Theater. The company, made up largely of prisoners, staged performances for non-prisoner audiences hundreds of times per year.[102] The social proximity of groups that were supposed to remain separate was a source of anxiety for both sides. How much appreciation could non-prisoner members of the audience show for the prisoner performers on stage? Even though many in the audience were recently released prisoners or exiles, too much applause would have implied too much admiration for the prisoners, and perhaps even an inversion of the accepted social hierarchy.[103] For many of those onstage or backstage, performing for an audience of social superiors also represented an uncomfortable dilemma. As former prisoner E. Kotliar relates, he once discussed the morality of being involved in the theater with artistic director Boris Mordvinov and screenwriter Aleksei Kapler. As he wrote, "[The conversation] was not about why the camp administration organized theatrical collectives of prisoners. We understood that this was not from humanity and not for cultural-educational work. We understood to what degree this was hypocrisy and lies. The conversation was about whether or not the artist had the moral right to participate in such a theater . . . would he become an accomplice to a cruel punitive system?"

Mordvinov's answer to this conundrum was to direct his performances to "free people of the second or third sort," former prisoners and other marginals who truly appreciated the performances.[104] No matter how the two sides adapted, whether by restraining applause for the performers or by playing to the less privileged among the audience, theater performances inevitably had the potential to disrupt social hierarchies and spatial divisions. These performances, which took place in the heart of the city, involved the participation of all the varied residents of Vorkuta and Vorkutlag: prisoners, exiles, guards, and members of the camp administration. By its very nature, the theater demonstrated many of the ways in which spatial and social divisions were both challenged and closely guarded.

CONCLUSION

The Second World War occupies a special place in the mythology of Vorkuta. In Soviet histories of the city, there was no period treated with greater pride. The 591 trainloads of coal that Leningrad received from Vorkuta from 1943 to 1945 were cited in a 1959 celebratory volume as "one of the most glorious pages in the history of Vorkuta."[105] In present-day Vorkuta, the city's contribution to the war effort continues to be touted as its greatest accomplishment.[106] This commemoration of Vorkuta's role in the war effort is not unusual. As many others have pointed out, the Second World War played an important role in legitimating the Soviet regime that only grew with the passage of time.[107] In this case, it is fairly easy to trace the deliberate construction of a myth surrounding Vorkuta and its function in the war. As described in the introduction to this chapter, the beginning of Vorkuta's entrance into public discourse was marked by a demonstration in 1943 to celebrate the shipment of coal to blockaded Leningrad. Trumpeted in Vorkuta's camp newspaper and briefly noted in *Pravda*, this demonstration represents the tentative beginnings of the city of Vorkuta, which occupied a separate symbolic space from Vorkutlag.

By 1946 the construction of the myth of Vorkuta and the selfless sacrifices of its "workers" to aid Leningrad was in full swing. "Northern Lights," the four-part series on the history of the city that appeared on the pages of *Pravda* in May 1946, treated the shipment of coal to Leningrad during the war as a central event in the city's history.[108] A year later, in November 1947, Vorkuta was featured in the popular Soviet newsmagazine *Ogonëk*. A two-page photo montage, under the headline "City above the Arctic Circle," depicted life in the city (figure 2.3). It featured images of Vorkuta's citizens at work and at rest, although coal and coal mines are present only in one photograph, which depicts a train with a coal car. Vorkuta's buildings and streetscapes were a particular point of focus, with several specimens of Stalinist neoclassical architecture on display. The center of the photo montage was the upper portion of a map of the Soviet Union, with "Vorkuta" clearly marked.[109] Vorkuta's urban geography was now an official part of Soviet public culture, just as the city now had a place on the map of the Soviet Union. These two publications told one story, in prose and pictures, of the transformation that the war had wrought on Vorkuta.

Yet these accounts of Vorkuta, and their subsequent recapitulations in Soviet and post-Soviet public discourse, were perversely incomplete. The war brought with it the integration of Vorkutlag into the Soviet effort of total war, and the effects of this change affected the lives of tens of thousands of men and women who had the misfortune of being sent to the city. The insatiable demand for coal, combined with a seemingly limitless "supply" of prisoners from the Soviet Union's western

ГОРОД ЗА ПОЛЯРНЫМ КРУГОМ

Фотоочерк специального корреспондента «Огонька» В. Евграфова

За годы сталинских пятилеток в Советской Арктике выросли новые города. Сбылась вековая мечта народов Севера: дикая, холодная тундра пробуждена к жизни. Один из очагов социалистической культуры в тундре — молодой город Воркута. Этот новый город был нанесен на карту Российской Советской Федеративной Социалистической Республики 26 ноября 1943 года. Но уже сейчас Воркута может соревноваться с другими городами Севера и по красоте и в темпах роста. Проходя по улицам юного города, мимо прекрасных зданий городского театра, Дома культуры, горного техникума, кинотеатра, средней школы, гостиницы, забываешь, что город расположен на 67-й параллели, в суровой тундре, где средняя годовая температура — минус 7 градусов, а зимой 114 дней свирепствует пурга и в течение 20 суток продолжается полная полярная ночь.

1. Железная дорога на 67-й параллели. 2. Памятник С. М. Кирову на площади Воркуты. 3. Заканчиваются работы по благоустройству улиц. 4. Городской театр. 5. Стадион «Динамо». 6. Гостиница.

Figure 2.3. Published images of Vorkuta, 1947. Source: V. Evgrafov, "Gorod za poliarnym krugom," *Ogonëk* 45 (1947).

borderlands, resulted not simply in a massive expansion of the camp and coal mining complex. They also combined to make the lives of prisoners incredibly "cheap" in the eyes of those officials who decided whether they lived or died. It is no coincidence that the moment of Vorkuta's greatest "glory" coincided with the most difficult conditions and highest death rate in the history of the camp complex. The war may have put Vorkuta on the map for millions of Soviet citizens to see, but those unlucky enough to experience Vorkutlag firsthand came to understand the tragic reality of the supposedly selfless sacrifices made for the war effort.

The war resulted not just in the expansion of the camp complex, but also in the creation of a city that was separate, at least in theory, from the camp complex. With only a few thousand residents at its foundation, the city of Vorkuta at first existed almost purely on paper. However, over the next four years Mal'tsev oversaw the construction of buildings and the creation of spaces that were nominally separate from the camp complex. In addition to acting in his official capacity as camp director, he acted unofficially as patron to architects and planners as he sought to build a city that reflected his self-image as a benevolent and enlightened local magnate. But for wartime population transfers, Vorkuta might have remained a city without residents. Soon "mobilized" ethnic Germans, former Soviet POWs, Soviet citizens who had lived under German occupation, and ex-prisoners would come to make up the bulk of the Vorkutiane. Although all began their time in Vorkuta within the barbed wire, by 1947 virtually all of them had been given the status of permanent exiles. It was a strange citizenry indeed, consisting largely of people who had been sent to the city against their will and were unable to leave.

The creation of a separate city and citizenry meant that borders between camp and city, and the zone and the outside, began to be delineated more clearly. But it was one thing to build city squares, parks, and theaters. The everyday lives of thousands of prisoners and non-prisoners bespoke a different reality, where interactions were constant and positions in the social hierarchy were murky. These ambiguities of identity and space were on display in the nightly performances of the Vorkuta Musical Drama Theater, where a company of prisoners and non-prisoners played for an audience of camp officials, guards, ex-prisoners, exiles, and their families. The theater that camp director Mal'tsev and prisoner Mordvinov created to provide escapist entertainment during the depths of the war paradoxically demonstrated both the distance that separated the world of the camp from the world of the city and the proximity and intimacy of these worlds and their inhabitants. Clearly, the relationship between Vorkutlag and the city of Vorkuta was still being negotiated. During postwar Stalinism it would continue to evolve in unprecedented ways.

3 In Search of "Normalcy"
Vorkuta during Postwar Stalinism

When development [of a Soviet prison camp city] has reached a certain state the distinction between camp and settlement, prisoner and free man, begins to disappear.

—*Bernhard Roeder,* Katorga

IN THE WINTER OF 1946–47, city architect Vsevolod Lunev was sent from Vorkuta to Moscow on official camp business. After a five-day train journey on the Northern Pechora main line, Lunev spent several days studying an indoor swimming pool that had recently been built in the Sokol'niki district. Lunev's patron, camp director Mikhail Mal'tsev, had charged him with the task of designing a similar structure for Vorkuta. Had the swimming pool been built, it would have occupied pride of place in the new city, on Moscow Square at the intersection of Moscow and Miner streets, behind a monument to Stalin. The ambitious project was soon scuttled, however, and an indoor pool would not be built in Vorkuta for another decade.[1] While in Moscow Lunev learned that Mal'tsev, the larger-than-life figure who had overseen Vorkuta's rapid expansion during the war, had been replaced.

Mal'tsev's successor, Aleksei Kukhtikov, had other plans. Reacting incredulously to the plan to build a swimming pool, Kukhtikov proposed another use for the site: a children's hospital.[2] Thus, Lunev was placed in charge of designing and overseeing the construction of Vorkuta's first children's hospital rather than its first indoor swimming pool. This was to be no mean feat, given the problematic soil conditions present at the site. Lunev's design, which followed the neoclassical design of his Musical Drama Theater, integrated three different types of foundations.[3]

Figure 3.1. Vorkuta children's hospital (detail). Photograph by the author, 17 May 2003. Note that the monument to Stalin depicted in figure 0.1 was in this location until 21 December 1961, when it was replaced with the monument to Kirov that had been located in a nearby square.

When the building was completed in 1950, it was considered to be an architectural jewel, occupying the focal center of Vorkuta's main square (see figure 3.1). Although it is no longer used as a children's hospital, it remains in use some sixty years after its construction.

The hospital, and the story of its design and construction, demonstrates both the continuities and ruptures between wartime and the period that followed. The children's hospital was similar to wartime projects in many respects, in that it was built on the whim of an all-powerful director and designed by a member of his patronage network. Lunev himself exemplified the wartime population of the city, as he had been transferred there involuntarily during the war, and while never technically a prisoner, he had spent several months living behind barbed wire. Now he occupied the somewhat ambiguous status of exile, free to move about the city of Vorkuta but unable to move elsewhere permanently. By far the clearest continuity with the war lay in the fact that the hospital was built by prisoners, who after each day of laboring at the construction site in the heart of the city were led back behind the barbed wire by an armed convoy. Yet, the children's hospital was different from previous projects for both symbolic and practical reasons. It projected the notion that Vorkuta had achieved a level of "normalcy" on par with other Soviet cities, with their concern for serving the civilian population, in particular children. The hospital also reflected the practical needs of the city, which was in the midst of a postwar baby boom. Between 1948 and 1952 over thirteen thousand children were born in Vorkuta, creating an enormous demand for new healthcare facilities to serve them.[4] Thus, the construction of the hospital points to a demographic transformation taking place. Further, the prisoners who built the hospital lived and worked in conditions that were significantly different from their wartime counterparts. With a drastic improvement in the food supply, death was far less likely than had been the case during the war.

This chapter examines Vorkuta during the period between the end of postwar reconstruction and Stalin's death, arguing that the city and camp complex experienced a version of the "return to normalcy" that was typical of cities and villages throughout the Soviet Union. As a number of historians have demonstrated, 1947–1948 represented an important turning point for postwar Soviet society as it entered "late" or "postwar" Stalinism. Demobilization wound down, the famine of 1946–1947 abated, rationing ended, and industrial production was restored to prewar levels.[5] According to Elena Zubkova, such changes were accompanied by a transformation in "public consciousness," as Soviet citizens shifted from an atmosphere of wartime sacrifice to the desire for the stability of peacetime.[6] Yet, despite all that changed during late Stalinism, a "return to normalcy" remained as much an aspiration as it was a reality. As Sheila Fitzpatrick has argued, the idea of going back to business as usual was problematic, given both the persistence of terror after the war and the fact that the 1930s hardly represented anything approaching normality to which society could return.[7] Both of these arguments are magnified in the case of Vorkuta, a city and camp complex that were both creations of terror and mass repression. Clearly, there was no "normal" state to which Vorkuta and its residents could return. Nevertheless, this did not prevent attempts to create "normalcy" in Vorkuta during late Stalinism.

The construction of the children's hospital to serve the growing population was only one of these efforts. In the camp complex, mortality rates plummeted as the food supply improved and a number of incentives were introduced that improved the living standard of many. At the same time, approximately half of the prisoners in the camp complex became subject to a new camp regime that was intended to increase the isolation and punishment of certain groups of prisoners. In the city, rising migration and natural population growth led the non-prisoner population to nearly double from 1947 to 1953, and some of the first efforts to recruit non-prisoners to the city were launched. A number of important institutions were established to serve the growing city population and to make the city more separate from the camp complex, at least in theory. Although such institutions would lack independence and power in the short term, in the longer term much of the groundwork was being laid for the expansion of Vorkuta as a company town. Finally, many efforts focused on the creation and maintenance of divisions between the city and camp complex, and between prisoners and non-prisoners. Such attempts to isolate the world of the city from the world of the camp were successful in many important respects, and there is little question that the separation of these two worlds was more complete during late Stalinism than at any other time in the previous two decades. However, as suggested by the epigraph above, the two worlds continued to interact on a daily basis in ways that officials found troubling. Continued interactions and confrontations between them exposed the limits of "normalcy" and the social tensions that were created as the company town grew alongside the camp complex, and anticipated the crisis that would follow Stalin's death in 1953.

FOOD, INCENTIVES, AND STABILIZATION

When Mikhail Baital'skii, who had been a prisoner in Vorkutlag from 1936 to 1941, returned to the camp complex in 1950, he was struck by just how much the complex had grown in the previous decade. As he commented sarcastically in his memoirs, "Yes, it is a big city! How it has changed, our Vorkuta! How many mines there are all around! And builders and miners! And souls! And bosses!"[8] The camp complex to which Baital'skii was involuntarily returned had just reached a population of 77,700 prisoners.[9] These prisoners worked in a series of mines and other supporting enterprises, most of which had been built during the Second World War. By 1950 there were eighteen working coal mines and seven in various stages of construction that together produced nearly 7 million tons of coal per year.[10] After the rapid expansion of the war and postwar reconstruction, Vorkuta was home to one of the largest camp complexes in the Soviet Union and to mines that provided a significant source of coal for the Russian Northwest.

Yet the dramatic expansion of the camp complex did not continue after the initial postwar reconstruction boom ended. Although ambitious plans were hatched in 1948 to build over twenty new mines in order to supply a new steel plant being built in Cherepovets on the Volga River, in fact only one mine was sunk during the tenure of director Aleksei Kukhtikov from January 1947 to April 1952.[11] With the restoration of the Donbas and significant progress in the postwar reconstruction of the coal industry, Vorkuta's expensive coal looked increasingly unattractive.[12] Previously, the primary force shaping the everyday lives of prisoners had been the war, the resulting shortages of food and other essentials, and an insatiable demand for coal. Now, the postwar context of increased food supply and attempts to improve prisoner productivity through incentives would lead to a marked degree of stabilization and greatly improved prospects for survival.

In the wartime Gulag, food shortages led to some of the highest death rates in the history of Soviet forced labor, particularly during the desperate winters of 1942–1943.[13] But after a brief spike in 1947 due to famine, mortality throughout the Gulag declined continuously from 1948 to 1953.[14] The Vorkuta camp complex was no exception to this trend. Mortality declined nearly twenty times from its apex of 147 deaths per thousand in 1943 to 7.5 deaths per thousand in 1953.[15] The most important cause of this decline in mortality was the steadily improving food supply in the camps. By the late 1940s, yearly reports from the camp director to his superiors no longer contained impassioned pleas for additional food, as had been the case in 1942–1943. Instead, these reports described significant but not life-threatening shortages of goods like sugar and milk.[16] Vorkutlag was able to continue its wartime policy of purchasing food directly from nearby regions, and this made up a significant proportion of its overall food supply. In 1948, for instance, the camp spent more than 22 million rubles on such purchases, including 12,000 tons of potatoes and vegetables, some two-thirds of the entire amount consumed by the camp that year.[17] Prisoners' diets remained deficient in many ways, but the majority of prisoners received adequate nourishment for survival.

In addition to the regular rations that they received, prisoners in the Vorkuta camp complex had additional opportunities to consume precious calories by the early 1950s. In order to increase the productivity of prisoner labor and make the forced labor system more "profitable," a system of wages for prisoners was introduced throughout the Gulag.[18] Between July 1950 and January 1952, all prisoners in the Vorkuta complex began to receive wages for their work.[19] By design, prisoners' wages were significantly lower than those paid to non-prisoners, even before the cost of their upkeep was deducted. As table 3.1 demonstrates, there was a wide variation of wages paid to prisoners within the camp complex. Nearly 30 percent of prisoners received under 75 rubles per month or the equivalent of 10 percent of the civilian wage (the effective minimum), whereas on the upper end, approximately 13 percent of prisoners earned over 300 rubles per month. By comparison, the average miner in the civilian economy earned a wage of 1,465 rubles per month in the second quarter of 1953.[20] Although this was far less than workers in the civilian economy were paid for performing the same work, these were considerable sums. In fact, prisoners in Vorkuta received some of the highest wages in the Gulag since most worked in a well-paid sector of the economy (coal mining) in a remote location (the Arctic), circumstances that were rewarded in the Gulag wage system as they were throughout the USSR.[21] Camp administrators considered the wage reform to be a success, as it appeared to improve prisoner productivity, the overall finances of the camps, and the physical condition of the prisoners.[22]

Measuring how much the wage reform improved the lives of prisoners is not as simple as determining the size of their wages, however. The table below tells only the official story of how wages were distributed throughout the camp. There was also an unofficial system, which informally redistributed much of this cash among the prisoners. Because the wage reform increased the amount of cash in circulation in the camps, payments of bribes, or *lapa* (literally, "paw"), between prisoners

Table 3.1. Distribution of wages paid to Vorkutlag prisoners, July–December 1950

Monthly Salary (rubles)	N	%
>1000	137	0.44
750–1000	267	0.86
500–750	883	2.85
300–500	2,762	8.90
200–300	4,595	14.81
150–200	4,372	14.09
100–150	4,385	14.13
75–100	4,442	14.32
<75	7,140	23.01
10% Guarantee	2,045	6.59

Source: GARF, f. R-9414, op. 1 ch. 2, d. 151, l. 73.

became more common.[23] Cash payments accompanied many transactions within the camp and were essential in order to secure favors or services from fellow prisoners who held superior positions in the camp hierarchy. Landing a desirable job or having the daily production figures of one's brigade padded usually involved the payment of lapa. As former prisoner Aleksandr Klein described it, "Having received money earned (after deductions this was little), a worker gave the 'lapa' (bribe) to the brigade leader. This was considered obligatory: the brigade leader had to give the 'lapa' to the foreman and the norm setters, who determined the percent of their brigade's plan fulfillment, from which, it is clear, the wages and, most important, the food ration depended. . . . Further, the foremen and the brigade leaders were required to give the 'lapa' to the duty officer." When Klein was able to secure himself a relatively soft job as a stoker and disinfector in the bathhouse, he received a wage of 56 rubles per month, of which he paid his superior 25 rubles. When he was later promoted to water carrier, his wage was 150 rubles per month, of which he paid his superior 70 rubles.[24] Thus, the formal wage system was subverted by the informal practices of the camp. Perhaps ironically, the money flowing upward through the hierarchy of the camp economy served to increase the unequal distribution of wages among the prisoner population, since those higher up in the camp hierarchy tended to receive both higher wages and larger amounts of lapa.

The buying power of prisoners was not just affected by the unofficial redistribution of wages. For one, limits were placed on how much prisoners were allowed to spend within the camp each month: 300 rubles per month in regular camps, and 100 rubles per month in "special" camps (see below).[25] Further, the availability of goods often trumped the availability of cash as a factor determining how useful the wages were, as was the case in the Soviet economy in general. Although stores were set up throughout the camp complex where prisoners could spend their money, the selection of goods usually left much to be desired. Joseph Scholmer, a German prisoner held in Rechlag, described the situation thus: "It is now possible to buy food in the camp, though only in limited quantities. The stocks of canteens consist mainly of jam, tinned fish, sugar, margarine, and cheap textile goods. Supplies do not come in regularly. Sometimes months go by in which sugar is unobtainable. Moreover, the town authorities have a tendency only to allow such goods as are too expensive for the 'free' population to appear in these stores. Boxes of chocolate are available, for instance, at 40 roubles [*sic*] a kilo."[26] Thus, in many cases prisoners had little choice but to spend their earnings on unnecessary or undesirable goods, although they were sometimes able to trade some of these items for other, more desired goods. Even more important for prisoners was the opening of additional cafeterias where prisoners could buy extra meals to supplement their regular rations. Although there was little difference between what was served in these cafeterias and regular prisoner rations, the cafeterias were nevertheless an important way for prisoners to add calories to their diet. Well-paid prisoners typically ate in both "free" and "for pay" cafeterias daily.[27] Thus, despite the lack of variety in what prisoners were able to purchase, the introduction of the wage system contributed significantly to the physical well being of the prisoner population.

Other new incentives undoubtedly improved the morale among certain parts of the prisoner population. The system of workday credits (*zachet rabochikh dnei*), which was introduced in Vorkutlag in September 1950, began to significantly shorten the sentences of prisoners convicted for less serious crimes.[28] Under this system, productive prisoners could receive between one and three days of time served for each day worked. As a result, over time sentences could be effectively cut by a third for prisoners who managed to overfulfill their quotas. By the end of 1950, over half of the prisoners in Vorkutlag were receiving workday credits that effectively shortened their sentences.[29] The workday credit system contributed to a significant increase in the release rate from Vorkutlag, which jumped from 8.5 percent in 1950 to 18.4 percent in 1951.[30] After Stalin's death in March 1953, the workday credit system would come to have even more significant effects on release rates.

Material incentives and improvements in the food supply meant that one of the deadliest periods in the history of Vorkuta had effectively ended by 1948. This did not, however, mean that prisoners did not struggle daily for survival. Even prisoners who occupied relatively privileged places in the camp hierarchy, such as mine safety worker Aleksandr Ugrimov, were all too aware of the daily possibility of death. As he wrote in his memoirs, "But deaths, especially of those close to me, I never saw in the camp. Of course, people died from illness, but more often from accidents in the mine; although I can't say that it was often. And it somehow happened imperceptibly; people tried not to notice, turned away—that possibility of 'kicking the bucket' and getting a tag on the big toe was too real for each of us; each of us had one thought: to survive, to hold out; hopelessness was interwoven with hope."[31] As Ugrimov pointed out, death was by no means absent from the camps, and illness and mining accidents still regularly resulted in fatalities. Yet, with outright starvation now only a remote possibility, it was possible to at least "try not to notice" those prisoners who died. The psychological atmosphere of the camp complex had clearly changed.

"SPROUTING NUMBERS"

Upon his return to imprisonment in Vorkuta in 1950, Mikhail Baital'skii noticed that the camp complex had not simply expanded, but had also qualitatively changed. He recalled in his memoirs, "There are many more guard towers, and the pea jackets worn by the 'souls' have sprouted numbers."[32] Baital'skii was calling attention to the fact that the introduction of incentives was not the only significant qualitative change in the lives of prisoners during late Stalinism. Many prisoners in the Vorkuta camp complex also faced another set of apparently contradictory changes to the terms of their existence: the introduction of the "special camp." A new camp with an initial quota of 10,000 prisoners was created alongside Vorkutlag by MVD order on 27 August 1948.[33] This new camp, dubbed Rechlag ("river camp"), was to be a so-called special camp, one of a new type of camp established to hold certain groups of prisoners in a stricter regime of isolation. Created on Stalin's order in February 1948, these "special camps" were designed to hold a veritable laundry list of those considered to be the most dangerous enemies of the Soviet state, including "spies, saboteurs, terrorists, Trotskyists, rightists, Mensheviks, SRs, anarchists, nationalists, white emigrants and participants in other anti-Soviet organizations and groups and those presenting danger by their anti-Soviet ties and enemy activities."[34] While the initial order had called for five of these camps to be built across the USSR to house 100,000 prisoners overall, the number of camps, as well as the number of prisoners held in them, quickly exceeded initial quotas. By October 1950, nine special camps had been created, with a theoretical capacity of 250,000 prisoners.[35] Rechlag was the sixth, and would eventually become one of the largest, holding some 35,000 prisoners by the beginning of 1952.[36]

In essence, the "special camp" reform extended the regime that had been applied to katorga prisoners since 1943 to a much larger group of prisoners.[37] In fact, katorga did not disappear with the introduction of the "special camps," and separate sections for katorzhane continued to operate in both Vorkutlag and Rechlag. Like katorga, the primary purpose of the special camps was to further isolate those considered to be the most dangerous criminals from the rest of the camp population and from society at large. Thus, much of the "special camp" regime was intended to increase this isolation. Prisoners in special camps lived in barracks that were locked at night, had bars over the windows, and were more cramped than was the standard elsewhere (if such a thing was possible!). Correspondence with the outside world was strictly limited, and prisoners were allowed to send only four letters per year and could receive letters only from family members. Special camp prisoners were not allowed to work with prisoners not in special camps, nor were they supposed to have any contact on the work site with non-prisoners.[38]

The special camps were designed not only to isolate, but also to punish. Special camp prisoners, as long as they were healthy, were to be used exclusively for heavy physical labor under armed guard. The workday for special camp prisoners was set at ten hours, as opposed to the standard nine.[39] Special camp prisoners were categorically excluded from having their sentences reduced for good behavior or productive labor, and it was initially forbidden to give them bonuses of any kind, although they were eventually allowed to receive wages in the winter of 1951. Finally, as noted above, special camp prisoners "sprouted numbers" that were painted on patches sewn to their uniforms. They were supposed to be referred to by these numbers rather than by their names. The introduction of numbers for prisoners in special camps was a further attempt to dehumanize and punish certain groups of prisoners.

Rechlag was not built from scratch. Instead, camp sections were transferred from Vorkutlag after minor modifications had been made to meet the new regulations. By 1951, Rechlag had taken on many of Vorkutlag's economic tasks, including some of its largest mines and construction projects.[40] All camp sections were located along the eastern and northern sections of the Vorkuta coalfield. Despite the emphasis on the isolation of Rechlag prisoners from "regular" prisoners and from the non-prisoner population, sections of Vorkutlag and Rechlag were interspersed with each other. Perhaps even more surprising is the fact that many of the camp sections transferred to Rechlag were in close proximity to the city. Rechlag prisoners were even assigned the task of city construction, which meant that special camp prisoners were led under armed guard through city streets on a daily basis. Just as camp sections were transferred to the new camp from Vorkutlag, so were the new camp's prisoners. According to the order creating the special camps in early 1948, all camps and prisons in the Soviet Union were required to review the files of their prisoners to determine who should be sent to the new camps.[41] With such a high percentage of counterrevolutionary and katorga prisoners, a significant proportion of Vorkutlag prisoners were designated for transfer to Rechlag. According to one estimate, by the beginning of 1950 over 70 percent of the prisoners in Rechlag had been transferred there from Vorkutlag.[42] Thus, the creation of a special camp in Vorkuta was more a matter of the reclassification of prisoners and space than it was the creation of a new camp.

For the administration of the camp complex, this reorganization created its own set of problems. From an economic standpoint, the reshuffling of people and space was clearly disruptive. Mine no. 1, the first mine to be transferred to Rechlag at the end of 1948, missed its yearly production target by 10 percent, which acting Rechlag director Fadeev attributed directly to the creation of Rechlag.[43] The new camp required the establishment of a separate administration, which strained the manpower of a camp complex that was already chronically short of personnel. Like any bureaucracy, Vorkutlag was loath to share its resources with the fledgling Rechlag, which made the reorganization even more difficult. Vorkutlag was slow to transfer personnel to Rechlag, and when it did, it used the opportunity to rid itself of its most undisciplined workers.[44] The reluctance of administrators in Vorkutlag to transfer housing stock (of which there was already a shortage) to Rechlag led to a "large housing crisis" for the new employees of the latter.[45] The stricter security requirements for special camps, which required more guards, were especially difficult to meet, since Vorkutlag was already forced to use thousands of prisoners to guard each other. Perhaps it is for this reason that Rechlag had its own director for only the first year of its existence. As of April 1950 Kukhtikov, who was already the director of Vorkutlag and Vorkutaugol', absorbed this responsibility.[46] In the short term, the creation of Rechlag required a difficult and disruptive reorganization.

The stricter regime of special camps, like that of katorga, placed increased psychological strains on the prisoners. The locking of barracks at night, limits on correspondence with the outside world, and the wearing of numbers on one's clothing all undoubtedly took their toll on the tens of thousands of prisoners in Rechlag. Elena Markova, a prisoner in a section of Rechlag that housed many mothers with newborn infants, recalls the anguish and anxiety created by the requirement that mothers remained locked in their barracks overnight away from their newborns.[47] Psychological strains were further intensified by the practice of assigning special camp prisoners only the most difficult and risky jobs available. In theory, at least, special camp prisoners were excluded from occupying privileged and less physically taxing positions in the camp as specialists or engineers. In practice, however, prisoners in special camps were not entirely excluded from such positions, and they were only slightly more likely than non-"special camp" prisoners to work in the mines.[48] Nevertheless, a concerted effort was made to make the psychological atmosphere in Rechlag even more oppressive for the prisoners.

Feelings of hopelessness were further magnified by one of the factors that most distinguished Vorkutlag from Rechlag: the likelihood of being released. As table 3.2 demonstrates, prisoners were far more likely to be released from Vorkutlag than from Rechlag. In fact, over time the difference between the two camps tended to increase. This contributed

Table 3.2. Absolute and relative number of prisoners released from Vorkutlag and Rechlag, 1949–1953

	Vorkutlag		Rechlag	
	N	%	N	%
1949	4,345	7.30	250	1.57
1950	4,074	8.56	573	1.96
1951	6,987	18.40	555	1.61
1952	6,706	17.08	926	2.61
1953	11,622	33.23	1,016	2.80

Source: GARF, f. R-9414, op. 1 ch. 2, d. 472; GARF, f. R-9414, op. 1 ch. 2, d. 479; GARF, f. R-9414, op. 1 ch. 2, d. 485; GARF, f. R-9414, op. 1 ch. 2, d. 495; GARF, f. R-9414, op. 1 ch. 2, d. 500.

to the perception on the part of prisoners in Rechlag that it was unlikely they would ever be freed. Although prisoners in each camp were serving sentences that were about the same length on average, there were three important differences that accounted for the much higher likelihood of being released from Vorkutlag. First, Vorkutlag typically had several thousand prisoners with sentences under five years, whereas Rechlag had only a few hundred at most.[49] Second, "special camp" prisoners, like all "counterrevolutionary" prisoners in general, tended to be categorically excluded from the periodic amnesties that released large numbers of prisoners from the postwar Gulag.[50] Third, "special camp" prisoners were not eligible to receive workday credits, making it far more likely that they would have to serve their entire sentence.

The handful of prisoners who were released from Rechlag each year faced the sobering prospect that it would be impossible for them to return home. As of February 1948, all prisoners who were released from special camps were sentenced to exile in certain remote regions of the Soviet Union, which included Kolyma, Novosibirsk oblast', Krasnoiarsk krai, and certain regions of Kazakhstan.[51] The prospect of eternal exile effectively eliminated even the miniscule chance of returning home to establish a relatively normal life. For the handful of prisoners released from Rechlag during the first year of its existence, the sentence of exile was unusually harsh, as former prisoners were forced to leave Vorkuta, an area where they might have social networks in place to help navigate the difficult transition to civilian life. By May 1949, however, the areas of Komi ASSR located to the east of Ukhta, which included Vorkuta, had been added to the areas to which released special camp prisoners could be exiled.[52] Still, the prospect of release into eternal exile gave special camp prisoners little to which they could look forward.

But despite the apparent hopelessness that Rechlag prisoners faced, this does not necessarily mean that physical survival was less likely. Official statistics show that from 1949 to 1954 (when Rechlag ceased to exist) prisoners in Rechlag died at a rate that was roughly equal to, and occasionally slightly lower than, that of their counterparts in Vorkutlag. The mortality rate for prisoners in Rechlag during this period reached its zenith in 1949 (11.31 deaths per thousand) and its nadir in 1951 (5.87 deaths per thousand). In Vorkutlag, the mortality rate was 11.64 deaths per thousand in 1949 and 9.50 deaths per thousand in 1951. Mortality in both camps tended to be roughly equal to that of the Gulag average, which ranged between a high of 12.10 deaths per thousand in 1949 and a low of 6.70 deaths per thousand in 1953.[53] If we compare the mortality rate of prisoners in the Vorkuta complex during this period to that of the war and its immediate aftermath, we see very strong evidence that by 1949 the food situation in Vorkuta had stabilized to a great extent and that the overall health of prisoners had improved significantly.

The intention of the special camp reforms was to *isolate* certain groups of prisoners, but an important consequence of the reform, perhaps unintended, was also to *concentrate* certain types of prisoners within the special camps. Take, for example, the crimes for which prisoners had been convicted. By 1950, 93 percent of the prisoners in Rechlag had been convicted of "counterrevolutionary" crimes, as opposed to only 59 percent for Vorkutlag.[54] Both numbers were well above the average for the Gulag as a whole, but Rechlag sections now held prisoners convicted of counterrevolutionary crimes almost exclusively. Even more striking is the way in which the special camp reform concentrated prisoners of certain nationalities within Rechlag. In 1950, only 16 percent of the prisoners in Rechlag were Russian, as opposed to 48 percent in Vorkutlag. Forty percent of the prisoners in Rechlag were Ukrainian, 5 percent were Latvian, 12 percent were Lithuanian, and 5 percent were Estonian; in Vorkutlag the figures were 22 percent, 1 percent, 3 percent, and 2 percent, respectively.[55] Thus, in the camp sections of Rechlag Russians were far outnumbered by other nationalities, in particular those from the western borderlands of the Soviet Union.

Rechlag and Vorkutlag also saw a significant influx of foreign nationals during late Stalinism, particularly German citizens. By 1950, there were 4,370 Germans in the complex, some 5.6 percent of the overall population.[56] Most were POWs who had been convicted by Soviet military tribunals of war crimes against Soviet citizens in 1949–1950.[57] Whereas the majority of German and other POWs had been repatriated by 1949, those convicted of war crimes were not sent home until much later.[58] Those that remained in the Gulag were concentrated in a small number of camps and colonies, including Vorkutlag and Rechlag.[59] Some of the POWs were held in isolation from the rest of the prisoners, including approximately three hundred held in the *Bezymianka* (literally, "nameless") camp point, which was technically part of Rechlag camp section 7.[60] While the camp section as a whole held only female prisoners, the Bezymianka camp point was located across the river from the rest of the section and held only men described in MVD correspondence as "German-fascist villains." According to Elena Markova, who was ordered to carry out sanitary inspection of the section in the winter of 1950, many of the prisoners were malnourished and seriously ill.[61] Many other German POWs, probably the majority, were scattered throughout Vorkutlag and Rechlag. The German prisoner Joseph Scholmer encountered sizable communities of Germans in camp sections 6 and 4 of Rechlag, where he was imprisoned.[62] Scholmer, who was himself a member of the German Communist Party, encountered SS guards who had worked in the Sachsenhausen concentration camp, unrepentant Nazis who used the phrase, "There's one we forgot—to gas!" when they encountered Jewish prisoners.[63] He also met several high-ranking former officers in the German army.[64] German prisoners were forbidden from receiving food packages or correspondence from home, a situation that made hunger and demoralization widespread.[65]

The concentration of large groups of national minorities in the "special camp" sections led to important changes in prisoner society. Conationals begin to organize themselves into voluntary "self-help" organizations for the purpose of mutual aid, protection, and survival. Describing such groups, Joseph Scholmer wrote, "Each group is built up on a national basis. There is a perfectly good practical reason for this. Only people of the same nationality are really in a position to judge whether a man is personally and politically suitable to be taken on for underground work. On the whole it can be said that such groups are made up of the elite of each nation's representation in the camps. The groups are organized around a nucleus which is purposely kept as small as possible to minimize the NKVD's [*sic*] chances of making contact with it."[66] Significantly, some of these prisoners had actively fought against the establishment of Soviet power as members of partisan organizations like the Organization of Ukrainian Nationalists (OUN) and the Ukrainian Insurgent Army (UPA), giving them shared experiences of resisting Soviet power as well as active experience organizing underground organizations.[67] As has been well documented both by memoirists and historians, these national self-help organizations became ubiquitous throughout the Gulag, particularly within the special camp system.[68]

These organizations transmitted information between prisoners, barracks, sections, and camp complexes. For prisoners who had access to these networks, they were able to call on what they assumed was a much more reliable source of information than the usual *parasha*, or camp gossip. Access to accurate information was essential for survival in the camp. The organizations also operated as mutual aid societies, sharing resources and favors in order to improve the survival chances of everyone in the group. The networks also existed in order to stop the infiltration of informants and collaborators within the camp population. Intimidation and violence were often applied to those suspected of collaborating with the authorities. By the early 1950s, there was a clear sense that these organizations were successful in many of their endeavors, particularly in disrupting informant networks. Administrators in Vorkuta consistently complained of the difficulty they had maintaining networks of prisoner informants and quelling violence between prisoners. Despite concerted attempts to infiltrate the organizations and diminish their influence through various means, in 1951 camp complex director Kukhtikov was forced to admit that incidents of camp violence were not decreasing, but in fact increasing.[69] The camp administration appeared to be at a complete loss to contain these underground nationalist organizations.

Despite the ubiquity of these organizations, open mass resistance by prisoners was notably absent in Vorkutlag and Rechlag during the late Stalinist period. Although there were a few documented cases of prisoner uprisings elsewhere in the early 1950s, the nationalist organizations in Vorkuta continued to operate underground, limiting their goals to improving the conditions of their co-nationals.[70] However, it is important to note that these organizations had already become well organized and ubiquitous during the late Stalinist period. In the summer of 1953, following the death of Stalin and the fall of Beriia, a large number of prisoners in Rechlag would participate in one of the largest prisoner strikes in Gulag history. The death of the Soviet Union's supreme leader and the arrest of one of his likely successors were central to making this uprising possible. However, the prisoner organizations that coordinated and carried out the strike were a product of the late-Stalinist Gulag.

Taken together, improvements to the food supply, incentives for prisoners, and the "special camp" reform represented an attempt to reintroduce "normalcy" into the camp system after the upheaval of the war. Restoring "normalcy" to the system meant improving its economic efficiency by ensuring that prisoners received a bare minimum of nourishment and that their labor was properly incentivized. It also meant instituting proper regulations of isolation and punishment for the new groups of prisoners that represented a perceived threat to Soviet society, including nationalist rebels from the western borderlands and former Red Army soldiers whose wartime activities rendered them suspicious in the eyes of the regime. Yet the combination of a general improvement in living conditions and the concentration of certain types of prisoners in the special camps combined to undermine any semblance of "normalcy" that they were intended to create. Instead, Gulag administrators were met with an increasingly organized and recalcitrant prisoner population. As Oleg Khlevniuk and Yoram Gorlizki have persuasively argued, those who worked in the Gulag system were increasingly aware that "the cumulative impact of Stalin's penal policies threatened to push the scale of the Gulag beyond sustainable limits."[71] Radical reforms to address a growing crisis in the Gulag would not be possible until Stalin's death, however.

BUILDING A COMPANY TOWN

Even more so than within Vorkutlag and Rechlag, the period of postwar Stalinism was marked by an attempt to establish "normalcy" in the city of Vorkuta. While the city had been established at the height of the Second World War by Mal'tsev, and nurtured through his patronage of the prisoner and non-prisoner population, by 1947–1948 it consisted of a handful of monumental structures, a park and boulevard, and a series of haphazard spaces and buildings originally built as part of the camps. Much the same could be said for the city's population. The war had brought to the city thousands of non-prisoners: prison-camp employees, ex-prisoners, and various exile populations that together made up a population of just over thirty thousand people at the beginning of 1948. Most of these "citizens" had been sent to the city as a result of various waves of wartime and postwar repression, and began their existence in Vorkuta behind the barbed wire in camp zones. Yet as their status was changed, the barbed wire was removed from around their homes and they became residents of the new city. In short, there was little that was "normal" about the space, population, or institutions of Vorkuta at the beginning of 1948. Over the course of the next five years, however, Kukhtikov and his superiors in the Gulag would seek to normalize the structures, spaces, and population of the city. In so doing, they would lay the foundation for Vorkuta as a Soviet company town.

The Vorkuta Children's Hospital, which was completed in 1950, signified a key transition taking place in the planning and construction of the city. Its planning and construction indicated continuities between Mal'tsev and Kukhtikov's strategies as city patrons. A monumental structure, it was designed by one of Mal'tsev's "clients," was built by prisoners, and was located in the city square that had been a focus of attention since the city's founding in 1943. Yet, in other respects, the children's hospital was different from anything that had been built before. Unlike the other monumental structures that surrounded it, it served a practical function for Vorkuta's growing population, providing healthcare for the thousands of children in the city. It was a direct investment in the city's future, especially the physical well being of its citizens. The children's hospital represented a change in priorities and practices within the city. Vorkuta would be increasingly oriented toward serving the needs of its citizenry rather than being the exclusive playground of the camp elite and its prisoner and non-prisoner clients.

The shift in priorities that the hospital represented continued after its completion. For the first time, long-term plans for the city were composed. A systematic geological survey of city territory revealed a large area of unfrozen soil just to the east of where city construction had already begun in Moscow Square. Bounded on three sides by two ravines and the Vorkuta River, this area presented much more agreeable soil conditions for building, since it was free of permafrost. Building on frozen soil required complicated and expensive designs in order to prevent a building's heat from thawing the soil and causing the structure to deform. Building on permafrost-free soil would allow for faster and cheaper construction. Thus, when city architect Lunev and prisoner L. E. Raikin set to work composing the city's first "General Plan" for long-term construction, they focused on this permafrost-free area for the future expansion of the city.[72] When a draft of their "General Plan" was approved in July 1951 by the Komi ASSR Council of Ministers, local and regional officials had agreed to a strikingly different vision of Vorkuta as a city. Rather than an awkward amalgam of architectural showstoppers and former camp barracks, a separate city of Vorkuta was imagined that would have a population of at least one hundred thousand by 1965.[73] Lunev and Raikin's plan envisioned the city having a three-ray composition in the style of major world capitals such as Rome and St. Petersburg, with all three lines emanating from a monument to be placed on the site of Vorkuta's first mine in Rudnik.[74]

Not surprisingly, the city that would be built over the next five decades bore little resemblance to any of the illustrious models mentioned by Lunev. Nor would future city planners adhere to the three-ray design of the original plan as Vorkuta expanded. Nevertheless, beginning in the early 1950s city construction shifted in accordance with the new plan. After finishing the hospital, prisoner construction crews moved into the open tundra, building simpler two-story wooden residential buildings on a new street, dubbed Lenin Street.[75] These structures, some of which still line the courtyards off one of Vorkuta's major thoroughfares, were far from humble, serving as the homes of the city and camps' administrative elites. They were, however, some of the first examples of purpose-built civilian housing within the city. The vast majority of Vorkuta's residents would continue living in dilapidated barracks originally built as part of the camp well into the 1960s. But the housing construction begun at the beginning of the 1950s was part of an attempt to establish "normalcy" for Vorkuta's residents.

The early 1950s shift in construction was accompanied by another important change that would form the foundation of the company town: the expansion of city institutions that were nominally independent from the camp complex. The most important of these institutions was the City Committee of the Communist Party, or Gorkom, founded in November 1951.[76] The Gorkom typically performed two sets of functions in Soviet cities. First, it was responsible for oversight of the ideological life of party members within an urban area. Second, and perhaps more important, as the most powerful institution of local government, it typically played the role of "supermayor."[77] Although in theory the Gorkom operated in parallel to state institutions, such as the city Gorispolkom that had been created in 1943, in keeping with the general Soviet practice of subordinating state to party institutions, the Gorkom usually represented the apex of local power. At its founding, Vorkuta's Gorkom was somewhat anomalous, as its capacity to carry out both of the above functions was significantly circumscribed. It was responsible for only 425 full and candidate party members.[78] Another 1,770 members were supervised by the political sections of Vorkutlag and Rechlag.[79] Nor did the Gorkom exercise any significant amount of power in local government, as it remained entirely subordinate to Kukhtikov as chief. Nevertheless, by establishing a more "normal" decision-making structure that resembled other Soviet cities, a key part of the institutional framework for the company town was created.

Another significant institutional change was the creation of a city newspaper. Although the prison camp complex had published a series of newspapers over the previous decade, including *Shakhter* (The miner) and *Zapoliarnaia kochegarka* (The polar stoker), these had been produced under the supervision of the camp political section and were intended strictly for distribution within the camp.[80] The first issue of *Zapoliar'e*, the official organ of the Gorkom, appeared on 3 August 1952. *Zapoliar'e*'s beginnings were quite humble, as a two-page publication that appeared only twice per week. It lacked not only office space, but also its own typographical equipment, and so was printed with the camp complex's printing equipment.[81] Despite its limitations, the publication of *Zapoliar'e* was indeed a milestone in the foundation of the company town. It suggested that the city now had a reading public ready to consume it. Unlike the camp press, which addressed prisoners and prison camp employees as such, this was the first newspaper to address Vorkuta's residents as citizens and members of the reading public. Thus, it was a key component of the attempt to establish "normalcy" in Vorkuta.[82]

None of the institutional changes that took place in the early 1950s effectively diminished Kukhtikov's power as head of KVU, Vorkutlag, and Rechlag. Nor were they intended to do so, as they were carried out with Kukhtikov's blessings. They were more than an attempt to establish "normalcy" in the city—they were also an acknowledgment that the city's population had become large and complex enough that it would need its own set of institutions for management and administration. The size of the city population expanded dramatically during the late Stalinist period, from 30,127 in December 1947 to 68,553 in January 1953.[83] Whereas during the war and its immediate aftermath the vast majority of the city's population increase had come from large-scale forced population transfers from other parts of the Soviet Union, the city's population more than doubled from 1948 to 1953 as a result of new factors. These included a dramatic increase in the birth rate, a rise in "free" migration, and the recruitment of skilled workers from outside the city. Important shifts in state policy and natural population growth made the demographic structure of Vorkuta in 1953 very different from how it had been in 1947, necessitating many of the institutional changes described above.

Former prisoners released from Vorkutlag constituted the majority of the considerable population increase. As Golfo Alexopoulos has noted, a surprisingly large number of Gulag prisoners were released from the camps every year while Stalin was alive, and Vorkuta was no exception to this trend.[84] From 1 January 1949 to 31 December 1952, approximately 22,000 prisoners were released from Vorkutlag and 2,300 prisoners were released from Rechlag.[85] Given the notoriously heavy limitations placed on the mobility of former prisoners under Stalin, the majority of released prisoners likely remained in Vorkuta. In most years the majority of new city residents were in fact released prisoners, making up as much as two-thirds of those who came to the city.

Given the strict limits on their mobility, most former prisoners were simply expected to remain in Vorkuta after release. Yet an important change took place in the early 1950s, one that set the stage for local recruitment policies over the next decade. For the first time, former prisoners whose skills were considered valuable to KVU were actively recruited to remain in the city. The local *tekhnikum* (technical school), which had graduated its first class of seventy-one technicians to work in the mines in 1948, began expanding in early 1951.[86] Exiles and former prisoners were specifically targeted to be part of the expanded student body and staff of the institution.[87] Skilled former prisoners were also offered monetary incentives to remain working in the city.[88] Thus, even before Stalin's death former prisoners who were recognized to have skills essential to the operation of KVU were offered material incentives to remain after their release. As we shall see, this trend would only intensify after Stalin's death.

Although the majority of new Vorkutiane during the period of postwar Stalinism were released prisoners, approximately one-third of new residents were *not* prisoners released from the camp. Migration to the city from other parts of the Soviet Union clearly constituted another important source of population growth. Such migrants came from two broad categories. First, there were "free" migrants, those who decided, based on individual or family circumstances, to move to the city. Those who chose to move to the city had a variety of reasons for doing so. Some came to the city in order to be close to family members who were imprisoned or who were unable to leave the city because of their status as former prisoners. Although it was officially forbidden for KVU to hire the family members of prisoners, this rule was frequently violated. In early 1952, the head of the Vorkutlag politotdel, Opalenko, acknowledged that family members of prisoners were being hired by KVU despite this prohibition. As he stated, "people are being hired without a special check [of their backgrounds]. There are cases of people being hired to work in the camp who have relatives imprisoned in Vorkutlag."[89] Such was the case with the Dolgopolov family: The father was a prisoner, and lived in the zone. Mother and daughter lived outside the zone in the city.[90] Although such "mixed families" were rarely harmonious, many nevertheless decided that coming to Vorkuta to be near an imprisoned family member was better than the alternatives.[91]

Others traveled to Vorkuta from rural villages and "special settlements," particularly within Komi ASSR, in search of greater economic opportunities. After the devastation of the Second World War and the postwar famine, life was particularly difficult for those living on collective farms, and many peasants across the Soviet Union chose to move to cities in order to break out of rural poverty.[92] Non-prisoners were in high demand in Vorkuta, and despite the brutal living conditions there were ample opportunities for both men and women to earn higher wages and be promoted through the ranks. The fact that most new arrivals would be living in former camp barracks would have done little to discourage those leaving the harsh conditions of the many "special settlements" in Komi ASSR. Regardless of the source of this migration, the traffic of non-prisoners to and from the city had become so great by 1950 that camp director Kukhtikov requested that train service from Moscow to Vorkuta be expanded so that there were three express trains in each direction per week.[93]

Expanding Vorkuta's population, and in particular its pool of skilled labor, was too important to be left to chance, however. Acknowledging that relying on the release of prisoners and on "free" migration was insufficient to provide KVU with a sufficiently skilled workforce, the MVD began deliberate efforts to bring more workers to the city through transfers, incentives, and recruitment. Such efforts began in 1951, when the USSR Council of Ministers passed a resolution aimed at the "creation of permanent cadres" by calling for the transfer and recruitment of personnel whose skills and expertise were in short supply in Vorkuta. Under the terms of the legislation, mining engineers were to be sent from the Ministry of Coal Industry (MUP) to assume top posts in KVU, specialist doctors were to be transferred by the Ministry of Health, and up to two thousand specialists were to be sent from regional departments of the MVD. In addition to this targeted recruitment and transfers, Sovmin ordered that all ministries transfer anyone to the Pechora coal basin who expressed a desire to work there.[94] Thus, skilled personnel from within and without the MVD system were sought for the city.

In order to make Vorkuta a more attractive destination, and to improve the retention of workers already there, this resolution called for significant improvements to the city. Implicitly acknowledging the sorry state of civilian housing in the city, Sovmin ordered the construction of 25,000 square meters of permanent housing in 1951. Furnished apartments were to be set aside for members of the mine management teams, including directors, chief engineers, chief mechanics, and head surveyors of mines, as well as the heads of each mine section. This coincided with the adoption of the city's first "General Plan" and the transition from devoting resources to a few expensive marquis projects on Moscow Square to the construction of larger numbers of more humble buildings on the new Lenin Street. Money was also set aside to provide paid vacations to sanatoria for non-prisoners. Ten million rubles were allocated by the trade unions for the outfitting of houses of culture, clubs, libraries, and physical fitness centers. Undoubtedly more significant for those considering whether or not to come to Vorkuta was the extension of various wage incentives that existed in other parts of the Soviet Union to specialists who came to Vorkuta.[95] Thus, significant efforts were made to make Vorkuta a more attractive destination for skilled workers. That Sovmin was the entity ordering such changes was not without significance—like the creation of the Gorkom and the city newspaper, it suggested that city management was no longer wholly the preserve of the MVD and its local representatives.

The results of these policies were poor, especially in the short term. Far fewer specialists were recruited than had been envisaged by the resolution, and retention of qualified specialists remained a thorny problem for years to come.[96] Leaving short-term results aside, however, it is clear that these new recruitment and retention policies are significant, if more in terms of intentions than of outcomes. It was part of an important shift taking place in the management of the Gulag in the beginning of the 1950s. As attention turned to improving the productivity and economic viability of the forced labor system, the increased use of non-prisoners in Gulag projects emerged as an important strategy. As Oleg Khlevniuk has pointed out, "Despite the apparent advantages of unlimited control of prisoners, the authorities increasingly preferred to deal with relatively free workers, who provided higher labor productivity and did not require a well-oiled system of guards and overseers."[97] In Vorkuta, the emphasis on using non-prisoners was an important step in a longer-term process of creating a company town alongside the camp complex. The explicit acknowledgment of the utility of non-prisoner labor, particularly in management and specialist positions, only served to intensify efforts to grow the population of the city as well as to expand and improve the built environment.

The greatest indication of a turn toward "normalcy" in Vorkuta was a postwar baby boom that significantly contributed to the population increase. When the area's population had consisted overwhelmingly of prisoners and exiles held in areas within the zone, birth rates tended to be quite low. Even though fairly strict gender segregation, difficult working conditions, and poor nutrition did not entirely prevent pregnancy and childbirth, the hundreds of children born in the camp every year did not have an appreciable effect on the size of the local population, since the typical Gulag policy was to send the children of prisoners to orphanages after they had reached the age of two.[98] But beginning in 1948, the city's birth rate began to have a significant effect on the size and structure of the local population for the first time. Vorkuta, like other Soviet cities, experienced a tremendous increase in the birth rate after the war. Over 13,000 children were born there from the beginning of 1948 until the end of 1952. In 1949 alone, nearly 3,000 children were born, and the natality rate reached 61.70 births per thousand.[99] This birth rate was nearly twice the urban average for RSFSR, which reached a peak of 33.4 births per thousand in 1949.[100] Improving medical facilities (such as the children's hospital) and more abundant food supplies meant that a decrease in mortality took place as well, from 13.58 deaths per thousand in 1948 to 8.22 deaths per thousand in 1952 among the non-prisoner population. From 1948 until the end of 1952, natural population growth averaged nearly 5 percent per year, a net total of over 10,000 people.[101] Thus, the first generation of native Vorkutiane was born, a key signpost in the establishment of "normalcy" in Vorkuta.

In many important respects, the period of postwar Stalinism saw the beginning of long-term trends that would continue to mark the city and its population well into the 1980s. The struggle to recruit skilled workers from outside the city, and to retain those already working there (including former prisoners), would continue to be a perennial issue for the city and its industries. Echoes of the first systematic attempt to establish "permanent cadres" in the city in 1951 would reverberate throughout the 1950s and beyond. High levels of migration would only increase throughout the 1950s and 1960s before eventually leveling off. While the city's birth rate would never approach the level of the postwar baby boom, it would remain high in the coming decades as the population of Vorkuta remained young and fertile. Thus, like urban planning, construction, and the establishment of institutions, population policies and trends of the early 1950s set the stage for Vorkuta's transformation into a company town following Stalin's death.

"NORMALCY" UNDERMINED

Efforts to establish "normalcy" in the city and camp complex were by their nature contradictory and incomplete. In the camp complex, "normalcy" meant a general improvement in the living conditions of prisoners, in addition to attempts to incentivize labor and increase the punishment and isolation of certain groups of prisoners. In the city, it meant efforts to create a planned company town, with its own set of institutions and a growing population of qualified and productive workers. For Vorkuta as a whole, "normalcy" meant the enforcement and maintenance of strict boundaries between the city and camp complex. The process of creating two Vorkutas as separate, parallel worlds, which had begun during the Second World War, was greatly accelerated during the period of postwar Stalinism. In theory, there were separate groups of prisoners and citizens who were prevented from interacting with each other, largely because the spaces that they inhabited were separate. While it is true that this theory came closest to being realized during late Stalinism, it remained an ideal vision fraught with contradictions. The scale of the effort to create and enforce separation between camp and city meant that when the two worlds met, the results were particularly violent and disruptive.

One set of relationships that undermined the separation of city and camp complex was necessitated by the continued economic interdependence between the city and the camp complex. As long as both prisoners and non-prisoners were used to work in Vorkuta's mines and industries, it would be impossible to maintain a strict separation between the two populations. This was particularly true underground in the mines, where prisoners and non-prisoners worked together away from the gaze of camp guards. Certain mining specializations, such as the "blasters" (*zapal'shchiki*) who were responsible for setting explosives to clear out new tunnels or to loosen coal for excavation, tended to be dominated by non-prisoners.[102] In order to maintain safety and efficiency in the mine, non-prisoner "blasters" had to be in constant communication with prisoner brigades. Underground, prisoner brigades reported directly to non-prisoner personnel who were not part of the camp administration. Mine directors, engineers, mechanics, geologists, and surveyors, just to name a few of the specialist personnel working in a mine, were all in constant and direct communication with brigade leaders and the heads of mine sections, who were usually prisoners. These routine interactions led to familiarity, if not a certain degree of intimacy and trust. One Rechlag prisoner, Aleksandr Aleksandrovich Ugrimov, even recalled being taught how to sew by elderly non-prisoner women who worked with him at a mine electrical substation.[103] The cooperation of prisoners and non-prisoners determined the success or failure of a mine to meet its monthly plan, giving both groups a mutual economic interest. In the case of dangerous mining operations, establishing trust between prisoners and non-prisoners was a matter of life or death.[104]

Even above ground, the economic interdependence of camp complex and city meant that the strict delineation of space was constantly violated. Because the company town was built by prisoners, this meant that prisoners walked the streets of the city on a daily basis, albeit under guard. In fact, most of the prisoner labor used for city construction during late Stalinism came from a section of Rechlag, the very prisoners who were supposed to be most strictly isolated from non-prisoners and non-prisoner spaces. Joseph Scholmer, a Rechlag prisoner working in a city construction brigade, recalls walking through the very heart of Vorkuta, Moscow Square, every morning. As he writes, "Every morning we used to march across the great square in the middle of the town where there was a bronze life-size statue of Stalin."[105] Such prisoners were strictly guarded and prevented from interacting with citizens. Nevertheless, the prisoners were able to observe life in the city, and vice versa. At one point Scholmer's brigade worked the night shift, and he recalled being able to observe the intimate family life of non-prisoners through the windows of their homes. As he wrote, "We were engaged on the digging of foundations. . . . The site was in the *Ulitsa Leningradksaya* [Leningrad Street], on the other side of which there was a row of two-storied houses erected by German prisoners-of-war. This was where the NKVD [*sic*] aristocracy of Vorkuta lived. Through the half-drawn curtains the prisoners could watch their tormentors having a quiet evening at home with their families. They saw the major taking off his tunic. He washed his hands and face in the kitchen sink. At half-past eight—we had begun working in the meantime—the family sat down to supper. They ate a large number of dishes and had a lot to drink."[106] Thus, the prisoners' gazes violated the "normalcy" of the city by intruding on the domesticity of a non-prisoner family. Indeed, the very presence of "special camp" prisoners on city streets violated the isolation of the camp from the company town.

Other common practices undermined the status distinctions between prisoners and non-prisoners. Illicit relations between prisoners and camp staff remained common during the period of late Stalinism, even in the stricter regime of Rechlag. There were cases of bribery of guards by prisoners, and the smuggling of food and vodka into the camp as well as packages and letters out of the camp.[107] In 1952, some guards were even allowing prisoners to meet family members at work sites, where they were supposed to be strictly guarded.[108] Such violations of camp regime remained so common that they were frequently cited by high-level administrators as serious issues to be addressed.[109] Prisoners and guards often smoked together, especially after the introduction of prisoner wages, since this meant that prisoners were more likely to have their own tobacco, or at least money to buy it.[110] Less common, but still endemic, were episodes of collective drinking where guards and prisoners shared alcohol.[111] According to Joseph Scholmer, such illicit interactions between prisoners and guards often took place owing to national or local bonds, with guards helping prisoners who came from the same part of the Soviet Union.[112] Such interactions violated social hierarchies and undermined efforts to prevent intimacy between prisoners and non-prisoners.

Sexual relationships between prisoners and non-prisoners appear to have remained as common as they had always been in Vorkuta, even in Rechlag. Local state security (MGB) chief Tyrin noted in November 1951 at a KVU party conference that "it is necessary to strengthen the fight against relationships between free people and prisoners, a significant proportion of which comes from female employees working in Rechlag who establish relationships with prisoners." Tyrin cited numerous examples of such relationships, including one between Kuznetsova, an engineer in charge of personnel training, and a prisoner named Butler. The implication in most of these cases, such as the one between a nurse named Kir'ian and a prisoner named Shiriakov, was that the relationships were sexual in nature. According to Tyrin, "close relationships with prisoners create a situation where international spies can operate here in Vorkuta."[113] More to the point, such relationships violated political and social taboos.

Yet it was not only illegal practices that undermined efforts at maintaining "normalcy." Some Gulag regulations allowed for a surprising degree of blurring of social boundaries. For example, the practice of "self-guarding" (*samookhrana*), which allowed camps to use certain types of prisoners as guards, became widespread in Vorkutlag (though not in Rechlag) in the late 1940s and early 1950s. In 1948, there were 1,352 prisoners working in the militarized guard, some 28 percent of all the guards working in the camp.[114] Although camp director Kukhtikov claimed to his superiors that this situation was "unusual" and a product of necessity, it did in fact become standard practice in Vorkuta.[115] It was used with such regularity, in fact, that it undermined status distinctions between prisoners and non-prisoners. As a Procuracy official reported to the General Procurator of the Soviet Union in December 1952, "the widespread use of self-guarding has reached such a point that command personnel have lost the feeling of a border between guard-prisoners with passes and non-prisoner soldiers, and so do not control the guard-prisoners and give these prisoners complete freedom."[116] Evidence from Vorkuta suggests that such concern from the Procuracy was well founded. For instance, on 30 June 1951, a prisoner working as a guard took six prisoners out of the zone and into the city of Vorkuta. The group proceeded to get drunk, and in a state of intoxication the guard-prisoner shot at three prisoners and seriously wounded one of them.[117] Thus, official practices like "self-guarding" facilitated interactions between prisoners and non-prisoners and blurred distinctions between the two categories.

If everyday interactions between prisoners and non-prisoners were constant low-level disruptions of "normalcy," the periodic spillover of violence from the camp into the city threatened to destroy it entirely. Now that the city had public spaces, including Victory Park and Boulevard, Kirov and Moscow squares, a musical theater, two movie theaters, and a hotel/restaurant, it was increasingly possible for recreation and leisure to take place in public spaces. Yet the presence of such spaces proved to be a double-edged sword, as they provided opportunities for proper, cultured recreation but also for non-prisoners to get into a great deal of trouble. The new city spaces were a locus for off-duty camp officials and guards to "relax" during their time off from working in the camp. Frequently, such "relaxation" involved the consumption of copious amounts of alcohol by armed men.

Sever (The north), the city's sole restaurant, was a common site for the dangerous mixture of alcohol and firearms. A particularly colorful incident took place on the evening of 24 August 1952. On that night, Viktor Ivanovich Tsyganov, the commander of a guard detachment, came to the Sever restaurant to enjoy an evening off. According to a report by the local militia on what took place that evening, Tsyganov became drunk, "violated the public order and conducted himself improperly." When confronted by the restaurant manager, Tsyganov drew his pistol, loaded it, and exclaimed, "I am going to take you out to be shot." The manager fled to the director's office to phone the militia, and Tsyganov ran into the vestibule to find him, at which point he fired off two shots before being detained by militia officers who arrived on the scene.[118] While dramatic, this particular incident was not unusual. In only one week in April 1952, no fewer than four high-ranking camp and KVU officials were arrested for drunk and disorderly behavior at the restaurant.[119] Thus, it was not only interactions between prisoners and non-prisoners that undermined the establishment of "normalcy," but also the behavior of camp officials and guards in the company town, who brought the violence of the camp with them.

CONCLUSION

Perhaps no single incident better illustrates the uneasy coexistence of prison camp and company town than the events of the night of Sunday, 22 June 1952. On that night, a massive brawl took place between intoxicated off-duty camp guards and various residents of Vorkuta, most of whom were students at the local vocational school. According to the subsequent investigation, the night's violence began when a few off-duty soldiers beat a mining tekhnikum student, apparently without provocation, at the local dance square. A drunken bystander, Major Chikalev, who was an employee of the city military registration office (*voenkomat*), attempted to detain one of the soldiers and enlisted the help of some twenty vocational school students who were on the scene. They chased the soldier to Victory Boulevard, whereupon they encountered a larger group of intoxicated off-duty soldiers, who then began to chase the students. Cheered on by yet another drunken bystander, hero of the Soviet Union and party member A. A. Shestakov, the soldiers removed their belts and began to beat any student they could find. As the militia later reported, the battle was far from even: "The youths . . . were not only unable to fight back in the brawl, but were completely unable to help their comrades in harm's way." Eight students from the vocational school were seriously injured, some of whom lost consciousness at the scene. Two bystanders who were completely unrelated to the incident were beaten as well, including a man who was on an evening stroll with his wife and young child.[120]

But the worst was yet to come. A camp patrol arrived on the scene, and, rather than defusing the violence, caused it to escalate. After firing their pistols and rifles into the air, members of the patrol arrested sixteen innocent bystanders, most of whom were students. Among those arrested was the secretary of the Komsomol organization of the vocational school, who was subsequently savagely beaten. As he later testified, "the first time I was struck with the club was in my face, which broke my nose to the point of bleeding, [and] I at that time was trying to cover my head with my coat so that they didn't break my skull. They continued to rain down blows on my head and neck, [and] when I sat in the corner they continued to kick me in my side and in other parts of my body."[121] After the beating, those arrested were threatened that "shooting you would be too little" and "you are guaranteed to get twenty-five years each."[122] Soon, a crowd of some 200–250 people had gathered at the local militia lockup to demand the release of those arrested. By ten o'clock the next morning the students had been freed, although eight of them required serious medical attention due to the beatings they received.[123]

Party and Komsomol officials who investigated the brawl acknowledged the existence of a troubling rift between young students in Vorkuta and members of the militarized guard. Thus, after investigating the incident and disciplining those found to be responsible, they responded with measures to improve relations between the groups.[124] Yet the incident demonstrated more than just divisions between students and guards. The alcohol-fueled violence of 22 June 1952 was indicative of a far more serious challenge that Vorkuta faced in the late 1940s and early 1950s. Despite concerted efforts to establish "normalcy" within the camp and the company town, the proximity of these two worlds and the porousness of the borders between them made it virtually impossible to isolate them from each other. The world of arbitrary violence that marked life in Vorkutlag and Rechlag was supposed to end as soon as one left the confines of the camp zone itself, whereupon the cultured and lawful world of the Soviet city was to begin. Yet the pervasiveness of bad behavior by camp officials and guards in city spaces shows that keeping the two worlds separate was not as simple as isolating prisoners from non-prisoners. Even as "normalcy" was being established to a greater degree than ever before, its precariousness was made evident by ongoing interactions between prisoners and non-prisoners and by the violent outbursts of camp officials in the city. The rising tensions between city and camp under postwar Stalinism would, as we shall see, explode after Stalin's death.

Late Stalinism saw the establishment of a new status quo in Vorkuta, Vorkutlag, and Rechlag. In the city, a number of new institutions were created to administer and serve the needs of a rapidly growing non-prisoner population. Efforts were made to recruit and retain non-prisoners with particularly valuable skills and expertise, although their effectiveness was still limited. Inside the camps, great attention was paid both to incentivizing the labor of productive prisoners and to increasing the isolation and punishment of those prisoners who were thought to represent the greatest threat to the Soviet state and society. These changes would have important unintended consequences that would prove to be particularly important in the years to come. In the city, much of the groundwork was being laid for the transition into a company town that relied primarily on the labor of non-prisoners. In the camps, the increased concentration of certain parts of the prisoner population, particularly those who came from the Soviet Union's western borderlands, created the conditions that would make mass prisoner resistance possible. Yet it would take the death of Stalin in March 1953 to unleash a genuine state of crisis in Vorkuta.

4 Vorkuta in Crisis
Reform and Its Consequences

-Ça y est. Le «moustachu», la «grande salope» est claquée.
—*Armand Maloumian,* Les fils du Goulag

ON 25 JULY 1953, Aleksandr Fedorovich Zasiad'ko, Minister of Coal Industry of the USSR (MUP), wrote a letter to Georgii Malenkov, chairman of the USSR Council of Ministers. The purpose of the letter was to inform Malenkov, now the de facto leader of the Soviet Union, of a serious situation that had arisen in Vorkuta. According to Zasiad'ko, labor discipline among the prisoners of Rechlag "continued to decline sharply," resulting in a corresponding reduction in coal production. Further, the minister had just learned that for the last three days the prisoners assigned to mine no. 7 had stopped working entirely, leaving the mine at a standstill. The prisoners were apparently demanding that a top official visit Vorkuta to listen to their demands. Concluding his letter, Zasiad'ko requested that Malenkov order the MVD to take "the most immediate measures to reestablish discipline among the special contingent of Rechlag."[1] Soon, the work stoppage that he described would spread to nearly half of the camp sections in Rechlag. By the end of July, over fifteen thousand prisoners would be on strike, making it one of the largest acts of mass resistance in the history of the Gulag.

The Soviet Union was in the midst of a profound crisis in the summer of 1953. Ever since Stalin had died at his *dacha* in the evening of 5 March 1953, the uneasy atmosphere of postwar "normalcy" had disappeared. The death itself had been traumatic enough, and was followed by weeks of collective mourning. Even Stalin's funeral in Moscow ended in tragedy, with scores trampled to death in the rush to view the body.[2] Immediately after his demise, Stalin's closest advisers had begun a succession struggle. In the months that it would take to resolve, the lack of certainty about who was at the helm would destabilize a political system that had been based on Stalinist dictatorship for a quarter century. In the midst of their intrigues and backroom dealings, Stalin's successors attempted reforms to address long-standing structural issues and to shore up public support for the government in the short term. These rapid changes converged to leave both government officials and ordinary citizens in a collective "state of anxiety" by the end of 1953, as historian Miriam Dobson has recently argued.[3]

Zasiad'ko's letter illustrates the particular manifestation of the post-Stalin crisis in Vorkuta. Among the reforms launched by Stalin's successors in the weeks after his death was a dramatic overhaul of the Gulag intended to drastically reduce the size of the prisoner population and improve the everyday operation of the prison camp system. This included, as we shall see, not only a massive prisoner amnesty, but also an attempt to reorganize the administration of the camps and the industries to which they were attached. In the short term, such reforms were profoundly destabilizing. The amnesty was chaotic and ill planned, resulting in a heightened sense of uncertainty for non-prisoners and increased expectations on the part of prisoners. The prisoner population became much more difficult to control, and acts of open defiance were increasingly common. At the same time, the reorganization of the Gulag created bureaucratic confusion and increased the potential for conflict among the officials responsible for running the camps and connected industries. It became difficult for even the most routine business to be carried out, and the confidence of many Gulag officials was undermined.[4] The prisoners' increased sense of possibilities, as well as the sudden ineffectiveness of the authorities, would make mass prisoner resistance more likely than it had ever been before. The stage had been set for the massive Rechlag prisoner strike of July–August 1953, which was only the most dramatic symptom of a crisis that gripped Vorkuta in the wake of Stalin's death.

Local mine, camp, and city officials were not simply passive participants in the ongoing conflict. Although most were initially overwhelmed by the upheaval of 1953, by the summer of 1954 the situation on the ground would stabilize somewhat. Despite the fact that the ongoing conflict for control of Vorkuta and its resources remained unresolved in Moscow, local officials sought ways to navigate the new realities that they faced. Adapting to an overhaul of camp regulations launched in the summer of 1954, they devised new methods of using prisoner labor in the mines that would be mutually beneficial for camp section chiefs and mine managers alike. One strategy was to grant thousands of prisoners the right to move freely without guard outside the camp. Another technique, which became increasingly prevalent in 1955–1957, was to allow thousands of prisoners to live outside the confines of the camp itself. Both of these practices, it was hoped, would alleviate the problems that had converged to cause the prisoner strike in 1953. In fact, the implementation of these informal arrangements would end up being more than a short-term expedient. By 1955–1957, the widespread practice of allowing prisoners to live outside the zone was transforming the identity of thousands of prisoners by ascribing them a status that was remarkably similar to that of many non-prisoners. In the process, many camp spaces were recast as part of the city. By improvising a solution to the crisis precipitated by Stalin's death in 1953 and made apparent by the Rechlag strike of 1953, local officials accelerated Vorkuta's transition from a camp complex into a company town in unanticipated ways.

REFORM AND CRISIS IN VORKUTA

When Stalin's death was announced in the newspaper and over loudspeakers in Vorkuta, Vorkutlag, and Rechlag, it set off a wave of emotions among the non-prisoners and prisoners.[5] Many mourned the loss of their leader, sometimes in spite of personal tragedies that they had suffered during his rule. According to the local camp newspaper *Zapoliarnaia kochegarka*, during Stalin's funeral on 9 March the streets of the city were filled with residents listening to the broadcast from the capital on loudspeakers.[6] Even inside Vorkutlag and Rechlag, some wept openly at the news.[7] Yet not all of these tears were of sorrow.[8] Many prisoners and non-prisoners, like the author of the epigraph to this chapter, Armand Maloumian, a Franco-Armenian prisoner in

Rechlag, were quietly celebratory. No matter their particular reaction, all were aware that something of great significance had taken place.

The awareness of the beginning of a new era was only reinforced when a steady stream of reforms to the Gulag system was announced in the last two weeks of March. The MVD was stripped of its major production, extraction, and construction industries, which were transferred to corresponding civilian ministries.[9] Several large construction projects being built by the Gulag were suspended, including the Chum-Salekhard-Igarka railroad, which would have linked Vorkuta with other camp complexes east of the Ural Mountains.[10] On 27 March the Supreme Soviet issued a broad amnesty that would reduce the size of the Gulag population by more than one million prisoners.[11] On the following day, control of most prison camps (excluding "special camps" like Rechlag) was transferred from the MVD to the Ministry of Justice.[12] These reforms were launched largely on the initiative of Lavrentii Beriia, who had been responsible for much of the state's repressive apparatus and camp system since the end of 1938.[13] Although there had long been a perceived need to reform the system of forced labor, such radical change had been impossible to effect under Stalin.[14] Now that the leader himself was gone, his former lieutenants had the opportunity to attempt changes that had been contemplated for some time. The reforms launched by Beriia would come to have a dramatic impact on Vorkuta.

Of the reforms, the one with the most immediate and dramatic effect was the amnesty of 27 March 1953. Popularly known as the "Beriia amnesty" or "Voroshilov amnesty," it was the largest in the history of forced labor in the Soviet Union.[15] Its terms were sweeping: excepting certain categories of prisoners, all those with sentences of up to five years were to be released outright and all other prisoners had their sentences halved. Pregnant women, as well as those with children under ten years of age, were released; juveniles, men over fifty-five, and women over fifty were also set free, as were the terminally ill. The amnesty did not apply to all prisoners, however. Those convicted of serious theft, banditry, attempted murder, as well as most "counterrevolutionary" crimes, were excluded. The categories of prisoners released generally followed the precedent set under Stalin, which is hardly surprising given that the architect of the 1953 amnesty, Beriia, presided over the others as well.[16] In terms of scale, however, the 1953 amnesty was without precedent: approximately 1.2 million, or one half, of the 2.4 million prisoners in the Soviet system of camps and colonies were released over a period of several months.[17]

While its impact was not quite as dramatic as it was in other camps, the amnesty nevertheless had a significant effect on Vorkuta. Because the camps had an unusually high percentage of those categories of prisoners excluded from the amnesty, far fewer prisoners were released from Vorkutlag and Rechlag than was the case elsewhere. Only 7,123 prisoners, or about 10 percent of the camp population, were released.[18] In fact, the 1945 amnesty decreed after Soviet victory in the Second World War had resulted in the release of a significantly larger proportion of the prisoner population. Still, the loss of 10 percent of the prisoners shrank the labor force significantly. The release of many prisoners convicted of less serious crimes was particularly disruptive. Such prisoners were frequently used for samookhrana, where prisoners serving short sentences for lesser crimes were permitted to guard prisoners considered to be more dangerous. So many prisoners who had worked as guards were released under the amnesty that many brigades could not be escorted to worksites.[19] The amnesty also affected the quantity and quality of the information that the camp administration collected from its network of prisoner informants. With many of its agents amnestied, the camp administration's ability to infiltrate underground prisoner organizations was compromised.[20] Thus, while the number of prisoners released from Vorkutlag and Rechlag was far below the average throughout the Gulag, the amnesty nevertheless resulted in shortages of key categories of prisoners on which the camp administration typically relied.

Among the approximately sixty thousand prisoners who remained in Vorkutlag and Rechlag, the amnesty inspired both disappointment and hope. Prisoners were acutely aware of its existence and its terms, since it had been announced so publicly. Most prisoners in Vorkutlag and Rechlag belonged to the categories explicitly excluded from the mass release, and so were critical of its seemingly limited nature. Rechlag director Derevianko would later note the overwhelmingly negative reaction of the prisoners, stating, "From the moment of the publication of the Supreme Soviet decree on the amnesty of prisoners . . . feelings of extreme discontent arose in the sections of Rechlag."[21] But the announcement of such a broad amnesty also raised the hopes of many prisoners in the camps. Even though they had been left out, the very fact that an amnesty had been announced was interpreted as a positive signal. If such a sweeping release was announced less than a month after Stalin's death, it was possible that other measures could soon follow. By opening up new possibilities for change, the amnesty created a crisis of rising expectations among prisoners following Stalin's death. The new hopes and frustrations that arose in response to the amnesty would play a key role in the outbreak of the prisoner strike in July.

The amnesty did not simply affect the prisoners who remained in Vorkutlag and Rechlag. It also impacted, whether directly or indirectly, the lives of the approximately 68,000 non-prisoners living in Vorkuta. Many of them were exiles or former prisoners who were themselves hoping to be released from their terms of exile. Thus, many shared the prisoners' emotions of frustration and hope. Yet the amnesty also inspired anxiety and fear among many non-prisoners, particularly after they saw how the amnesty was carried out. When the first group of prisoners was released on 15 April 1953, mayhem and violence followed. This group, which numbered 853 prisoners, was brought to a central location at the railroad depot to await transportation out of the city. Although this had been done at night in order to send the amnestied on their way in the early morning hours, there was a six-hour delay to prepare paperwork. In the meantime, hundreds of the amnestied had scattered about the city, drinking and getting into trouble. A brawl broke out, and by the time the train had left after its long delay, seven were hospitalized for serious injuries.[22] Despite explicit orders to separate men from women, virtually nothing was done to protect the latter from sexual violence at the hands of the former. On one train departing from *Seida*, a southern outpost of Vorkutlag, two women were gang raped by male prisoners traveling in their car. In at least one other case, women were raped and then thrown off the train onto the tracks.[23] Reports on the violence perpetrated by the amnestied prisoners circulated throughout Vorkuta, contributing to an atmosphere of anxiety verging on panic.[24]

The dramatic violence associated with the release of the first group of prisoners under the amnesty does not provide a complete picture of how it was carried out, however. A number of measures were soon taken to prevent the repetition of such problems, including the strict separation of male and female prisoners, banning the sale of alcohol nearby transit points, and having armed guards accompany the departing trains of prisoners.[25] These measures prevented a repetition of the violence of 15 April when subsequent groups were released. Many of the amnestied in fact never left the city, choosing instead to continue working in the mines. The vast majority of these prisoners made a peaceful transition to civilian life. Although there was friction and even occasional violence between amnestied prisoners and other local residents, particularly camp guards, this was most often the result of aggression against the amnestied, not the other way around.[26] Yet the perception that the amnestied prisoners were dangerous remained. In the minds of those who had seen or heard about the mayhem of 15 April, the camp authorities had lost control of the unruly prisoners, whose release endangered the security of non-prisoners. As was the case across the Soviet Union, most of the crime perpetrated by the amnestied was directed against other former prisoners. Nevertheless, the chaos associated with the amnesty created the widespread perception that peaceful Soviet citizens were at risk.[27] Thus, the amnesty played an important role in undermining the uneasy "normalcy" that had characterized postwar Stalinism in Vorkuta, in that it created anxiety and discontent among prisoners and non-prisoners alike.

While dramatic, the amnesty probably had less long-term significance in Vorkuta than some of the other changes that Beriia introduced in March 1953. With an eye toward improving the performance of the Gulag both as an economic empire and as a penal system, he introduced a profound reorganization of the way that it was organized administratively. The Gulag administration, and most camps and colonies throughout the Soviet Union, were transferred to the oversight of the Ministry of Justice from the MVD. The Ministry of Justice, it was hoped, would do a better job of ensuring that proper security was enforced and that conditions conducive to the rehabilitation of prisoners were maintained. Thus, the Ministry of Justice assumed responsibility for nearly all the camps and colonies in the Soviet Union, with the notable exception of the "special camps," which remained under MVD oversight. In order to improve the economic viability of the Gulag's vast economic empire, oversight for its industries and enterprises was transferred to the corresponding civilian ministries. These civilian ministries, it was argued, would do a better job of ensuring that they were run in an efficient fashion and met their yearly production plans. The economic "chief administrations" that had been set up under the NKVD to manage groups of industries in 1940–1941, which occupied an administrative level between the top Gulag leadership and individual camps, were abolished.[28] Industries that had been attached to camps were thus no longer subordinated to the "chief administrations," the Gulag, or the MVD. The result of this reorganization was that Vorkuta's mines and camps now came under the purview of three ministries. The MVD, which had previously been responsible for the mines and both camps, was now responsible for Rechlag only. The Ministry of Justice gained control of Vorkutlag. The Ministry of Coal Industry assumed responsibility for Vorkutaugol' and its coal mines. Where one ministry had reigned supreme in Vorkuta, now three shared control of the camps and the mines.

This meant a definitive end of the era of *edinonachal'e*, or "one-man rule," in Vorkuta.[29] Ever since the creation of Vorkutlag in 1938, local control of Vorkuta's industries and camps had been vested in a single director. While the potential for alternative centers of power within the area had been created by the incorporation of the city of Vorkuta in 1943, and again by the creation of a Gorkom in 1951, in practice men like Tarkhanov, Mal'tsev, and Kukhtikov wielded an enormous amount of power and answered only to their superiors in the MVD. Now, this authority was split into three different positions. Stepan Ivanovich Degtev, who had become head of Vorkutlag, Rechlag, and KVU in April 1952, was stripped of two of these portfolios. He remained chief of KVU, whereas his responsibilities as camp director were handed over to two other officials, G. M. Prokop'ev (Vorkutlag) and A. A. Derevianko (Rechlag) that summer.[30] At first, the independence of Vorkutlag and Rechlag was fairly nominal, as Derevianko and likely Prokop'ev were former deputies of Degtev. Nevertheless, this was a significant change: the virtually unlimited power of the local director was no more. The three most important organizations in Vorkuta were now run by different men, each of whom reported to a different ministry. A significant potential for competition and conflict had been created.

The most significant friction and conflict among the three ministries and their local representatives revolved around the issue of prisoner labor. Under previous arrangements, Vorkutlag and Rechlag, as suppliers of camp labor, had been closely tied to KVU's mines, the primary consumers of prisoner labor. While the mines and the camp sections were run by different sets of officials, all of them had been subordinate to a single boss. Now, they were split into entirely different hierarchies that were part of separate ministries.[31] In order to facilitate the continued supply of labor from camps to enterprises, the two sides entered into reciprocal contracts. Such contracts established the rates at which the enterprise would compensate the camp for the labor of its prisoners, set ground rules for the safety, isolation, and guarding of prisoners, and committed both sides to improving the productivity of prisoner labor.[32] In theory this was a significant improvement over the previous system. Two sets of officials were responsible for the two separate penal and productive aspects of the prisoner's existence, and this would ensure that both were fulfilled satisfactorily. Contracts would then insure that both supplier and consumer of prisoner labor worked together to help each organization meet its respective goals.

In practice, however, the new arrangements were awkward and ill suited to accomplishing what had in the past been routine bureaucratic operations. Take, for example, a problem that arose in the summer of 1953. KVU was experiencing a severe shortage of wooden supports for tunnels in its mines. This was a common problem, as there was no timber in Vorkuta's immediate environs. The lack of sufficient wood at this time was attributed to a severe labor shortage at a remote satellite section of Vorkutlag that processed timber for the mines. Ameliorating the labor shortage would previously have required little more than an order from the single director to transfer more prisoners to the section. Now, however, it required a negotiation among three ministries and their local representatives in Vorkuta. KVU needed the tunnel supports, and therefore wanted Vorkutlag to devote more workers to manufacturing them. Because of the recent amnesty, Vorkutlag did not have enough prisoners to fully staff the camp section where they were produced. Rechlag had a sufficient number of prisoners, but was under the control of a different ministry. Solving this simple matter required correspondence among three sets of local officials and their superiors in Moscow, eventually involving both a deputy minister of MUP and the Minister of the MVD. In the end, Rechlag agreed to temporarily provide five hundred female prisoners to Vorkutlag, who would work to supply the needed timber to KVU.[33] If the resolution of such a simple matter required a complex and drawn-out negotiation, how would local and central authorities react to a genuine crisis?

Bureaucratic conflict among the three ministries now responsible for Vorkuta even included debate about who would provide uniforms for officials. Several officers who were transferred from the MVD to MUP in the summer of 1953 wrote letters to their new superiors complaining that they had been deprived of their privilege of receiving a new MVD officer's uniform each year. These complaints eventually reached the desk of MUP deputy minister A. Lalaiants, who intervened on behalf of his new employees. In a letter to MVD minister Kruglov, Lalaiants argued that they remained entitled to receive the uniforms since the Sovmin resolution transferring Gulag industries to civilian control stipulated that transferred officials would receive all the privileges and rights of their previous jobs until the end of 1953. The response from MVD deputy minister I. Serov was curt and unequivocal: only current MVD officers were entitled to wear MVD uniforms, and those transferred to MUP had lost that right; therefore the MVD was unable to provide the uniforms.[34] This exchange over providing uniforms was not only typical of the constant bureaucratic bickering that now characterized the correspondence between the ministries—but it also suggested that the transfer of officials away from the purview of the MVD was more than a matter of changing a boss, a title, or a job description. It also entailed a change of status and potential loss of prestige for those transferred from the police organs to a civilian ministry. The uniform of an MVD officer carried great symbolic weight in Vorkuta, and these officials were loath to relinquish this symbol of their privileged status.

By the summer of 1953, open conflict had broken out between MUP on one side and MVD/MinIust on the other. In repeated letters to the top government leadership, such as the one described at the beginning of this chapter, MUP minister Zasiad'ko deplored the poor discipline among the prisoners who worked in the mines. The problem, as he described it, came from the fact that camp officials had now completely absolved themselves of responsibility for prisoner productivity and coal output. Thus, in June 1953 Zasiad'ko wrote to Beriia requesting that the principle of edinonachal'e be restored temporarily through the end of 1954 in order to improve productivity. Under his proposal camp officials would be made subordinate to KVU officials who worked for the coal ministry.[35] Gulag chief I. Dolgikh and Minister of Justice K. Gorshenin, his superior, strongly criticized Zasiad'ko's proposal, vigorously denied his claims of declining productivity, and argued that the separation of economic and penal functions was in fact exactly what was needed to ensure that the camps and the mines ran as intended.[36] For the moment, Dolgikh and Gorshenin's arguments carried the day. This was not simply a philosophical disagreement over the proper way to ensure both economic efficiency and security—rather, it was part of a growing turf war between MUP on one side and MinIust/MVD on the other for control of this particular piece of the former Gulag empire.

The chief adjudicator in this dispute, Lavrentii Beriia, did not live to see it resolved. On 10 July 1953 it was publicly announced that Beriia had been arrested and relieved of his posts in the state and party.[37] His arrest was a bombshell that further destabilized a city and camp complex already in a state of crisis. The amnesty had introduced uncertainty among prisoners and non-prisoners, and the arrest of its architect made the future of the Gulag even more difficult to ascertain. For local officials and their superiors in the Moscow-based ministries, vertical and horizontal lines of power became even more confused. As historian Vladimir Kozlov has rightfully pointed out, in the summer of 1953 officials at all levels feared for their jobs.[38] In a political system where reading signals was of the utmost importance, the new context of the post-Stalin period made it difficult not just to read signals, but also to figure out who was sending them. By the summer of 1953, the administrations of the mines and the camp complex were in a state of virtual paralysis.

THE 1953 RECHLAG STRIKE

It was in this context that the 1953 Rechlag prisoner strike began. On 19 July 1953, just nine days after Beriia's ouster was announced, 350 prisoners in camp section 2 of Rechlag refused to report for work. When guards came to take them to line up for morning roll call, they remained inside their barracks, demanding a visit from the camp director and procurator. When these two men arrived later that day, the prisoners informed them that they had requests and complaints that could only be resolved by the Central Committee of the Communist

Party. Until a representative of this body arrived, they would not work, nor would they allow themselves to be transferred to another camp section.[39] One of the most remarkable events in the history of the Gulag had begun. Soon, the strike would spread throughout much of Rechlag. By 29 July, when the strike was at its height, 15,604 prisoners, some 40 percent of the Rechlag population, would be on strike. Although it would end by 2 August, this strike, along with two others in Gorlag (Noril'sk) and Steplag (Kengir) that took place in 1953–1954, stands as the largest known act of mass resistance in the history of the Gulag.

Historians have rightly noted that the strikes were a culmination of trends in the postwar Gulag. For some time, there had been a growing sense of crisis within the Gulag administration, particularly regarding the system's apparently declining profitability. In fact, Beriia's reforms of March 1953 were in large part a response to these concerns.[40] There had also been a rising tide of prisoner resistance in the camps since the end of the Second World War. The "special camps" held many former nationalist rebels who had actively fought the Sovietization of their territories. Red Army veterans also made up a significant part of the population of such camps. Both of these populations were significantly less passive than their prewar counterparts, and were well equipped to organize various forms of resistance against the camp administration. Thus, changes in the prisoner population encouraged resistance and made the prisoners much more difficult for the camp administration to manage.[41] Both of these postwar trends are important for explaining the underlying causes of the strike. Yet the specific context of 1953 is also of crucial importance to comprehending what took place.[42] Stalin's death and the momentous changes that followed it undermined the authority of camp officials and increased the sense among prisoners that resistance could result in concrete achievements. The reforms of the Gulag placed prisoner labor at the center of a conflict between ministries as they struggled for control of Vorkuta and other camps. Whether they were aware of it or not, when the strike leaders decided to withhold their labor in order to improve their lot, they were hitting the local administration at one of its most vulnerable points. Thus, the Rechlag prisoner strike of 1953 was more than just the climax of a postwar crisis of the Gulag and the rise of prisoner resistance. It was part of an ongoing struggle by many actors to come to terms with, and find their place in, the emerging post-Stalinist order. Seen in this light, the strike appears not as a simple conflict between two opposing sides, but as a complex event that exposed deep fissures that ran through both the prisoner and the non-prisoner populations.

THE OUTBREAK AND SPREAD OF THE RECHLAG STRIKE

The 350 prisoners who refused to report for work on 19 July 1953 were newcomers to Rechlag. They were part of a group that had been transferred from Peschanlag near Karaganda in an attempt to end a wave of unrest there in 1952.[43] There was nothing unusual about such a transfer of "troublemakers" between camps—it was standard practice to move members of prisoner networks in order to disrupt their activities. There was also nothing unusual about the fact that the so-called *Peschanlagovtsy* had been held in "quarantine" for three weeks after arriving in Rechlag, which meant that they were held in a relatively isolated section of camp section 2 and were not taken out to work. What was unusual was that when they were given their work assignments in mine no. 7, the entire group of prisoners refused to report for roll call.

Rechlag director Derevianko, who met with the prisoners on that first day of the strike, reacted cautiously to their demand for a visit from a member of the Central Committee of the Communist Party. An experienced official, he had good reason to take such an approach in this case.[44] Beriia's ouster had been announced less than two weeks before this, and the prisoner strike in Gorlag, the existence of which Derevianko was undoubtedly aware, had just ended.[45] Further, while he was used to dealing with acts of resistance, mass work refusals of this type were still relatively uncommon.[46] When meeting with the prisoners, Derevianko immediately struck a conciliatory stance rather than threatening a crackdown. He then contacted his superiors and other officials, requesting that they advise him on the best course of action to take. He sent a telegram to his boss, Minister of the USSR MVD Kruglov, asking for instructions on how he should respond to the prisoners' demands. He contacted the Komi ASSR MVD, the relevant regional authority, to inform them of what was going on in the camp. Derevianko also discussed the matter with Komi Obkom secretary Osipov, who happened to be in Vorkuta at the time. Osipov, in turn, sent a telegram to Sovmin chair Georgii Malenkov, the effective leader of the USSR after Beriia's ouster.[47] Osipov's telegram likely was the first news that the top leadership received about the strike. Almost immediately, the strike ceased to be an internal matter, and numerous officials were involved in discussing the most effective means to respond to it.

The response from Moscow was anything but swift. Kruglov, Minister of the USSR MVD, did not reply to Derevianko's request for instructions for five days. In the meantime, the 350 Peschanlagovtsy continued their strike. Although initially the rest of the prisoners in camp section 2 continued to report for work, this soon changed. As Rechlag prisoner Aleksandr Aleksandrovich Ugrimov wrote about this time, "The whole camp boiled like a cauldron," and after seeing that the camp administration was not reacting decisively to the strike of the new arrivals, the strike spread to the rest of the section on 22 July. That morning, messengers ran through the barracks urging prisoners not to report for work.[48] Approximately 1,500 prisoners from two shifts refused to report for duty and repeated the earlier demand for a visit from a Central Committee member. By the following day, 23 July, nearly 3,000 prisoners, the majority of the prisoner population of camp section 2, were on strike.[49] Derevianko still had not yet received a reply from Kruglov.

The response arrived on 24 July, five days after the strike began. In addition to dispatching an "operational group" from Moscow to Vorkuta, Kruglov instructed Derevianko to offer a number of concessions to the prisoners in order to placate them.[50] These included a reduction of the length of the work day to nine hours from ten and the removal of numbers from clothing. In addition, prisoners now received permission to send one letter per month, send money home to families, spend up to 300 rubles per month in the camp, and meet with relatives.[51] These changes amounted to a repudiation of some of the most cruel and hated aspects of the "special camp" regime that had been in effect since Rechlag was established in 1948.[52] The concessions proved to be ineffective, however, and the prisoners in camp section 2 continued their strike.

In fact, the concessions likely played a role in encouraging the spread of the strike outside camp section 2. Hoping to head off further unrest, the improvements were announced not only to the striking prisoners, but also throughout Rechlag. Rather than satisfy the prisoners' desires for improvements in their living conditions, the announcement of the concessions instead conveyed the sense that the camp administration was weak and therefore the prisoners could make further gains. Almost immediately, prisoners in camp sections 3 and 6 joined the strike, bringing the number of striking prisoners to 8,700; mine nos. 7, 12, 14, 16, and the construction of the TETs-2 power station were now at a standstill. The next day, on 25 July, camp section 10 joined as well. On 28 July, the strike spread to section 13, and on 29 July, to camp section 4.[53] The strike remained geographically concentrated in camp sections along the northern section of the ring of Vorkuta's mines near the settlements of Promyshlennyi, Severnyi, and Oktiabrskii, likely because it was easiest for neighboring camp sections to communicate with each other and coordinate strike activities. The sole exception to this was camp section 6, located in close proximity to the city itself. According to an official estimate, 15,604 prisoners in six of seventeen camp sections in Rechlag were now on strike, ten days after the strike began.[54] The strategy of offering concessions had clearly backfired.

As events in Vorkuta spun out of control, the strike became a point of contention in the ongoing turf war between MUP and MVD/MinIust. Just as the strike was beginning, MUP was in the midst of presenting a proposal to Malenkov that contained requests to dramatically increase investment in Vorkuta's mines and to bolster the authority of KVU officials over the camp complex and the prisoner population.[55] MUP minister Zasiad'ko learned about the strike from KVU director Degtev soon after it began, and used it as an opportunity to criticize the MVD and MinIust to Malenkov. According to Zasiad'ko, the strike was yet another manifestation of the MVD's chronic inability to provide labor for KVU's mines. Zasiad'ko asked that the MVD be ordered to take immediate measures to restore discipline. Kruglov of the MVD and Gorshenin of MinIust responded largely with accusations of their own, countering that ongoing unrest in the camps was a result of the poor organization of labor and inadequate housing provided by KVU, and therefore was ultimately MUP's fault.[56] Malenkov's response was to let the MVD sort the situation out on its own, although he did instruct the Party Presidium to discuss the future of the special camps that summer.[57] The struggle for control of Vorkuta, itself a symptom of a growing crisis of authority, clearly contributed to the slow and indecisive response to the strike.

Indeed, it was not just the act of mass resistance by prisoners that seemed to confound the authorities. The form of this resistance was also extremely important. The fact that the prisoners had chosen to withhold their labor, and therefore threatened to reduce the output of the coal mines, raised the stakes of the strike and broadened the number of organizations with a stake in its successful termination. Whether they were aware of this or not, the prisoners were withholding something that had been at the center of administrative conflict in Vorkuta for months. In this sense, the strike was a weapon that hit the local authorities and the larger ministries to which they belonged in the most vulnerable of places. Although they could not have been privy to the turf war taking place in Moscow, the prisoners' leaders interpreted the weak and conciliatory response to their strike as an indication that this particular form of resistance could be used with continued success. The longer the strike met with a weak response from the authorities, the greater the potential payoff seemed to be. The strike both exploited the crisis of authority in Vorkuta and contributed to the prisoners' raised expectations.

US VERSUS THEM?

On the surface, the uprising demonstrated the cleavages that divided Vorkuta. If there was ever a moment when prisoners were definitively divided from the non-prisoners (particularly the camp administration and guards), this would be it. The defiant refusal of the prisoners to work and their demands for concessions from the administration put them, at least in theory, in stark opposition to the camp, city, and mine administrations. On the surface, prisoner memoirs and official accounts alike tend to emphasize a picture of the strike as a standoff between two clearly opposed sides. However, a closer examination of these sources suggests a much more complex and nuanced picture of the fault lines created by the strike. In fact, the strike actually reveals that interactions and relationships between prisoner and non-prisoner populations remained much the same as they had been previously. Although the strike and the upheaval that preceded it added to social tensions and anxieties, camp and city remained tightly connected with one another.

While it is true that prisoners and the camp administration adopted a posture of mutual opposition, there was in fact a high degree of cooperation between the striking prisoners, the camp administration, and mine officials throughout the strike. This is most clearly illustrated by the fact that some prisoner mine personnel continued to work during the uprising, despite the fact that many of them maintained open solidarity with the strikers. To have shut down the coal mines of Vorkuta for a period of only a few days might have resulted in a disaster that could have endangered the lives of many and disrupted coal production for months. Without the operation of water pumps, many parts of the mines would have been flooded and would have had to be abandoned. Ventilation systems had to continue to work in order to prevent a dangerous collection of carbon dioxide or methane gas below ground. In order to prevent disaster, it was imperative for some prisoners in each striking camp section to report to work as usual.

In camp section 2, representatives for the prisoners and the camp administration immediately agreed to cooperate in order to maintain safety in the mines. Aleksandr Ugrimov, who ran an electrical substation in mine no. 7 throughout much of the strike, later recalled in his memoirs, "The leadership of the strike adopted a wise decision. It was said that it was necessary to keep the mine and the equipment in normal order, and because of this the people who are responsible for this should leave [the zone] and—by their wishes—remain there or return. Of course, such decisions could only have been made by agreement with the camp administration."[58] Both sides agreed to allow prisoners working in essential safety systems to travel back and forth from the mine during the strike. A certain degree of cooperation between the striking prisoners and the camp administration was present throughout the strike in virtually all sections, as both sides agreed that maintaining safety was paramount.[59] The willingness to cooperate demonstrates that the strike was not an all-or-nothing proposition for many of the actors on both sides of the barbed wire. Given the uneasy political situation in the country, neither side was willing to raise the stakes of the conflict too far. This was particularly imperative for the prisoners. If they had neglected the safety systems and allowed an accident to take place, it would have undermined their representatives' arguments that the strike was an act of loyal Soviet citizens carried out in the name of legality.

In fact, neither side of the standoff was as unified as its leaders wanted the other side to believe. Although a clear majority of prisoners in the six striking camp sections supported the strike, some prisoners chose to leave the zone rather than participate. Each day during the strike, the camp administration invited prisoners who did not support the strike to leave the zone. Not wanting to have dissenters in their midst, the prisoners generally allowed them to leave. As prisoner memoirs attest, there were a number of reasons why prisoners chose not to participate in the strike. According to Ugrimov, "More than a few prisoners answered that call [to leave the zone]: production bosses, people holding on to, above all, their 'warm places,' stool pigeons, and simply self-seekers and cowards. Perhaps there were also those who were firmly confident that all of this was a provocation by the camp administration that would necessarily end in cruel repression; and there were also those who were not connected to the comradely work of collective brigades."[60] Thus, there was a whole range of people who had much to lose by participating in the strike, including those with privilege, those who occupied positions of authority, prisoner informants, and those who were simply convinced that the strike was a bad idea. Ugrimov also singled out those who felt little solidarity with other prisoners because they did not share common work experiences. Despite the fact that prisoner solidarity had generally increased in the "special camps" owing to the increased concentration of certain categories of prisoners and improved prospects for survival, the camp population remained divided into various identity groups in terms of nationality, position in the camp hierarchy, and occupation. Such divisions often worked against unity even during the strike.

Even among the prisoners who remained in the zone, not all supported the strike. MVD operatives in Rechlag continued to receive regular reports throughout the strike from prisoner informants. A typical report from an unnamed agent dated 25 July began in the following fashion: "The initiators of the events in the second camp section are prisoners who came from Karaganda. The 'headquarters' of the sabotage is barracks 41 and the head of the sabotage is the Polish Colonel Kendzerskii."[61] Such reports gave the camp administration an opportunity to monitor the situation within the camp and to determine the identity of the leaders. While the accuracy of these reports is obviously questionable, the fact that prisoner agents continued to report throughout the strike demonstrates that prisoner solidarity was far from complete.

For its part, the non-prisoner population was hardly unified in opposition to the strike either. This is not surprising given the diversity of city residents. While the city was home to thousands of camp and mine officials whose livelihood depended on the exploitation of prisoner labor, it also included thousands of former prisoners, former POWs, and exiles who had at one time been held within the barbed wire. Surveillance reports compiled during the strike, despite their problematic nature, suggest that attitudes toward the strike ranged from stark opposition to strong support.[62] Enthusiastic expressions of opposition to the strike were common, even among populations that might have been expected to sympathize with the prisoners. As one ethnic German exile reportedly stated, "Let's say that they were even unjustly convicted, but to carry out a strike—that is unworthy of Soviet people, it is necessary to simply hang the strike organizers." Another former prisoner stated, "A strike is a crime. I think we should do with them what we used to do with Trotskyites in my time: take them all to *kirpichnyi* [the brick factory, site of 1938 shootings] and shoot them." Some criticized the local administration for its moderate reaction to the strike. One exile engineer apparently stated that "a large amount of guilt for it [the strike] belongs to the local administration, which was unable to decisively and quickly localize the expression of discontent and seize the ringleaders."[63] Some apparently feared that the prisoners might break out of the zone and attack the non-prisoner population. One ex-prisoner stated, "It has become scarier to live in the city. The katorzhane [*sic*] could suddenly break out of the zone by force and fall upon the peaceful population."[64] Thus, many non-prisoners expressed strong opposition to the strike.

Other non-prisoners, however, demonstrated clear sympathies for the striking prisoners. This was the general conclusion of a report prepared by deputy minister of the Komi MVD Noginov, one of the first outside officials to arrive on the scene in late July. Noginov observed that "the majority of residents who are former prisoners . . . look upon the actions of the prisoners sympathetically." As one former prisoner from western Ukraine apparently stated, "There have not been any real successes, just a minor softening [of the regime] in questions of everyday life. But a yoke remains a yoke . . . in all of this there seems to be a victory, in that we are seeing the strength of our unity . . . and how the authorities are forced to yield in the face of it." For this former prisoner, the strike was a key moment that would demonstrate to the prisoners what they could achieve through collective action. Expressions of support for the prisoners were apparently especially common in neighborhoods of the city with large concentrations of former prisoners. Some in the local MVD feared that the population of one neighborhood (Rudnik) had become so embittered toward camp soldiers and officers who frequently provoked them and started fights that they would use opportunities presented by the strike to "inflict reprisals."[65] While this is likely an exaggeration of the willingness of non-prisoners to bring the strike out of the zone, it demonstrates how much the strike heightened tensions throughout Vorkuta, which was already used to periodic outbreaks of violence.

Other non-prisoners demonstrated support for the uprising, although not always in an active fashion. According to police reports, some miners pointed out that other mines were already shut down and urged their prisoner colleagues to strike. Others attempted to leave work themselves in order to show solidarity with the strikers, although this was prevented by city authorities.[66] But sympathy for the strikers rarely translated into active support. Many non-prisoners simply passed along information about the situation in other mines and other parts of the camp, communication that facilitated the spread of the strike between camp sections.[67] Others made use of their time off at idling mines and enterprises to drink. While such behavior was criticized by local authorities, one should be cautious about ascribing political meaning to such activities. Overall, active support appears to have been rare among the non-prisoner population.

Non-prisoner reactions to the strike shared a common thread of anxiety. Vorkuta, like other cities and towns across the Soviet Union, had been gripped by uncertainty since the spring of 1953. Stalin's death, the Beriia reforms, and Beriia's arrest had all deeply affected the lives of Vorkuta's residents. The strike only served to heighten tensions and uncertainties and made "normalcy" seem ever more elusive. It virtually shut down several mines, which resulted in a loss of income for thousands of non-prisoners. It disrupted the operation of the camps, which further undermined the job security of those working in Vorkutlag and Rechlag. It even potentially undermined the status of former prisoners in the city, many of whom feared that a crackdown on the strike participants might affect them as well. According to surveillance reports, an amnestied prisoner working in the planning department apparently stated, "It had only just gotten easier, and now the katorzhane [*sic*] aren't working, they are just making things difficult for themselves, and now they [the authorities] might pounce on others (he has in mind the amnestied) [editorial comment in original]."[68] Although prisoners and non-prisoners looked on the strike from a variety of perspectives, all felt the atmosphere of uncertainty gripping Vorkuta in the summer of 1953.

COMMITTEES AND COMMISSIONS

Despite the lack of absolute unity, the swift spread of the strike throughout much of Rechlag demonstrates the degree to which it was well organized and coordinated. In each section, an informal prisoner government coordinated prisoners' actions, communicated information throughout the camp section, and articulated demands. The basis for prisoner leadership lay in underground nationalist prisoner organizations that had become increasingly prevalent in the postwar Gulag. Such organizations, which were generally constituted along national lines and had been established in the postwar period, operated behind the scenes in many camps in order to improve prisoners' chances of survival and to protect them from forces that might prey on them, including cruel camp officials, prisoner-informants, criminal groups and other national organizations. In Rechlag these organizations had long existed, although they had rarely coordinated overt mass resistance. In the context of the extraordinary events of the summer of 1953 the leadership of these organizations stepped in to lead the strikes. As strike participant Joseph Scholmer wrote, "This strike would not of course have been possible if the underground resistance groups had not already been in existence. . . . They provided the personnel and the necessary technical basis for any sort of offensive action. . . . The strike had at its disposal a piece of machinery that had been built up with the greatest care and could be relied upon to function smoothly."[69] Although the prisoner organizations had to be hastily adapted to running the strikes, their backbone had been present for years.

Many of the characteristics of the organizations remained unchanged despite the novel circumstances in which they were operating. The leadership continued to behave in a conspiratorial and secret manner throughout the strike. Many participants did not know who was actually in charge of the strike. Aleksandr Ugrimov, for instance, admitted in his memoirs that early in the uprising he had only a rough idea of who was in charge. As he wrote, "I never once saw our leaders. It was said that the center [of the leadership] included representatives from various nationalities, and that the head was some Colonel-Pole from that transport [from Peschanlag]."[70] Rather than addressing the prisoners directly, runners were chosen to communicate decisions from the underground leadership to the mass of prisoners throughout the camp section.[71] There was, however, one significant difference in the operation of the committees that is alluded to in the above quotation: rather than represent the members of one nationality only, the strike leadership tended to incorporate members of multiple national organizations. Thus, the underground self-help organizations were adapted for the new circumstances.

As the strike progressed, it became increasingly difficult for the committees to balance a series of priorities: first, to consult and make decisions about how the strike should proceed; second, to communicate decisions to the mass of prisoners and convince them to follow what was decided; third, to maintain secrecy among the leaders of the underground organizations in order to prevent the camp administration from learning too much about them. These priorities came into conflict especially once prisoners began active negotiations with the authorities. If the actual leaders of the strike came forward to negotiate, they might be compromising themselves and the underground organizations that they had spent years building. In some cases, the strike leaders were willing to take this risk. In camp section 10, for instance, Edward Buca, one of the important "underground" leaders of the strike, was persuaded to reveal himself as a leader of the strike and represent the prisoners in negotiations.[72] More often, however, separate "official" strike committees were created to represent the prisoners in negotiations. These committees usually comprised prisoners willing to profess a strong loyalty to the Soviet system rather than the more radical nationalist prisoners. In camp section 3, for instance, the strike committee was led by V. D. Kolesnikov, a former state security officer who had been convicted only in the spring of 1953 and had spent a mere twenty-seven days in the camp section before the strike broke out. Known as a former air force colonel among the prisoners, his reputation had led him to be elected to leadership of the strike committee against his own objections.[73] While Kolesnikov negotiated with the authorities, the true leaders of the strike remained underground.

Such a strategy reflected the pragmatism of the strike leaders. Using an "official" committee allowed the nationalist organizations to maintain some level of secrecy. But there were risks to adopting this strategy. By appointing more moderate prisoners to the "official" committees, the underground leaders created an alternative center of power within the prisoner population. Over time, conflict often arose between these two committees. Historian Vladimir Kozlov has aptly described the prisoner governments as having "dual centers" (*dvoetsentrie*) of power.[74] Generally speaking, the underground leadership tended to steer the strike in a more radical direction, whereas the official strike committees were more moderate and conciliatory. Such arrangements reflect not only the complexity of prisoner organizations, but also the diversity of outlooks among the prisoners.

The "official" prisoner strike committees were created, by and large, in the last days of July, when representatives from Moscow began to meet with the prisoners. Although the prisoners had consistently demanded that a member of the Central Committee travel to Vorkuta to negotiate with them, instead a group was dispatched that came primarily from the MVD. The so-called Moscow commission was led by army general Ivan Ivanovich Maslennikov, a longtime deputy minister of the USSR MVD. Of the commission's twelve members, eight were relatively high-ranking officials in the USSR MVD, including M. V. Kuznetsov, the chief of the prison section of the MVD, who had led the commission that had met with prisoners during the strike in Gorlag. The other members were M. D. Samokhin, who represented the USSR Procuracy, Noginov, the deputy minister of Komi USSR MVD, Rechlag director Derevianko, and the head of the local militarized guard division, Mironov.[75] Despite the presence of one member from the USSR Procuracy, a body whose main function was to exercise judicial oversight, the overwhelming predominance of MVD and Gulag officials within the commission suggests that it was not created in order to seriously investigate the prisoners' complaints. Rather, its task was to bring the strike to a swift and decisive conclusion.

During the two days the commission met with the prisoners on 29–30 July, a similar scenario played out in each of the sections. Maslennikov and the commission members entered the zone and asked to hear the prisoners' complaints. After the prisoners had massed in an open space, the commission read a prepared speech to the prisoners, announcing that the group had been sent from Moscow "to examine the situation that has arisen 'on the ground' and to decide the questions that have been broached by the prisoners of Rechlag." The commission then proposed that the prisoners immediately return to work and "end the sabotage" so that their demands could be responded to in good time. The speech reiterated the concessions already given to the prisoners, and added three more that awaited approval in Moscow: that bars be removed from the windows of barracks, that barracks be left unlocked overnight, and that the workday credit system (zachet) be extended to Rechlag prisoners. The speech proposed that the prisoners return to work the next day, otherwise the commission would not be able to resolve the issues that concerned them. Strike leaders were then given the opportunity to address the commission.[76]

The activities of the Moscow commission warrant a number of observations. First of all, the tone of the commission's speech to the prisoners is striking. Although Maslennikov was clear that the strike should be considered "sabotage," and therefore illegitimate, his speech was generally conciliatory.[77] Again, the first move when approaching the prisoners was to offer a series of minor improvements in camp regime as concessions. This was a clear departure from the way that Gulag officials had responded to acts of prisoner resistance during Stalin's lifetime. On the other hand, it is also apparent that this commission had fairly circumscribed authority in dealing with the prisoners. Although they were charged with the task of listening to the prisoners' demands and complaints, they did not have the power to respond to them beyond offering a list of concessions that they had brought from Moscow. Further, no real negotiation would actually take place. After offering concessions and hearing prisoners' complaints, the commission would then deliver an ultimatum to each section beginning on 31 July: return to work voluntarily or the strike would be ended by force.

Given the opportunity, finally, to express themselves to officials from Moscow, representatives of the "official" strike committees in each camp section addressed the commission. A number of important themes emerge from the small collection of speeches preserved in the Gulag archives and in the memoirs of strike participants. One is the repeated assertion that the majority of prisoners were not in fact "enemies of the people," criminals bent on resisting the authority of party and state. In fact, prisoner representatives went out of their way to emphasize the degree to which they were loyal citizens of the Soviet state. As Vladimir Levando, a member of the group of Peschanlagovtsy who began the strike in camp section 2, stated to Maslennikov, "most of us are the same age as Soviet power or people of the [nineteen] teens . . . who have lived during Soviet power, led by our powerful Communist Party." Levando and other leaders took pains to assert that most of the prisoners were products of the Soviet system who had simply become victims of circumstance during the Second World War. Thus, as he continued, "Among us there is practically no one who was repressed by Soviet organs before the Great Patriotic War, and the war appears as the only reason for our imprisonment."[78] The strike leaders consistently represented the strike as an action taken by loyal Soviet citizens.

Prisoners' speeches also tended to focus on the issue of legality. Anatolii Musaevich Kniazev, another leader of the strike in camp section 2, went to great lengths to enumerate the various violations of legality perpetrated under Derevianko's watch by guards and officials in Rechlag. This included deliberately cruel treatment of disabled and ill prisoners, corrupt bookkeeping practices, and savage, unprovoked beatings of prisoners.[79] Thus, some prisoner leaders focused on the illegal treatment of prisoners in the camp. Others, like Levando, instead made the case that prisoners had been wrongly convicted in the first place. Levando thus sought to focus attention not on local corruption, but on the systematic abuse of power and misapplication of Soviet law within the MVD and MGB.[80] Perhaps the most sweeping condemnation of the system came from a written statement attributed to "the prisoners of the 10th camp section." This document argued that the entire prison system was a flawed and corrupt creation, and thus demanded the release of all "political prisoners" from the camps, the opportunity for foreigners to return home, and the guarantee that none of the strikers would be punished.[81] Overall, the speeches and statements sought to legitimize the strike as a legal protest against various illegal practices on the part of both local officials and the central judicial organs.

The representatives who spoke on behalf of the prisoners did not shy away from leveling accusations at specific people. Derevianko emerged as the chief local villain responsible for allowing and encouraging the cruel treatment of prisoners. Some speeches alleged that the illegal practices in the camp had been approved by him, often unbeknownst to leadership in Moscow. Thus, some strike leaders adopted a time-honored Soviet rhetorical technique, which perhaps had its roots in pre-revolutionary times: calling on powerful and incorruptible higher forces (the party) to intervene and punish corrupt local officials.[82] But other leaders alleged that the Rechlag director had not acted alone—rather, he had merely been the local representative of an even bigger villain, Lavrentii Beriia, the recently arrested leader. In speeches that echoed the language of the Soviet press, Beriia was described as an "agent of world imperialism, adventurer, careerist-executioner."[83] Aside from giving the prisoners a legitimate target for their anger, Beriia was clearly a convenient scapegoat, as he had been publicly denounced for a series of crimes against the Soviet state. By tying their local issues to the fall of Beriia, prisoner representatives attempted to inscribe their protests into a broader Soviet discourse. Kniazev's speech went the farthest in this regard, placing the crimes of Beriia in opposition to the positive leadership of Stalin.[84] In fact, the rhetorical strategy adopted by the prisoners was not unlike that of many ordinary Soviet citizens who wrote letters to leaders in the summer of 1953, echoing the language of *Pravda* and linking Beriia to the personal injustices that they had suffered.[85]

This points to perhaps the most surprising aspect of the uprising, as well as the ones that preceded it in Gorlag and followed it in Steplag: by and large, the representatives of the prisoners "spoke Bolshevik" in their interactions with local and central authorities.[86] Prisoner leaders framed their strike using strikingly Soviet language, casting themselves as loyal Soviet citizens rather than as outsiders. This seems surprising given the fact that the majority of prisoners held in Rechlag came from the western borderlands of the Soviet Union. Many of these prisoners had grown up outside the Soviet system, and therefore had only recently become familiar with how to "speak Bolshevik." Some had even participated in guerrilla warfare against Soviet forces during or after the Second World War in order to prevent the Sovietization of their homelands. There are a number of ways to interpret the professions of loyalty by the prisoners and their appropriation of Soviet language and rhetorical devices. One approach would be to accept the discourse at face value, accepting the language of the prisoners as proof of their complete Sovietization.[87] Another would be the opposite, to interpret professions of loyalty as purely instrumental appropriations of Soviet discourse adopted to mask profoundly anti-Soviet motivations.[88] A more nuanced alternative, advanced by Steven Barnes in his analysis of the Steplag uprising of 1954, rejects both of these positions. For the many Red Army veterans in the camps who were fiercely loyal to the Soviet system and intent on remedying its injustices, professions of loyalty were expressed sincerely.[89] For former nationalist rebels, however, the fact that they chose to "speak Bolshevik" simply demonstrated that during their time in the Gulag they had learned how to speak publicly in the Soviet Union. According to Barnes, "they began to mouth the words" of Soviet discourse, even if they did not do so sincerely.[90] Thus, the speeches made use of a powerful and flexible discourse that could express loyalty to the system while criticizing the activities of certain officials like Derevianko and Beriia.

THE END OF THE STRIKE

Having heard the prisoners' complaints and demands, the Moscow commission acted swiftly to end the strike. On 30 July, a plan composed by commission members Maslennikov and Kuznetsov to end the strikes was approved by MVD minister Kruglov.[91] On the following morning of 31 July at 10:00 a.m., the commission began its operation to end the strike where it had begun, in camp section 2. Loudspeakers that had been set up on the watchtowers surrounding the zone delivered an ultimatum demanding that the prisoners return to work.[92] Ugrimov noted that the machine guns mounted on the watchtowers that had been partially hidden were now brought into full view. Faced with the first decisive ultimatum delivered by the authorities since the strike began, the prisoner committee decided to cooperate. Messengers instructed all in the zone to give up in order to prevent bloodshed.[93] The prisoners of camp section 2 then voluntarily left the zone. Once outside, they were divided into groups of one hundred and taken under guard into the tundra. Following the plan approved by Kruglov, those responsible for leading the strike were removed and taken elsewhere. The rest of the prisoners were then taken back into the zone, divided into work brigades, and taken out to work.[94] Thus, the first group of prisoners to go on strike was also the first to end it.

Whereas the indecisiveness of local, regional, and central authorities had allowed the strike to spread, the pursuit of a decisive course of action resulted in its swift conclusion. News of the broken strike in camp section 2 traveled quickly throughout Rechlag. According to Scholmer, the Moscow commission announced that the strike had ended in camp section 2 in order to encourage others to give up as well. Although the prisoners were initially skeptical of these claims, they were convinced by the sight of full coal cars passing their section.[95] Over the next two days the prisoners in sections 3, 4, and 13 returned to work of their own volition.[96] In these three sections the alleged ringleaders were arrested as they were escorted to their work sites. In camp section 16 the prisoners also returned to work, apparently turning in the strike leaders to the authorities.[97] In nearly every case the strike ended peacefully, with the prisoners deciding that it was better to return to work than risk a violent confrontation with the authorities.

Events ran a different course in camp section 10, however, with tragic consequences. On 1 August the Moscow commission began its operation there as it had on the previous day in camp section 2, announcing an ultimatum to the prisoners and opening the gates of the camp to allow the prisoners to leave. Yet unlike in camp section 2, the strike committee instructed the prisoners to remain in the camp. The ultimatum was soon repeated over the speaker system, to no avail. From this point forward, the situation in the camp zone became chaotic. Some prisoners attempted to leave the zone and end the strike, but were stopped by a large mass of approximately 350–400 prisoners who were determined to resist and formed a barrier.[98] Fifty unarmed guards were sent into the zone to aid those who wanted to leave, but they were repelled by the mass of prisoners. Next, the main gates were opened and a fire truck was sent into the zone to use water cannons to break up the strike. However, the fire brigade was repelled as well. At this point the decision was taken to fire on the prisoners, an action that finally broke the strike.[99] According to official totals, 42 prisoners were killed and 135 wounded, of which at least 11 more died subsequently from their wounds.[100] The overwhelming majority of those killed were "Westerners" from the Ukraine and the Baltic states, demonstrating the important role that such prisoners played in the strike.[101] With the bloody repression of the prisoners in camp section 10 over, the Rechlag strike concluded.

It is unclear why the strike in camp section 10 ended in a hail of gunfire, whereas the matter was settled with little overt violence in the other five striking sections. The camp authorities had approached each section in a similar manner, adhering as closely as possible to a prepared script, where the application of violence was seen as a last resort. Why had the prisoners in camp section 10 chosen to remain on strike despite the ultimatums they received? It is possible that the leaders did not believe that the strike had already ended elsewhere. If they were unable to independently confirm that the strike had ended in other sections on the previous day, they may have suspected that the Moscow commission was misleading them when it reported that other prisoners had gone back to work. A more important factor, perhaps, was that much of the "underground" leadership of camp section 10 had decided to become the official representatives of the prisoners rather than remain hidden. This decision likely made the leaders less inclined to compromise—having already revealed the leadership of the underground nationalist prisoner organizations, there was little hope that such organizations could "live to fight another day" after the strike ended. By exposing the identities of the leadership, the prisoners had effectively raised the stakes of the strike. Thus, they chose not to voluntarily return to work when threatened. This is not to say, of course, that the strike leaders in camp section 10 were somehow responsible for the deaths of their comrades—if the Moscow commission had been willing to delay or forgo opening fire on the prisoners, the strike might not have ended in a bloodbath.

After each section was pacified, Derevianko took action to isolate the suspected leaders of the strike. Twenty-nine prisoners identified as strike organizers were detained in a special regime prison in Vorkuta to await trial.[102] At least 14 of them would be convicted under articles 58–14 and 58–11 of the Russian criminal code and given sentences of ten to twenty-five years.[103] Outside the small group of organizers, a much larger group of "active participants" also faced further punishment and isolation. Two hundred eighty prisoners were transferred to special regime prisons outside Vorkuta for terms of one year. Nearly 900 others were transferred to newly organized sections of Rechlag, where they were held in greater isolation from the rest of the camp population. Of the approximately 15,600 prisoners who had gone on strike, just over 90 percent were returned to their previous status.[104] Clearly, Gulag authorities had learned one important lesson from the strike: transporting a large group of "troublemakers" to another camp, as had been the case with the Peschanlagovtsy, would simply spread the problem.

PRISONERS WITHOUT BORDERS

The end of the strike did not mean an end to the crisis in Vorkuta. Although the Moscow commission's report on the strike boasted that Rechlag had returned to business as usual by early August, smaller-scale prisoner unrest continued unabated.[105] As MUP minister Zasiad'ko complained to Sovmin chairman Malenkov in a letter on 21 January 1954, "mass instances of early departure from [work in] the mines, direct refusals to perform work, and also concealed resistance and sabotage on the part of the 'special contingents' do not cease."[106] High-level officials in the ministries struggling for control of Vorkuta, as well as their local representatives in Vorkuta, continued to exchange accusatory letters about who was responsible for the continuing collapse of labor discipline.[107] The strike had even intensified conflicts within the MVD, as central and local officials sought to absolve themselves of blame for continued prisoner resistance. For instance, at a meeting of "special camp" directors in Moscow in March 1954, Derevianko argued that it was the unfulfilled promises made by the Moscow commission in July 1953 that accounted for continued unrest.[108] The Rechlag director had been heavily criticized in the commission's report, and this was likely an opportunity for him to settle the score. Ongoing prisoner unrest and the steady stream of mutual recriminations clearly demonstrated that two of the most important factors that had made the strike possible—increased expectations on the part of prisoners and dysfunction on the part of administrators—continued after the strike.

Although some progress was made in 1954 to solve the ministerial gridlock in Vorkuta, the effort remained incomplete. Structural reform of the Gulag was renewed in 1954, in large part through a repeal of many of Beriia's experimental reforms. On 21 January 1954, Sovmin returned the oversight of all camps and colonies to the MVD from MinIust. Now Rechlag and Vorkutlag were once again under one ministry.[109] The reforms went even further, abolishing the "special camps" entirely, and thus on 26 May the MVD ordered that Rechlag be eliminated and combined with Vorkutlag. Derevianko was relieved of his responsibilities, and Vorkutlag director Prokop'ev took over responsibility for the reunified camp complex.[110] Beriia's March 1953 decision to split the economic and punitive functions of the Gulag was also largely reversed over the course of 1954, and many Gulag industries were transferred from civilian ministries back to the MVD.[111] However, not all industries were restored to the MVD. KVU remained subordinate to MUP and Vorkutlag remained under the MVD. Therefore, the system of contract labor continued unchanged.[112] While it is not entirely clear why MUP retained control of the mines, this is likely because plans were already afoot for KVU and the Pechora coal basin to make the transition to a primarily non-prisoner labor force. Yet concrete measures to facilitate this change would not emerge until 1955, leaving Vorkuta stuck between two masters.

For local mine and prison camp officials, the strike had driven home an important lesson. The separation of the mines from the camps left each set of officials ultimately responsible for separate aspects of the prisoners' existence, the productive and the penal. Yet the strike had demonstrated that these aspects were closely intertwined because a breakdown in one inevitably meant a breakdown in the other. By the summer of 1954, KVU and Vorkutlag officials were finally ready to work together, as far as was possible given the ongoing turf war in Moscow. One important opportunity to do this arrived in connection with the first major internal reorganization of the camp system of the 1950s. The "Regulations on Corrective Labor Camps and Colonies of the Ministry of Internal Affairs of the USSR," approved by the USSR Council of Ministers on 10 July 1954, contained a broad, comprehensive set of rules to govern many aspects of life in the camps, from medical treatment, to the organization of labor, to political-educational work among prisoners.[113] Among other things, these new regulations were intended to rationalize the regime under which prisoners were held. By dividing prisoners into three different levels of regime—strict, common, and light—the new rules were designed to isolate and punish the truly dangerous and unrepentant, and to reward those prisoners who posed little threat and were on the path of rehabilitation.[114] It was in these regulations that camp section chiefs and mine directors found new ways to work together for their mutual benefit.

The light regime, which was reserved for those prisoners who had served at least one-third of their sentences, strictly adhered to the camp rules, and worked dutifully, held intriguing possibilities both for reducing prisoner unrest and improving productivity. Prisoners in such camp sections were guarded less strictly and were entitled to various incentives that had not previously been available, such as the opportunity to spend days off outside the camp. Two aspects of the light regime made it particularly attractive to officials in Vorkuta. First, it removed many of the existing limitations on de-convoying prisoners, that is, granting them passes to move outside the zone without a guard convoy. The "regulations" also restored the opportunity to grant prisoners permission to live outside the camp zone itself. Although designating prisoners as de-zoned had been fairly common throughout the history of the Gulag, it had been prohibited since 1947.[115] Now, prisoners who "demonstrated, by their conduct and relationship to work, that they no longer needed to be held under guard" could be given permission to live outside the camp zone for the remainder of their terms. Unlike before 1947, permission to live outside the zone was explicitly identified in the regulations as a widely applicable labor "incentive," whereas previously it had been done informally where zones had not existed, or as a privilege for individual prisoners. Further, de-zoned prisoners were now allowed to send for their families to live with them. They were to be paid full wages, in most ways equivalent to those paid to non-prisoner workers. Although they were required to present themselves to the camp administration "regularly" for registration, they could be granted temporary absences from their place of residence.[116] In many important respects their status was similar to the category of "colonists" of the early 1930s.

Granting prisoners the right to move freely or to live outside the zone was an arrangement that suited both Vorkutlag and KVU. It offered benefits for each side without having to cede authority or take on onerous new responsibilities. De-convoyed and de-zoned prisoners were less of a strain on the limited resources of the camp than prisoners who lived inside the zone. Neither type of prisoner needed to be brought to work under guard, which was of great benefit to camp sections that had been suffering from a severe shortage of guards since the late 1940s. By 1953–1955, the shortage had become so severe that each day hundreds of prisoners could not work in the mines simply because there were not enough guards to bring them to the work site and back.[117] De-zoned prisoners also did not eat in the camp canteens, instead purchasing their own food from their wages. Since they lived in housing outside the camp, de-zoned prisoners could help relieve the chronic overcrowding of camp barracks, allowing camp officials to boast in their yearly reports that prisoner housing was improving. Perhaps most important, prisoners who lived outside the zone or who had passes allowing them free movement were much less likely to be involved in organized acts of mass resistance, thereby preventing another prisoner strike. Because this did not involve a fundamental change in the relationship between Vorkutlag and KVU, it could all be accomplished without ceding significant authority or accepting extra responsibility for mine output.

For their part, mine managers saw the granting of passes or the right to live outside the zone as an opportunity to gain what Zasiad'ko had been arguing for on their behalf since 1953: greater control over their workforce. De-convoyed prisoners would not be dependent on whether or not there were sufficient guards to bring them to work—they would make their way to the mines themselves. De-zoned prisoners could live in the same settlements as non-prisoners and utilize the transportation options already in place. Thus, managers were convinced that prisoners granted the privilege of moving freely or living outside the zone would show up for work more regularly. When at work in the mines, such prisoners were likely to be much more productive, as they would be working for wages nearly equivalent to those paid to non-prisoners.[118] Like the camp officials, mine officials were also convinced that prisoners granted these privileges would be unlikely to revolt, and this would help restore workplace discipline. Thus, mine officials also saw this as an opportunity to reverse the decline of labor productivity in the mines and to prevent another prisoner strike.

Vorkutlag's administration wasted little time granting passes and the right to live outside the zone in 1954. At first, granting passes was a far more common practice. Oleg Borovskii, a prisoner in Rechlag since 1949, received a pass in 1954 so that he could build an x-ray machine in another camp section. In the summer of 1954 he took his first steps outside the camp zone, unguarded and unaccompanied. He described the experience with great emotion: "Walking around the city for a few hours, I was surprised that no one paid any attention to me, although at first it seemed that every soldier or guard that I met would ask for my documents. Soon kiosks selling newspapers, ice cream, and beer opened. I was unable to resist temptation and drank a glass of beer, which seemed to me to be fantastically tasty and intoxicating, then ate two portions of 'Eskimo' ice cream and froze my lips and throat terribly. I sat a little while longer on a bench and dreamed of the time when I would be freed forever, and I would leave Vorkuta with Mira [his wife], as quickly and as far away as possible."[119] He was allowed to be outside the camp from 6:00 a.m. until midnight every day. Although he was only officially allowed to travel between camp sections 1 and 10, he used the opportunity to more or less live with his wife Mira, an ex-prisoner living in Vorkuta—that is, until he was caught taking a train to see his wife by an officer in the camp administration and his pass was revoked.[120] By 1 January 1955 there were already 7,781 de-convoyed prisoners, representing over 10 percent of the prisoner population.[121] Thus, granting prisoners passes was initially the preferred option for solving the conflict between Vorkutlag and KVU over prisoner labor.

Although initially the number of de-zoned prisoners was quite modest, they would soon far outnumber the de-convoyed. On 7 August, less than a month after the "regulations" went into effect, Vorkutlag director Prokop'ev approved his first list of 45 prisoners to be transferred outside the zone. His order, including the list of prisoners, was announced over the Vorkutlag camp radio so that the newly de-zoned could serve as examples to which all prisoners could aspire.[122] Lists of prisoners to be transferred outside the zone continued to cross Prokop'ev's desk, and the number rose quickly in the second half of 1954; by 1 January 1955 there were already 2,102 de-zoned prisoners in Vorkuta (table 4.1).[123] In 1955 the number of de-zoned prisoners increased even more quickly. From January through August, over 7,000 prisoners were granted permission to live outside the barbed wire. As table 4.2 shows, the monthly rate varied considerably, from a low of 379 in March to a high of 2,646 in April. The camp administration was now routinely allowing an average of *10 to 30 prisoners per day* permission to live outside the zone. The absolute and relative numbers of de-zoned prisoners reached their height in March 1956, when well over 13,000 prisoners were living outside the zone, nearly one-third of the total Vorkutlag population. Although the actual number of de-zoned prisoners declined over the course of 1956 because of mass releases, their numbers remained significant through the middle of 1957: on 1 July 1957, over 6,000 prisoners, representing just over 13 percent of the camp population, lived outside the zone. By 1960, the practice had

Table 4.1. Absolute and relative number of de-zoned prisoners in Vorkutlag, 1955–1960 (Selected Dates)

Date	N	%
1-Jan-55	2,102	3.35
1-Mar-56	13,639	29.00
16-Aug-56	10,752	22.79
10-Oct-56	8,741	18.48
1-Jan-57	7,309	14.74
1-Jul-57	6,296	13.24
1-Dec-58	1,029	4.74
1-Jan-59	854	4.11
1-Jan-60	320	2.09

Source: GURK NARK 2, f. 1875, op. 1, d. 176, l. 57; GURK NARK 1, f. R-1307, op. 1, d. 520, l. 1; GURK NARK 1, f. R-1307, op. 1, d. 531, l. 3; GURK NARK 1, f. R-1307, op. 1, d. 539, l. 9; GURK NARK 1, f. R-1307, op. 1, d. 75, l. 25; GURK NARK 1, f. R-1307, op. 1, d. 543, l. 1; GARF, f. R-8131, op. 32, d. 6566, ll. 6–7.

Table 4.2. Prisoners granted de-zoned status in Vorkutlag, January–August 1956

Month	N
January	722
February	749
March	379
April	2,646
May	746
June	911
July	399
August	511
Total	7,063

Source: GURK NARK 1, f. R-1307, op. 1, d. 531, l. 40.

virtually ceased, with only 320 prisoners, approximately 2 percent of the prisoner population, living outside the zone.

As the prevalence of de-zoned prisoners grew, so did the lists of prisoners being approved. For example, on 10 November 1955, 750 prisoners from camp section 10 were simultaneously given permission to live outside the camp zone.[124] This is clear evidence that by 1955 the practice of allowing prisoners to live outside the zone was not being granted as stipulated in the 1954 "regulations," as a privilege for a handful of prisoners who demonstrated good behavior. With hundreds of prisoners approved simultaneously, the decision could not have been based on a careful consideration of an individual prisoner's file. In fact, permission was being granted for other reasons. In some cases individual prisoners were asking for and receiving permission on the basis that they wanted to live with members of their families that had already come to Vorkuta.[125] But most often the process of granting the privilege to prisoners originated in the mines and other enterprises that Vorkutlag supplied with prisoner labor under contract. In many of the long lists of prisoners submitted for Vorkutlag director Prokop'ev's approval, the only characteristic given for each prisoner was his or her occupation.[126] Prisoners' names were being submitted for permission to live outside the zone not because of good behavior or because they qualified by having served at least one-third of their sentences, but because of their skills and economic importance to the mines and factories in which they worked. In some cases, entire work brigades were moved outside the zone at the request of the mines and enterprises to which they were attached. In others, entire camp sections (usually those attached to mines) were moved outside the zone.[127] Clearly, camp officials and enterprise managers saw the opportunity to transfer thousands of prisoners outside the zone as a mutually beneficial opportunity and one that promoted cooperation in the midst of the ongoing "turf war" between MUP and the MVD.[128]

The fact that local authorities were bending the rules was apparent to officials in the Komi ASSR Procuracy, whose inspectors reported gross violations of official policy. Some de-zoned prisoners had not yet served one-third of their sentence, which was required, whereas others had been convicted of crimes that made them ineligible.[129] In one section of Vorkutlag in September 1956, over 40 percent of the de-zoned prisoners did not legally qualify for the privilege.[130] Procuracy officials were well aware that permission was not being given as an incentive for good behavior, but in order to improve the economic performance of the industries and enterprises that Vorkutlag supplied with labor. As one report stated, "The administrations of camps transfer a significant number of prisoners . . . to live outside of camp zones not as an incentive, but motivated by the needs of production."[131] It does not appear that the procuracy's criticisms had any teeth, however, as few prisoners (if any) were transferred back into the camp zone as a result of these comments.[132] The granting of de-zoned status to large groups of prisoners in Vorkutlag continued unabated, undoubtedly with the tacit approval of the USSR MVD.[133]

Moving tens of thousands of prisoners outside the zone was a convenient arrangement for both KVU and Vorkutlag that prevented conflicts over prisoner labor. For all practical purposes it restored the authority of mine managers over their workers while allowing camp section officials to retain their authority over prisoners still living in the zone. Thus, locals had found a way to ease the administrative crisis that had grown in the wake of Stalin's death, at least in this important respect. It was less effective, however, in lessening the increased expectations of prisoners. In fact, the steady stream of prisoners out of the camps and into the surrounding settlements seems to have created a widespread expectation that all prisoners should be allowed to live outside the zone. Prisoners like Mikhail Baital'skii, who waited months to be de-zoned, even after his wife had already come to live in Vorkuta, were understandably frustrated at the perceived lack of logic to the process.[134] When a brief prisoner strike broke out in camp sections 5 and 15 in July 1955, this one involving approximately 1,200 prisoners and lasting less than a week, one of the most prominent demands was that all "counterrevolutionaries" be given the right to live outside the zone.[135] Contrary to the hopes of camp administrators and mine managers, further improvements and incentives seem to have only fueled prisoner unrest.

CAMP INTO CITY, "SLAVES INTO SERFS"

By 1956, it was clear that the practice of granting passes and permission to live outside the zone had moved well beyond being a temporary expedient. This is apparent when one turns to the thorniest issue raised when hundreds, and then thousands, of prisoners were given permission to live outside the zone: where to house them. According to the 1954 "regulations," Vorkutlag was responsible for providing housing for these prisoners outside the zone. Yet Vorkuta and the surrounding mine settlements suffered from a desperate shortage of housing that had plagued the area since the 1930s.[136] The rapid increase in the number of de-zoned prisoners threatened to strain the already overburdened civilian housing stock, sending camp and mine officials scrambling to find them places to live. In some cases, the prisoners themselves were responsible for finding rooms to rent.[137] In others, camp authorities were able to conclude agreements with surrounding settlements to secure living space for prisoners.[138] Yet securing housing space was sometimes such a problem that the camp administration actually rescinded orders allowing prisoners to live outside the zone because there was simply nowhere for them to live.[139]

Enterprise managers soon began to improvise in order to secure housing for those whom they wanted transferred outside the camp. One strategy was for enterprises to set aside land, building materials, and time for potential de-zoned prisoners to build their own housing. Once the housing was completed, the camp or mine officials would then petition for the prisoners who took part to be granted permission to live in it.[140] Yet this method was not widely practicable owing to a shortage of building materials. In the end, the only method that could accommodate thousands of prisoners moving outside the zone was to move the boundaries of the zone itself. The fencing and barbed wire that enclosed the territory of the camp were simply moved, so that barracks that had once stood within the camp zone were now outside it. As a Vorkutlag procuracy official noted, "Prisoners living outside the zone live in the main in the same barracks in which they previously lived, only now these barracks are located outside the zone."[141] Moving the boundaries of the zone to convert camp buildings for civilian use had been going on at least since the early 1940s, and much of the housing stock in the city of Vorkuta consisted of former camp barracks. But in this case, the prisoners continued to live in the same barracks, only now they were no longer located within the camp and were called "dormitories" instead.

It is here that we see the improvisations of camp and mine officials transforming into something far more than a stopgap measure to ensure a steady labor supply. By 1956–1957, Vorkutlag and KVU's strategy of allowing prisoners to live outside the zone had become part of a process by which spaces of the camp complex were becoming part of the company town. As the barbed wire receded, entire camp sections became part of the "outside" and moved from the camp to the city. It was no longer the case that prisoners were being relocated outside the zone—rather, the zone itself was shrinking. By improvising a solution

Figure 4.1. Ex-prisoner Anna Szyszko in the tundra near a camp zone, ca. 1955–1957. Photograph courtesy of KARTA Center Foundation, Warsaw.

to both administrative conflict and the prisoner unrest, KVU and Vorkutlag were moving beyond short-term labor concerns to the long-term issue of how to convert a camp complex into a city. The widespread use of de-zoned prisoners was transforming the landscape of Vorkuta (figure 4.1).

The practice of allowing thousands of prisoners to live outside the zone also had profound effects on prisoner status and identity. While it remained clear that the de-zoned were still prisoners, in practice their rights and privileges closely resembled those of the many former prisoners and exiles living in the city. They were paid equivalent wages to non-prisoner workers and lived in housing outside the zone. Many sent for their families to join them in Vorkuta. Some were even granted permission to travel long distances throughout the Soviet Union.[142] In short, de-zoned prisoners had already accomplished significant parts of the process of making the transition from prisoner to non-prisoner before their terms had expired. This was advantageous not only to the prisoners, but also to their employers. Looking ahead, managers realized that in the near future thousands of skilled and reliable prisoners would be released from the camp. In the absence of compulsion, there were no guarantees that they would stay in Vorkuta. Perhaps they could be convinced to remain if they already had jobs and housing, and had settled with their families. Thus, de-zoning thousands of prisoners became part of a long-term strategy to build a skilled and reliable workforce from the prisoner population by "tying" prisoners to their enterprises. Both former prisoners and historians have suggested that this was an attempt to convert "slaves into serfs."[143] Although it is problematic to apply either category to prisoners in Vorkuta, such a description of the process captures the notion that the status of tens of thousands of prisoners came to more closely resemble that of exiles rather than prisoners. No matter its intentions, there is no doubt that this process helped tens of thousands of prisoners navigate the difficult transition from imprisonment to freedom.

The use of prisoner labor contracted from the camps to the mines would decline significantly in the second half of the 1950s, as would the use of de-zoned and de-convoyed prisoners. Two related developments would precipitate this fundamental shift. First, the waves of mass releases from the Gulag that had been initiated by the 27 March 1953 amnesty finally began to have a significant effect on the population of Vorkutlag. From 1955–1958, tens of thousands of prisoners were released from Vorkutlag, and the size of the camp population fell to less than forty thousand by 1958. Thus, the potential pool of prisoner labor shrank significantly. Second, MUP minister Zasiad'ko finally got his wish for definitive control over both Vorkuta's mines and its labor force. In August 1955, the Council of Ministers passed a comprehensive resolution on the future of the Pechora coal basin, declaring that as of 1958 only "permanent cadres" (non-prisoners) would work underground in the mines. Neither of these developments spelled an end to prison camps in Vorkuta, let alone the use of prisoner labor contracted out to enterprises. Major construction projects, from schools to mines, continued to make use of prisoner labor through the 1980s. But the changes went a long way toward resolving the crisis that had begun in 1953. With a sharp reduction in the use of prisoner labor contracted from the camps to the mines, the turf war between MUP and the MVD ended. With the release of tens of thousands of prisoners from Vorkutlag, the hopes and expectations of many prisoners were met, even if, as we shall see, the freedom that they were granted had its limitations.

With the decisions to greatly reduce the size of Vorkutlag and to use only non-prisoner labor in the mines, much of the uncertainty precipitated by the events of 1953 was resolved.

Yet this did not mean an end to the upheavals and transformations taking place in Vorkuta. Administrative uncertainty would be replaced by a new set of challenges over the next decade and a half. Like the crises in 1953–1955, they would also revolve around the issue of labor. Given the significant reduction in the size of the prisoner population and the imperative to switch entirely to the use of non-prisoner labor in the mines by 1958, MUP was now faced with the prospect of finding tens of thousands of workers to replace the labor of prisoners. Workers from other parts of the Soviet Union would be actively recruited or encouraged to migrate to the city with incentives. At the same time, former prisoners and exiles would continue to represent a significant proportion of mine employees going forward. It was these outside recruits, as well as prisoners and exiles, who would define the social fabric of the company town that Vorkuta would become for the remainder of the Soviet period.

5 The "Second Birth" of Vorkuta
Forging the Company Town

At the edge of the square some blackened pillars stick up from the snow. People say these pillars used to support a guard tower. They say that once long ago, back in Stalin's time, there was a prison camp on the site of our settlement. It is hard to imagine that here, where we now work, dance, go to movies, laugh at one another, and cry, there was once a prison camp. I try not to think of those times; to me they are utterly incomprehensible.
—*Vasilii Aksenov, "Oranges from Morocco"*

ON 5 JUNE 1956 Vorkuta's railroad station was abuzz with activity. An important delegation was arriving. *Zapoliar'e*, the local newspaper, described the scene: "Twelve young men and twelve young women were warmly welcomed at the station by representatives of the coal company . . . and city society. . . . Sounds of a brass orchestra welcomed the slowing train. Here at the station a spontaneous meeting arose, opened by the secretary of the city committee of the Komsomol, comrade Mazur. He congratulated them on behalf of all the youth of the city for their decision to help the polar residents develop the incalculable riches of the earth's interior, and build new enterprises, sociocultural institutions, and comfortable housing."[1] Speeches were delivered, first by the Komsomol secretary of the construction department where the volunteers would work, and then by a seventeen-year-old representative of the arriving workers. Then, singing, the twenty-four youths were driven to their new living quarters in the Gorniatskii settlement. The first group of Komsomol volunteers from Syktyvkar, the capital of the Komi ASSR, had arrived. New challenges and opportunities awaited them as construction workers in Vorkuta.

Thirteen years before, a meeting had taken place at the same train station in order to commemorate the first shipment of Vorkuta's coal to Leningrad. Taking place at the height of the war in 1943, that meeting had celebrated the new city's contribution to the war effort and ritually marked its connection to the national transportation network. Although the June 1956 meeting marked the movement of people, not goods, and the direction of travel was reversed, there are striking similarities between them. The arrival of the Komsomol volunteers signified an important stage in the city's transformation from Gulag town to company town. In place of coerced labor by prisoners, young and enthusiastic volunteers would work in Vorkuta's mines, construction crews, and factories. Soon, the barbed wire of the camps and crude barracks would be replaced by practical and comfortable new housing.

In line with the emerging policies of the new Khrushchev government, recruitment practices were becoming, at least in theory, less coercive than they had been during and after the war. As part of his attempt to revive the Soviet system and rekindle the enthusiasm of the population for communist ideals, Khrushchev and his closest advisers attempted a thoroughgoing reform of labor recruitment policies in order to make them based on choice rather than compulsion. The arrival of the Komsomol volunteers in June 1956, and the fanfare that surrounded it, publicly marked Vorkuta's embrace of the new times and new policies. On the one hand, such recruitment policies were necessitated by Khrushchev's abandonment of mass repression as a tool of population management. Millions of prisoners and special settlers across the Soviet Union were being released, and an injection of new labor was necessary to replace them. In Vorkuta alone, over 105,000 prisoners were released between 1953 and 1958. Yet the new recruitment campaigns of the 1950s were about more than simply replacing one population with another. The young volunteers who were recruited to Vorkuta were seen as a vehicle through which an entire community could be transformed. By bringing young, enthusiastic, uncorrupted citizens to replace prisoners and exiles, the intention was to transform the very nature of city society. In the place of prisoners with shady pasts and suspect political ideas, the new youth could purify public and private spaces and expunge the city's troubled past.

The recruitment of new workers was a key part of a thoroughgoing attempt to transform Vorkuta into a company town, a process that faced obstacles beyond simply bringing enough people to the city to replace departing prisoners and exiles. Like most Soviet cities, Vorkuta did not have sufficient infrastructure to properly absorb thousands of new recruits. But the structural shortage of housing and other urban infrastructure that was ubiquitous in the postwar Soviet Union was only magnified by Vorkuta's remoteness, extreme natural environment, and its legacy as a Gulag town, which bequeathed little more than ramshackle barracks. Thus, the struggle by local officials to improve living conditions for recruits was a key element of Vorkuta's transformation. So was a program, launched in 1959, to completely rebuild Vorkuta's mines in accordance with contemporary international standards. Without a seemingly unlimited supply of forced laborers, local managers and their superiors in Moscow now had to think about improving the profitability of the mines in order to offset the new expenses of higher wages and investment in infrastructure. Further, safe working conditions mattered much more to a labor force of non-prisoners. The program of mine reconstruction would drag out for decades, but would result in a profound transformation in the working lives of Vorkutiane.

As the epigraph above suggests, attempts to transform the city and its population in the second half of the 1950s and early 1960s also exposed deep anxieties. The period was marked by sustained uneasiness about the integration of new recruits and their capacity to transform Vorkuta into an ideal Soviet community. Although there was some evidence that the new recruits were transforming the character of work and leisure spaces, local leaders were disturbed to observe that just as often it was the fresh recruits who were being influenced by the former prisoners and exiles with whom they lived and worked. Thus, attempts to transform Vorkuta into a Soviet company town demonstrate not only the profound optimism of the new times, but also the profound anxieties unearthed by the attempt to transform Soviet society after Stalin.[2]

IN SEARCH OF "PERMANENT CADRES"

By the time of the arrival of the first group of Komsomol volunteers from Syktyvkar in June 1956, large-scale outside labor recruitment had already been under way for some time. Local officials in Vorkuta and their counterparts in Moscow had been struggling over the issue of labor supply since the first weeks after Stalin's death. Although there were still nearly fifty thousand prisoners in Vorkutlag at this time, well

Figure 5.1. View of mine 9–10 and its surroundings, ca. 1955–1957. Photograph courtesy of KARTA Center Foundation, Warsaw.

over fifty thousand prisoners had been released in the previous three years. In August 1955, MUP and its local representatives had been told unequivocally that the vast majority of prisoners would have to be replaced with non-prisoner labor. In a resolution entitled "On measures for urgent assistance to the Pechora coal basin," the USSR Council of Ministers decreed that Vorkuta's mines would make the transition to non-prisoner labor. According to the resolution, MUP was now solely responsible for providing the entire underground staff of Vorkuta's mines.[3] Although prisoners would continue to be used in the future, particularly in mine construction projects, the personnel responsible for running KVU's mines were now going to be "permanent cadres," a euphemism for non-prisoners.

The 1955 Sovmin resolution placed a difficult task on KVU administrators. In the next two and a half years, they would have to find specialists and workers to replace over twenty thousand prisoners working in the mines, who made up nearly 70 percent of the workforce.[4] This was in addition to replacing thousands of exiles who would soon be granted the right to leave Vorkuta under the terms of various amnesties. Many jobs vacated by prisoners would be filled by ex-prisoners or former exiles who decided to remain in the city after their release. But KVU administrators could not rely entirely on ex-prisoners to replace the prisoner labor that they had been receiving under contract. Although much could be done to convince former prisoners to stay, it was clear that many would choose to depart when they were able. Further, these former prisoners were in many respects a problematic population with suspect pasts and political views. Thus it was not only necessary to find new blood for the city, it was also desirable.

In fact, MUP had already been recruiting non-prisoner labor to the mines for some time. After assuming responsibility for KVU at the end of March 1953, MUP immediately began recruiting workers to the city. For the next two years, KVU would rely primarily on a system known as "organized recruitment" (*organizovannyi nabor* or *orgnabor*), which had been used since the 1930s to recruit rural and urban dwellers for particular industries. Under this system, recruiters fanned out to villages and towns to entice peasants and workers to sign contracts agreeing to work for fixed terms in the enterprises that the recruiters represented. Although KVU had limited experience using this system, MUP was long accustomed to obtaining labor in this fashion. In 1950, for instance, over one hundred thousand people were recruited via orgnabor to work in MUP coal mines across the Soviet Union.[5]

The orgnabor system had well-known flaws that became apparent once it came into use in Vorkuta.[6] As had been common since the 1930s, there was a clear mismatch between the promises made to the recruits and what they actually experienced after they arrived. Housing set aside for them was in deplorable condition, if it existed at all. A city deputy from the Zapoliar'nyi settlement wondered at a Gorispolkom meeting in March 1954, "Why did we recruit people when we knew perfectly that there weren't conditions for them to live?"[7] At the same meeting, the head of the city militia complained that he was being told to punish deserting workers, whereas he felt that deceitful recruiters were the ones truly to blame.[8] The other problem that plagued orgnabor was the suspect quality of the recruits, many of whom seemed more interested in recreation than labor. Grigorenko, secretary of the party organization of mine no. 4, complained in early 1955, "Of 100 men at our mine [recruited via orgnabor], only 32 work, and the rest of them drink and do not go to work."[9] Some recruits simply left the city soon after arrival, whereas many others were fired for drunkenness or absenteeism.[10] Although 2,906 workers were recruited for KVU under orgnabor in 1955, it appears that few became productive workers.[11]

When KVU began recruiting workers in earnest after the August 1955 resolution, orgnabor was almost entirely abandoned. This was in line with a shift in labor recruitment policy throughout the Soviet Union, as Stalinist recruitment methods were scaled back in favor of those intended to better harness the enthusiasm of Soviet youth.[12] One important technique of the mid-1950s was to recruit demobilized soldiers to agricultural and industrial projects that needed a fast injection of large amounts of labor. Khrushchev was overseeing a massive reduction of the Soviet armed forces, which shrank by over one million men from 1955 to 1958, creating a vast pool of mobile labor.[13] At the same time, the new Soviet leader was keen to launch ambitious new projects, such as the settling of the so-called Virgin lands in Kazakhstan. Although the recruitment of demobilized soldiers to Khrushchev's pet agricultural project received far more press, in fact many soldiers were recruited to former Gulag sites like Vorkuta. As table 5.1 shows, from 1955 to 1960 over fifteen thousand former soldiers were recruited to Vorkuta, with about four thousand arriving each year during the peak from 1956 to 1958.[14] This made demobilized soldiers the largest source of labor actively recruited by KVU from outside the city in the second half of the 1950s.

Another recruitment method introduced under Khrushchev was the so-called social call-up (*obshchestvennyi prizyv*). Modeled to a large degree after successful drives to recruit youth to settle the Virgin lands, it was announced as a national campaign on 16 May 1956.[15] The "call-up" was addressed to all Soviet youth, imploring them to "send their best comrades for the construction of electric generating stations, metallurgical, chemical, oil-refining, and machine-building factories, mines, coal mines, railroads," in the east, north, and the Donbas.[16] This voluntary recruitment was explicitly intended to make up for a decreased reliance on orgnabor. Privately, officials acknowledged that many of the recruits would replace prisoners and exiles being released from the Gulag.[17] Although Vorkuta was not a destination for the Union-level campaign, it was part of a regional call-up that saw thousands of young volunteers sent to industrial projects across Komi ASSR, many of which were former Gulag sites. The first Komsomol volunteers ar-

Table 5.1. KVU hiring from armed forces, 1955–1967

Year	KVU Total	From Armed Forces N	From Armed Forces %
1955[a]	13,586	1,224	9.01
1956		4,000	
1957		3,800	
1958	23,171	4,432	19.13
1959	21,028	934	4.44
1960	19,502	1,120	5.74
1961	15,076	349	2.31
1962	16,865	766	4.54
1963	13,003	817	6.28
1964	14,042	588	4.19
1965	14,423	871	6.04
1966	11,977	761	6.35
1967	10,730	727	6.78

Source: GURK NARK 1, f. R-1675, op. 1, d. 2281, l. 22ob.; *Zapoliar'e*, 3 December 1957; GURK NARK 1, f. R-1675, op. 1, d. 2281, ll. 12–15, 19–21; GURK NARK 1, f. R-1675, op. 1, d. 2305, ll. 1–10b; GURK NARK 1, f. R-1675, op. 1, d. 2312, ll. 1–10b; GURK NARK 1, f. R-1675, op. 1, op. 1, d. 2324, ll. 1–2; GURK NARK 1, f. R-1675, op. 1, d. 2346, l. 1.; GURK NARK 1, f. R-1675, op. 1, d. 2366, ll. 1, 4, 43; GURK NARK 1, f. R-1675, op. 1, d. 1719, ll. 136, 142–43, 156.

[a] Row includes data for mines only.

rived on 5 June 1956 and would continue to stream into the city over the next few years.[18]

There were also concerted efforts to recruit mining specialists, those who had graduated from institutes of higher education or from technical schools, to come to the city. Since the 1930s, most graduates from such schools were given work assignments that they were required to fulfill after graduation (*raspredelenie*). This practice, which was continued during the Khrushchev era, was designed to ensure that a sufficient number of specialists were sent to all parts of the Soviet Union, especially its most far-flung and peripheral places. As part of the Gulag, Vorkuta had received few, if any, mining specialists from this system.[19] But in 1953, when MUP assumed responsibility for Vorkuta's mines, the ministry began to send graduates from its educational institutions to the Pechora coal basin. From then on, hundreds of specialists were sent to the city each year to fill important posts as "engineering and

Table 5.2. Specialists sent to KVU via raspredelenie, 1954–1967

Year	Higher Education	Technical Education	Total
1954	74	355	429
1955	106	337	443
1956	149	278	427
1957	96	241	337
1958	121	334	455
1959	89	259	348
1960	142	216	358
1961	121	208	329
1962	80	174	254
1963	88	169	257
1964	50	113	163
1965	99	162	261
1966	104	123	227
1967	61	103	164

Source: GURK NARK 1, f. R-1675, op. 1, d. 1780, l. 38; GURK NARK 1, f. R-1675, op. 1, d. 1709, l. 16; GURK NARK 1, f. R-1675, op. 1, d. 1710, l. 2; GURK NARK 1, f. R-1675, op. 1, d. 1711, l. 2; GURK NARK 1, f. R-1675, op. 1, d. 1712, l. 3; GURK NARK 1, f. R-1675, op. 1, d. 1713, l. 3; GURK NARK 1, f. R-1675, op. 1, l. 32.; GURK NARK 1, f. R-1675, op. 1, d. 1715, l. 4; GURK NARK 1, f. R-1675, op. 1, d. 1716, l. 2; GURK NARK 1, f. R-1675, op. 1, d. 1717, l. 9; GURK NARK 1, f. R-1675, op. 1, d. 1718, l. 7.

technical workers" (ITR). The number of specialists sent via raspredelenie reached its zenith in 1958 (455) before declining to its nadir in 1964 (163) (table 5.2). Although the overall number of specialists arriving in Vorkuta actually increased over time, the number who arrived there because of raspredelenie had declined significantly by the middle of the 1960s.

Ultimately, however, the numbers of recruits sent from central and regional campaigns and programs were not sufficient to satisfy the acute demand for labor. KVU sought other ways to bring more non-prisoners into the working population. From 1955 to 1958, a concerted effort was made to bring more working-age women into the workforce, particularly in the coal mines. Although women were typically underrepresented both in the Gulag population and in frontier towns like Vorkuta that were oriented toward male-dominated industries, the population of working-age women grew fairly quickly in the second half of the 1940s and first half of the 1950s. Combining prisoner and non-prisoner populations, the percentage of women in the overall population of Vorkuta grew from only 17 percent in 1947 to 27 percent in 1954. Among the non-prisoner population, the gender balance was more even, with women representing 36 percent of non-prisoners in 1947 and 45 percent in 1954.[20] Although some of this increase came from women released from imprisonment or exile, most of the increase came from a rising birth rate and growing migration to the city in search of opportunities. It would not be until 1969 that gender parity would be reached, however.[21]

Women had been working in Vorkuta's mines since the mid-1930s, a practice that had been common throughout the Soviet Union at least since the first five-year plan.[22] For example, K. Plastinina, one of the first graduates of the mining-oil tekhnikum in Chib'iu (Ukhta), had, as a non-prisoner, worked her way from being a miner in 1936 to serving as a mine director from 1954 to 1957. She continued working at KVU until 1973, serving much of that time as the head of cadres for KVU.[23] As mass releases accelerated in 1955, there was increasing incentive to hire women in order to stabilize the workforce. For example, in mine no. 40, one of the largest and most productive in Vorkuta, women made up a significant proportion of the workforce. As of July 1958, 129 women worked underground in the mine, representing perhaps as much as 10 percent of all underground workers. Most were single, childless, under the age of thirty, and lacked postsecondary education, although significant minorities were married and had children. Only 6 of them were former prisoners. Although a few had been working underground for over five years, most were in fact new to their jobs, as the median service tenure in July 1958 was only twelve months.[24] Thus, KVU managers were clearly relying on young women as an important labor source as they shifted from contract labor from the camps to non-prisoner labor.

In fact, hiring women to work in the mines was part of a deliberate and sustained local campaign. From 1955 to 1958 Vorkuta's local newspaper frequently contained editorials and profiles of women in Vorkuta, emphasizing the important contributions of female miners, particularly around the symbolic dates of International Women's Day (8 March) and Miner's Day (29 August). The 28 August 1955 issue featured a profile of Mariia Kirillovna Marchenko, who in her twelve years in Vorkuta had worked her way up from a duty officer, to the head engineer of mine no. 12, to the head of the production department of *Zapadugol'*, an organization that ran half of the mines in Vorkuta.[25] Her story is particularly significant because it not only emphasized Marchenko's contributions as an underground laborer, but it also presented a narrative of female social mobility, suggesting that women could also enjoy the common male career path from miner to engineer.

But by the 1960s, the public campaign to celebrate women working in mines disappeared. Female miners disappeared from Vorkuta as well, never to return. Protective legislation adopted nationally in July 1957 forbade women from working underground in mines in all but a few exceptional cases.[26] The purpose of the legislation was at least twofold: first, to protect the health and safety of female workers, who were overrepresented in fatal accidents; second, to restore coal mining as an exclusively male occupation. Women had been making inroads in mining, particularly since the Second World War, when a shortage of male skilled workers led to their recruitment. Yet data collected by the government suggested that male miners were far more productive than their female counterparts, and so the central government intervened to restore coal mining as a male-dominated industry.[27] Although KVU managers delayed the implementation of the legislation as long as they possibly could, by 1960 virtually no women worked underground in the mines.[28] Mine managers lost an important source of labor, and women lost the opportunity to work in some of the most prestigious and highest-paid jobs in the city. The 1960s would see numerous attempts at creating jobs for the growing female population of the city, but the result was a creation of a paltry number of poor-paying jobs.[29] Throughout the 1960s, local women lobbied for the right to work once again in the mines, but to no avail.[30]

Although attempts to hire women to work underground would be entirely abandoned by 1960, working outside official recruitment campaigns to increase the size of the workforce in Vorkuta was a harbinger of things to come. In October 1959, in a speech in Vladivostok, Khrushchev signaled a shift in recruitment policies that would be enshrined in law in early 1960.[31] One change was that lucrative wage bonuses would be scaled back, replaced instead by increased investment in improving living conditions, a change that Soviet economists had concluded would improve labor retention.[32] At the same time that wage bonuses were reduced, the requirement that a worker sign a contract in order to receive northern bonuses was removed.[33] Now, former prisoners and those who migrated to cities in the northern regions and Siberia without being recruited received the bonuses as well.[34] By eliminating the main incentives for signing a recruitment contract, these changes effectively undercut the recruitment system that had been in place for the past five years. Thus it appears that the policy of mass, campaign-style recruitment that had characterized the period from 1955 to 1960 was largely abandoned. After 1960, few demobilized soldiers were hired by KVU. By this time, the steady stream of volunteers coming to the city on "Komsomol passes" had virtually dried up as well. Migration based on recruiters and contracts, not to mention public campaigns, had given way to a more "spontaneous" movement of workers. One of the great social experiments of the Khrushchev era, the attempt to rely on recruitment campaigns, had largely drawn to a close. In its place, the regime instead intended to rely on relatively unregulated migration of individual families in search of better opportunities.

MOTIVATIONS

Until the middle of the 1950s, coming to Vorkuta was rarely a matter of choice. The majority of Vorkuta's "residents" were brought there under guard, on foot, on barges and in freight cars, and even nonprisoners frequently arrived in Vorkuta as the result of coercion. With this in mind, the idea that thousands of people would choose to move to Vorkuta might strike one as strange. Prison camp aside, Vorkuta has one of the most difficult climates of any city in the world. Temperatures there are known to reach −50° C, and the sun does not rise for months at a time in winter. But tens of thousands did choose to come to the city. In the middle of the 1950s there were various "push" factors at work that led people to uproot themselves and look for opportunities elsewhere, and Vorkuta was one of many possible destinations. Despite its harsh climate and harsher history, there were a number of things that Vorkuta offered, or at least appeared to offer, to new recruits. Such characteristics were factors that might "pull" potential recruits to the city. Crudely speaking, it is a combination of these "push" and "pull" factors that led thousands to try their luck making a new life in Vorkuta.

By far the most common "push" factor was poverty. Many of the soldiers who were being demobilized from the armed forces in the middle of the 1950s came from dismal conditions on collective farms.[35] Recruiters who came to units offering jobs and housing in cities did not have a difficult time convincing young men who grew up in the hungry years of the Second World War and its aftermath that what they offered was a superior alternative to village life. As Stepan Petrovich Sirosh, who came to Vorkuta in 1957 from the army, explained, "You judge for yourself [why I left]. I was born in 1934 in the village of Maksimovichi in Polesskii raion. That is in the north of Kiev oblast', not far from the border with Belorussia. What sort of years those were in Ukraine is well known from history. My family was de-kulakized and we lost our father. There were five children in the family. Then there was war and occupation. Two children, a sister and brother, died before the war. [Then came the] difficult postwar years. My father returned in 1945 and died two years later: his health had been destroyed."[36] For Sirosh, like many others who were recruited from the army for all sorts of projects around the Soviet Union, returning home to a life of almost certain poverty was not an attractive option.

The same held true for many of the Komsomol volunteers recruited from within Komi ASSR. The region was sparsely populated, and aside from a few cities that had grown up around prison camp complexes, predominantly rural. In 1959, it had a population density of 2.0 persons per square kilometer, the lowest density of any region in European Russia and well below the RSFSR average of 6.9 persons per square kilometer.[37] Despite low population density, Komi actually had a relatively high level of urbanization: in 1959, 59 percent of the region's population lived in cities and towns. This urbanization figure becomes even more startling when one considers that twenty years earlier in 1939, only 9 percent of the population had lived in urban areas.[38] Komi ASSR had obviously undergone rapid urbanization, and most of the population was concentrated in only a few large urban centers, all of which, with the exception of the capital Syktyvkar, had originated as prison camp complexes. Thus, opportunities to move from countryside to city, and for social mobility in general, usually involved moving to one of these cities. As the largest and fastest-growing urban area in Komi, Vorkuta was an attractive destination for many young people looking to leave the poverty of farm and village for industrial employment.

But what could recruiters offer that would draw people specifically to Vorkuta? Foremost among the "pull" factors was the so-called long ruble: workers recruited to Vorkuta enjoyed significant financial incentives that only increased with the length of tenure. The Soviet state had long practiced a policy of providing "northern bonuses" (*severnye nadbavki*) to those who signed contracts to work in designated regions.[39] They called for a 10 percent wage bonus to be paid after each six months of uninterrupted work in the North for anyone who had signed a contract with an enterprise. The first bonus was paid after six months of work, and the bonuses were cumulative, up to 100 percent of the nominal wage. Thus, after two and a half years of work the bonus would be an extra 50 percent of wages, and after five years it was effectively doubled. Those who worked in Vorkuta's mines enjoyed even greater financial incentives on top of the "northern bonuses." From 1945 to 1955, workers in KVU had their wages indexed to 1.5 times those paid to workers in the Donbas, a "regional coefficient" (*raionnyi koefitstient*) intended to compensate workers for greater hardship and a higher cost of living. After 1955, this wage index was increased to 1.8.[40] The "regional coefficient" worked in concert with the northern bonuses, so someone who worked in the mines of Vorkuta for five years would, in theory at least, have enjoyed an income that was 3.6 times that of a miner in the Donbas. Although real wages tended to be lower than the rate that was guaranteed by law, this hardly reduced the effectiveness of wage differentials as an incentive for migration to the city. Such wage bonuses were decreased somewhat in early 1960, so that bonuses accrued only half as quickly, were capped at 80 percent of wages, and did not include the "regional coefficient" in their calculations.[41] But even these reduced wage bonuses were quite attractive, and further, the bonuses scheme that had existed prior to 1960 was largely restored in 1967.[42]

Aside from wages, workers in the North enjoyed other monetary and non-monetary benefits. They were entitled to significantly longer vacations and extra social insurance payments in case of injury. In addition, one year of work in the North counted for two toward receiving a state pension—and this was in addition to significant pension incentives for those who worked underground. On the way to their new jobs, they were entitled to receive twice the usual travel expenses and per diem payments for the journey. In addition, they were paid twice the one-time wage payment that all new recruits received.[43] Thus, recruits who signed contracts to work in KVU were offered both short- and long-term incentives.

The importance of the "pull" factor of high wages is underscored not only in memoirs, but also in public discourse of the time. For instance, on 30 April 1958, *Za ugol'* (the "wall newspaper" of mine no. 1) published letters exchanged between army friends discussing whether or not to come to Vorkuta.[44] In reply to the inquiries of friends who were contemplating the journey, those in Vorkuta devoted significant attention to their earnings as well as those of their acquaintances. One letter written to a former army comrade reads, "I work as an assistant combine operator and my monthly salary is 2,700. Sasha Voronik, who works as a tunneler, he earns 1,500 rubles . . . and Viktor Amel'chenko sometimes earns 2,800 and even 3,000 rubles in a month."[45] In newspaper articles such as these, Vorkuta was cast as a Soviet "boom town," a place where those who were willing to work hard could make their fortunes.

But the lure of the "long ruble" was not the only motivation for recruits, either as depicted in the Soviet press or in personal decisions. Public rhetoric often focused in fact on another important draw of the city: the opportunity to actively help fulfill the lofty goals of the Soviet state by participating in the construction of a new city. The text of the "social call-up" in 1956 drew an explicit link between individual participation and the overall fulfillment of the goals just set by the Twentieth Party Congress, and it also connected new construction projects with those of the 1930s. It stated, "Remember the heroic construction of Komsomol'sk-na-Amure—the city of youth in the Far East."[46] For a generation of young people who had participated neither in the Second World War nor the monumental transformations of the 1930s, this was an opportunity to write a part for oneself in the great narrative of Soviet construction. The Khrushchev regime was eager to tap into such enthusiasm.

For some volunteers, like Iurii Terekhov of Syktyvkar, the "social call-up" clearly resonated. They were overcome by the exciting opportunities that the call-up promised. As Terekhov wrote in *Zapoliar'e* soon after his arrival in July 1956, "Ten days later [after the "call-up" was published] I had a Komsomol *putevka* in hand . . . those were exciting days. [I felt] joyful and excited before the big new life on the construction projects of the sixth five-year plan." While he had worked previously as a driver, now he was working as a mason, building houses. The pride that Terekhov felt was almost palpable: "It is wonderful to realize that a building has been built with your participation, that there are bricks there laid by your own hands."[47] Put in this manner, it is easy to see how a national recruiting campaign could appeal to an individual.

Other motivations for coming to Vorkuta were not often reflected in official documents. Some recruits came to Vorkuta for what they understood to be its rather permissive atmosphere. Mikhail T., who came to Vorkuta as a young man in 1962, is one of those people. After graduating from the Novocherkassk Polytechnic Institute, he found life in Southern Russia to be very difficult. As he related, "There was such anti-Semitism, frightening. I wanted to go anywhere at all in order not to stay in Rostov oblast'." A cousin in Vorkuta, whose parents were former prisoners, suggested that he come to Vorkuta. As Mikhail T. discovered, "The climate there was entirely different." While there may have been anti-Semitism on an everyday level, he found no discrimination against Jews in terms of job prospects, which he attributed to the high representation of Jews in KVU management positions.[48] Anti-Semitism, and its relative absence in Vorkuta, was both a "push" and a "pull" factor in this case.

When considering the motivations for recruits, it is important to remember that they had access to a limited amount of information about the city, and even this limited information was often of suspect quality. Recruiters were notorious for misleading or lying to potential recruits, especially regarding the living conditions on offer for new arrivals.[49] The Soviet press could hardly be relied on to provide an accurate picture of life in Vorkuta. Stories in the central press about the city were rare, and when they did appear they focused on the city's achievements in production.[50] Press accounts that did go into detail about life in the city tended to romanticize the more exotic aspects of life there rather than reflect the level of hardship that its residents faced.[51] Such public accounts claimed, of course, that the city had been built by Komsomol volunteers, not by a mass of prisoners and exiles. Potential recruits who wanted a more accurate picture of the city had to rely on firsthand accounts of those who had been there, or much more often, rumor. Although unofficial sources of information did help some, like Mikhail T., make informed decisions about going to Vorkuta, in most cases such information could not have prepared them for what they found on arrival.

Finally, one must underline that individuals and families who wished to move in search of better opportunities faced limitations on where they were allowed to settle. Although many of the overtly coercive population policies of the late-Stalin era were abandoned, internal migration in the 1960s and 1970s came to be governed by an increasingly complex and strict system of what Victor Zaslavksy called "territorial stratification" that divided the Soviet Union's cities and villages into three categories: "the village, the open city, and the closed city."[52] The system of *propiska*, which allowed local authorities to determine who could settle in a given city, as well as stricter control of enrollments at educational institutions, led to tighter controls on migration to closed cities. These cities, which included "all capitals of Soviet national republics, almost all cities with a population in excess of 500,000, and several smaller towns and regions which, for various reasons, are especially attractive for migration," were at the top of a system of territorial hierarchy, and their residents by extension were at the top of the Soviet Union's social hierarchy.[53] This system of stratification, while less overly coercive than the Stalinist labor policy, actually resulted in fewer opportunities for social mobility, especially for those migrating from the Soviet countryside.

Vorkuta, as an open city, occupied the middle rung in this scheme. There were relatively few administrative limits for those who wanted to settle there; the thousands of ex-prisoners who remained in the city after release certainly attest to that. But among the many thousands of open cities in the Soviet Union, Vorkuta must certainly have been among the more desirable places to migrate. Despite poor living conditions and the harsh climate, high wages, abundant employment (for men at least), and the opportunity to acquire valuable skills through a growing network of training institutions all added up to excellent opportunities for social mobility for Soviet citizens who found themselves in the middle or on the bottom of the territorial hierarchy. In fact, as we shall see, this is an important explanation for why labor turnover in KVU began to decline significantly after campaign-based recruitment was virtually abandoned in favor of controlled migration at the beginning of the 1960s. Simply put, it was a more effective means of ensuring an adequate labor supply.

INTEGRATION AND ANXIETIES

Convincing tens of thousands of new recruits to come to Vorkuta was a key part of transforming it into a company town. As it turned out, this was in fact a relatively easy and successful part of re-peopling the city. Much more difficult, however, was the problem of how to integrate these new recruits into the city, its surrounding settlements, and the workplaces throughout the area. In a speech to the city party committee plenum on 25 September 1956, Sherstnev, the new director of KVU, set this as the most important task of all authorities in Vorkuta. Going over the poor production figures of the first nine months of 1956, he lamented, "The reasons for the shortfall [in coal] are clear. . . . We are guilty of repeating the mistakes of last year. As prisoners were given early release, we did not take care of the replenishment and training of cadres. . . . Now we can receive demobilized soldiers, who are already arriving—and to receive them in the proper way, to quarter, train, and send them to extract coal, that is the goal of all of our organizations."[54] As director of the most important and powerful economic organization in the emerging company town, Sherstnev recognized that the city's long-term success depended upon keeping a sufficient number of recruits in the city and training them to be productive workers.

But integrating recruits was about more than simply maintaining an adequate supply of trained workers. City, party, and industrial authorities were also intent on forging citizens and workers of a specific type. In particular, they were concerned about protecting the recruits from the potentially negative influence of the many former prisoners and exiles who remained in the city. Thus, when Sherstnev spoke of recruits being integrated "in the proper way," he had in mind not only that they be treated properly so that they would stay, but also that they join proper socialist collectives and avoid pernicious influences that still abounded in Vorkuta.

Social integration, at least in theory, began with the arrival of recruits at the train station. As the example cited of the first Komsomol volunteers at the beginning of this chapter shows, welcoming recruits had a strong element of ritual for both those doing the welcoming and those being welcomed. Representatives from the city accepted the new arrivals with pomp and circumstance, and the recruits voiced their intentions to become part of work, Komsomol, and city collectives. There were also important practical elements to the station meetings. The recruits were arriving in a new and unfamiliar city, often in the dead of winter, at a train station that was several kilometers away from mines and construction sites. Most arrived without any inkling of where they would work or live. Without some sort of welcome, they were lost. As *Zapoliar'e* instructed, "It is the duty of Komsomol organizations and managers to meet them [arrivals] with dignity and to surround them with complete attention from the very first days."[55]

Yet on 9 June 1956, a scant four days after the first group of Komsomol volunteers had arrived from Syktyvkar to such fanfare, the second echelon of young workers had no official reception at all. The lead editorial in the local newspaper subsequently scolded, "We are not going to guess whose fault it was, but no one met them [the arriving workers] at the train station. And only after one of the new arrivals phoned the Komsomol Gorkom were cars dispatched to the station."[56] Despite official rhetoric and a few high-profile success stories, integration of recruits was severely hampered by a lack of resources and lack of attention (if not outright negligence) on the part of local officials who were ostensibly responsible for it.

Most recruits and migrants did not arrive as members of official delegations; instead, they stepped off the train individually, with their families, or as part of small groups of army comrades. For such men and women, having personal contacts in the city to meet them was of utmost importance. A. Grinik, who came to Vorkuta after serving in the Red Army at the end of 1956, had a much more positive experience than most arrivals because of his personal contacts in the city. As he remembered, "I was lucky: in the Zapoliar'nyi settlement . . . lived two friends from my village. They met me, warmed me up, fed me, and found me a place in a good dormitory, which solved practically all of my day-to-day problems."[57] For another veteran, N. P. Nizhegorodtsev, it was sufficient that the sergeant in his army unit had a relative in Vorkuta. He and four army buddies wrote to the sergeant's relative in Vorkuta. The relative met them and provided them with a temporary place to stay until they got settled.[58] Those who had someone expecting them were more likely to have good experiences upon arrival, and therefore were more likely to stay for the long term.

The next step for the newcomers was to secure employment in the city. For many, finding a job was the simplest part of moving to the city. After all, there was a constant demand for labor in the mines and other enterprises. Further, most new arrivals had been actively recruited by a particular enterprise or mine, meaning that in theory they had a job waiting for them. For many this went off without a hitch, and newspaper articles in 1956 often described finding work as a virtually painless process. According to one newspaper story, three friends demobilized from the Red Army arrived in Vorkuta in 1956 and were given the following inspirational speech in the cadres department of KVU: "Our mines need mining cadres. How would you feel if we send you to one of the oldest mines—to *Kapital'naia*? [mine no. 1]." After accepting their assignment, the three new arrivals soon found themselves being trained as tunnelers, first passing the ten-day "technical minimum" and then completing on-the-job courses from instructors. When they had problems underground, more experienced colleagues gave them advice and provided positive examples. Quite quickly, as the headline from *Zapoliar'e* proudly declared, "they became miners."[59]

Yet despite the chronic labor shortage, many recruits had difficulty finding jobs in the city. Four demobilized soldiers wrote to *Zapoliar'e* in October 1956 complaining that the process of finding a job was anything but smooth. "From the first day of our arrival in Vorkuta," they wrote, "we have had to tolerate many hardships until we were, finally, assigned work."[60] It was not uncommon for a demobilized soldier to arrive after a long journey at the mine that had ostensibly recruited him only to discover that there was no opening for him to fill. Gridasov, a demobilized soldier who arrived at mine no. 25 in 1956, spent three days tracking down the head engineer and mine director in order to ask them for the job he had been promised, only to be rebuffed by both. Further, he had been reproached, "why had he come here and who had sent him?"[61] Many recruits who had been promised a specific job in a specific mine instead drifted from mine to mine in search of work for days or weeks.

It was not simply lack of preparation that resulted in new arrivals having difficulty finding jobs. Some managers, it appears, actively discriminated against the new recruits. Speaking at a city party meeting in April 1959, one official stated, "It is entirely unclear where our managers' dislike for young people comes from."[62] To some, the source of this "dislike" was obvious: networks of former prisoners throughout the city were reluctant to accept outside recruits. One Komsomol official stated at a meeting on 30 March 1956 that "the chiefs of the production lines and masters are mostly former prisoners, and so they are only interested in qualified ex-prisoners, and so they try to avoid youth."[63] Of course, it was not simply a matter of ex-prisoners preferring to hire other ex-prisoners. Rather, many managers who had not been prisoners themselves preferred to hire former prisoners rather than those who came in the recruitment drives of the 1950s. Recruits were more likely to require that scarce resources be allocated for their housing and training. New arrivals had fewer local roots and so were more apt to depart after only a short stay. Thus, some managers treated new recruits as if they were unwelcome in the new company town.

Once on the job, many found that wages and working conditions were not as promised. While newspaper articles regularly claimed that miners were earning as much as 3,000 rubles per month, ordinary workers rarely earned that much.[64] In fact, the average wage of a worker in a KVU mine in 1956 was only 1,660 rubles per month. Despite the "regional coefficient" that dictated workers in Vorkuta would earn 1.8 times the wages of their counterparts in the Donbas, in reality the average wage was less than 1.5 times greater. Chronic underfulfillment of production plans meant that wages stayed relatively low for ordinary miners. There was a marked contrast in the wages of ordinary miners and those of ITR and upper management, who were paid comparatively lucrative sums, an average of 3,945 and 6,200 rubles, respectively.[65] If promises of high wages had been an important "pull" factor in attracting recruits, the disappointing paychecks they later received could just as easily convince them to leave the city.

There were steady complaints about working conditions as well. One common criticism leveled by city and party officials was that managers were treating recruits in the same manner that they had treated prisoners and exiles, leading to understandable dissatisfaction among recruits. A worker in mine no. 1 observed in a speech at the city Komsomol conference on 20 October 1956 that new recruits were being treated like prisoners. Despite the shift to a free workforce, "those who worked under the MVD have retained the same methods of work: cursing, threats, and rush jobs."[66] Komsomol volunteers from Iaroslavl' oblast' sent to work on rebuilding the Northern Pechora main line near Vorkuta had similar complaints of poor treatment. A report from the secretary of the Komi Obkom of the Komsomol attributed the "roughness" of officials to the fact that many were used to working with prisoners.[67] Thus, many recruits had to contend with far lower wages and more difficult working conditions than they had been promised.

Unlike the many ex-prisoners hired by KVU in the 1950s and 1960s, most recruits lacked the skills to perform their jobs safely and productively. Most came directly from the army and from collective farms, and so very few of them had any experience that would prepare them for their jobs in Vorkuta. Thus, training was a particularly important part of integration. For one thing, individual wages and the measure of a mine's performance depended primarily on output. Poorly trained workers would produce little, and given the high degree of division of labor and mutual dependence involved in coal mining, one poorly trained worker could slow down not only his or her brigade, but also entire shifts. The training was more than just a matter of money, because it was closely related to the maintenance of safety in the mines and on assembly lines. A poorly trained worker not only endangered his own life, but also those of everyone around him. Accidents not only marred the performance of individual brigades, but in a worst-case scenario could also bring an entire mine's operation to a halt.

Given the scale of recruitment and the constant turnover of personnel, training for recruits was often extremely limited. Underground workers were required to undergo ten days' training in basic safety, the so-called technical minimum. This course, which was also required of prisoners, was intended to give a basic understanding of the dangers of carbon dioxide and methane gas, how to operate a miner's lamp, and how to use an emergency respirator. But ten days' training was hardly sufficient to teach even the basic outlines of a mining specialty. As one experienced miner complained in a letter to the local newspaper in late 1956, "But their [demobilized soldiers] dreams [of becoming trained miners] have so far not come true. I must say openly that neither the mine managers nor the trade union or Komsomol organizations are sufficiently showing concern for the new miners. Currently in the mines there are no real courses of production training."[68] The high number of accidents in the mines was a reflection of the inadequacy of the training: in 1957 alone there were over five thousand accidents throughout Vorkuta's mines.[69] Not all were due to inexperience, of course, but the poor quality of training for recruits certainly did not help matters.

Despite initial difficulties in providing adequate training for recruits, this does appear to have been an area of success for local authorities. Over the course of the seven-year plan (1959–1965), KVU underwent a transformation in both the scale and quality of training that its workers, especially new recruits, were offered. Several mines expanded existing training facilities or built new ones. Whereas in 1959 there were spots for 790 workers in classes, by 1965 this number had nearly doubled to 1,389.[70] A tremendous number of new workers were trained in mining specializations over the seven-year period, over 33,000 in 1958–1960 alone (table 5.3). Although the number of new workers being trained declined significantly after 1960, this appears to be more a reflection of the decline in the number of workers hired every year rather than of a decline in the scale of training. The increase in the number of workers receiving training to increase their qualifications demonstrates that training continued to be a priority after 1960. While the quality of such training was undoubtedly uneven, it appears to have had an effect on improving safety. By 1963, KVU was averaging around two thousand accidents per year, less than half of the rate for 1957.[71] While such figures on accidents are perhaps not entirely trustworthy, they do indicate a significant long-term decline.

Table 5.3. Training and retraining in KVU, 1958–1965

Year	New Cadres	Increased Qualifications	
		Workers	ITR
1958	13,289	7,293	0
1959	11,413	5,819	0
1960	10,145	7,485	178
1961	6,886	11,609	428
1962	7,040	9,259	270
1963	6,274	7,524	254
1964	5,825	6,462	1,487
1965	6,958	5,802	2,164

Source: GURK NARK 1, f. R-1675, op. 1, d. 1716, ll. 152–53.

The city's educational institutions also expanded significantly at this time, providing occupational and social mobility for thousands of new recruits. The mining tekhnikum, which had opened in 1944 to provide training for mining technicians, expanded both its curriculum and its student body in the 1950s and 1960s. By 1962, there were 744 students enrolled in full- or part-time classes at the main campus and at a new branch that had been established in the Komsomol'skii settlement. Vorkuta's first and only institute of higher education opened in 1959, a branch of the Leningrad Mining Institute. The institute allowed workers and specialists in the city to be trained in a broad range of specializations. While there were only 50 full-time students in 1962–1963, more than 1,000 were studying part time. Together with the tekhnikum, the local branch of the institute provided an avenue of social mobility for Vorkuta's residents, playing an important role in ensuring the availability of skilled personnel and in reducing turnover.[72]

The successful integration of new recruits into Vorkuta was about more than simply establishing a new pool of non-prisoner labor to supply Vorkuta's mines and industries. The officials who oversaw the change from prisoner to non-prisoner labor were also engaged in another, equally important task: keeping the new recruits safe from the pernicious influence of the former prisoners and exiles who remained in the city. For such officials, the new recruits represented both great opportunities and great risks. On the one hand, they could serve as a vanguard to help transform the city from its previous incarnation as a prison camp complex into an ideal Soviet company town. On the other, the risk that the new recruits might be corrupted by the thousands of former prisoners and exiles in the city seemed very real, adding a particular edge to the struggle to recruit and retain workers.

Anxieties about the potentially negative influence of former prisoners on the new recruits were frequently expressed at city party meetings, particularly in the late 1950s. Gorkom First Secretary Popov, one of the most powerful officials in the city, expressed repeated anxieties about the dangers of allowing recruits to mix with former prisoners. In a speech at a Gorkom plenum on 3 June 1958, he stated, "The composition of our population is very difficult and this gives us the responsibility to protect the youth who have come to us from this evil." In particular, he was concerned about new recruits' interactions with "former Ukrainian nationalists and other people who served sentences for political crimes," which had resulted in the expression of heterodox views and "serious anti-Soviet outbursts."[73] Popov was perhaps more familiar than most with the "danger" presented by former prisoners—he had been the head of the camp politotdel throughout much of the 1950s. As such, he was used to dealing with unruly and resistant prisoners, particularly those from the western borderlands, many of whom remained in Vorkuta after they were released because they were unable to return home.

Fear of corruption of recruits reached its height in 1958–1959 and was roughly coterminous with a major purge of former prisoners from the ranks of local specialists. This fear was expressed, for example, by the head of mine no. 1 at a party plenum on 28 April 1959. As he stated, "If we don't carry out work in the education of young people, they will fall under the influence of people who are alien to us, and of ideologies that are alien to us."[74] Local KGB and party officials cited a number of cases where prisoners or former prisoners exerted a negative influence on recruits. In one case, an eighteen-year-old female recruit entered into "relations" with a prisoner and showed a notebook of his, which was full of "notes of a counterrevolutionary nature," to her friends.[75] Even more serious was the behavior of Zagorodnikov, a demobilized soldier who came to work in mine no. 14 in November 1957 at the age of twenty-two. Having "fallen in among prisoners and former prisoners," he made anti-Soviet statements. Later, upset because of low wages at the mine, he persuaded other demobilized soldiers to participate in what Gorkom first secretary Popov described as a "strike": Zagorodnikov led a group of five demobilized soldiers to the KVU management, where they demanded higher wages. The five men were not dealt with harshly, as they were accused only of absenteeism and presumably punished by administrative means.[76] Nevertheless, there was clear concern that incidents of anti-Soviet speech by recruits was the result of their interactions with former prisoners.

Despite the obstacles that stood in the way of the successful integration of recruits, as well as anxieties about the pernicious influence of ex-prisoners, local leaders could boast of numerous success stories. Newcomers like demobilized soldier Boris Fedorovich Boitsov eagerly took on leadership roles in the mines not long after their arrival. Boitsov, the leader of a "Komsomol youth" brigade in mine no. 5, entered into "socialist competition" with the then-famous miner Nikolai Mamai of the Don Basin and pledged that his brigade would produce

2 tons of coal above the norm every day in 1958.[77] By the beginning of the 1960s, Averin, the first secretary of the Vorkuta Gorkom, bragged about many successful recruits who had come to the city in the second half of the 1950s. In a speech delivered in 1963, he singled out successful recruits like Sergei Antonovich Miloserdnyi for praise. Miloserdnyi had a typical biography: demobilized in 1957, he arrived in mine no. 7 without any skills to speak of. After completing a course as an electrical mechanic, he began working in the mine. Not satisfied with his training, however, he studied at the mining tekhnikum and completed his course of study in 1962.[78] Although adjustment to life in Vorkuta was not easy, many recruits and migrants persevered through hardships to become valued members of work collectives.

BUILDING THE COMPANY TOWN

Securing adequate housing in Vorkuta was one of the most intractable problems faced by migrants and recruits in the late 1950s and 1960s. In theory, comfortable housing was supposed to be supplied by the enterprise to which each worker had been recruited. If we return to the story of the first set of Komsomol volunteers that began this chapter, we find that some were lucky enough to live in comfortable, although far from luxurious, conditions in purpose-built dormitories. As one member of the arriving group described, "When we arrived we were immediately housed in a new and comfortable dormitory, with five in each room. The newly painted windows and doors sparkled with cleanliness, the curtains in each room gave them a particular coziness and a homey friendliness. New bedside tables, tables, and beds complete with bedding were remarkable for their tidiness and conducive to relaxation. On tables in the 'red corner' lay issues of recent magazines and newspapers, and sets of checkers."[79] A visit by newspaper correspondent (and ex-prisoner) Aleksandr Klein over a year later confirmed that despite some lack of maintenance (most light bulbs in corridors had burned out), the dormitory was still "bright, clean, [and] cozy."[80]

Yet such living conditions were far from the norm for new recruits. A steady stream of complaints filled the pages of the local newspaper in the second half of the 1950s and first half of the 1960s regarding the sorry state of housing across the city, particularly for freshly minted city residents. Typical of such letters was one from February 1957, entitled "Is this really a dormitory," which complained of "dilapidated barracks" that were being passed off as dormitories.[81] A recollection of a longtime resident of the city who came as a recruit in 1957 gives this description of the barracks where he was assigned to live: "The heating system was frozen, metal beds without bedding were half covered in ice. And we slept on bare metal mesh from December almost until spring. We were given mattresses only in March, and in May, blankets and pillows. There was no water. In the evening you would bring water, and two hours later it would freeze."[82] Complaint after complaint was written in this vein, underlining the extremely poor state of most housing stock in the city, the lack of fuel to adequately heat barracks, and desperate shortages of furniture and bedding.

As was typical Soviet practice, mine managers, party officials, and trade union representatives were taken to task for the poor conditions in their workers' housing. Party officials drew a clear connection between poor housing conditions and the frequent departure of new recruits.[83] Yet the problem was not so much dereliction of duty by the officials who were made scapegoats for the housing crisis as it was the result of a lack of resources and infrastructure. The majority of housing stock in the city had not been built as worker dormitories, but instead had served as prisoner barracks. They were shoddily constructed and often did not take into account the permafrost soil conditions, so the buildings began to deform and buckle as the soil thawed. Not only were they old and in poor condition, but the barracks had been built in order to pack as many prisoners as possible into multiple rows of bunks. In many cases, there was neither sufficient time nor materials to properly "convert" such barracks for non-prisoner workers. Yet even given the sorry state of former camp barracks, workers still clamored to be assigned to them, especially if those barracks had been subdivided into individual apartments.[84] The alternatives to such converted camp barracks were even less desirable, as virtually any empty space in the city was mobilized to house recruits, including clubs, warehouses, and outbuildings.[85]

A feverish campaign to build more subdivided wooden barracks to house new recruits from 1955 to 1958 soon gave way to a new, more promising solution to the housing crisis.[86] In 1958, the city banned the construction of wooden barracks, turning instead to the solutions offered by Khrushchev's national housing campaign.[87] In 1957, Khrushchev had officially launched a new initiative that promised to end the chronic shortage of housing across the USSR in only twelve years' time. The product of several years of internal discussions and debates, it specified that the long-term housing problem would be solved primarily by building separate apartments for families in four- or five-story buildings erected using the latest techniques in prefabricated construction. Although its goals were hopelessly utopian and unrealistic, the campaign set in motion a remarkable transformation of the Soviet Union's housing stock over the following three decades.[88] For all the continued shortages of apartments and flaws in the buildings themselves, the housing boom would eventually make it possible for the majority of Soviet citizens to live in their own separate apartments. For a society that had been living in barracks, dormitories, and communal apartments for decades, this represented a fundamental change in everyday life.[89]

Long-term plans for bringing mass-produced housing to Vorkuta began in 1959, when new legislation was introduced calling for nearly 1 million square meters of new housing stock to be built in Vorkuta and its southern neighbor Inta by 1965.[90] Most of the new housing was to come in the form of rapidly built apartment blocks that utilized prefabricated panels produced by a concrete block factory in Vorkuta that was retrofitted in 1959–1960 in order to manufacture them.[91] In many respects, the national housing campaign's emphasis on using prefabricated panels was well suited to Vorkuta because most of the materials that went into such panels could be found locally, whereas wood, the previous construction material of choice, had to be brought in via train. The abrupt shift in construction techniques did not occur without hiccups, however. Although the factory began producing panels in the spring of 1960, putting them together into a livable building presented an ongoing challenge that would take another two years to resolve. The foremost difficulty that builders faced was to prepare suitable foundations in the Arctic soil. Because they were working largely on permafrost, builders found that it took four months just to prepare the foundations.[92] At long last, in May 1962, the first prefabricated panel building was finally completed near the intersection of Moscow and Lenin streets, a three-story, twenty-four-unit building that effectively stood on the border between the old and new city centers. This building, completed far behind schedule, marked the beginning of a new era of construction. Located within sight of the children's hospital at the opposite end of Moscow Street, it symbolized a dramatic shift in priorities, construction techniques, and the labor force. Rather than have prisoners build expensive and ornate architectural showpieces, construction crews of non-prisoners were now erecting simple but functional housing intended for mass consumption.

As construction crews tried to figure out how to adapt new construction techniques to an Arctic city, city planners were reconceiving the layout of the company town. Lunev and Raikin's original long-term plan for the city, formulated in the early 1950s, had taken into account neither the new construction techniques nor the growth in population after mass releases of prisoners. But by 1962 there was a new design for Vorkuta. The plan, which was featured in the prominent architectural journal *Arkhitektura SSSR*, emphasized the unique problems of urban construction in the Arctic. It envisioned the construction of three microdistricts (*mikroraiony*) in the city around the downtown core on either side of Lenin Street. While it included the reconstruction of two- to three-story wooden buildings that had been built in the late 1940s and early 1950s for members of the upper administration of the camp and mining complex, the primary focus was on new construction. To the east, in an area where soil conditions appeared to be more favorable, large-scale housing complexes were planned that included four- to five-story brick, concrete block, and prefabricated concrete panel apartment buildings, schools, kindergartens, and commercial developments. Taking into account the unusual climatic conditions in Vorkuta, special attention was paid to protecting interior spaces from wind and blowing snow. Thus, buildings in Vorkuta were to be unusually wide when facing the prevailing direction of the wind.[93]

By the late 1960s, the new city plan was well on its way to being realized. From 1966 to 1968, for example, approximately 30,000 square meters of new housing in prefabricated panel buildings opened each year, an increase that went a long way toward allowing ordinary families in Vorkuta to move into separate apartments, although it was well off the pace needed to meet the lofty goals set in 1959.[94] In the 1970s and 1980s, even more ambitious housing plans were launched, using updated designs for taller apartment blocks.[95] Yet despite the steady pace of new construction, the process of building more and better permanent housing stock in the city and surrounding settlements lasted decades and did little to alleviate the chronic shortages that recruits had experienced since the 1950s. Separate apartments in the new prefabricated buildings could be obtained only by long waiting lists or by making use of special connections. It would not be until the population of the city fell considerably in the 1990s that the housing shortage was actually resolved.

HOW "PERMANENT"?

The August 1955 resolution, "On measures for urgent assistance to the Pechora coal basin," set out the agenda for resolving the labor supply crisis and years of incessant bureaucratic friction between the ministries responsible for Vorkuta. The resolution spoke of establishing "permanent cadres" in Vorkuta, an expression that operated both in a literal and a euphemistic sense. Literally, the goal was to create a stable labor supply to ensure that KVU and other enterprises could rely on an adequate number of trained workers at all times. Euphemistically, the idea was to end KVU's reliance on prisoners as a labor force. In order to meet these goals, thousands of young peasants, workers, and soldiers were recruited in the mass mobilization campaigns of the second half of the 1950s. Great resources and energy were expended to recruit them. Once they arrived in Vorkuta, a campaign was fought to integrate them, "in the proper fashion," into life and work in the city. How successful were these campaigns of recruitment and integration?

In terms of replacing prisoners with non-prisoners, the recruitment policy was a qualified success. Not surprisingly, the switchover did not happen by the target date of the end of 1957. In 1958, some mines still relied to a limited degree on prisoner labor. For example, mines 30 and 32 had 173 prisoners working underground that were supplied by camp section 11.[96] But by 1960, virtually no prisoners were employed by KVU. This was a stark contrast with the situation five years before, when over 33,000 prisoners had worked in KVU, constituting nearly 60 percent of its workforce.[97] Of course, there were still prisoners in Vorkuta after 1960, and prisoner labor continued to play an economic role in the city. In 1965 approximately 2,000 prisoners worked in the city overall, but almost all of them were used in construction projects and none whatsoever were involved in coal extraction.[98] By 1960 labor recruitment, in combination with aggressive policies to retain former prisoners and exiles, had virtually ended the need for prisoner labor to be contracted from the camps.

Evaluating the relative success of labor recruitment policies from the perspective of creating a stable workforce in the city is more complicated. According to company personnel records, labor turnover was quite high during the recruitment campaign, particularly during its first years. According to available data, nearly 60 percent of all mine workers left their jobs every year between 1955 and 1958 (table 5.4). Figures were even higher for construction workers, who saw turnover rates of 75 percent in 1958 and 81 percent in 1960. Thus, during the years when campaign-style outside recruitment was at its height, particularly among demobilized soldiers, turnover rates were at their highest levels. Just as the above discussion of the challenges of integration would lead one to suspect, mass recruitment was quite successful in drawing a sufficient number of outsiders to the city, but the percentage of those who actually stayed was fairly dismal. Still, such rates of labor turnover did not even approach those of the 1930s, when Soviet industries had typically experienced a turnover rate of more than 100 percent in a given year, even according to official statistics.[99]

Turnover rates began to decline in 1959 and would continue to trend lower throughout most of the 1960s. Overall turnover hovered around 40 percent between 1959 and 1962, before falling to a new plateau of approximately 30 percent that would last from 1963 to 1967. While it is difficult to definitively determine the reasons for the decline in turnover, it is likely the result of multiple factors. First, living and working conditions improved somewhat for most workers, making it less likely that they would decide to leave. Second, some degree of social cohesion emerged in the company town, as former prisoners and new recruits found ways of living and working together. Third, the proportion of women in the local population had risen significantly, increasing the likelihood of recruits starting families and putting down roots in the city.[100] Last, mass recruitment itself was phased out around 1960 in favor of controlled migration. This was likely to have reduced turnover, since those that came to the city were not subject to the empty promises made by recruiters, and thus likely had a better idea of what they were getting into. Worker absenteeism, which had been astronomically high in the 1950s, generally followed the same path of decline from the late 1950s to the late 1960s, thus reinforcing the picture presented by the turnover data.[101]

Table 5.4. Labor turnover by sector in KVU, 1955, 1958–1967 (workers only)

	Year	Total (Jan. 1)	Hired	Departed	Net Change	Turnover (%)
Mine Workers	1955	9,226	13,586	5,477	8,109	59.36
	1958	29,401	23,171	17,513	5,658	59.57
	1959	35,059	14,910	16,118	−1,208	45.97
	1960	34,429	12,898	13,979	−1,081	40.60
	1961	33,881	10,607	13,077	−2,470	38.60
	1962	31,411	10,971	12,510	−1,539	39.83
	1963	29,872	9,283	9,988	−705	33.44
	1964	30,858	10,472	10,049	423	32.57
	1965	31,861	11,353	9,977	1,376	31.31
	1966	31,124	8,578	8,884	−306	28.54
	1967	30,818	7,298	7,946	−648	25.78
Construction Workers	1955					
	1958	2,577	2,291	1,950	341	75.67
	1959	2,918	1,964	2,139	−175	66.53
	1960	2,720	2,682	2,216	466	81.47
	1961	2,862	1,395	1,827	−432	63.84
	1962	2,430	1,034	1,347	−313	55.43
	1963	2,117	504	930	−426	43.93
	1964					
	1965					
	1966	1,955	713	783	−70	40.05
	1967					
Overall	1955					
	1958					
	1959	45,538	21,028	22,086	−1,058	39.47
	1960	46,636	19,502	19,333	169	41.46
	1961	47,005	15,076	18,036	−2,960	38.37
	1962	44,045	16,865	17,698	−833	40.18
	1963	43,212	13,003	14,060	−1,057	32.54
	1964	42,155	14,042	12,922	1,120	30.65
	1965	43,345	14,423	14,114	309	32.56
	1966	44,003	11,977	14,047	−2,070	31.92
	1967	41,571	10,730	11,381	−651	27.38

Source: GURK NARK 1, f. R-1675, op. 1, d. 2281, ll. 12–15, 19–22ob.; GURK NARK 1, f. R-1675, op. 1, d. 2305, ll. 1–10b.; GURK NARK 1, f. R-1675, op. 1, d. 2312, ll. 1–10b.; GURK NARK 1, f. R-1675, op. 1, d. 2324, ll. 1–2; GURK NARK 1, f. R-1675, op. 1, d. 2346, l. 1; GURK NARK 1, f. R-1675, op. 1, d. 2366, ll. 1, 4, 43; GURK NARK 1, f. R-1675, op. 1, d. 1719, ll. 136, 142–43, 156.

Turnover rates among ITR personnel did not follow similar trends. Overall, they were far lower than the turnover rates for regular workers. The highest turnover rate between 1953 and 1967 came in 1954, when it reached nearly 24 percent.[102] The lowest known rate of turnover within this period actually came in 1956 (just under 14 percent), at a time when the turnover rate among rank-and-file workers was at its highest.[103] Generally speaking, specialists were much less likely to leave their jobs in Vorkuta because, unlike many workers, they often received very high wages (typically more than double the average wages of workers). Further, specialists were more likely to receive better housing and other non-cash perks such as paid vacations. Although KVU's management would continue to bemoan the difficulties they had retaining valuable specialists, they were in fact much easier to hold on to when compared with ordinary workers.

TOWARD THE "SECOND BIRTH" OF THE PECHORA COAL BASIN

With Vorkuta well on its way to making a successful transition to an entirely non-prisoner workforce, those at KVU and MUP who were responsible for plotting the long-term future of coal mining in the Pechora coal basin faced another important challenge: how to make continued investment in coal mining in Vorkuta sustainable in a starkly new political and economic environment. The labor force no longer consisted primarily of prisoners and exiles that provided seemingly cheap or free labor. Now, workers demanded high pay and benefits like reasonably good housing and paid vacations to resorts in the south. Labor, therefore, became a much more expensive input for the coal mining trust. Higher labor costs made increased productivity imperative in order to avoid squandering expensive human resources. Planners recognized that productivity improvements required more than just monetary incentives and propaganda—mine designs would have to be improved in order to mechanize as much as possible and cut down on wasteful practices. Further, coal had become a plentiful resource in the Soviet Union. Unlike during the Second World War and its aftermath, when coal from Vorkuta had been needed to meet strategic needs regardless of cost, it now seemed to be prohibitively expensive, even by internal measures that did not take into account the extraordinary cost of maintaining a large city above the Arctic Circle. In the 1950s there was little to be done about these problems, as the clear priority of local managers was simply to ensure that they had enough workers to replace released prisoners. But with the labor question largely settled by the early 1960s, KVU and MUP administrators were forced to confront the reality that the area's mines were extracting expensive coal for which there was little demand. If production was to continue to expand in the 1960s and beyond, they would have to fight a two-pronged battle to show that coal could be mined more cheaply and to demonstrate that there was sufficient demand to justify further investment.

A new long-term plan for coal mining coalesced at the end of the 1950s as part of Khrushchev's ambitious seven-year plan (1959–1965). Responding to intense lobbying by MUP, a joint resolution of the RSFSR Sovmin and Bureau of the Central Committee called for an ambitious program of mine reconstruction to be completed by the middle of the 1960s. Seven of Vorkuta's smaller and older mines would be combined into three large, efficient, modern ones. A further six mines were to be completed or built from scratch during this period. Finally, six more mines were to have new shafts dug and new levels opened.[104] This grandiose plan, which apparently followed a model successfully executed in France, represented nothing less than an attempt to entirely rebuild the mines of KVU to meet current international standards.[105] Hailed in the local press as the "second birth" of the Pechora coal basin, the plan was a key component in the city's transition from prison camp complex to company town.[106] Now that the city had largely made the transition to a non-prisoner labor force, and embarked on an ambitious project of urban reconstruction using mass-produced panel housing, the time had come to also upgrade the city's industry to match.

The 1959 mine rebuilding plan offered the opportunity, at least in theory, for MUP and KVU to demonstrate that the mines could successfully operate in the political and economic context of the new era. But justifying the time and expense of rebuilding the coal mining complex also hinged on finding new customers for Vorkuta's expensive but high-quality coal. As KVU director Sherstnev pointed out in the newspaper *Sovetskaia Rossiia* in August 1959, coal from Vorkuta was being used in a wasteful fashion by its customers. Although nearly one-third of the coal that was extracted in the Pechora coal basin was of suitable quality for coking, only about one-sixteenth of it was actually being used for metallurgy. Instead, the majority of coal from the mines was used to generate heat and electricity, which made little sense given that cheaper coal could be used for the same purposes.[107] The solution was to use the coal in the growing Soviet steel industry, and in fact from the 1960s onward the city's most important customer became the Cherepovets Metallurgical Kombinat, a massive steel complex that had been built in the 1940s and 1950s to produce steel and related products using iron ore from the Kola Peninsula and coking coal from Vorkuta. Coking coal was also shipped to factories in Moscow, Lipetsk, Cheliabinsk, and Nizhnii Tagil.[108] Although a substantial proportion of its production was still used to generate heat and electricity, the relationships established in the 1960s and 1970s made Vorkuta an integral part of the supply chain in the Soviet steel industry.[109] A system of mines that had seemed unsustainable in 1960 would be reborn in the next decade and a half, reinforcing Vorkuta's raison d'être in new times.

CREATING A HUMAN "COMPOTE"

Looking back on the second half of the 1950s and the 1960s, the city of Vorkuta resembles a giant social experiment. As the city underwent one of the most intense phases of the transition from Gulag town to company town, the political, social, and economic landscape transformed rapidly. Driven by the need to replace tens of thousands of prisoners and to meet the goal of using only non-prisoner labor in the mines, managers hired thousands from an ever-expanding labor pool. Demobilized soldiers, Komsomol volunteers, young women, college and technical school graduates, and former prisoners and exiles all joined the city's workforce. The Khrushchev regime, attempting to replace Stalin-era labor recruitment policies with much less coercive substitutes, attempted to channel the enthusiasm of thousands of young people in order to replace departing prisoners. Many of the new recruits left after only days, weeks, or a few months in the city, frustrated by wages and living conditions that were not as advertised. Yet thousands chose to remain, and by the early 1960s the city's population and the workforce in its mines began to stabilize as the workforce began to rely almost exclusively on "spontaneous" migration. Although adjustment to life in Vorkuta was not easy, some recruits persevered through hardships to become permanent residents.

Although relations between the various groups hired to replace prisoners were not always harmonious, by the early 1960s local authorities could boast of significant successes in integrating the recruits, particularly into workplace collectives. By encouraging the creation of new work collectives like "Komsomol-youth" brigades, they did more than harness the enthusiasm of Vorkuta's fresh new citizens. Combined into work brigades where overall success depended on cooperation, people with different backgrounds and motivations learned to work together despite their differences. According to Mikhail T., the specialist discussed above who came to Vorkuta to avoid rampant anti-Semitism in southern Russia, the peculiar mixture of people in Vorkuta in the early 1960s combined into what he called a "human compote." As he explained, "Communists, Komsomol members, recruits from the army, and prisoners—this created a kind of conglomeration . . . and such [good] human relationships . . . then it seemed to be a normal state of affairs." People from different backgrounds, he said, had vastly different personal goals: some wanted to become engineers, others wanted to make careers for themselves, some wanted to make money and return home, while others were hoping for a full rehabilitation. But the achievement of all of these goals depended on one thing: coal production. The company town of Vorkuta was, above all, a place of opportunity, and this brought together people from disparate backgrounds with disparate goals.[110]

Mass labor recruitment may have been, in retrospect, an inefficient solution to the labor supply problem that threatened to paralyze Vorkuta's mines in the wake of post-Stalin reforms. Particularly from 1955 to 1960, mass recruitment was a revolving door, spitting out nearly as many people as it took in, frustrating recruits and locals alike. But it did, at least for the short term, bring enough manual laborers and specialists to the city so that the mines were able to operate as their supply of prisoner labor vanished in an astonishingly short length of time. Ex-prisoners may have provided the backbone of the workforce during the latter half of the 1950s, but recruits were a key part of the raw material from which the rest of the labor force was forged. In that sense, labor recruitment was a successful stopgap measure.

Mass labor recruitment had a number of other, mostly unintended consequences. First, the infusion of young recruits at the end of the 1950s made the city extraordinarily young, a demographic consequence that profoundly shaped it during the 1960s and onward. By 1960, the mean age of Vorkuta's residents was a mere twenty-six years of age, down from thirty-two in 1948.[111] Second, the rapid turnover of recruits actually strengthened the position of ex-prisoners in Vorkuta's social structure. Managers' perception of ex-prisoners as more skilled, experienced, and reliable than the newcomers improved their opportunities by softening the obstacles that formal discrimination put in their way. Perhaps most important, the grafting of a new generation of young people onto the pre-existing social fabric of Vorkuta led to the creation of a strange new social structure in which ex-prisoners and ambitious young outsiders mixed in all areas of life. The implications of this combination caused a great deal of trepidation among local officials, especially for those who feared that unrepentant ex-prisoners would corrupt ideologically pure Soviet citizens. But despite these fears, social and political deviance never truly threatened to dominate the city. Rather, ex-prisoners and recruits together formed a community that was profoundly different from the camp complex that had preceded it.

By the 1960s, a new social, political, and economic order had emerged in Vorkuta based around a renewal of central investment in coal mining, urban infrastructure, and the social mobility offered by the lucrative wages and favorable benefits for miners. For peasants and those coming from small towns, not to mention former prisoners and exiles, a stint of twenty-five or thirty years in Vorkuta could mean significant improvement in a family's economic and social status. After such a stint, savings accrued could be used to ensure a comfortable retirement in central Russia or to provide a solid beginning elsewhere for one's children. Sociologist Vladimir Il'in described this practice as the "traditional Vorkuta strategy": newcomers "arrived, earned excellent money, and left for warmer places for the continuation of life in a good house with a good car and a pension."[112] The nature of the city as a place where one could make a lot of money and earn an early pension meant that it was simply assumed that many miners and others would not retire there, but would instead relocate with their families after reaching an early pension age (typically fifty or fifty-five for men, and forty-five or fifty for women).[113] Apartments in Vorkuta could be left to children who stayed on after their parents left in order to earn their own nest eggs. Alternatively, housing could be swapped for an apartment in another city, since there was always a steady stream of people who wanted to move to Vorkuta to try their fortune.[114] Thus, by the 1960s Vorkuta had experienced a dramatic turnabout. Once a place of profound social immobility, and a population comprised largely of prisoners and exiles, it was now a Soviet company town that offered significant opportunities to thousands of migrants every year. Although the legacies of the camp complex remained, former prisoners and migrants together participated in Vorkuta's profound and dramatic transformation.

6 From Prisoners to Citizens? Ex-prisoners and the Transformation of Vorkuta

—Then there's another thing—people do live in the camps you know, and they come out of the camps as people. And they don't live or come out too badly at that. They have real friends, they read good books, study things.
—*Yury Dombrovsky,* The Faculty of Useless Knowledge

ON 25 DECEMBER 1954 a young engineer named Leonid Pavlovich Markizov moved to Vorkuta. This was not Markizov's first time in the city—he had been a prisoner there from 1951 to 1954. Granted parole in October 1954, he was given a choice of where in the Soviet Union he wished to settle. Markizov chose Chkalovskaia oblast' in the Virgin lands of Kazakhstan, where his wife and family had moved earlier that year. Markizov was reunited with his family on a state farm, but found conditions there so appalling that he did not even stay long enough to find work. "In a word," writes Markizov, "we saw the situation for what it was and decided to go to Vorkuta, where there was work." Less than two months after he had been released from Vorkuta, he returned to the place where he spent three long years behind barbed wire. In Vorkuta he was hired as a department head in a mine construction bureau, a position that put him in an elite category of engineers. His family joined him the following March. The Markizovs lived in Vorkuta until 1972, when they moved to Syktyvkar because Leonid Pavlovich finished a graduate degree and found a better job in the capital of Komi ASSR.[1]

Markizov's story may seem incongruous at first glance. Why would a former prisoner of one of the most notorious prison camp complexes in the Soviet Union choose to return there so soon after he was released?

After years of struggling for survival in the extreme Arctic climate and the brutal conditions of the postwar Gulag, why would anyone choose to return there, let alone invite his family to settle down with him? It might be easy to dismiss this story as an isolated case if it were not for the fact that thousands of former prisoners made similar decisions. Although it is impossible to measure exactly how many former prisoners chose to remain in Vorkuta after they were released in the 1950s, best estimates suggest that former prisoners and their families made up as much as one-third of the city population of approximately 175,000 at the end of the 1950s.[2] These former prisoners would, along with the tens of thousands of new recruits arriving in the second half of the 1950s and the 1960s, profoundly shape the character of the emerging company town.

Vorkuta, like other cities, towns, and villages in the post-Stalin-era Soviet Union, was hardly a haven for ex-prisoners. There, as elsewhere, prisoners faced significant obstacles as they attempted to establish new lives for themselves outside the barbed wire. These obstacles included legal discrimination, police surveillance, distrust by their neighbors, and official employment discrimination. The legal, political, and social framework within which former prisoners attempted to fully reenter Soviet society was hardly conducive to a smooth transition. Indeed, the overwhelming consensus in the historiography examining the issue of former prisoners in Soviet society after Stalin is that in most cases they were forced to remain on the margins.[3] Yet the transition from an economy based primarily on forced labor in Vorkuta and other cities like it made successful reintegration much more likely. Many ex-prisoners had already secured jobs and housing in the city before they were released, as was the case with the thousands of de-zoned prisoners who were given permission to live outside the camp zone after Stalin's death. Others were able to use social networks of which they had become a part while imprisoned in order to secure these things for themselves and their families. The release of tens of thousands of prisoners in such a short period of time, combined with the transition of Vorkuta's mines to non-prisoner labor, created an enormous demand for workers, particularly those with skills and experience. The various recruitment schemes that brought new workers to the city resulted in high turnover rates, making reliable former prisoners a valuable commodity for managers and bosses. The result was that tens of thousands of former prisoners were able to build relatively successful, normal Soviet lives for themselves in Vorkuta.

Former prisoners played a key role in Vorkuta's transition from prison camp complex to company town. Although they were discriminated against and often viewed with suspicion by party officials, KGB operatives, not to mention their neighbors and coworkers, the overwhelming need for their labor meant that they remained a major presence in the years and decades following Stalin's death. Far from remaining on the social and economic margins of the city, thousands of former prisoners became, as the epigraph above suggests, a vital part of the community. Despite the best efforts of officials to create an ideal Soviet company town with entirely new citizens, institutions, and culture, former prisoners would have a profound influence on Vorkuta's continuing development. Although reintegration was a constant struggle for all actors involved, Soviet society proved to be surprisingly well suited to the task of welcoming prisoners back into the fold, particularly in cities like Vorkuta where forced labor had played such an important role in the local economy.

MASS RELEASES

The years following Stalin's death saw a significant reduction in the size of the Gulag population. Beginning with the dramatic release of approximately half of the Soviet Union's 2.4 million prisoners under the 27 March 1953 amnesty, over 4.1 million prisoners were released in the five years following Stalin's death in March 1953.[4] Large-scale releases had been a feature of the Gulag as an institution since the early 1930s; 20–40 percent of the prisoners were released each year throughout most of the Stalin era.[5] This structural tendency has led historian Golfo Alexopoulos to characterize the Gulag as having a "revolving door."[6] Yet never before had the system experienced such a sustained series of large-scale mass releases. Even though new prisoners continued to enter the system, sometimes in very significant numbers, by the end of the 1950s the Soviet forced labor system was merely a fraction of its former size.[7] While this hardly amounted to a "dismantling," "crash," or "end" of the Gulag as it is typically treated in the historiography, it did signify a dramatic transformation of both the size and nature of the Gulag as an institution.

The prisoner population of the Vorkuta camp complex fell dramatically from 1953 to 1960. Blanket amnesties, for example, led to the release of well over ten thousand prisoners. The 27 March 1953 amnesty resulted in the release of just over seven thousand prisoners from Vorkutlag and Rechlag.[8] The effects of this amnesty in Vorkuta, at least in terms of raw numbers, were not nearly as dramatic as they were elsewhere, since only approximately 10 percent of the prisoners were released. But other amnesties aimed at particular categories of prisoners, often "counterrevolutionaries" who were no longer deemed to be a threat, soon followed. An amnesty of convicted wartime collaborators, which was declared by the Presidium of the Supreme Soviet on 17 September 1955, freed more than six thousand prisoners from Vorkutlag.[9] German and Japanese war criminals who remained in the Gulag long after their countrymen had been released and repatriated, some of whom were held in Vorkuta, were released under amnesties in September 1955 and December 1956, respectively.[10] Other prisoners were released under amnesties aimed at freeing juveniles, the elderly, pregnant women, and women with small children, such as those offered in September 1955 and November 1957.[11]

Commissions joined amnesties as another important method of reviewing cases and of releasing prisoners. The first of these was created on 4 May 1954, when the Central Committee approved a proposal to create commissions to "re-examine cases against those convicted of counterrevolutionary crimes, held in the camps, colonies, and prisons of the USSR MVD, and those living in exile."[12] Cases against most prisoners convicted of "counterrevolutionary" crimes were to be re-examined by central or regional commissions, depending on where and by what body the prisoner had been convicted.[13] In 1955, the decisions of these commissions resulted in the release of nearly eleven thousand prisoners from Vorkutlag.[14] This set of commissions was superseded by others established on 19 March 1956 to examine cases against those serving sentences for "political crimes, malfeasance, and economic crimes." Unlike the earlier commissions, which operated on the central and regional level, these new commissions were to consider cases on the spot, in camps, labor colonies, and prisons.[15] The Vorkutlag commission freed over five thousand prisoners and reduced the sentences of at least two thousand others over the three-month period that it operated from 15 May to 15 August 1956.[16]

The process of mass releases from Vorkutlag was not entirely controlled by the center or its representatives, however. Local authorities had a great deal of influence on the implementation of parole (*uslovno-dosrochnoe osvobozhdenie*), for instance. This institution, which had been eliminated in 1939, was reintroduced in July 1954.[17] Prisoners who showed an "honest work relationship and exemplary behavior" could now be set free upon completion of two-thirds of their sentences. Candidates for parole were nominated by the camp administration, after which time their cases were discussed by camp section cultural committees before being considered in a camp section court.[18] From 1954 to 1957, approximately 7,400 prisoners were paroled from Vorkutlag in this manner, the vast majority of them in 1955.[19] A further 4,500 prisoners were paroled from Vorkutlag in 1954–1955 because they suffered from mental or chronic illness.[20] In a similar process, the camp administration was allowed to release prisoners who had been convicted as minors and who had served at least one-third of their sentences.[21] In 1954–1955, over 3,000 prisoners were released under this measure.[22] Thus, parole and related measures allowed local authorities a great deal of influence over deciding who would be released.

Although we are accustomed to think of the mass releases of the mid-1950s as the result of mass amnesties and the like, in fact only about half of those prisoners released from the Vorkuta camp complex from 1953 to 1960 were released under amnesties, commissions, or parole. The other half simply served out the balance of their sentences.[23] Many, like Rifat Khabibulovich Gizatulin and Evdokiia Ivanovna Cherneta-Gizatulina, had been sentenced to ten years during the war, and thus their sentences expired in the first half of the 1950s.[24] Others benefited from the fact that their sentences had been reduced by commissions and parole boards, even if their convictions had been upheld. Many were given extra credit for time served under the system of workday credits (zachet), whereby prisoners could be credited up to three days' time served for each day of productive labor. This system, which had been introduced for most prisoners in Vorkutlag in September 1950 and had been extended to all prisoners under the new regulations of July 1954, could shorten sentences by months or years. For example, Oleg Borovskii, who had been given a ten-year sentence in 1949, was in fact released in August 1956 because two years of workday credits counted as five years toward time served.[25]

By 1955–1956 amnesties intended to reduce the size of the Soviet Union's massive exile population were also enacted. Throughout the Soviet Union, the size of the "special settler" population was reduced dramatically, with over 2.5 million "special settlers" freed between 1 July 1954 and 1 July 1957.[26] As mass releases of prisoners gathered steam, hundreds of thousands of exiles wrote to Soviet officials requesting their release as well. M. I. Litaver, an ethnic German who had been sent to Vorkuta in 1943 to work in the mines, wrote such a letter to Nikolai Bulganin in the first half of 1955. As he explained, he had been awarded the Order of Lenin for his exemplary labor in Vorkuta's coal mines, yet he was unable to leave the city.[27] Litaver and thousands of other ethnic Germans who had been exiled to Vorkuta during the war soon had their wish, as they were released from their terms of exile by a Supreme Soviet Decree of 13 December 1955. Several thousand ethnic Germans in Vorkuta were no longer required to regularly report to the local MVD for registration, although they were being released without the right to reclaim any property or to return home.[28] On 10 March 1956 the Supreme Soviet abolished a 1948 law that required that prisoners convicted of certain especially dangerous crimes be sentenced to eternal exile after their terms expired.[29] As a result, some 2,500 former prisoners were released from their terms of exile in Vorkuta.[30] Various other categories of exiles were also allowed to leave the city in 1955, including Communist Party members and their families, Second World War veterans, invalids, and those exiled for collaborating with the German occupation during the Second World War.[31] By the end of 1956, few residents of Vorkuta were tied to the city by terms of exile.

Overall the prisoner population of the Vorkuta camp complex shrank rapidly from 1953 to 1960, with over 105,000 prisoners released in the period from 1953 to 1958 alone (figure 6.1). While this process in Vorkuta generally followed the overall population trends in the Gulag, the most dramatic reductions in the size of the prisoner population took place later than in most camps. For example, only about 17 percent of the prisoner population in Vorkutlag and Rechlag were released over the course of 1953. By comparison, in that same year nearly 65 percent of all prisoners in the camps and colonies of the Gulag system were released. The rate of release from the Vorkuta camps increased only slightly in 1954 to 19 percent, whereas release rates throughout the Gulag approached 50 percent. But in the following two years,

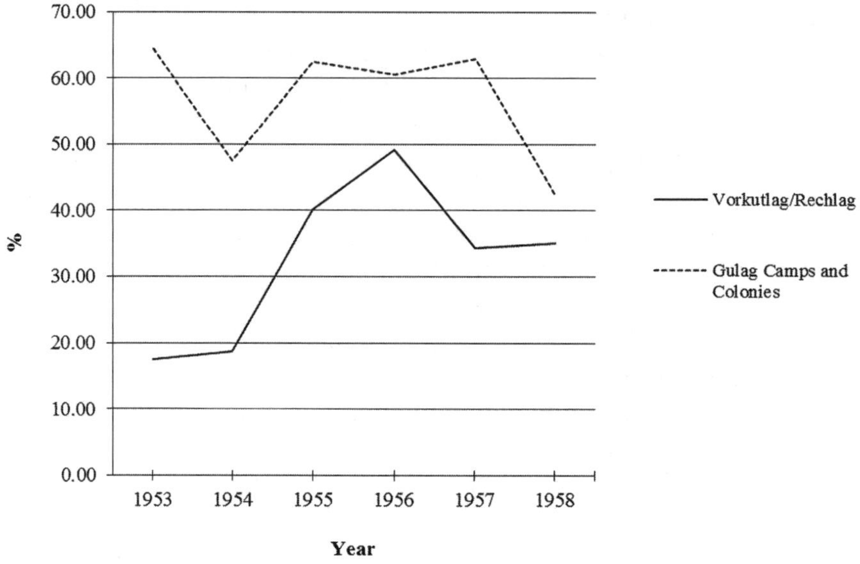

Figure 6.1. Percentage of prisoner population released, 1953–1958. Data from Appendix A, table A.5.3; GARF, f. R-9414, op. 1 ch. 2, d. 519, ll. 124–28, 177. Release figures for 1958 are estimated based on data from 1 January to 1 October.

1955–1956, releases reached their peak in Vorkuta, with between 40 to 50 percent of prisoners released in each of these years. The release rate remained substantial in 1957–1958, when approximately 35 percent were released per year. Both the lower rates of release and the fact that most of the prisoners were released later in the 1950s was largely due to the unusually high proportion of "counterrevolutionary" prisoners held there.

Prisoners remained in the remnants of Vorkutlag for decades after the 1950s, although the size of the prisoner population would never again approach the levels it reached under Stalin. By 1958 the camp population was half of what it had been in 1953, this despite the fact that nearly sixty thousand new prisoners were transferred to Vorkutlag from 1955 to 1957.[32] From 1960, when Vorkutlag became known as the Vorkuta "corrective labor colony" (often referred to by the cryptic designation "P.O. Box OS-34/11"), there were never more than a few thousand prisoners at any given time.[33] Most of these prisoners were residents of Komi ASSR who had been convicted of serious criminal offenses such as rape and murder. Forced labor continued to play an important if much reduced role in the local economy, as it did in many regions across the Soviet Union where camps had been prevalent under Stalin.[34] No prisoners were used directly in coal mining after 1960, but most were engaged in construction, both of coal mines and aboveground buildings.[35] Prisoners were a logical choice for construction crews given the fact that low pay and poor conditions made these some of the least desirable jobs in the city. As recent work on the Soviet prison system after Stalin has demonstrated, the Gulag did not disappear with the end of Stalinist terror, although it did change significantly, both quantitatively and qualitatively.[36]

THE RECEPTION OF PRISONERS

For many of the prisoners released from the Vorkuta camp complex from 1953 to 1960, being set free was followed by feelings of euphoria.[37] Aleksandr Solomonovich Klein's poem "Miracle" (*chuda*), written after his release from Vorkutlag in 1955, conveys the emotions that he felt as he first left the camp. The poem opens with incredulity and celebration:

> I walk—and do not believe:
> alone,
> without guards?
> And there is joy,
> and tenderness,
> and shyness in me,
> And everything surprises,
> and it seems strange,
> That I do not have to
> wear a number
> on my back.[38]

Klein associates child-like delight and curiosity with his newfound freedom. It is as if he were now the inhabitant of an entirely new world, a world free of guard towers and camp dogs. As a result of this "miracle" of release, he can explore this new world without fear of violence. Yet the poem ends on an ambiguous note. In the final stanza Klein writes, "But my hands / out of habit / I hold behind my back."[39] The disbelief that accompanied euphoria at the beginning of the poem has reemerged as uneasiness, symbolized by the author's habitual holding of his hands behind his back, as a prisoner would. Like other ex-prisoners, Klein faced an uncertain future outside of the zone. After years of imprisonment, he had to contend with the difficult and often contradictory process of starting a civilian life in Soviet society.

Former prisoners faced misunderstanding, prejudice, and sometimes open hostility from the society that they were attempting to rejoin. Even in a city like Vorkuta, where much of the population consisted of former prisoners and exiles, mass releases of prisoners were greeted by some of the non-prisoner population with a mixture of fear and trepidation. What would happen when thousands of prisoners were set free in the city? Would the streets be safe when convicted murderers and thieves wandered the streets? Would those former prisoners who had been convicted of serious political crimes, such as anti-Soviet agitation or terrorism, spread sedition and anti-Soviet views among the general population? Would the prisoners be able to readjust to Soviet society? Would they even want to?

This picture was complicated by the fact that Gulag prisoners did not necessarily identify with each other as belonging to the same group. To be sure, having been a "zek" was an important identity marker for former prisoners, and it could play an important role in post-Gulag social interactions.[40] But on the other hand, former prisoners often identified first and foremost with a certain subgroup of the camp population. For many, the key identity factor was belonging to a particular nationality, especially for those prisoners who had belonged to underground self-help organizations in the camps that had been organized on the basis of national identity.[41] Others identified with criminal castes, such as the *vory-v-zakone*.[42] Many prisoners felt that there was a stark division between those who had been convicted of political offenses and those who had been convicted of other types of crime—this is the famous distinction between "politicals" and "criminals" that is so often found in Gulag memoirs. By that same token, other non-prisoners did not necessarily perceive released prisoners as a homogenous mass. Particularly in a place like Vorkuta, where so much of the population consisted of former prisoners or camp officials, it was likely that the general population would see former prisoners as continuing to belong to the same identity groups that they had in the Gulag. The result was that the perception and reception of former prisoners was far more complex and nuanced than would appear at first glance.

The first wave of releases after Stalin's death, the so-called Beriia amnesty of 27 March 1953, certainly did little to calm fears about what would happen when thousands of prisoners were set free. These releases were accompanied by incidents of violence, although as elsewhere it was primarily directed against other prisoners rather than against the non-prisoner population. Tensions between the local population and newly released prisoners were further exacerbated by violence between camp guards and amnestied prisoners. On the one hand, many former prisoners had scores to settle now that they were free; on the other, camp guards were reluctant to give up the arbitrary authority that they had so recently wielded over the prisoners. Under such circumstances, violent confrontations were fairly frequent. On 17 May 1953 a recently released prisoner who was leaving a store with a loaf of bread was accosted by drunken, off-duty camp guards and beaten with a belt. After being beaten, the ex-prisoner returned with nearly forty former prisoners who lived in a nearby converted camp barracks, hoping to dispense some "payback." Faced with a large crowd of angry ex-prisoners, the guards summoned some sixty of their comrades to what soon became an all-out brawl. Belts, bricks, knives, and picks were among the weapons used, although miraculously there do not appear to have been serious injuries among the ten wounded participants.[43]

The blame for the incident landed squarely on the guards and camp officials who had instigated the violence without provocation. This was not surprising, as it was not particularly unusual for camp guards, usually in a state of intoxication, to victimize erstwhile peaceful city residents, as had been happening for a number of years. But even if they did not bear the official blame for the violence, former prisoners, especially those who were perceived to have come from the ranks of the Gulag's "criminals," remained the subjects of suspicion and fear, if not outright hostility. The outbreak of violent confrontations between former prisoners and others only served to heighten tensions and increase mutual suspicions.

Public fears about the potential criminality of ex-prisoners were only confirmed by newspaper reports on crime and punishment in the city. Beginning in July 1953 Vorkuta's local newspaper published brief descriptions of court proceedings under the heading "From the Courtroom."[44] Many of the articles publicized cases of former prisoners being convicted of new crimes, usually petty theft, apartment burglary, or hooliganism. For instance, an article on 21 October 1956 described how one recently released prisoner was sentenced to twenty-five years' imprisonment for a series of twelve thefts in May–July 1956.[45] Such fears that former prisoners represented a risk to public safety were not completely unfounded; one report to the Gorkom in September 1960 pointed out that 31 percent of all crimes in the first half of that year were committed by ex-prisoners.[46]

Some former prisoners were themselves fearful of the danger that other ex-prisoners posed. In particular, former prisoners who identified themselves as "politicals" or "counterrevolutionaries" were often afraid of being victims of violent crimes at the hands of former "criminal" prisoners. Former "political" Oleg Borovskii recalled that in 1956 there was widespread fear of being robbed and beaten by members of the criminal world who had recently been released from the Gulag, especially during the twenty-four-hour darkness of the polar night. As he wrote, "We . . . strong men left [work in] the city [for an outlying settlement] in small groups . . . some of us even [armed] with knives."[47] Thus, it was not simply a matter of non-prisoner suspicions of ex-prisoners, but also of mutual suspicions between different groups of released prisoners.

Hostility and suspicion were not directed only at "criminals," however. Local and regional state and party officials, particularly those representing the state political police (KGB), voiced fears at party meetings that some former counterrevolutionaries represented an active danger to Soviet society. The potential threat posed by former prisoners came into particular focus after the Hungarian uprising, which had broken out on 23 October 1956 and been crushed by Soviet tanks and troops less than two weeks later.[48] In its wake, on 19 December 1956 a letter drafted by the Central Committee was sent to all party organizations in the Soviet Union at the republican, regional, local, and district levels. The letter called for all party organizations to strengthen their vigilance and actively fight against recent manifestations of "active operations of anti-Soviet and enemy elements" that were taking place in the context of recent unrest in Hungary. Among the potential sources of threat identified in the letter, recently released prisoners were singled out. Although the letter acknowledged that the majority of prisoners were making honest and successful efforts to readjust to civilian life, it pointed out that there were a few "former Trotskyites, right opportunists, and bourgeois nationalists" who were continuing their anti-Soviet activities. Using fairly strong language, the letter urged that "party organizations and Soviet organs must take the most decisive measures to intercept [them] and act as we always have against people who are enemies of our system."[49]

The language of the letter was echoed directly in a speech that the first secretary of the Vorkuta Gorkom, V. A. Shikhov, delivered a month later at a city party conference. As he stated, "Among them [former prisoners], especially former Trotskyites and bourgeois nationalists, there are people who are evilly disposed against Soviet power, who gather around themselves anti-Soviet elements, who attempt to resume their hostile and anti-Soviet activities." In order to thwart these people, the party was to take a two-pronged approach: first, it had to educate "the population and former prisoners" in order to inoculate them from pernicious influences; second, it had to keep a watchful eye and act swiftly to thwart truly anti-Soviet elements.[50] Although there were no drastic measures taken against former prisoners, the Central Committee's letter and general anxieties about the Hungarian events did lead to increased scrutiny of the activities of some former prisoners and to an intensification of KGB surveillance.

This surveillance was focused on three types of potential opposition among former prisoners: political, nationalist, and religious. The first category, that of political opposition, was the most amorphous of the three. Politically suspicious activities included criticism of Soviet foreign policy, particularly in Hungary.[51] It also included allegations of distributing anti-Soviet material, as in the case of a former prisoner who gave his notebook containing "anti-Soviet poetry" to a young woman who came to the city as a volunteer.[52] Listening to foreign radio broadcasts, such as the BBC, was also a particular focus of the KGB.[53] That said, such garden-variety anti-Soviet activities were not given nearly as much attention as nationalist and religious opposition.

Suspicion of former prisoners for dangerous political speech and action extended not only to ex-prisoners, but to their families as well. While Stalin was still alive, romantic associations or sexual relations with former prisoners usually resulted in serious consequences for party and Komsomol members. For example, in January 1952 the local Komsomol took up the case of a young woman who "attempted to marry a former prisoner convicted under Article 58–10." She was not kicked out of the Komsomol, but she was formally reprimanded and the Komsomol Gorkom asked her employer to demote her.[54] Such practices continued well into the late 1950s, suggesting a significant degree of continuity in the treatment of non-prisoners who associated with former prisoners. In 1958, for instance, several female party members who had married former prisoners were singled out for harsh words at Gorkom meetings. It does not appear that any of them were expelled from the party for their relationships, but the negative attention sent a clear message that the loyalties of those party members who married former prisoners were highly suspect.[55]

As was the case in the western borderland regions of the Soviet Union, suspicious activity by former nationalists was a particular area of interest for the KGB in Vorkuta.[56] By the early 1950s the majority of the prisoner population in the Vorkuta camp system was not Russian, and so non-Russians made up a majority of the prisoners released in the 1950s. Local KGB officials noted a wide range of potentially subversive nationalist activity in Vorkuta and its environs in the decade following Stalin's death. In 1956, a group of almost two hundred former prisoners from Latvia gathered in a cemetery in Inta (Vorkuta's near southern neighbor) for the unveiling of a monument commemorating Latvians who had died in the camps. According to Kurashov, the head of the local KGB, the gathered ex-prisoners delivered "anti-Soviet speeches" and sang "bourgeois" Latvia's national anthem to the accompaniment of a brass orchestra.[57] Thus, a gathering intended to honor dead comrades became, in the eyes of the KGB at least, a politicized event with dangerous nationalist overtones.

Networks connecting prisoners of common nationality within the camps were frequently reconstructed outside the camps, making them an easy target for those with suspicions that unrepentant nationalist rebels were on the loose in the city. The fact that many convicted nationalists were forced to return to Vorkuta in the late 1950s after unsuccessful attempts to return to their homes in the western borderlands only contributed to the atmosphere of suspicion and unease.[58] For local KGB representatives, the re-deportations of former prisoners served to reinforce prejudices and suspicions about non-Russian former prisoners, particularly those from western Ukraine. For the prisoners deported, being sent back to Vorkuta was a painful reminder of how the Soviet Union's system of identity politics ascribed labels and stigmas that were remarkably persistent. This could only have strengthened social networks of co-nationals in the decades after Stalin.

What made allegedly nationalist activity especially dangerous in the eyes of party and KGB officials was the potential danger of anti-Soviet, nationalist contagion being spread from former prisoners to the many young recruits who came to the city to work in the 1950s and 1960s. Take, for instance, a birthday celebration that took place in an apartment in 1958. At this gathering, former prisoners from Lithuania "sang nationalist songs, songs from bourgeois Lithuania."[59] What worried party officials most was that this celebration was for a newly arrived demobilized soldier, not for a former prisoner. Thus the significance was far greater because it suggested the possibility that an impressionable youth was being corrupted by incorrigible nationalists who had rightfully served time for fighting Soviet power in the Baltics. In light of the directives received from the Central Committee, this birthday party represented a dangerous attempt to indoctrinate a loyal Soviet citizen.

The final area of potential opposition that was the focus of the KGB in Vorkuta during the second half of the 1950s was a result of Khrushchev's revival of antireligious propaganda and his sustained campaign against religious belief in the Soviet Union.[60] In Vorkuta, religious "sectarians" became a frequent target for KGB surveillance in connection with this campaign. In 1957 the city's KGB representative reported that religious groups of all kinds, including Jehovah's Witnesses, Baptists, and Mennonites, were active in Vorkuta. Not surprisingly, former prisoners and their families figured prominently in reports on their alleged activities. Jehovah's Witnesses were singled out in particular. As one report stated, "Jehovah's Witnesses gather illegally in many parts of the city in order to carry out religious services, recruit new members to their sect, distribute religious literature among citizens and believers, and maintain ties with coreligionists in other regions of the Soviet Union and with missionaries from capitalist countries." Religious groups often met in the apartments of former prisoners, many of whom had already served sentences in the 1940s and early 1950s for their heterodox religious beliefs. Men like Korol' Prokop'evich Nishchii, an ex-convict who now worked as a blacksmith in mine no. 30, led regular weekly gatherings that included as many as twenty-six participants. But the most threatening activity of the Jehovah's Witnesses was the outspoken refusal of many to participate in elections.[61]

As in most cases of potentially dangerous "anti-Soviet" activity, the local KGB and party organization pursued a policy of arresting ring-leaders and aggressive measures to stop the spread of religious propaganda. Prophylactic measures included the publication of material in the local newspaper meant to attack and debunk the sectarians. For instance, a major feature appeared in the local newspaper in March 1959 telling the story of Krivchuk, a former prisoner who had become a Jehovah's Witness while serving time in a camp for Ukrainian nationalist activity. Drafted into the army soon after his release in 1955, he had been arrested a second time, this time for recruiting Jehovah's Witnesses from among his fellow soldiers. Now living in Vorkuta, "having finally broken with the Jehovah's Witnesses, he began to work. . . . He is cheerful, outgoing, and grateful to his comrades at work, who have accepted him into their working family." The lesson here was that inner peace was not to be found in religion, but through labor in a collective.[62] Despite repression and propaganda, the presence of "sectarians" persisted, especially Jehovah's Witnesses; in 1961 one leader named Kazak, who worked in mine no. 9, was arrested in connection with the confiscation of large amounts of religious literature found in his home.[63] Surveillance of ex-prisoners suspected of illegal religious activities persisted throughout the 1960s.

In fact, KGB surveillance of former prisoners continued well past the Khrushchev era. In 1967, former prisoner Pavel Negretov was formally questioned by the KGB in connection with his wife's planned trip to visit family in West Germany. The questioning began when he was met at a bus stop by an unknown man who later identified himself as a KGB agent and called him in for questioning. Although the conversation was ostensibly about his wife's trip, it quickly became clear to Negretov that he was being harassed for his activities during the Second World War. During the war, he had joined the "The National Workers' Union of the New Generation," a proto-fascist organization that originated among Russian émigrés in the West, an association that had earned him a fifteen-year sentence in the Gulag. Now, some twenty years later, the Vorkuta KGB asked Negretov to write a letter denouncing the group, which had been reincarnated as the "National Workers' Union," an anti-Communist organization. Negretov flatly refused.[64] For Negretov and other former prisoners, continued KGB surveillance served as a constant reminder of their outsider status. Those suspected of potentially anti-Soviet political, nationalist, and religious activities faced suspicion, surveillance, harassment, and even arrest, long after they had been released.

IN SEARCH OF REHABILITATION

The prospects of former prisoners in Soviet society were further complicated by their legal status. Just being released from the Gulag did not restore one's full rights as a Soviet citizen. Prisoners whose sentences had not been overturned, or who had not received an official "rehabilitation" from the state, faced a variety of limitations on their civil rights.[65] Foremost among these limitations was the fact that prisoners convicted of "especially dangerous crimes" who had not been "rehabilitated" generally did not receive full passports that entitled them to live anywhere in the Soviet Union. Instead, they received a so-called passport with a minus, which prevented them from living within 101 kilometers of major cities or in potentially sensitive border zones.[66] Prisoners without rehabilitations were generally unable to join or rejoin the Communist Party, an important limitation on their social mobility. They were not entitled to even the paltry monetary compensation that rehabilitated prisoners could claim under Soviet law (two months' wages). Their time spent in prison, camp, and exile was not counted in calculations toward bonuses or pensions.[67] In short, former prisoners who did not receive their rehabilitation were second-class citizens from a legal perspective.

Whether or not a former prisoner was fully rehabilitated depended to a large degree on how the particular prisoner had been released from the camp. Those whose sentences expired or who had their sentences reduced by the central and local commissions that worked in 1954–1956 were generally released without receiving a rehabilitation. Those who were paroled or were released under amnesties were generally not rehabilitated either. Of the more than one hundred thousand prisoners released from the Vorkuta camps from 1953 to 1960, only those released by the central and local commissions of 1954–1956 had some chance of immediately receiving a full rehabilitation. One such prisoner was Vasilii Egorovich Romanovskii, who was arrested in 1953 for allegedly plotting to kill Stalin. Because the only evidence used to convict him was that he visited the Armory Palace in the Kremlin, the commission reconsidering cases in Vorkuta in May 1956 decided unanimously to rehabilitate and release him.[68] But Romanovskii was in the clear minority, as these commissions granted full rehabilitations in a very small number of cases.[69] The overwhelming majority of prisoners released from the Vorkuta camps were not rehabilitated upon release. Further, because the mass releases were overseen by a number of different state agencies and carried out using a variety of mechanisms, there was a great deal of confusion regarding the legal status of those released.[70]

Thus, for the vast majority of former prisoners, receiving a rehabilitation meant writing letters, appeals, and petitions to central authorities.[71] Some, like Leonid Markizov, were rehabilitated within only a few years of their release after a successful appeal.[72] Others, like Aleksandr Klein, waited over a decade.[73] But many others, like Iurii P., Galina S., and Pavel Negretov, were not rehabilitated until the 1990s.[74] The variety of outcomes depended not just on the particular circumstances of each individual writing the appeal. It was also influenced by a number of other factors. As Miriam Dobson has pointed out, the process of deciding appeals was highly personalistic, thus making the outcome of an appeal highly dependent on the personality of the official who received it.[75] Also, the judicial apparatus struggled to keep up with the pace of requests for the reconsideration of cases. By the end of the Khrushchev era, it was estimated that the Ministry of Justice had only succeeded in reviewing the cases of just under one-third of all of those people convicted of "counterrevolutionary crimes" from the 1920s until Stalin's death. Finally, the overall political situation in the Soviet Union had a significant effect on the prospects of an appeal for rehabilitation. Although the process of the rehabilitation of individual or group cases did not cease under Brezhnev, the pace slowed considerably.[76]

Of the legal restrictions that many prisoners faced, undoubtedly the most vexing was the limitation in their passports. According to historian Marc Elie, approximately half of the prisoners released from the

Gulag during the Khrushchev era received such passports.[77] For those prisoners who came from Moscow, Leningrad, or other major cities, receiving a limited passport rendered a return home impossible. Such was the case for Galina S., a longtime Moscow resident before she was arrested in 1952 and sent to Vorkuta to serve out her sentence. When she was released, she was issued her release papers and passport (with limitations) by the head of the "special section" of her camp section. As was required, he asked her where she planned to go. She replied, "Moscow," to which the official responded, "They won't register you there." But her daughter lived in Moscow and she was determined to go. After nearly a month in the capital it became clear to her that the advice of the official had been accurate: she could not get registered, even though her daughter and sister were residents. Without a full rehabilitation, her prospects in Moscow were few. "Where else could I go," she told me, "but Vorkuta?"[78] However, since most of the prisoners in the Vorkuta camps did not come from major cities, passport limitations restricted their mobility but did not affect their ability to return home after release.

Thousands of former prisoners also had to navigate the process of international repatriation. Just as Vorkutlag and Rechlag held unusually high numbers of prisoners of non-Russian nationalities, they also held thousands of prisoners who claimed citizenship in another state. At the beginning of 1953, for example, the camps held 2,626 foreign citizens, most of whom came from Germany, Poland, and Hungary.[79] For them, release was only the first step in the process of obtaining permission to return to their homeland. Some foreign prisoners returned home directly upon release, as was the case with Joseph Scholmer, who arrived back in East Germany in early 1954 after his release from Vorkuta in December 1953.[80] Many, however, had to go through the process of obtaining permission for repatriation after release from the camp. By 1955, for example, scores of Polish ex-prisoners were requesting permission for repatriation to Poland. Such a process required not only clearance from the MVD, but also from the Ministry of International Affairs. Thus, requests sent from Vorkuta could take a long time to wend their way through offices in Moscow.[81] However, repatriation soon began to pick up speed, with an entire echelon of Polish prisoners departing from the railroad station in December 1955.[82] Unlike the case with non-Russian Soviet citizens, many of whom remained in Vorkuta for decades, few if any foreign citizens remained in the city by the end of the 1950s.

EMPLOYMENT DISCRIMINATION

Discrimination in the workplace was another significant obstacle that many former prisoners in Vorkuta faced. Ex-prisoners were a frequent target of state policies aimed at excluding them from important positions in a variety of fields. Engineering and technical workers (ITR) were subject to formal discrimination in the late 1950s and early 1960s. These managers, engineers, and technicians were the experts on which the proper and efficient operation of the mines depended. Because of their importance, local, regional, and central party bodies were concerned with their qualifications and political reliability. As a result, the cadres department of KVU collected data on specialists that it did not collect on ordinary workers. These data were used throughout the 1950s and 1960s to practice discrimination against specialists who were former prisoners and exiles. This discrimination may have been to some degree systematic, but it followed no simple formula. There was no blanket policy against hiring ex-prisoners for ITR positions. Nor was it random. Rather, it ebbed and flowed in accordance with party oversight, which was done, like so many other things in the Soviet Union, "campaign style."[83]

Formal discrimination against ex-prisoners was discussed in party meetings under the rubric of the "selection, allocation, and preparation of cadres" (*podbor, rasstanovka i vospitanie kadrov*). Campaigns to purge the ranks of specialists of ex-prisoners were carried out in 1950–1951, 1954–1955, 1959, and 1966, usually initiated as a result of discussions at the level of central and regional party bodies.[84] The purge of 1959 provides a good example because it is well documented. The campaign in Vorkuta began at a Gorkom plenum on 21 March 1959. Launched in a speech by the second secretary Vorob'ev, it took place in accordance with decisions made at the Twenty-first Party Congress. The logic behind the purge was explained in the following manner: "Comrades! The Communist Party teaches that in order to make the most objective measure of a worker one must first know his political and professional qualities. . . . Many of our managers, while making promotions to important posts, forget these Leninist instructions and are guided by only one of these qualities, either choosing on the basis of professional qualities, forgetting about political qualities, or the other way around." In other words, specialists needed a combination of know-how *and* political reliability in order to be suitable candidates for important posts.[85]

As evidence for this, Vorob'ev pointed out that of 2,405 ITR positions in KVU, 712 were filled by people "formerly convicted of serious crimes against the motherland." By contrast, there were only 163 Communist Party and 456 Komsomol members in ITR positions. In terms of "professional qualities," the ITR workers of KVU were wanting as well: over half were *praktiki*, people with no formal training. As Vorob'ev continued his speech, it became increasingly clear that lack of requisite political and professional qualities often coexisted. As an example, Vorob'ev pointed out that none of the section heads in mine no. 26 had any formal mining training, and at the same time, all had been convicted of serious crimes.[86] This blurring of categories between politically unreliable and technically unqualified was a consistent feature of campaigns against former prisoners. Its logic was probably self-evident to contemporaries. Most ex-prisoner specialists had not come to coal mining after graduating from mining institutes or technical schools, but rather had been brought to the city as prisoners. Consequently, many lacked formal training.

Vorob'ev proceeded to provide concrete examples of appointment "mistakes" throughout a range of mines. One personnel decision that he found particularly disturbing took place at mine no. 9/10 in 1957. In that case, Efimov, a Communist Party member who had worked as a section head from 1950 to 1957, was demoted for mismanaging work in his section. He became a deputy to Artym, an ex-prisoner (allegedly a West Ukrainian nationalist) with no formal training. According to Vorob'ev, making a communist the deputy of an unqualified ex-prisoner was a blatant violation of party policy.[87]

The resolution of the Gorkom plenum called for several measures to be taken in order to rectify the situation. First and foremost, in the first half of 1959, relevant authorities were to fill decisive positions in all organizations with people who were known to be both "technically literate and faithful to our party." Particular attention was to be paid to promoting young specialists, especially those who were not yet employed in ITR jobs despite having formal training. All party organizations were to participate in the ritual of criticism and self-criticism regarding the management of cadres. Secretaries of party organizations in Vorkuta were to discuss the Gorkom resolution in closed party meetings. The management of KVU, as well as individual enterprises (like mines 26 and 9/10), were singled out as those that needed to change their hiring practices most of all.[88]

How successful was this campaign against ex-prisoners? The 1959 purge, from the point of view of local party leadership, was somewhat successful, although it seemed to fall short of expectations. Directors of individual enterprises continued to be singled out and criticized for their poor implementation of the new policy. In June 1959, the director of mine no. 26 was called in front of the Gorkom and disciplined for not implementing the new policy properly.[89] Even in 1961, two years after the original plenum discussion, the Gorkom was having trouble enforcing it. On 28 March 1961 the head of construction department 19, Meleshko, was given a formal reprimand by the Gorkom for ignoring the resolution. In addition to not firing ex-prisoners under his employ, he had even gone so far as to hire newly released prisoners after the resolution had been passed.[90] According to a status update from the Gorkom bureau on 20 May 1961, two years after the plenum resolution, 312 ITR positions in KVU were filled by ex-prisoners, as opposed to 712 before the campaign began. While this was a significant reduction in the number of ex-prisoners in ITR jobs, Gorkom officials were not satisfied, and various managers were warned and disciplined.[91]

Thanks to reasonably systematic recordkeeping within KVU on the number of ex-prisoners working as specialists, it is possible to discern overall trends in discrimination from 1955 to 1966, as depicted in table 6.1. These data suggest a general downward trend in the employment of ex-prisoners as specialists, although increases in the employment of ex-prisoners in 1961 and 1966 underscore the episodic nature of discrimination. Whereas in 1955 nearly half of KVU's ITR workers were ex-prisoners, by 1966 the number was about 14 percent. This confirms what other evidence suggests: as the prison camps in Vorkuta shrank, fewer and fewer ex-prisoners held responsible posts in the city. This was partly due to the fact that as time passed, more and more qualified ex-prisoners left the city or retired. It could also, to some degree, reflect informal practices used to keep ex-prisoners "off

Table 6.1. Former prisoners occupying ITR positions in KVU, 1955–1966

Occupation (descending importance)		Date (dd.mm.yy) 15.07.55	01.01.59	01.01.60	01.12.60	01.12.61	01.12.62	01.12.64	01.01.66
Mine Director	N	0	0	0	0	0	0	0	0
	%	0.00	0.00	0.00	0.00	0.00	0.00	0.00	0.00
Head Mine Engineer	N	2	2	1	0	0		0	0
	%	12.50	9.52	6.25	0.00	0.00	0.00	0.00	0.00
Deputy Head Mine Engineer	N	3	1	1	0	0		0	2
	%	18.75	5.26	6.25	0.00	0.00	0.00	0.00	3.85
Head Mine Mechanic	N	5	8	3	1	0		0	1
	%	26.32	38.10	18.75	5.56	0.00	0.00	0.00	5.88
Deputy Head Mine Mechanic	N		13	2	3	1	1	0	11
	%		50.00	6.45	13.04	7.69	5.56	0.00	18.33
Mine Geologist	N		7	2	0	1	1	0	
	%		77.78	28.57	0.00	12.50	11.11	0.00	
Mine Economist	N		1	0	7				
	%		5.88	0.00	53.85				
Section Head (Extraction and Tunneling)	N	41[a]	42	11	10	11	2	9	8
	%	34.75	36.21	12.36	10.87	11.58	2.13	10.00	7.34
Mining Master	N		240	71	60	64	42	29	58
	%		33.29	11.97	10.20	11.59	7.61	6.65	11.39
ITR Overall	N	1034[b]	712	312	247	397	271	342	474
	%	46.95	29.60	13.09	10.56	14.23	10.21	11.88	14.07

Source: GURK NARK 1, f. R-1675, op. 1, d. 1778, l. 15; GURK NARK 1, f. R-1675, op. 1, d. 1709, ll. 147–49; GURK NARK 1, f. R-1675, op. 1, d. 1710, ll. 35–36; GURK NARK 1, f. R-1675, op. 1, d. 1711, ll. 29–30; GURK NARK 1, f. R-1675, op. 1, d. 1712, ll. 32–34; GURK NARK 1, f. R-1675, op. 1, d. 1713, ll. 21–23; GURK NARK 1, f. R-1675, op. 1, d. 1714, ll. 61–62; GURK NARK 1, f. R-1675, op. 1, d. 1716, ll. 39–40.

[a] Includes 16 prisoners.

[b] Includes 261 prisoners.

the books" (see below). But formal discrimination was the dominant factor.

Data in this table also suggest the existence of a "glass ceiling" for ex-prisoners. A selection of ITR jobs at various levels in the hierarchy (in descending order of importance) shows how far former prisoners could advance in the KVU hierarchy and how this changed over time. No former prisoner held the job of mine director during this eleven-year period, although in 1954 two of ten mine directors had been ex-prisoners.[92] A few former prisoners managed to occupy the second most important job in a mine (head engineer), but this ceased after 1960. Former prisoners did work in slightly less important positions, like head mechanic (or assistant head mechanic), in greater numbers and further into the 1960s. But by 1964, the only ITR positions at a mine that were realistically within the reach of former prisoners were decidedly less prominent, such as section head or mining master. Whereas in 1954 a former prisoner had been the director of one of KVU's two "trusts" (in other words, he managed half of Vorkuta's mines), by 1966 few prisoners were entrusted with management of even a mine section.[93]

Despite the general decline in the use of ex-prisoners in ITR positions and the "glass ceiling," it is important to underline the limited success of discrimination in keeping former prisoners out of important posts. Even on 1 January 1966, 56 of mine no. 1's 277 ITR positions were filled by former prisoners (about 20 percent), many of them formerly convicted of "counterrevolutionary crimes."[94] Overall, official discrimination succeeded in keeping former prisoners out of the highest ITR positions, but it did not keep them out of less important jobs. Why was it that campaigns to remove political unreliables from positions of responsibility met with limited and uneven success? One part of the answer is undoubtedly the ambiguous language of the resolutions passed by the Gorkom. It was never explicitly stated against whom the campaign was directed, nor was anyone expressly forbidden from hiring or employing former prisoners. This ambiguity could only have been underscored by the fact that the Gorkom, in September 1959, was criticizing KVU for not hiring enough newly released prisoners in accordance with a Supreme Soviet decree from earlier in the year.[95] Thus, enterprise managers received decidedly mixed messages from the Gorkom.

In fact, the limited success of the formal policy of discrimination exposes widespread informal practices that undermined it. In some cases, former prisoners were simply too valuable to fire or demote. Although many lacked formal training, they were often more experienced than the young, formally trained specialists who were sent to Vorkuta. In an atmosphere of a general labor shortage and high labor turnover rates, it seemed foolish to fire long-term residents and dependable specialists in favor of new arrivals who might not stay in Vorkuta for long. The livelihood of virtually every person working in a mine, from the director to those working at the coal face, depended on meeting production quotas. The work of ex-prisoner specialists was essential in meeting these targets. It was one thing for Gorkom officials to institute a policy of formal discrimination, but these same officials also demanded that mines meet output plans. In the end, it was individual enterprise managers who conducted hiring, and they had to balance conformity with party campaigns and plan fulfillment. For their part, KVU top brass never seemed wholly committed to implementing discrimination policy. In the midst of the 1959 campaign, even the head of the cadres department of KVU, K. Plastinina, herself a longtime resident of Vorkuta, admitted that ex-prisoners were still employed in ITR positions and that they were also still being hired to fill vacancies. Those former prisoners who "recommended themselves positively by their work" often remained unpurged.[96]

Mine directors and those in charge of personnel deployed various techniques to minimize the potentially negative effects of purges on their enterprises. One strategy was to name an ex-prisoner specialist to a relatively low post, but appoint him the "acting" (*ispol'niaiushchii obiazannosti*) occupant of a higher post. This was one way to make it appear as though an enterprise employed few ex-prisoners as specialists. Another strategy was to comply with party orders to demote a specialist, but then promote her later on. Mikhail T., a young specialist who came to Vorkuta in 1962 from Novocherkassk, described how this worked in the case of an ex-prisoner who had once been a high-ranking civilian official in the German occupation administration of Kharkov. This ex-prisoner was an unacceptable candidate for an important post in a mine because he was considered politically unreliable. Yet he was an extraordinarily competent manager and so worked as the deputy mine director in charge of supplies in mine no. 27. As Mikhail T. explained,

> The order came to remove him [from his post]. He is removed from that position, and he begins to work as a master in the lumber depot. Time passes, and the mine begins to choke without lumber [for tunnel supports] . . . the lumber depot works in three shifts, and there is still not enough lumber for the mine. . . . So he [the ex-prisoner], whether it is allowed or not, is reappointed deputy mine director in charge of supplies. Time passes, and lumber appears in the mine. More time passes, and he suggests that the lumber depot only work in two shifts. They work in two shifts, and there is still lumber for the mine. More time passes, and two shifts are no longer needed, one will suffice. The lumber depot works in one shift and there is sufficient lumber in the mine. The party organs once again order that he must be removed—"how can there be a deputy mine director with that kind of biography [*anketa*]?" They remove him . . . the lumber depot begins to work in two shifts, then in three, and there isn't enough lumber in the mine.[97]

Using a cycle of demotion and promotion of former prisoners, managers navigated the dual pitfalls of punishment for not following party directives and penalties for falling short of plan targets.

WHY VORKUTA?

The previous two sections have explored some of the handicaps that ex-prisoners faced after release in Vorkuta. As I have pointed out, some aspects of life in Vorkuta made these obstacles potentially less important for the experiences of ex-prisoners in the city than they might have been elsewhere. Yet the story of why so many former prisoners remained in Vorkuta is not simply a negative one, that things were not quite as difficult for ex-prisoners there as they were elsewhere. The city of Vorkuta also had significant things to offer ex-prisoners that were positive inducements for them to settle there over the short or long term.

One advantage was that Vorkuta, like other cities in the former Gulag empire, was familiar to most ex-prisoners—not simply the environment, but also the people. When Valentin Frid was released from a camp in Inta (a city near Vorkuta) on 8 January 1954, he was relieved to learn that he would be allowed to live in that city rather than being sent elsewhere. He writes, "It was very lucky [to be released in Inta and not exiled elsewhere]. Here everything was familiar, here there were friends, here there were greater opportunities to find tolerable work." The advantages of being released in a place where one had friends and acquaintances became immediately apparent to Frid in his first days on the "outside." With no place to live, he stayed temporarily in the house of another ex-prisoner, a convicted thief named Vasia Nikulin, whom he had met in the camp.[98] Living there was a harrowing experience because of Nikulin's proclivity for drinking binges (not to mention a vicious dog), but in January it was essential to have a warm place to stay, and without the kindness of this acquaintance Frid might have been left without a roof over his head.

Nanci Adler, in her groundbreaking book on Gulag survivors, rightfully points out that "the deforming effects of the camps continued to wreak havoc on the ex-prisoners, along with their social networks."[99] But, as the story above shows, prisoners' experiences in the camps led to the creation of new social networks that could facilitate adjustments to life after release.[100] These social networks were especially valuable in cities like Vorkuta that had been dominated by prison camps. Here ex-prisoners were everywhere, if not a majority then a sizeable minority of the population. They were more likely to be in positions of power than elsewhere, and so therefore were able to help their camp acquaintances obtain scarce resources like housing. Even if two people had not been imprisoned together, sharing the experience of imprisonment in the Gulag could be enough to strengthen otherwise weak social bonds.

The case of Galina S. shows both the power and the limits of ex-prisoner social networks. Unable to return permanently to her home in Moscow because of limitations in her passport, recently widowed, and with a newborn baby, she lived in a fellow ex-prisoner's apartment for some time after she was released. Her first job was as a guard in a store. Her boss was a fellow ex-prisoner who hired her out of sympathy for her struggles as a single mother. The job required her to work one twenty-four-hour shift and then gave her three days off at a stretch, an arrangement that allowed her to take care of her baby. But assistance from other ex-prisoners was not adequate for her to obtain permanent housing or a stable financial situation. For that, she got married, to a man who had been recruited to come to Vorkuta to run a new cafeteria, and who had been introduced to her by the woman in whose apartment she was staying. Her husband had a good job and had been offered housing when he was recruited. After their nuptials, the young family moved into a "family dormitory," essentially a large communal apartment, but one in which she, her husband, and her baby shared their own room. About five years later, in 1962, they moved into two rooms in a communal apartment that they shared with one other family. In 1971 they moved into a two-room separate apartment across the street. Recalling the marriage decades later, she maintained that the main reason for getting married was her husband's access to housing. As a single mother with a small child, she had little other choice.[101] In this case, contacts among ex-prisoners helped her find temporary work and housing, but were inadequate when it came to obtaining long-term housing and financial stability.

The case of Pavel Negretov is similarly instructive. Released in November 1955, he had no real place to live for a year and a half. He split his nights between the apartment of his childhood friend Vitalii (an ex-prisoner), the laboratory where he worked, and the apartments of colleagues while they were on vacation (many of whom were also ex-prisoners). He wrote, "In this manner I spent the entire summer of 1956 living in the apartment of Olga Pavlovna Bazhovaia, my boss, who was away on two years' worth of vacation." It was not until he and his wife Ursula married in May 1957 that he obtained permanent housing and they moved into a dormitory room with Ursula's sister.[102] By 1962 the couple had moved into a two-room apartment in a former camp barracks, such as the one depicted in figure 6.2. In January 1967 they moved into a separate apartment in a new five-story reinforced concrete apartment block.[103]

Many ex-prisoners found jobs through the networks they had built inside the zone. If a prisoner left Vorkuta for a new city he would likely have to rely on strangers to hire him. Even when returning to a place of former residence, there was no guarantee that previous ties would still be extant or useful in finding a job. But in Vorkuta, former prisoners often relied on friends and acquaintances they had acquired while in the camps. An anonymous letter sent to the Ministry of Coal from a worker in mine no. 25 in 1954 contended that an ex-prisoner named Niurin, who worked as the head accountant in the mine, was directly responsible for the mine hiring a number of his ex-prisoner friends. The letter specifically alleged that Niurin had conspired with Bak, a good

Figure 6.2. Young people on a motorcycle in front of typical converted barracks, ca. 1955–1957. Photograph courtesy of KARTA Center Foundation, Warsaw.

friend of his from Vorkutlag, under the following conditions: Niurin hired Bak for a lucrative position and paid him a travel allowance of almost 6,000 rubles. The allegedly conspiratorial behavior took place when the two met in Moscow after release. Obviously, this anonymous letter was meant to denounce Niurin and Bak. But it merely confirmed what was a widespread, and perfectly legal, practice: former prisoners often hired their friends.[104]

In Vorkuta some former prisoners held positions where they were responsible for hiring others. Even though employer and potential employee might not be personally acquainted, they did share a common experience in the camps, and this could be a deciding factor in the hiring process. Gadzhiev, a machine operator from mine no. 40, complained that some ex-prisoners had exclusive say in the hiring process and were using it to hire ex-prisoners. As he stated at a session of the Gorkom plenum in 1959, "There are still former prisoners who command Komsomol members and Communists. In my opinion it is necessary to make it so that they cannot personally decide on hiring or firing workers, because otherwise they will hire 'their own' as they are freed from the camps."[105] Hiring "their own" is exactly what a Komsomol representative alleged was happening at the Vorkuta machine-repair factory in 1956: in that factory, "most of the shop managers and masters are former convicts, and because of this they are interested in hiring only qualified workers from among prisoners, and avoid [hiring] youths."[106]

As the use of the expression "qualified worker" in the last example suggests, it was not simply a matter of ex-prisoners preferring to hire other ex-prisoners. Managers of mines and enterprises who had never been prisoners were often desperate to retain the former convicts who were being released from Vorkutlag or from exile in huge numbers. The alternative sources of labor were prisoners provided by Vorkutlag, who were becoming increasingly unruly and unproductive, or new recruits from outside the city, who were often unskilled and unlikely to stay in the city for long once they realized how difficult life there could be. In order to retain released prisoners, mine directors made requests in 1955–1956 to be allowed to offer northern bonuses, wage incentives to which only outside recruits were normally entitled, to former prisoners who remained.[107] These requests made their way to the USSR Council of Ministers via both the Ministry of Coal Industry and the Komi Obkom, resulting in a Council of Ministers circular on 7 May 1956 that allowed mine directors to sign contracts with released prisoners and exiles.[108] Now able to offer northern bonuses to ex-prisoners, mines and enterprises in Vorkuta were far better able to retain the services of prisoners being released from Vorkutlag.[109] Further, rehabilitation law allowed for a prisoner's term of imprisonment in the Far North to be counted toward calculating one's bonus, a significant inducement for prisoners to remain after release.[110]

For some, at least in hindsight, the transition from prisoner to "free" worker was relatively seamless. This was apparently the case for Stepan Mikhailovich Semegen, a prisoner who worked in mine no. 27 beginning in 1953. When interviewed for a book of recollections about this mine published in 2002, he described his personal transition in very simple terms, stating, "In 1957–1958 the substitution of prisoners for free workers gradually began, and as of April 1958 I also began to work as a free worker. But my production status was not affected by this: I had been a tunneling brigade leader, and remained one."[111] This may be a dramatic oversimplification of the transition from prisoner to comrade, but it does show that from the standpoint of work, it did not necessarily make an enormous difference. Many former prisoners continued working in the same mines, had the same jobs, and even led the same work brigades. In fact, continuity among brigade leaders and foremen was quite high; even as late as 1964, almost one-fifth of the brigade leaders and foremen working in mine no. 1 were former prisoners, most of whom had been released from 1955 to 1957.[112]

Unfortunately, systematic data on the number of former prisoners hired by KVU have not been preserved in the company records. Still, it is possible to get an impressionistic view of the quantitative scale of this phenomenon. According to company records, of 13,268 prisoners released in 1954, 2,823 remained in Vorkuta. All but 312 of them were still gainfully employed as of 1 January 1955.[113] In 1958, 3,161 people were hired directly by KVU after release from Vorkutlag.[114] Such calculations do not include the many who returned to the city after trying their luck elsewhere. Still, it is clear that over the course of the 1950s many thousands of ex-prisoners chose to remain in Vorkuta. Even in 1960, when Vorkutlag had shrunk significantly, 652 ex-prisoners were hired directly after release by KVU.[115] The eagerness of managers to hire experienced former prisoners and the presence of potentially useful social networks in the city were important factors that prisoners weighed when choosing where to settle after release. These factors combined to make Vorkuta, like other former Gulag communities, magnets that attracted a large proportion of the Soviet Union's millions of ex-prisoners in the Khrushchev era.

CONCLUSION: EX-PRISONERS AND THE COMPANY TOWN

In 1957 Iurii P. left his native Ukraine for Vorkuta. Like many others who settled there he was recently released from the Gulag. But his story was different: although he spent almost six years in Soviet prisons and camps, he came nowhere near Vorkutlag. After being released from a camp in Kuibyshev in 1956, he returned to his hometown in the western Ukraine. He found work in a sugar factory but found life at home difficult because of the KGB. They asked him to inform on a local man who had emigrated from the United States, and when he refused, the KGB began to harass him. In 1957, a school friend of his, an ex-prisoner then living in Vorkuta, was visiting on summer vacation and presented Iurii P. with a solution: "He said, you know what, come to Vorkuta—there, everyone is like you and me. And no one is going to keep you under surveillance."[116] Iurii P. came to Vorkuta, and his wife and daughter soon followed. From 1957 to 1959, he worked in mine no. 2, and from 1959 until his retirement in 1983, in mine no. 40 (now known as *Vorkutinskaia*). Whereas his home village in the Ukraine had rejected him, Vorkuta accepted him as a citizen.

This man's story, like those of many other ex-prisoners, resonates with an officially endorsed parable that cast Vorkuta as a place where ex-prisoners could be successfully reintegrated into Soviet society. Perhaps the best example of this story is a version that was told in the pages of *Zapoliar'e* on 7 December 1960, entitled "The Road to the Big Life." Stretching across three of the paper's four pages, this article related the life of Victor Babkin, an ex-prisoner living in Vorkuta. Arrested for theft as a teenager in Moscow oblast' and sentenced to fifteen years' imprisonment in the late 1940s, he was freed early by a commission. After his release, this is how he described his new life as a coal miner: "At the mine he was simply hired. No one asked about the past, in his brigade he was considered an equal and respected for his diligence." By 1959, Viktor had been elected leader of a brigade, joined the Komsomol, and was nominated as a candidate member of the Communist Party. His brigade had been given a great honor, the title of "Brigade of Communist Labor." This is how he reflected on his new life: "Viktor thought for a long time about his comrades, real friends, with whom he had resolved to live by the principle 'one for all and all for one.' What broad horizons this life had opened up before him—a big life, rushing into the future."[117]

As I have argued, beginning life on the "outside" for most ex-prisoners in Vorkuta was more difficult than suggested by the narratives of Iurii P. or Viktor Babkin. Former prisoners faced serious obstacles in establishing new lives after release: prejudice, surveillance, and discrimination in the workplace. These were obstacles that former prisoners had to contend with all over the Soviet Union. Yet there is much that rings true even in the parable of Babkin, because as Vorkuta underwent its transition from Gulag town to company town, there were opportunities for ex-prisoners that were unlikely to have existed where they had originally come from. Given the social, economic, and political upheaval taking place around them, enterprise managers actively sought ex-prisoners as the anchors who could ensure that production targets were met. Former prisoners were hired for many jobs without any questions asked about their backgrounds. This was an important factor in the individual decisions of ex-prisoners who chose to remain in the city. Another of no less importance was the familiarity of the city and its inhabitants. During their time in the zone, prisoners made important personal connections that proved to be useful on the "outside."

For former prisoners in Vorkuta, there would always be reminders of the camps. Many lived in, worked at, or saw the physical vestiges of Vorkutlag and Rechlag on a regular basis. An interaction with a former camp official, even a decade after release, might bring back unhappy memories of imprisonment, as happened to Galina S. when her husband invited a former camp chief to their home to share a bottle of vodka.[118] Embittered by the continued discrimination that he faced, Pavel Negretov wrote two publications that appeared abroad in the 1970s and 1980s, one an article on the Gulag origins of Vorkuta, the other a memoir of his life in camp and city.[119] As Nanci Adler concluded in her study of Gulag survivors from among the urban intelligentsia, "The consequences of their experience as prisoners and the further consequences of their status as ex-prisoners hindered all efforts toward readjustment and reassimilation."[120] But in Vorkuta, hindrances hardly rendered readjustment or reassimilation impossible. Many former prisoners grew proud of their city and their own contributions to its construction. In personal narratives related by ex-prisoners like Leonid Markizov and Iurii P., this pride is what frames the story of their post-Gulag lives in Vorkuta, not the obstacles they faced as ex-prisoners. Even Negretov wrote with pride about some city institutions, particularly the local newspaper, to which he frequently wrote during the decades after his release.[121] Such framing suggests that it was indeed possible for former prisoners to be reintegrated into Soviet society, at least in former Gulag cities like Vorkuta.

Together with new recruits who came to the city from all over the Soviet Union, former prisoners became citizens of the new company town. Some were joined by their families from elsewhere in the Soviet Union, whereas others established new ones. They lived in dormitories, many of which were hastily converted former camp barracks, or rented a corner of a private room or apartment. They went to work in the mines, many of them holding the same jobs that they had performed as prisoners. They raised children, went on vacations, and saved money for the future. Like new recruits, they too practiced what sociologist Vladimir Il'in described as the "traditional Vorkuta strategy."[122] In short, they were integrated, and integrated themselves, into the city. There were limitations on their occupational mobility, and they continued to be viewed with suspicion by many high-level local officials. Nevertheless, tens of thousands of former prisoners became Vorkutiane and committed themselves to living their lives in the shadow of the former camp complex. Vorkuta continued to be transformed in the following decades, but the important role played by former prisoners in the economic and social life of the city would not diminish.

Epilogue

ON 4 NOVEMBER 1975 journalists, miners, engineers, managers, and the top party leadership of Vorkuta and the Komi ASSR crowded into an unfinished assembly hall. They were celebrating an auspicious occasion, the arrival of the first hopper of coal from a new mine. The gathering was supposed to be held outside in the mine's courtyard, but a sudden blizzard necessitated a change of venue. Top city and regional party officials, as well as construction bosses, delivered speeches. The head of the group was Aleksandr Alexandrovich Popov, second secretary of the Komi Obkom, who had risen to the position after serving as the head of the Vorkuta Gorkom and the Vorkutlag politotdel years before. Smashing a bottle of champagne over the first hopper of coal, those gathered marked the unofficial opening of the *Vorgashor* mine. Under construction for just over a decade, this was not only the largest and most modern coal mine in the history of Pechora coal basin, but it was also the most productive mine in all of European Russia.[1]

The opening of the Vorgashor mine was the culmination of a more than a decade-and-a-half-long project to rebuild, expand, and generally improve the efficiency of Vorkuta's mines during the Khrushchev and Brezhnev eras. The reconstruction project, which had been launched in 1959, had appeared at times to be yet another of Khrushchev's expensive boondoggles. Those carrying out the reconstruction of Vorkuta worked from poor designs, which were frequently changed mid-course. Work proceeded much more slowly than expected because of shortages of construction equipment and of labor, much of which was supplied by prisoners in the remaining "corrective labor colonies."[2] At the time of Khrushchev's ouster in late 1964, the reconstruction project had been over budget and behind schedule. Although the Brezhnev team that replaced Khrushchev was highly critical of the way in which the reconstruction had been carried out, it nevertheless renewed its commitment to the project in June 1965, promising new investment.[3] In the end, the first of the rebuilt mines opened in 1970. The last became fully operational only in 1976, some eighteen years after the rebuilding process had begun.[4] Despite the considerable cost and time overruns, by the middle of the 1970s KVU now boasted large, modern, and productive coal mines, including the new *Vorgashor* complex. By the end of the 1970s, KVU's mines were producing just over 20 million tons of coal per year, approximately double the amount that had been extracted in 1953.[5]

Continued investment in mine construction helped establish a new social and economic equilibrium during late socialism. After the wrenching upheavals of the 1950s and early 1960s, Vorkuta expanded during the 1970s. Whereas population growth had been relatively flat in the 1960s, from 1970 to 1989 the population of Vorkuta and its surrounding settlements grew from 185,383 to 216,176.[6] New residents were attracted to the city by steadily improving living conditions. Taller and more energy-efficient reinforced concrete panel apartment blocks continued to be built, and in fact spread beyond the city proper into the mining settlements on its outskirts. In 1976, the city embarked on its most ambitious housing construction project ever, a neighborhood called "Timan." Occupying a total area of 47 hectares, it was intended to house 16,000 people in buildings rising as high as nine stories, an impressive engineering feat considering the poor soil conditions that prevailed.[7] High wages and generous benefits for miners continued, ensuring that new migrants, as well as the former prisoners and recruits who had settled in the city in the 1950s and 1960s, could take advantage of what had become the "traditional Vorkuta strategy": earn high wages in the mines, receive an early pension, buy an apartment in a city to the south, and relocate. The 1970s and 1980s, it would seem, constituted the golden age of Vorkuta as a company town.

Yet this state of relative equilibrium depended on the political economy of late socialism, which promised slow but steady improvements in living standards in exchange for political and social acquiescence. When Mikhail Gorbachev began to launch a series of political and economic reforms in 1986, the disruption of equilibrium in Vorkuta came swiftly, manifesting itself in a series of high-profile strikes beginning in 1988. At first, the strikes appeared to be at the vanguard of the reform movement, arguing for swifter political and economic change that many miners thought would result in greater prosperity. But after the collapse of the Soviet Union in 1991 and the launch of economic reforms by El'tsin and his team, the economic status of Vorkuta's residents began to decline swiftly. Strikes and work stoppages continued throughout the 1990s and into the beginning of the twenty-first century, but now they were bent on restoring the equilibrium of late socialism. But no amount of political activism by miners was able to reverse or even stall the city's rapid decline. The closure of mines and settlements, rising unemployment, and rampant nonpayment of wages all contributed to a dramatic decline in the size of the city's population. By the turn of the twenty-first century, the city was considering the possibility of large-scale population transfers, and foreign pundits were predicting that it would soon disappear entirely. The purchase of KVU in 2003 by the steel conglomerate Severstal', a company controlled by one of Russia's wealthiest oligarchs, headed off some of the direst predictions. Nevertheless, significant questions about the city's long-term future remain.

VORKUTA IN CRISIS

Mikhail Gorbachev's program of radical economic and political reforms severely disrupted the equilibrium that had been established in Vorkuta under late socialism. Under the banner of perestroika, Gorbachev sought to democratize the Soviet Union, introduce market reforms into the economic system, change the structure of the Soviet empire, and scale back rampant militarization. The result was, in the words of political scientist Archie Brown, a case of "reform precipitating crisis" with wide-ranging consequences for all citizens of the Soviet Union.[8] In Vorkuta, this crisis first appeared in the summer of 1989, when miners began to strike in response to efforts to improve economic efficiency by tying wages more closely to worker productivity. The miners realized that these reforms would lead to lower wages, and soon formed an "Intermine Strike Committee" that presented forty-three points to Moscow, a list that included a broad range of economic and political demands. Notably, the economic demands included in the list were both forward and backward looking. On the one hand, they called for greater state support and subsidies for miners, but on the other they demanded greater autonomy for the mines, including greater control over marketing of coal and increased profit sharing.[9] Although the coexistence of these two sets of demands was clearly paradoxical, it demonstrated what many ordinary Russians thought about market reforms in the late 1980s. They believed that the introduction of market elements would result in higher wages and better access to goods, but they wanted the Soviet government to maintain, or perhaps even increase, its investment in the social safety net.

Initially, the 1989 strike met with apparent success. A commission was set up to negotiate with the strikers, and Gorbachev himself sent a telegram to the miners to offer concessions. Even though the government did not deliver on everything promised in negotiations, the miners and their strike organizations were convinced that they had achieved a major victory.[10] Yet the economic and political crisis precipitated by Gorbachev's reforms only deepened, culminating in the collapse of the Soviet Union itself in December 1991. Vorkuta was now a city in the Russian Federation, a new country led by Boris El'tsin, who had been elected president in early 1991 and had emerged as a hero during a failed coup that hastened the empire's collapse. Vorkuta's miners supported El'tsin and were optimistic that the end of the Soviet Union would finally bring about many of the reforms that they desired. In particular, they were enamored of the new regime's promise to carry out a quick transition to a market economy, a process that many believed would work out in their favor. Once coal was being sold at market price and the mines and miners received their fair cut of the profits, many of Vorkuta's residents believed that their standard of living would improve.

Yet when the economic reforms launched by El'tsin and his government actually began to take effect, it quickly became clear that the spread of the "market" would not be the panacea that many imagined. Although great short-term profits were reaped from selling coal abroad, corruption and the spread of criminal organizations in Vorkuta meant that miners gained little from it.[11] The late payment of wages, which allowed industries to essentially take interest-free loans from their workers, became a systemic part of the Russian economy by the mid-1990s. In Vorkuta it was not unusual for a mine to owe workers an entire year's salary. Although miners were paid a "subsistence minimum" wage and allowed to buy goods in "company stores" on credit against their unpaid wages, they were much worse off than workers elsewhere in Russia. At a time when most of the country came to rely on produce from small private agricultural plots, residents of Vorkuta and other northern cities had no choice but to purchase food in private shops, where shortages and high prices prevailed. Instead of benefiting from the transition to a market economy, most miners were reduced to a subsistence existence, unable to save toward the nest eggs that they had hoped to build by working in Vorkuta, but also unable to afford to leave the city.[12]

Money-losing enterprises not directly connected to mining began to shut down, and unemployment spread. Greenhouses that had been established to grow fresh fruit and vegetables to supply the city were shuttered. A chicken processing plant was closed, as was a clothing factory. A distillery that had supplied the city and other parts of Komi with vodka, beer, and nonalcoholic beverages was downsized, with most of its operations packed up and relocated to Syktyvkar. With the closing of the local dairy, the production of milk products plummeted from a yearly average of over 18,000 tons in 1986–1990 (which was the third highest of any region in Komi) to only 1,200 tons from 1996 to 2000 (the lowest total of any region in Komi).[13] Such factories and enterprises had primarily employed women, and had been built in the 1960s and 1970s for the express purpose of increasing employment opportunities for women. Their closure exacerbated long-term structural unemployment or underemployment of women in the city, and a 1995 survey revealed that 70 percent of the unemployed in the city were women.[14] Many families that had relied on dual incomes were now forced to survive on a single salary, and even this was not guaranteed as wage arrears mounted.

Mine closures soon followed the shuttering of unprofitable local industries. In 1993, the state-owned Russian coal monopoly, Rosugol', asked the World Bank to develop a plan for privatization and restructuring.[15] Taking into account the sorry state of the post-Soviet coal sector, as well as a longer-term global decline in coal mining, the World Bank recommended both the privatization of the entire coal sector and a significant reduction in production.[16] Although in the long term productivity would be improved through modernization, in the short term a large number of unprofitable mines would have to be closed. Khalmer'-Iu, a mine located some 30 kilometers from Vorkuta proper, was the first mine in Russia to be closed under the plan in 1994. The closure of the surrounding settlement of Khalmer'-Iu soon followed. By 1998, three more mines in Vorkuta had shut down because of their perceived unprofitability, and a fourth closed after a tragic gas explosion killed twenty-seven miners and caused considerable damage.[17] In 2003 and 2009 two more mines closed, bringing the total number of operational mines down to only five from thirteen in 1991. In the process, thousands of men and women lost their jobs. Even in 1997, before a number of mines were shut, the size of KVU's workforce was only 55 percent of what it had been in 1988.[18] Privatization itself dragged out for nearly a decade, until Vorkutaugol' became a private company in 1998. Yet over 85 percent of the resulting private company remained in the hands of the Russian state, suggesting that this privatization was in name only.[19] Despite initial hopes that the arrival of capitalism would be a boon to coal mining, by the end of the 1990s Vorkuta was in the midst of a deep economic slump with little end in sight.

DEPOPULATION AND SOCIAL BREAKDOWN

The crisis unleashed by Gorbachev's reforms in the second half of the 1980s, which continued to deepen in the 1990s, initiated unprecedented demographic and social change in Vorkuta. The end of various controls on the price of goods and subsidies for living in the Far North and the massive unemployment that followed from the closure of mines and other industries took a devastating toll throughout the 1990s. The result was that patterns of migration were altered, which would come to have significant effects on the demographic structure of the population. By the end of the 1990s the citizenry of Vorkuta looked far different than it had a decade earlier.

The collapse of the Soviet Union quickly reversed the process of modest but steady population growth that had characterized the 1970s

Figure 7.1. Abandoned buildings in the Rudnik settlement. Photograph by the author, 29 July 2004.

and 1980s. Economic and political turmoil, inflation, wage arrears, and looming privatization all contributed to a sharp rise in net migration from the city in the early 1990s. In 1994, for example, 9,800 people came to the city and 18,000 left, a net outflow of 8,200 people. But this was apparently much less than it would have been had all those who wanted to leave the city been able to do so. Surveys administered in 1994 and 1995 suggested that in fact many more people wished to leave the city immediately, but were prevented from doing so by the dire state of their household budgets. KVU was no longer building cooperative apartments for retirees as it had in the late 1980s. Prices on apartments had increased astronomically outside the city, whereas the value of real estate in the city had plummeted because of concerns about Vorkuta's future. The cost of moving one's family and possessions by rail had also increased significantly. Perhaps most important, the balance of savings accounts, which had been carefully accumulated over the course of years and decades to buy an apartment in another city, was wiped out by the hyperinflation of the early 1990s. While the poor state of the economy led to a significant population decline, it also prevented a mass exodus from the city.[20]

Like many other post-Soviet cities, Vorkuta experienced a dramatic increase in crime in the 1990s. The higher crime rate was fueled not only by economic and social displacement, but also by the new opportunities for generating enormous wealth created during the 1990s. Organized crime in Vorkuta grew dramatically, fueled by large infusions of cash and consumer goods that resulted from coal exports to foreign and domestic buyers. As new economic practices emerged there were increased opportunities for private entrepreneurs to participate as middlemen in lucrative transactions and reap significant rewards. Profits, in turn, could be used to recruit new foot soldiers to continue extracting *krysha* from industries and businesses, a tax for "protection."[21] According to sociologist Vladimir Il'in, by 1996 two "shadow organizations" had formed around two sets of brothers who fought to control both the export of coal and import of consumer goods to the city. Competition led to increased violence and a rash of murders.[22] According to official statistics, which undoubtedly underreported criminal activity, the number of crimes reported per ten thousand citizens jumped from 160 in 1990 to 230 in 2000, an increase of nearly 50 percent over ten years.[23]

The breakdown of traditional social and economic ties and grim prospects for the future took a particularly harsh toll on the city's young people. Youth culture in the city under late socialism had hardly been peaceful, and several city residents told me that organized brawling between groups of young men from different settlements had been a common form of entertainment in the 1980s. But this was relatively tame compared to what was to come. By the late 1990s and early twenty-first century skinhead and neo-Nazi groups had become widespread in Vorkuta.[24] Illegal drug use quickly became rampant as well. Sociologist Hilary Pilkington, who was part of a team of international researchers that studied drug use in several Russian cities across multiple regions, found drug use to be considerably higher in Vorkuta than in other comparable regions.[25] Despite Vorkuta's considerable distance from areas where narcotics are grown and its isolation from major drug trade routes, the city's remoteness and the lack of economic prospects for young people made recreational drug use appealing for many.

By the end of the 1990s Vorkuta had shrunk significantly. The closure of mines and settlements, increased unemployment, economic instability, crime, and increased drug use had all taken their toll. By the beginning of January 1998 the population had fallen to only 175,000 people.[26] In 2002 only 134,200 people remained in Vorkuta and its environs.[27] What had once been a sizable, successful, and growing Soviet company town was now subject to the worst aspects of capitalism, Russian style: widespread unemployment, a shrinking population, corruption and violence, and a rise in drug use and other social ills. Vorkuta appeared to be a city dying a rapid and difficult death, with few prospects for the future.

A NEW COMPANY TOWN?

Given the rapid decline of the city and its coal mines in the 1990s, it is not surprising that pronouncements of its impending demise began to appear in the domestic and foreign press around the turn of the twenty-first century. On 27 May 1998, for example, the central newspaper *Izvestiia* described the plight and bleak future prospects of the city in an article entitled "Frozen Forever: A Curse Hangs over the Fate of Polar Miners."[28] Bemoaning the fact that the Russian government appeared to have given up on subsidizing Russia's coal industry, the article's author described Vorkuta as a dying city. Soon foreign publications were carrying the story of Vorkuta's rapid decline as well, albeit with a different framing. Journalist Anne Applebaum, for example, published a piece in the British journal *The Spectator* in July 2001 that described the city's ugliness, declining economy, and rapid depopulation. But rather than bemoaning its loss, she instead pointed to the perversity of its existence in the first place, calling it "The Great Error." What she appeared to find most troubling about the city was the degree to which its citizens, even former prisoners and their children, remained attached to a place that was "widely famed for atrocity and stupidity" and "notoriously unpleasant and ugly."[29] Commentators both within Russia and outside its borders agreed that Vorkuta was dying, even if they disagreed about whether or not this was a good thing.

Yet the story of Vorkuta in the post-Soviet era has not been one of continuous decline. Despite the disastrous course of the 1990s and the grim outlook for the future, the city's prospects appeared to change in the summer of 2003 when its coal mines were purchased by a private company. Severstal' (Northern Steel), an international steel conglomerate controlled by Russian oligarch Aleksei Mordashov, purchased KVU in order to secure its supply of high-quality coking coal.[30] The company, which owned steel plants in Russia, Italy, France, and the United States, emerged from the privatization of Vorkuta's most important customer, the Cherepovets Metallurgical Factory in the Vologda region. The mines were now part of the international economic network of one of Russia's wealthiest oligarchs rather than an economically weak, and only nominally private, state-controlled company. Vorkuta was once again a company town, albeit under very different circumstances.

With the mines in the hands of their most important customer, production stabilized after a severe decline in the 1990s. Although one additional mine was closed after the takeover by Severstal' (Aiach-Iaga in 2009), investment in new equipment and new sections of the remaining mines meant that production remained steady, with a total raw output of 12.6 million tons in 2010, roughly the same as the amount produced in 2000.[31] Further, the company won a bid in December 2011 to develop part of a new coal field, Usinsk-1, located southwest of the city near the Northern Pechora main line.[32] As of 2012, the company planned to build a mine with a projected capacity of 4 million tons of coal per year on the site, which would increase the area's annual coal output by as much as a third.[33] This investment is evidence of a perceived economic need to continue significant coal extraction in Vorkuta and its environs. It remains to be seen how many people will be employed in the new mine and where they will live. While it is conceivable that mine workers could live in the city and commute to the mine by rail or bus, it seems more likely that workers will live in housing built near the mine itself, which is located some distance from the city. Thus, the economic boost to the city itself might be somewhat less than if a mine were built closer to the center.

Under Severstal', the mines began to once again subsidize some city services. Such support practically ceased in the 1990s, as KVU's poor economic performance and ambiguous status meant that it was unable to support the public sector as it had during late socialism. Ownership by a large company with deep pockets meant that new capital was available to help support the city. For example, in 2010 Severstal' signed an agreement with Komi Republic promising to provide 60 million rubles of support for Vorkuta from 2011 to 2013. According to the company's own press releases, it spent over 40 million rubles (approximately $1.3 million) in 2011 on schools, public buildings, sport, and on maintaining city streets. This included, for example, paying to remove snow from city streets in advance of the annual New Year's celebration.[34] But the size of such payments paled in comparison to the level of subsidies that KVU provided during Soviet times, when the company had been responsible for a large proportion of city services, including building and maintaining housing stock, and providing health and child care. While it seems likely that Severstal' will continue to subsidize the city to a small degree in order to remain in the good graces of regional and local government, a return to the previous level of support appears remote given the company's obligation to turn a profit for shareholders. Ownership by an oligarch may have improved the prospects for Vorkuta's coal mines, but the new, post-Soviet company town is clearly very different from its Soviet predecessor.

If coal production stabilized in the 2000s, the same cannot be said for demographics. The population continued to decline, falling to 95,900 citizens according to the 2010 census.[35] Thus, the population in 2010 was less than half of what it had been before the Soviet Union collapsed twenty years before. After a round of layoffs in the second half of the decade, the number of people employed by KVU fell to 9,683 in 2010.[36] By comparison, in its heyday in 1967 KVU employed just over 45,000 people in the mines, mine construction, and various subsidiary industries.[37] Although there have been numerous attempts to relocate pensioners and other unproductive parts of the population elsewhere, the results have been mixed at best. For example, from 2002 to 2007 the World Bank committed up to $80 million in loans to help resettle households with pensioners or multiple children from Vorkuta and two other areas of the Far North, Noril'sk and the Susuman district of Kolyma. Each of these regions had once been the site of a large prison camp complex, but had become company towns in the decades after Stalin's death. While the program provided funds for 5,358 Vorkuta residents to buy apartments and resettle in other cities, this does not appear to have had a significant effect on the overall population structure of the city.[38] Although the absolute number of pensioners in the city has declined, their relative share in the population has actually increased slightly from 28 percent in 2000 to 32 percent in 2010.[39] While Severstal' has promised to fund the relocation of all families of those who have died in mining accidents, there seems to be little political will to carry out the kind of large-scale resettlement program that would be needed to significantly alter the structure of city's local population.

The city has experienced significant improvements in at least two areas of life in the 2000s. By 2010 the overall crime rate in the city had fallen to half of its all-time high (reached in 2006), so that crime was near the 1990 level.[40] Perhaps most important, the falling population and the gradual abandonment of poor-quality housing meant that both the quality and quantity of housing in the city increased dramatically. Whereas there was only 15.5 square meters per person in the city in 1990, in 2010 this had nearly doubled to 29.2 square meters, roughly the level promised by Khrushchev when the mass housing campaign was launched at the end of the 1950s.[41] Transportation problems were also improved because so many residents of distant settlements moved into the city center, closer to shopping, schools, and services. The process of consolidating and closing settlements continued under the leadership of Severstal', and in 2011 it was announced that two hundred remaining families in the Komsomolskii settlement would be relocated to nearby Vorgashor.[42] As the population contracts and mining continues to be concentrated in a smaller number of high-capacity mines, it is likely that the process of spatial consolidation will also continue.

The overall stabilization of Vorkuta and its mines since 2003 suggests that the most pessimistic scenarios for the city's future were somewhat off the mark. If the city is dying, its demise will be a slow one. With large reserves of high-quality coking coal remaining and the potential for current mines to operate for decades, it is unlikely that the city will be abandoned anytime in the near future. Further, urban spaces, once built, have a kind of inertia about them—it is one thing to close outlying settlements, but to leave Vorkuta entirely would require significant political will, not to mention the resources to relocate tens of thousands of people. While post-Soviet Russia may have scaled back its commitment to internal colonization in the North, enough imperial aspirations remain to justify holding on to northern cities like Vorkuta. Nevertheless, it is clear that a return to the heyday of late socialism is not on the horizon. The equilibrium that was established over the course of the 1960s and 1970s was definitively destroyed by perestroika and the economic reforms of the 1990s. The city's population will likely continue to contract in the future, as fewer and fewer miners are required to work in increasingly automated mines. As new coalfields such as the one at Usinsk-1 are developed, the city is likely to move toward a model that more closely resembles the shift system (*vakhtovaia sistema*) often used in oil and natural gas extraction in remote areas.[43] Under this system, groups of men and women work for fixed terms, living in temporary housing before returning home to families elsewhere. Although labor costs are high, there is little need to maintain expensive urban infrastructure. But in order to fully introduce such a system, tens of thousands of residents, primarily pensioners and children, would have to be relocated elsewhere. After decades of heavy-handed population management by the Soviet state, there seems to be little appetite for such a project.

MEMORY AND MEMORIALIZATION

In December 1988, Vorkuta's first memorial to victims of the Soviet Gulag was dedicated (see figure 7.2).[44] Designed by city architect Vitalii Troshin, it took the form of a column covered in black and white marble, topped by a rock surrounded by barbed wire. Its inscription was simple: "In memory of the victims of political repression." Placed off a quiet residential street on Miner's Embankment, its location could not have been more poignant. It stood on the banks of the Vorkuta River, looking across to Rudnik, the neighborhood where the first camp section and mine had been built in the early 1930s. For the first time in the city's history, there was public acknowledgment of Vorkuta's origins as a Gulag town, a place where hundreds of thousands had been imprisoned and tens of thousands had died. The citizenry, many of whom had a personal connection to the camps, now had a conspicuous location at which to commemorate the experiences of those who had suffered in the camps. The monument, which had been built at the initiative of the city government and activists, received financial support from the city and from private citizens.

The opening of this monument demonstrated a high level of enthusiasm in the late 1980s for confronting Vorkuta's past. Its existence marked a significant shift from the policies of the previous three

Figure 7.2. 1988 Vorkuta Gulag Memorial. Photograph by the author, 17 May 2003.

decades, when discussions of the Gulag had virtually vanished from public discourse. Like most other cities in the Soviet Union, Vorkuta had been the subject of numerous memorial volumes and retrospectives from the 1950s to the 1980s.[45] Although it had been possible to celebrate the city's early "achievements" and prominent "citizens," the fact that Vorkuta had been a massive prison camp complex, and that its greatest heroes had been prisoners, exiles, or camp administration officials, was never mentioned.[46] Although there had been a brief interval during the waves of "de-Stalinization" under Khrushchev when it had been possible to discuss the Gulag in a circumspect fashion, from the time of his ouster in 1964 until the middle of the 1980s, it became a forbidden topic.

The official silence surrounding the Gulag ended during Gorbachev's perestroika. By the spring of 1988, he had ended political censorship in the USSR as part of a policy of *glasnost'* (openness), resulting in a flood of publications on the Gulag.[47] Vorkuta's local newspaper began to publish stories with revelations about disturbing chapters in the city's past. Articles examining particularly dramatic events in the history of the Gulag town, such as the "Kashketin executions" of 1938 and the Rechlag prisoner uprising of 1953, were particularly popular.[48] The Vorkuta Museum (now the Vorkuta Museum-Exhibition Center), which had been collecting unpublished memoirs, photographs, and artifacts for decades, began to organize exhibits that confronted the city's origins as a camp complex. Regular visits by school groups spread awareness among those who had grown up during the official silence of late socialism. By 1988 local activists, among them many former prisoners and exiles, had established a local chapter of Memorial, an organization dedicated to documenting repression and terror, as well as to assisting its victims.[49] The residents of Vorkuta were active participants in what was beginning to look like a national movement of reckoning with the Stalinist past.

The 1988 monument on the Miner's Embankment, in fact, was meant to be only a preliminary effort to establish many public memorials to the Gulag in Vorkuta. In 1989, the city government commissioned émigré sculptor Ernst Neizvestnyi, best known within the Soviet Union for creating Khrushchev's headstone, to design a memorial complex for the city. After visiting Vorkuta, Neizvestnyi designed a massive complex called "Stone Tears," which juxtaposed human masks, fire, and water.

Although the complex was clearly avant-garde in its design, its scale was well in line with Soviet standards for memorial complexes, which tended toward the gigantic. As designed, it would have stood 100 meters tall, dwarfing surrounding structures, definitively transforming the urban landscape. In fact, Neizvestnyi planned to build additional memorial complexes in Magadan and Sverdlovsk (Ekaterinburg)—together with the one in Vorkuta, they would make up a "Gulag Triangle." Although agreements were signed between the sculptor and the city, economic and political turmoil in the early 1990s erased both the funds that had been collected to build it and the political will of central, regional, and local authorities to support its construction. Only the Magadan monument, the "Mask of Sorrows" (*Maska skorbi*), was ever built, finally completed in 1996.[50]

The rapid collapse of the "Stone Tears" project indicated another shift in attitudes toward Gulag memorialization, both among officials and the general public. As was the case across the Soviet Union, interest in coming to terms with the Gulag fell precipitously with the collapse of the Soviet Union and the continuation of almost uninterrupted economic shocks throughout the 1990s. With the city and its industries so clearly under threat, discussion turned to the future of the city and its coal mines rather than its past. While a number of additional Gulag memorials would be built in the first half of the 1990s, the active support of the city government disappeared. The new memorials were built outside the city core, largely at the initiative of foreign organizations and governments that wished to commemorate the suffering of their own citizens in the Soviet camp system. Thus, monuments dedicated to Ukrainian, Lithuanian, German, and Polish prisoners were opened between 1990 and 1995.[51] With the exception of two Polish monuments, all were located in or near an old cemetery near the Iur-Shor mine and settlement, some 11 kilometers from the city center. The final resting place of the fifty-three prisoners who had been killed on 1 August 1953 when soldiers opened fire on striking prisoners in camp section 10 of Rechlag, the cemetery had been restored in the late 1980s, and proper grave markers were erected for each of the prisoners who had been killed (see figure 7.3). While the restored cemetery and the cluster of national memorials became important sites of memory, both the remote location and the national orientation of the monuments symbol-

Figure 7.3. Grave marker of Elmars Andreevich Petersons, killed during the 1953 prisoner strike. Photograph by the author, 1 August 2004.

ized the degree to which coming to terms with Vorkuta's troubled past quickly became marginalized in the post-Soviet period.

In fact, throughout the first decade of the twenty-first century there were disturbing signs of attempts to marginalize the city's history as a Gulag town. Igor Shpektor, who was mayor of the city throughout much of the 1990s and 2000s, announced plans in 2005 to build a replica Gulag camp section near the city to generate revenue from tourists. According to his project, well-heeled visitors would pay for the thrill of staying in replica barracks, eating camp food, and even participating in an escape attempt from guards armed with paintball guns.[52] Even though this perverse scheme never came to fruition, it demonstrated the degree to which city authorities had given up on the idea of establishing a major memorial complex in the city. The energies of city planners have instead been directed toward memorializing other aspects of the city's past. For example, "Victory Park," opened in 2001 to commemorate the Soviet victory in the Second World War, emphasized Vorkuta's links to the Soviet victory over Nazi Germany. Another monument, called "The Sword and the Shield," was unveiled in Vorkuta's City Park in August 2010, honoring "international peacekeepers, soldiers, and police officers killed in local wars and conflicts." Designed by Vitalii Troshin, the same architect who was responsible for the 1988 Gulag memorial, it was dedicated to the memory of local residents who were killed while fighting in the wars in Afghanistan and Chechnya.[53] Instead of confronting the city's troubled past as one of the Soviet Union's most notorious prison complexes, these memorials instead emphasized Vorkuta's participation in the creation and maintenance of the Soviet and Russian empires.

The struggle over the memorialization of the Gulag and remembering Vorkuta's past is but one example of a national struggle to come to terms with some of the more difficult aspects of Russia's Soviet legacy. Indeed, the fact that Vorkuta was entirely a creation of the Soviet system, and so deeply connected to terror and forced labor, makes it a particularly vivid case of such a struggle. In effect, those examining the history of Vorkuta need to reconcile at least three key aspects of the city's history: first, that it was created as a camp complex, where hundreds of thousands of forced laborers fought for survival on a daily basis; second, that it became a Soviet company town, where its citizens (including former prisoners and exiles) enjoyed a reasonably good standard of living and significant opportunities for social mobility; third, that its local economy completely collapsed in the post-Soviet era, causing poverty, depopulation, and a host of social problems.[54] Attempts to come to terms with these three aspects of the city's history have often resulted in widely divergent ideas. On the one hand, there are those who wish to present Vorkuta as a place solely connected with victimhood and suffering. Anne Applebaum takes this argument to the logical extreme, treating the city as no more than a horrendous mistake.[55] While such an approach is surely justified in many respects, particularly from the perspective of former prisoners and their families, it also ignores the fact that many former prisoners settled in the city after release and made new lives for themselves there. Calling the city nothing more than an "error" threatens to rob the many participants in the city's rebuilding, former prisoners among them, of their agency. On the other hand, there are many, like the city authorities who have commissioned memorials emphasizing the city's contributions to the Soviet and Russian empires, who wish to marginalize or ignore the place of the Gulag in Vorkuta's history, an approach that is much more deeply problematic. In failing to acknowledge the role of forced labor throughout the city's history, it not only trivializes the involuntary sacrifices made by the many prisoners and exiles held in Vorkuta, but it also attempts to justify the worst policies of the Stalinist state, arguing that mass terror was necessary in order to build and maintain a powerful Soviet empire.

Both approaches, in their own way, ignore the degree to which the Gulag was embedded in the Soviet system. As I have argued throughout this book, Gulag camps were part of the communities that surrounded them, connected by myriad economic and social links. Although prison camp complexes were supposed to be completely isolated spaces, borders between the zone and the outside were porous and often in flux. The same was true for status and identity in the Gulag town, which was far more complex than a simple division between prisoners and "free" people. Instead, social status was highly variable and depended on one's place in a complex official hierarchy and on informal practices and relationships that were a part of life in the camps just as they were in Soviet society more broadly. In the same manner that Gulag camps operated as an integral part of the Soviet system, the Soviet system of forced labor was closely intertwined with Soviet history and remains so decades after the Soviet Union's demise. The Gulag did not disappear after Stalin's death in the 1950s, no matter how many efforts were made to consign the system to the distant Stalinist past. The profound ways in which the system of forced labor had shaped the country remained omnipresent. Former prisoners and exiles, not to mention former camp bosses and guards, attempted to make the transition to civilian life, many of them in former Gulag towns. Tens of thousands of industrial enterprises that had been built by prisoners remained in use for decades. Like Vorkuta, entire cities owed their existence to the Gulag, and their urban landscapes were filled with objects built by prisoner or exile labor. Strict censorship may have caused public discussions of the Gulag to disappear in the 1960s, but no amount of government intervention could begin to erase the traces of the system and their continued effects on life in the Soviet Union.

This book, then, has been an attempt to reassemble the separate fragments of Vorkuta's history. It has attempted to give voices to some of the hundreds of thousands of people who played a role in the city's history: prisoners from all over the Soviet Union and Eastern Europe, exiles from villages across the Soviet Union, prison camp officials and guards, Komsomol volunteers, demobilized soldiers, and the many people who came to the city during late socialism in search of economic opportunities. It has examined the tragedies, triumphs, and absurdities of life in the Gulag town and the company town. In so doing, it suggests that in order to better understand the Soviet experience, historians must look at the smaller, peripheral places that dotted the Soviet Union's massive expanses. It is in such places where one can most clearly see the degree to which the Gulag was entwined with Soviet society and Soviet history.

Appendix A
Prisoner Data Set

Most data series presented in this appendix were compiled from statistics collected by the Gulag administration. The information comes from quarterly reports on the population of individual camps. In general, I have used reports from the first quarter of each year, so the numbers represent the totals on 1 January. The exceptions to this are as follows: data for katorga prisoners from 1945 are from 1 April; all data for 1952 are from 1 April; data for Rechlag in 1954 are from 1 April. There is no data for 1940, 1941, and 1951. Statistics for 1944 are missing data on katorga prisoners. As this was a relatively small group of prisoners (approximately five hundred by year's end) it does not significantly skew the data series.

Because Tables A.1.1–A.4.3 use the same data set, I have specified the sources only in Tables A.1.1–A.1.3. Empty cells denote absence of data. All other peculiarities and irregularities are noted below each individual table.

Table A.1.1. Number of prisoners in Vorkutlag, 1939–1948

	1939		1942		1943		1944	
	N	%	N	%	N	%	N	%
Men	15,279	94.92	26,979	94.37	26,438	95.12	23,231	91.97
Women	817	5.08	1,491	5.22	1,355	4.88	2,027	8.03
Unknown	0	0.00	118	0.41	0	0.00	0	0.00
Total	16,096	100.00	28,588	100.00	27,793	100.00	25,258	100.00

	1945		1946		1947		1948	
	N	%	N	%	N	%	N	%
Men	36,045	85.71	46,523	91.67	54,499	90.05	56,552	90.21
Women	6,011	14.29	4,226	8.33	6,020	9.95	6,136	9.79
Unknown	0	0.00	0	0.00	0	0.00	0	0.00
Total	42,056	100.00	50,749	100.00	60,519	100.00	62,688	100.00

Source: GARF, f. R-9414, op. 1 ch. 2, d. 360; GARF, f. R-9414, op. 1 ch. 2, d. 370; GARF, f. R-9414, op. 1 ch. 2, d. 378; GARF, f. R-9414, op. 1 ch. 2, d. 411; GARF, f. R-9414, op. 1 ch. 2, d. 428; GARF, f. R-9414, op. 1 ch. 2, d. 446; GARF, f. R-9414, op. 1 ch. 2, d. 459; GARF, f. R-9414, op. 1 ch. 2, d. 469.

Table A.1.2. Number of prisoners in Vorkutlag and Rechlag, 1949–1954

		1949		1950		1952		1953		1954	
		N	%	N	%	N	%	N	%	N	%
Vorkutlag	Men	59,193	89.29	46,617	88.50	36,956	92.04	33,889	91.94	31,583	95.45
	Women	7,097	10.71	6,059	11.50	3,195	7.96	2,972	8.06	1,504	4.55
	Unknown	0	0.00	0	0.00	0	0.00	0	0.00	0	0.00
	Total	66,290	100.00	52,676	100.00	40,151	100.00	36,861	100.00	33,087	100.00
		N	%	N	%	N	%	N	%	N	%
Rechlag	Men	6,774	100.00	23,627	94.42	31,417	88.69	31,731	89.51	33,598	90.43
	Women	0	0.00	1,397	5.58	4,007	11.31	3,720	10.49	3,555	9.57
	Unknown	0	0.00	0	0.00	0	0.00	0	0.00	0	0.00
	Total	6,774	100.00	25,024	100.00	35,424	100.00	35,451	100.00	37,153	100.00
		N	%	N	%	N	%	N	%	N	%
Overall	Men	65,967	90.29	70,244	90.40	68,373	90.47	65,620	90.75	65,181	92.80
	Women	7,097	9.71	7,456	9.60	7,202	9.53	6,692	9.25	5,059	7.20
	Unknown	0	0.00	0	0.00	0	0.00	0	0.00	0	0.00
	Total	73,064	100.00	77,700	100.00	75,575	100.00	72,312	100.00	70,240	100.00

Source: GARF, f. R-9414, op. 1 ch. 2, d. 471; GARF, f. R-9414, op. 1 ch. 2, d. 478; GARF, f. R-9414, op. 1 ch. 2, d. 492; GARF, f. R-9414, op. 1 ch. 2, d. 506.

Table A.1.3. Number of prisoners in Vorkutlag, 1955–1958

	1955		1956		1957		1958	
	N	%	N	%	N	%	N	%
Men	59,013	94.03	49,111	97.43	49,477	99.66	39,664	99.77
Women	3,744	5.97	1,297	2.57	169	0.34	91	0.23
Unknown	0	0.00	0	0.00	0	0.00	0	0.00
Total	62,757	100.00	50,408	100.00	49,646	100.00	39,755	100.00

Source: GARF, f. R-9414, op. 1 ch.2, d. 511; GARF, f. R-9414, op. 1 ch. 2, d. 513; GARF, f. R-9414, op. 1 ch. 2, d. 517; GARF, f. R-9414, op. 1 ch. 2, d. 524.

Table A.2.1. Convictions of prisoners in Vorkutlag (selected crimes), 1939–1948

	1939		1942		1943		1944	
	N	%	N	%	N	%	N	%
Treason	107	0.66	1,024	3.58	1,998	7.19	4,505	17.84
Espionage	965	6.00						
Diversion	72	0.45	613	2.14	914	3.29	1,140	4.51
Wrecking	597	3.71						
Terror	480	2.98	465	1.63	619	2.23	523	2.07
Anti-Soviet Agitation	2,569	15.96	3,541	12.39	3,405	12.25	2,175	8.61
Total (CR crimes)	11,024	68.49	14,387	50.33	13,931	50.12	14,262	56.47
	N	%	N	%	N	%	N	%
Hooliganism	426	2.65	1,575	5.51	954	3.43	586	2.32
Speculation	250	1.55			458	1.65	404	1.60
Malfeasance, Economic Crimes	530	3.29	1,612	5.64	1,080	3.89	789	3.12
Banditry	509	3.16	1,395	4.88	1,800	6.48	1,698	6.72
War Crimes	29	0.18	871	3.05	1,739	6.26	2,622	10.38
1932 Theft Law	407	2.53	349	1.22	598	2.15	593	2.35
1947 Theft Law (Personal)								
1947 Theft Law (State)								
Other Theft	704	4.37	2,471	8.64	1,450	5.22	1,338	5.30
Total (other crimes)	5,072	31.51	14,201	49.67	13,862	49.88	10,996	43.53
Total (all crimes)	16,096	100.00	28,588	100.00	27,793	100.00	25,258	100.00

	1945		1946		1947		1948	
	N	%	N	%	N	%	N	%
Treason	12,586	29.93	20,576	40.54	32,935	54.42	35,707	56.96
Espionage	5,802	13.80	1,122	2.21	1,447	2.39	381	0.61
Diversion	52	0.12	73	0.14	75	0.12	71	0.11
Wrecking	232	0.55	225	0.44	201	0.33	141	0.22
Terror	404	0.96	473	0.93	375	0.62	362	0.58
Anti-Soviet Agitation	3,237	7.70	4,756	9.37	4,035	6.67	2,359	3.76
Total (CR crimes)	26,473	62.95	31,370	61.81	42,939	70.95	43,840	69.93
	N	%	N	%	N	%	N	%
Hooliganism	356	0.85	246	0.48	593	0.98	609	0.97
Speculation	273	0.65	171	0.34	275	0.45	300	0.48
Malfeasance, Economic Crimes	860	2.04	356	0.70	785	1.30	2,383	3.80
Banditry	1,448	3.44	1,760	3.47	2,891	4.78	3,328	5.31
War Crimes	3,406	8.10	2,068	4.07	2,989	4.94	2,347	3.74
1932 Theft Law	768	1.83	814	1.60	1,124	1.86	1,267	2.02
1947 Theft Law (Personal)							7	0.01
1947 Theft Law (State)								
Other Theft	2,107	5.01	1,144	2.25	2,326	3.84	3,987	6.36
Total (other crimes)	15,443	36.72	11,754	23.16	16,199	26.77	18,840	30.05
Total (all crimes)	42,056	100.00	50,749	100.00	60,519	100.00	62,688	100.00

Table A.2.2. Convictions of prisoners in Vorkutlag and Rechlag (selected crimes), 1949–1954

		1949		1950		1952		1953		1954	
		N	%	N	%	N	%	N	%	N	%
	Treason	33,427	50.43	24,660	46.81	16,118	40.14	15,998	43.40	14,505	43.84
	Espionage	390	0.59	308	0.58	14	0.03	0	0.00	3	0.01
	Diversion	72	0.11	43	0.08	2	0.00	0	0.00	0	0.00
	Wrecking	127	0.19	90	0.17	10	0.02	7	0.02	8	0.02
	Terror	296	0.45	211	0.40	86	0.21	1	0.00	10	0.03
	Anti-Soviet Agitation	2,614	3.94	2,173	4.13	1,150	2.86	754	2.05	519	1.57
	Total (CR crimes)	41,318	62.33	30,948	58.75	18,856	46.96	23,191	62.91	20,813	62.90
		N	%	N	%	N	%	N	%	N	%
Vorkutlag Only	Hooliganism	725	1.09	551	1.05	516	1.29	610	1.65	1,240	3.75
	Speculation	460	0.69	441	0.84	190	0.47	130	0.35	17	0.05
	Malfeasance, Economic Crimes	2,365	3.57	1,916	3.64	169	0.42	236	0.64	23	0.07
	Banditry	2,828	4.27	2,213	4.20	1,352	3.37	1,339	3.63	1,478	4.47
	War Crimes	2,325	3.51	1,779	3.38	639	1.59	353	0.96	59	0.18
	1932 Theft Law	1,524	2.30	1,439	2.73	1,248	3.11	949	2.57	368	1.11
	1947 Theft Law (Personal)	2,344	3.54	2,498	4.74	3,622	9.02	2,908	7.89	4,127	12.47
	1947 Theft Law (State)	5,040	7.60	5,356	10.17	4,582	11.41	4,047	10.98	2,526	7.63
	Other Theft	2,996	4.52	2,052	3.90	16	0.04	44	0.12	0	0.00
	Total (other crimes)	24,972	37.67	21,728	41.25	21,295	53.04	13,670	37.09	12,274	37.10
	Total (all crimes)	66,290	100.00	52,676	100.00	40,151	100.00	36,861	100.00	33,087	100.00

		N	%	N	%	N	%	N	%	N	%
	Treason	6,250	92.26	21,069	84.20	26,651	75.23	25,234	71.18	28,814	77.55
	Espionage	156	2.30	459	1.83	1,473	4.16	2,729	7.70	1,576	4.24
	Diversion	40	0.59	116	0.46	133	0.38	141	0.40	84	0.23
	Wrecking	0	0.00	33	0.13	146	0.41	118	0.33	17	0.05
	Terror	84	1.24	441	1.76	697	1.97	839	2.37	1076	2.90
	Anti-Soviet Agitation	78	1.15	1,198	4.79	1,139	3.22	1,194	3.37	1,315	3.54
	Total (CR crimes)	6,774	100.00	23,330	93.23	31,685	89.45	35,418	99.91	37,131	99.94
		N	%	N	%	N	%	N	%	N	%
Rechlag Only	Hooliganism	0	0.00	0	0.00	19	0.05	0	0.00	0	0.00
	Speculation	0	0.00	0	0.00	0	0.00	3	0.01	0	0.00
	Malfeasance, Economic Crimes	0	0.00	0	0.00	0	0.00	2	0.01	0	0.00
	Banditry	0	0.00	11	0.04	16	0.05	4	0.01	1	0.00
	War Crimes	0	0.00	0	0.00	0	0.00	0	0.00	0	0.00
	1932 Theft Law	0	0.00	0	0.00	3	0.01	3	0.01	1	0.00
	1947 Theft Law (Personal)	0	0.00	0	0.00	0	0.00	2	0.01	17	0.05
	1947 Theft Law (State)	0	0.00	0	0.00	2	0.01	6	0.02	0	0.00
	Other Theft	0	0.00	0	0.00		0.00	1	0.00	0	0.00
	Total (other crimes)	0	0.00	1,694	6.77	3,739	10.55	33	0.09	22	0.06
	Total (all crimes)	6,774	100.00	25,024	100.00	35,424	100.00	35,451	100.00	37,153	100.00

(*continued*)

Table A.2.2. (*continued*)

		1949		1950		1952		1953		1954	
		N	%	N	%	N	%	N	%	N	%
	Treason	39,677	54.30	45,729	58.85	42,769	56.59	41,232	57.02	43,319	61.67
	Espionage	546	0.75	767	0.99	1,487	1.97	2,729	3.77	1,579	2.25
	Diversion	112	0.15	159	0.20	135	0.18	141	0.19	84	0.12
	Wrecking	127	0.17	123	0.16	156	0.21	125	0.17	25	0.04
	Terror	380	0.52	652	0.84	783	1.04	840	1.16	1,086	1.55
	Anti-Soviet Agitation	2,692	3.68	3,371	4.34	2,289	3.03	1,948	2.69	1,834	2.61
	Total (CR crimes)	48,092	65.82	54,278	69.86	50,541	66.88	58,609	81.05	57,944	82.49
		N	%	N	%	N	%	N	%	N	%
Overall	Hooliganism	725	0.99	551	0.71	535	0.71	610	0.84	1,240	1.77
	Speculation	460	0.63	441	0.57	190	0.25	133	0.18	17	0.02
	Malfeasance, Economic Crimes	2,365	3.24	1,916	2.47	169	0.22	238	0.33	23	0.03
	Banditry	2,828	3.87	2,224	2.86	1,368	1.81	1,343	1.86	1,479	2.11
	War Crimes	2,325	3.18	1,779	2.29	639	0.85	353	0.49	59	0.08
	1932 Theft Law	1,524	2.09	1,439	1.85	1,251	1.66	952	1.32	369	0.53
	1947 Theft Law (Personal)	2,344	3.21	2,498	3.21	3,622	4.79	2,910	4.02	4,144	5.90
	1947 Theft Law (State)	5,040	6.90	5,356	6.89	4,584	6.07	4,053	5.60	2,526	3.60
	Other Theft	2,996	4.10	2,052	2.64	16	0.02	45	0.06	0	0.00
	Total (other crimes)	24,972	34.18	23,422	30.14	25,034	33.12	13,703	18.95	12,296	17.51
	Total (all crimes)	73,064	100.00	77,700	100.00	75,575	100.00	72,312	100.00	70,240	100.00

Table A.2.3. Convictions of prisoners in Vorkutlag and Rechlag (selected crimes), 1955–1958

	1955		1956		1957		1958	
	N	%	N	%	N	%	N	%
Treason	35,226	56.13	13,708	27.19	3,095	6.23		
Espionage	1,489	2.37	575	1.14	17	0.03		
Diversion	76	0.12	157	0.31	24	0.05		
Wrecking	6	0.01	103	0.20	14	0.03		
Terror	1,002	1.60	546	1.08	214	0.43		
Anti-Soviet Agitation	1,258	2.00	998	1.98	115	0.23		
Total (CR crimes)	47,073	75.01	19,167	38.02	3,680	7.41	2,751	6.92
	N	%	N	%	N	%	N	%
Hooliganism	2,742	4.37	3,848	7.63	8,953	18.03	5,446	13.70
Speculation	62	0.10	253	0.50	680	1.37		
Malfeasance, Economic Crimes	26	0.04	958	1.90	1,018	2.05		
Banditry	1,677	2.67	1,470	2.92	1,524	3.07	1,377	3.46
War Crimes	83	0.13	957	1.90	2,023	4.07	1,206	3.03
1932 Theft Law	251	0.40	124	0.25	83	0.17		0.00
1947 Theft Law (Personal)	6,187	9.86	10,637	21.10	15,538	31.30	8,120	20.43
1947 Theft Law (State)	2,375	3.78	7,689	15.25	9,612	19.36	6,960	17.51
Other Theft	407	0.65	169	0.34	64	0.13		0.00
Total (other crimes)	15,684	24.99	31,241	61.98	45,966	92.59	37,004	93.08
Total (all crimes)	62,757	100.00	50,408	100.00	49,646	100.00	39,755	100.00

Table A.3.1. Sentence length of prisoners in Vorkutlag (years), 1942–1948

	1942		1943		1944		1945	
	N	%	N	%	N	%	N	%
<1	158	0.55	63	0.23	182	0.72	481	1.14
1–3	1,780	6.23	787	2.83	1,553	6.15	2,100	4.99
3–5	12,678	44.35	8,387	30.18	4,746	18.79	5,399	12.84
5–10	12,868	45.01	15,723	56.57	17,878	70.78	33,408	79.44
10–15	483	1.69	348	1.25	813	3.22	468	1.11
15–20	0	0.00	0	0.00	0	0.00	0	0.00
20–25	0	0.00	0	0.00	0	0.00	0	0.00
Unknown	531	1.86	2,485	8.94	86	0.34	200	0.48
Total Prisoners	28,588[a]	100.00	27,793	100.00	25,258	100.00	42,056	100.00
Mean Sentence Length	5.79		6.37		6.68		6.79	

	1946		1947		1948	
	N	%	N	%	N	%
<1	166	0.33	330	0.55	260	0.41
1–3	199	0.39	3,576	5.91	4,670	7.45
3–5	2,352	4.63	4,678	7.73	5,779	9.22
5–10	40,055	78.93	50,171	82.90	20,464	32.64
10–15	253	0.50	383	0.63	31,507	50.26
15–20	0	0.00	0	0.00	0	0.00
20–25	0	0.00	0	0.00	0	0.00
Unknown	7,724[b]	15.22	1,381	2.28	8	0.01
Total Prisoners	50,749	100.00	60,519	100.00	62,688	100.00
Mean Sentence Length	7.31		6.89		9.26	

[a] This does not equal the total number of prisoners on 1 January of that year according to Table A.1.

Table A.3.2. Sentence length of prisoners in Vorkutlag and Rechlag (years), 1949–1954

	1949		1950		1952		1953		1954	
	Vorkutlag Only									
	N	%	N	%	N	%	N	%	N	%
<1	14	0.02	27	0.05	0	0.00	4	0.01	0	0.00
1–3	3,325	5.02	1,195	2.27	239	0.60	216	0.59	125	0.38
3–5	6,396	9.65	5,126	9.73	1,010	2.52	455	1.23	1,114	3.37
5–10	23,295	35.14	18,340	34.82	14,487	36.08	3,715	10.08	2,789	8.43
10–15	15,758	23.77	11,916	22.62	12,207	30.40	8,908	24.17	14,255	43.08
15–20	14,337	21.63	11,153	21.17	9,642	24.01	11,415	30.97	10,813	32.68
20–25	3,165	4.77	4,919	9.34	2,566	6.39	12,148	32.96	3,991	12.06
Unknown	0	0.00	0	0.00	0	0.00	0	0.00	0	0.00
Total Prisoners	66,290	100.00	52,676	100.00	40,151	100.00	36,861	100.00	33,087	100.00
Mean Sentence Length	10.98		11.72		12.27		16.68		14.61	
	Rechlag Only									
	N	%	N	%	N	%	N	%	N	%
<1	0	0.00	0	0.00	0	0.00	0	0.00	0	0.00
1–3	0	0.00	0	0.00	0	0.00	1	0.00	0	0.00
3–5	256	3.78	515	2.06	208	0.59	100	0.28	5	0.01
5–10	1,723	25.44	7,512	30.02	12,819	36.19	11,669	32.92	11,821	31.82
10–15	2,149	31.72	5,959	23.81	6,942	19.60	7,032	19.84	6,854	18.45

(continued)

Table A.3.2. (*continued*)

	1949		1950		1952		1953		1954	
	Rechlag Only									
	N	%	N	%	N	%	N	%	N	%
15–20	2,155	31.81	5,552	22.19	5,877	16.59	6,010	16.95	5,934	15.97
20–25	491	7.25	5,486	21.92	9,578	27.04	10,639	30.01	12,539	33.75
Unknown	0	0.00	0	0.00	0	0.00	0	0.00	0	0.00
Total Prisoners	6,774	100.00	25,024	100.00	35,424	100.00	35,451	100.00	37,153	100.00
Mean Sentence Length	13.24		14.14		14.18		14.68		15.08	
	Overall									
	N	%	N	%	N	%	N	%	N	%
<1	14	0.02	27	0.03	0	0.00	4	0.01	0	0.00
1–3	3,325	4.55	1,195	1.54	239	0.32	217	0.30	125	0.18
3–5	6,652	9.10	5,641	7.26	1,218	1.61	555	0.77	1,119	1.59
5–10	25,018	34.24	25,852	33.27	27,306	36.13	15,384	21.27	14,610	20.80
10–15	17,907	24.51	17,875	23.01	19,149	25.34	15,940	22.04	21,109	30.05
15–20	16,492	22.57	16,705	21.50	15,519	20.53	17,425	24.10	16,747	23.84
20–25	3,656	5.00	10,405	13.39	12,144	16.07	22,787	31.51	16,530	23.53
Unknown	0	0.00	0	0.00	0	0.00	0	0.00	0	0.00
Total Prisoners	73,064	100.00	77,700	100.00	75,575	100.00	72,312	100.00	70,240	100.00
Mean Sentence Length	11.19		12.50		13.16		15.70		14.86	

Table A.3.3. Sentence length of prisoners in Vorkutlag (years), 1955–1958

	1955		1956		1957		1958	
	N	%	N	%	N	%	N	%
<1	0	0.00	9	0.02	78	0.16	276	0.69
1–3	184	0.29	4,363	8.66	6,843	13.78	2,134	5.37
3–5	1,840	2.93	6,971	13.83	11,042	22.24	6,843	17.21
5–10	15,358	24.47	14,314	28.40	17,407	35.06	16,253	40.88
10–15	16,456	26.22	8,089	16.05	6,740	13.58	6,298	15.84
15–20	12,415	19.78	10,180	20.20	5,345	10.77	5,755	14.48
20–25	16,504	26.30	6,482	12.86	2,191	4.41	2,196	5.52
Unknown	0	0.00	0	0.00	0	0.00	0	0.00
Total Prisoners	62,757	100.00	50,408	100.00	49,646	100.00	39,755	100.00
Mean Sentence Length	14.63		11.32		8.41		9.68	

Table A.4.1. Nationality of prisoners in Vorkutlag (selected nationalities), 1942–1948

	1942		1943		1944		1945	
	N	%	N	%	N	%	N	%
Russian	16,222	56.74	17,420	62.68	16,050	63.54	21,971	52.24
Ukrainian	3,107	10.87	3,380	12.16	2,832	11.21	11,543	27.45
Belorussian	887	3.10	696	2.50	558	2.21	1,535	3.65
Georgian	349	1.22	276	0.99	233	0.92	208	0.49
Armenian	398	1.39	335	1.21	327	1.29	383	0.91
Tatar	605	2.12	472	1.70	385	1.52	742	1.76
Latvian	363	1.27	186	0.67	145	0.57	112	0.27
Lithuanian	271	0.95	199	0.72	149	0.59	167	0.40
Estonian	427	1.49	204	0.73	201	0.80	138	0.33
Jewish	1,135	3.97	893	3.21	788	3.12	676	1.61
German	412	1.44	422	1.52	773	3.06	1,220	2.90
Polish	846	2.96	302	1.09	225	0.89	290	0.69
Chinese	381	1.33	311	1.12	301	1.19	316	0.75
Korean	24	0.08	28	0.10	64	0.25	65	0.15
Other	3,161	11.06	2,669	9.60	2,227	8.82	2,690	6.40
Total	28,588	100.00	27,793	100.00	25,258	100.00	42,056	100.00

	1946		1947		1948	
	N	%	N	%	N	%
Russian	19,471	38.37	27,642	45.67	27,720	44.22
Ukrainian	14,453	28.48	16,035	26.50	17,870	28.51
Belorussian	2,115	4.17	2,994	4.95	3,143	5.01
Georgian	91	0.18	131	0.22	212	0.34
Armenian	287	0.57	275	0.45	306	0.49
Tatar	446	0.88	711	1.17	788	1.26
Latvian	1,425	2.81	2,023	3.34	1,485	2.37
Lithuanian	5,897	11.62	3,831	6.33	3,624	5.78
Estonian	825	1.63	1,816	3.00	1,611	2.57
Jewish	489	0.96	327	0.54	420	0.67
German	1,164	2.29	1,266	2.09	1,365	2.18
Polish	1,782	3.51	1,199	1.98	1,160	1.85
Chinese	145	0.29	44	0.07	89	0.14
Korean	55	0.11	110	0.18	93	0.15
Other	2,104	4.15	2,115	3.49	2,802	4.47
Total	50,749	100.00	60,519	100.00	62,688	100.00

Table A.4.2. Nationality of prisoners in Vorkutlag and Rechlag (selected nationalities), 1949–1954

	1949		1950		1952		1953		1954	
	Vorkutlag Only									
	N	%	N	%	N	%	N	%	N	%
Russian	32,108	48.44	25,272	47.98	19,939	49.66	17,105	46.40	15,459	46.72
Ukrainian	15,766	23.78	11,434	21.71	9,323	23.22	9,335	25.32	9,147	27.65
Belorussian	3,030	4.57	2,451	4.65	2,548	6.35	2,492	6.76	2,333	7.05
Georgian	202	0.30	145	0.28	115	0.29	97	0.26	83	0.25
Armenian	303	0.46	251	0.48	204	0.51	185	0.50	181	0.55
Tatar	527	0.79	442	0.84	671	1.67	623	1.69	565	1.71
Latvian	1,382	2.08	346	0.66	892	2.22	933	2.53	854	2.58
Lithuanian	2,808	4.24	1,422	2.70	1,063	2.65	1,015	2.75	714	2.16
Estonian	973	1.47	923	1.75	665	1.66	617	1.67	427	1.29
Jewish	443	0.67	415	0.79	231	0.58	196	0.53	189	0.57
German	3,338	5.04	4,755	9.03	1,318	3.28	1,236	3.35	892	2.70
Polish	973	1.47	276	0.52	446	1.11	420	1.14	362	1.09
Chinese	19	0.03	7	0.01	0	0.00	0	0.00	3	0.01
Korean	53	0.08	30	0.06	1	0.00	2	0.01	8	0.02
Other	4,365	6.58	4,507	8.56	2,735	6.81	2,605	7.07	1,870	5.65
Total	66,290	100.00	52,676	100.00	40,151	100.00	36,861	100.00	33,087	100.00
	Rechlag Only									
	N	%	N	%	N	%	N	%	N	%
Russian	1,154	17.04	4,126	16.49	6,023	17.00	5,242	14.79	5,491	14.78
Ukrainian	3,150	46.50	10,058	40.19	14,525	41.00	14,202	40.06	15,459	41.61
Belorussian	298	4.40	1,061	4.24	1,487	4.20	1,493	4.21	1,548	4.17
Georgian	9	0.13	79	0.32	99	0.28	6	0.02	103	0.28
Armenian	30	0.44	107	0.43	150	0.42	7	0.02	172	0.46
Tatar	30	0.44	100	0.40	107	0.30	113	0.32	137	0.37
Latvian	264	3.90	1,132	4.52	1,950	5.50	1,966	5.55	2,118	5.70
Lithuanian	805	11.88	2,972	11.88	4,333	12.23	4,344	12.25	4,454	11.99

(continued)

Table A.4.2. (*continued*)

	1949		1950		1952		1953		1954	
	Rechlag Only									
	N	%	N	%	N	%	N	%	N	%
Estonian	364	5.37	1,361	5.44	1,974	5.57	2,038	5.75	2,118	5.70
Jewish	24	0.35	121	0.48	275	0.78	255	0.72	373	1.00
German	124	1.83	1,989	7.95	276	0.78	441	1.24	427	1.15
Polish	234	3.45	834	3.33	601	1.70	1,117	3.15	1,130	3.04
Chinese	18	0.27	32	0.13	0	0.00	0	0.00	0	0.00
Korean	23	0.34	56	0.22	0	0.00	5	0.01	5	0.01
Other	247	3.65	996	3.98	3,624	10.23	4,222	11.91	3,618	9.74
Total	6,774	100.00	25,024	100.00	35,424	100.00	35,451	100.00	37,153	100.00
	Overall									
	N	%	N	%	N	%	N	%	N	%
Russian	33,262	45.52	29,398	37.84	25,962	34.35	22,347	30.90	20,950	29.83
Ukrainian	18,916	25.89	21,492	27.66	23,848	31.56	23,537	32.55	24,606	35.03
Belorussian	3,328	4.55	3,512	4.52	4,035	5.34	3,985	5.51	3,881	5.53
Georgian	211	0.29	224	0.29	214	0.28	103	0.14	186	0.26
Armenian	333	0.46	358	0.46	354	0.47	192	0.27	353	0.50
Tatar	557	0.76	542	0.70	778	1.03	736	1.02	702	1.00
Latvian	1,646	2.25	1,478	1.90	2,842	3.76	2,899	4.01	2,972	4.23
Lithuanian	3,613	4.94	4,394	5.66	5,396	7.14	5,359	7.41	5,168	7.36
Estonian	1,337	1.83	2,284	2.94	2,639	3.49	2,655	3.67	2,545	3.62
Jewish	467	0.64	536	0.69	506	0.67	451	0.62	562	0.80
German	3,462	4.74	6,744	8.68	1,594	2.11	1,677	2.32	1,319	1.88
Polish	1,207	1.65	1,110	1.43	1,047	1.39	1,537	2.13	1,492	2.12
Chinese	37	0.05	39	0.05	0	0.00	0	0.00	3	0.00
Korean	76	0.10	86	0.11	1	0.00	7	0.01	13	0.02
Other	4,612	6.31	5,503	7.08	6,359	8.41	6,827	9.44	5,488	7.81
Total	73,064	100.00	77,700	100.00	75,575	100.00	72,312	100.00	70,240	100.00

Table A.4.3. Nationality of prisoners in Vorkutlag (selected nationalities), 1955–1958

	1955		1956		1957		1958	
	N	%	N	%	N	%	N	%
Russian	21,691	34.56	23,826	47.27	29,318	59.05	24,325	61.19
Ukrainian	19,905	31.72	13,480	26.74	9,663	19.46	7,236	18.20
Belorussian	3,449	5.50	2,340	4.64	2,536	5.11	1,173	2.95
Georgian	184	0.29	439	0.87	791	1.59	682	1.72
Armenian	369	0.59	336	0.67	504	1.02	384	0.97
Tatar	607	0.97						
Latvian	2,839	4.52	1,690	3.35	683	1.38	483	1.21
Lithuanian	4,476	7.13	2,298	4.56	1,136	2.29	755	1.90
Estonian	2,241	3.57	1,102	2.19	588	1.18	442	1.11
Jewish	490	0.78						
German	756	1.20						
Polish	1,256	2.00						
Chinese	0	0.00						
Korean	4	0.01						
Other	4,490	7.15	4,897	9.71	4,427	8.92	4,275	10.75
Total	62,757	100.00	50,408	100.00	49,646	100.00	39,755	100.00

Table A.5.1. Prisoners released from Vorkutlag, 1942–1958

	1942	1943	1944	1945	1946	1947	1949	1950
N	6,042	5,624	4,271	11,335	7,603	5,496	4,345[a]	4,074
%	21.43	21.20	15.51	28.14	13.67	8.67	7.30	8.56

	1951	1952	1953	1954	1955	1956	1957	1958
N	6,987	6,706	11,622	12,252[b]	25,210	24,801	17,062	13,985
%	18.40	17.08	33.23	19.74	44.55	49.58	38.17	35.18

Source: GARF, f. R-9414, op. 1 ch. 2, d. 382, l. 1; GARF, f. R-9414, op. 1 ch. 2, d. 400, l. 6; GARF, f. R-9414, op. 1 ch. 2, d. 416, l. 5; GARF, f. R-9414, op. 1 ch. 2, d. 434, l. 5; GARF, f. R-9414, op. 1 ch. 2, d. 450, l. 5; GARF, f. R-9414, op. 1 ch. 2, d. 606, ll. 5–6; GARF, f. R-9414, op. 1 ch. 2, d. 472; GARF, f. R-9414, op. 1 ch. 2, d. 479; GARF, f. R-9414, op. 1 ch. 2, d. 485; GARF, f. R-9414, op. 1 ch. 2, d. 495; GARF, f. R-9414, op. 1 ch. 2, d. 500; GARF, f. R-9414, op. 1 ch. 2, d. 508; GARF, f. R-9414, op. 1 ch. 2, d. 512; GARF, f. R-9414, op. 1 ch. 2, d. 514; GARF, f. R-9414, op. 1 ch. 2, d. 518; GARF, f. R-9414, op. 1 ch. 2, d. 525.

[a] Estimated based on figures for February–December.

[b] Includes releases from both Vorkutlag and Rechlag, which explains the dip in percentage of the prisoner population released despite relative stability in the absolute number of releases.

Table A.5.2. Prisoners released from Rechlag, 1949–1953

	1949	1950	1951	1952	1953
N	250[a]	573	555	926	1,016[b]
%	1.57	1.96	1.61	2.61	2.80

Source: As Table A.5.1.

[a] Estimated based on figures for February–December.

[b] Estimated based on figures for January–March.

Table A.5.3. Prisoners released from Vorkutlag and Rechlag, 1942–1958

	1942	1943	1944	1945
N	6,042	5,624	4,271	11,335
%	21.43	21.20	15.51	28.14
	1946	1947	1949	1950
N	7,603	5,496	4,595	4,647
%	13.67	8.67	6.10	7.32
	1951	1952	1953	1954
N	7,542	7,632	12,638	12,252
%	9.82	11.36	17.45	19.74
	1955	1956	1957	1958
N	25,210	24,801	17,062	13,985
%	44.55	49.58	38.17	35.18

Source: As Table A.5.1.

Table A.6.1. Mortality rate in Vorkutlag, the Gulag, and the USSR, 1942–1947 (in deaths per thousand)

Year	Vorkutlag			Gulag	USSR (non-front)
	Prisoners	KTR	Overall		
1942	46.65		46.65	249.00	27.72
1943	147.14		147.14	224.00	16.50
1944	48.58	377.96	97.01	92.50	15.10
1945	38.02	197.62	86.38	59.50	14.10
1946	19.08	42.08	27.93	22.00	15.80
1947	19.14	47.66	31.02	35.90	20.30

Source: Vorkutlag: As Table A.5.1. Gulag figures: Afanas'ev and Kozlov, eds., *Istoriia stalinskogo Gulaga*, 4: 55. Figures for the USSR come from Poliakov, *Naselenie Rossii v xx veke*, 2: 87, 96.

Table A.6.2 Mortality in Vorkutlag, Rechlag, and the Gulag, 1949–1954 (in deaths per thousand)

Year	Vorkuta Complex			Gulag
	Vorkutlag	Rechlag	Overall	
1949	11.64	11.31	11.57	12.10
1950	9.64	8.36	9.19	9.50
1951	9.50	5.87	7.95	9.20
1952	8.94	6.74	7.90	8.40
1953	8.06	6.95	7.50	6.70
1954	8.71	8.97	8.85	6.90

Source: Vorkutlag/Rechlag: As Table A.5.1. Gulag figures: Afanas'ev and Kozlov, eds, *Istoriia stalinskogo Gulaga*, 4: 55.

Appendix B
Non-Prisoner Data Set

The data presented in this appendix have been compiled from the Komi Republic State archive (GURK NARK 1), *fond* R-1941, *Vorkutinskaia gorodskaia inspektora gosstatistiki.* There are numerous errors and inconsistencies, which I have attempted to correct wherever possible. Although it is far from perfect, the statistical picture that emerges from these data is as accurate and complete as possible given the way in which the data were collected and preserved.

Table B.1. Non-prisoner population of Vorkuta, 1945–1970

1945	24,218
1946	31,590
1947	35,549
1948	30,127
1949	36,250
1950	41,800
1951	50,459
1952	59,721
1953	68,553
1954	76,359
1955	84,114
1956	100,815
1957	129,698
1958	153,474
1959	175,857
1960	183,295
1961	183,383
1962	183,682
1963	186,851
1964	192,377
1965	197,093
1966	198,751
1967	204,126
1968	203,000
1969	201,600
1970	185,383

Source: GURK NARK 1, f. R-1941, op. 1, d. 3, ll. 2, 22; GURK NARK 1, f. R-1941, op. 1, d. 7, ll. 2, 15; GURK NARK 1, f. R-1941, op. 1, d. 14, l. 10b.; GURK NARK 1, f. R-1941, op. 1, d. 22, ll. 4–5; GURK NARK 1, f. R-1941, op. 1, d. 31, ll. 4–40; GURK NARK 1, f. R-1941, op. 1, d. 43, l. 13; GURK NARK 1, f. R-1941, op. 1, d. 43, l. 12 and GURK NARK 1, f. R-1941, op. 1, d. 53, ll. 1–2, 8; GURK NARK 1, f. R-1941, op. 1, d. 64, l. 57; GURK NARK 1, f. R-1941, op. 1, ll. 28–33, 42; GURK NARK 1, f. R-1941, op. 1, d. 75, ll. 1–2, 33; GURK NARK 1, f. R-1941, op. 1, d. 83, l. 6; GURK NARK 1, f. R-1941, op. 1, d. 95; GURK NARK 1, f. R-1941, op. 1, d. 100, l. 12; GURK NARK 1, f. R-1941, op. 1, d. 169, l. 28; GURK NARK 1, f. R-1941, op. 1, d. 191, ll. 1, 11–18, 28–29; GURK NARK 1, f. R-1941, op. 1, d. 205, l. 36; GURK NARK 1, f. R-1941, op. 1, d. 224, ll. 1–2, 5, 29, 31; GURK NARK 1, f. R-1941, op. 1, d. 235, ll. 43–43ob.

Note: Figures for 1945–1946, 1952, and 1954–1956 have been calculated based on the best available statistics on population growth.

Table B.2. Migration to and from Vorkuta, 1945–1970

	1945	1946	1947	1948	1949	1950	1951	1952	1953
In	8,859	9,484	13,793	9,987	7,145	10,887	11,768	10,995	13,622
Out	1,936	5,525	5,572	5,401	3,504	4,123	4,854	5,054	7,748
Net	6,923	3,959	8,221	4,586	3,641	6,764	6,914	5,941	5,874

	1954	1955	1956	1957	1958	1959	1960	1961	1962
In	12,288	26,731	49,870	38,876	41,429	31,151	32,511	23,082	18,418
Out	6,610	10,030	16,414	19,455	27,592	27,209	29,484	27,233	19,042
Net	5,678	16,701	33,456	19,421	13,837	3,942	3,027	−4,151	−624

	1963	1964	1965	1966	1967	1968	1969	1970
In	19,793	18,754	18,448	17,377	17,214	18,119	15,279	16,150
Out	18,959	17,132	16,771	17,964	18,389	19,541	17,745	16,638
Net	834	1,622	1,677	−587	−1,175	−1,422	−2,466	−488

Source: GURK NARK 1, f. R-1941, op. 1, d. 3, l. 2; GURK NARK 1, f. R-1941, op. 1, d. 7, ll. 2, 15; GURK NARK 1, f. R-1941, op. 1, d. 14, l. 2; GURK NARK 1, f. R-1941, op. 1, d. 22, l. 64; GURK NARK 1, f. R-1941, op. 1, d. 31, ll. 4–40; GURK NARK 1, f. R-1941, op. 1, d. 40, ll. 33–36; GURK NARK 1, f. R-1941, op. 1, d. 53, l. 8; GURK NARK 1, f. R-1941, op. 1, d. 64, l. 57; GURK NARK 1, f. R-1941, op. 1, ll. 28–33; GURK NARK 1, f. R-1941, op. 1, d. 75, l. 33; GURK NARK 1, f. R-1941, op. 1, d. 83, l. 6; GURK NARK 1, f. R-1941, op. 1, d. 83, ll. 1–20; GURK NARK 1, f. R-1941, op. 1, d. 95, l. 4; GURK NARK 1, f. R-1941, op. 1, d. 100, l. 1; GURK NARK 1, f. R-1941, op. 1, d. 107, l. 1; GURK NARK 1, f. R-1941, op. 1, d. 117, l. 2; GURK NARK 1, f. R-1941, op. 1, d. 127, l. 5; GURK NARK 1, f. R-1941, op. 1, d. 137, l. 5; GURK NARK 1, f. R-1941, op. 1, d. 146, l. 5; GURK NARK 1, f. R-1941, op. 1, d. 158, ll. 5–11; GURK NARK 1, f. R-1941, op. 1, d. 169, ll. 5–11; GURK NARK 1, f. R-1941, op. 1, d. 180, ll. 8–22; GURK NARK 1, f. R-1941, op. 1, d. 191, ll. 1–3, 6–8, 19–20, 23–26; GURK NARK 1, f. R-1941, op. 1, d. 205, ll. 1–36; GURK NARK 1, f. R-1941, op. 1, d. 224, ll. 1–27; GURK NARK 1, f. R-1941, op. 1, d. 236, ll. 1–8, 14, 20, 24.

Table B.3. Natality, mortality, and natural population growth among non-prisoner population of Vorkuta, 1945–1970

		1945	1946	1947	1948	1949	1950	1951
Live Births	(N)	626		1,688	1,947	2,919	2,579	2,888
Natality	(births per 1000)	25.85		47.48	64.63	80.52	61.70	57.23
Deaths	(N)	177		405	409	466	567	540
Mortality	(deaths per 1000)	7.31		11.39	13.58	12.86	13.56	10.70
Natural Growth	(N)	449		1,283	1,538	2,453	2,012	2,348
Natural Growth	(%)	1.85		3.61	5.11	6.77	4.81	4.65
Total Population		24,218	31,590	35,549	30,127	36,250	41,800	50,459

		1952	1953	1954	1955	1956	1957	1958
Live Births	(N)	2,722	2,458	2,524		3,311	5,030	5,256
Natality	(births per 1000)	45.58	35.86	33.05		32.84	38.78	34.25
Deaths	(N)	491	526	447		370	675	647
Mortality	(deaths per 1000)	8.22	7.67	5.85		3.67	5.20	4.22
Natural Growth	(N)	2,231	1,932	2,077		2,941	4,355	4,609
Natural Growth	(%)	3.74	2.82	2.72		2.92	3.36	3.00

Total Population		59,721	68,553	76,359	84,114	100,815	129,698	153,474

		1959	1960	1961	1962	1963	1964	1965
Live Births	(N)	5,278	5,468	5,065	4,274	3,810	3,790	3,503
Natality	(births per 1000)	30.01	29.83	27.62	23.27	20.39	19.70	17.77
Deaths	(N)	629	641	667	534	514	645	634
Mortality	(deaths per 1000)	3.58	3.50	3.64	2.91	2.75	3.35	3.22
Natural Growth	(N)	4,649	4,827	4,398	3,740	3,296	3,145	2,869
Natural Growth	(%)	2.64	2.63	2.40	2.04	1.76	1.63	1.46
Total Population		175,857	183,295	183,383	183,682	186,851	192,377	197,093

		1966	1967	1968	1969	1970
Live Births	(N)	3,179	3,067	2,880	2,964	2,933
Natality	(births per 1000)	15.99	15.03	14.19	14.70	15.96
Deaths	(N)	576	558	590	620	654

(*continued*)

Table B.3. (*continued*)

		1966	1967	1968	1969	1970
Mortality	(deaths per 1000)	2.90	2.73	2.91	3.08	3.56
Natural Growth	(N)	2603	2509	2290	2344	2279
Natural Growth	(%)	1.31	1.23	1.13	1.16	1.24
Total Population		198,751	204,126	203,000	201,600	183,735

Source: GURK NARK 1, f. R-1941, op. 1, d. 3, l. 22; GURK NARK 1, f. R-1941, op. 1, d. 13, l. 29; GURK NARK 1, f. R-1941, op. 1, d. 22, ll. 17, 20, 32, 44, 52, 58, 64; GURK NARK 1, f. R-1941, op. 1, d. 31, ll. 4–40; GURK NARK 1, f. R-1941, op. 1, d. 40, l. 9; GURK NARK 1, f. R-1941, op. 1, d. 53, ll. 1–2; GURK NARK 1, f. R-1941, op. 1, d. 64, l. 57; GURK NARK 1, f. R-1941, op. 1, ll. 3–4; GURK NARK 1, f. R-1941, op. 1, d. 75, ll. 1–2; GURK NARK 1, f. R-1941, op. 1, d. 90, ll. 30–31; GURK NARK 1, f. R-1941, op. 1, d. 95, ll. 18–19; GURK NARK 1, f. R-1941, op. 1, d. 100, ll. 14–15; GURK NARK 1, f. R-1941, op. 1, d. 107, ll. 28–29; GURK NARK 1, f. R-1941, op. 1, d. 117, ll. 33–34; GURK NARK 1, f. R-1941, op. 1, d. 127, l. 5; GURK NARK 1, f. R-1941, op. 1, d. 137, ll. 1–2; GURK NARK 1, f. R-1941, op. 1, d. 146, ll. 1–2; GURK NARK 1, f. R-1941, op. 1, d. 158, ll. 1–2; GURK NARK 1, f. R-1941, op. 1, d. 169, ll. 1–2; GURK NARK 1, f. R-1941, op. 1, d. 180, ll. 8–22; GURK NARK 1, f. R-1941, op. 1, d. 191, ll. 1–3, 6–8, 19–20, 23–26; GURK NARK 1, f. R-1941, op. 1, d. 205, ll. 1–36; GURK NARK 1, f. R-1941, op. 1, d. 224, ll. 1–2; GURK NARK 1, f. R-1941, op. 1, d. 237, ll. 1–2.

Appendix C
Production Data Set

Table C.1. Yearly coal production in Vorkuta, 1931–2000 (millions of tons)

Year	Coal	Year	Coal	Year	Coal	Year	Coal
1931	0.001	1941	0.309	1951	7.980	1961	12.379
1932	0.004	1942	0.706	1952	8.874	1962	12.219
1933	0.006	1943	1.574	1953	9.488	1963	11.921
1934	0.033	1944	2.275	1954	10.401	1964	11.532
1935	0.104	1945	2.906	1955	10.118	1965	12.127
1936	0.103	1946	3.054	1956	11.057	1966	12.347
1937	0.095	1947	3.933	1957	11.605	1967	13.072
1938	0.189	1948	4.608	1958	12.021	1968	13.521
1939	0.240	1949	5.715	1959	12.459	1969	13.971
1940	0.252	1950	6.805	1960	12.449	1970	14.126
Decade Total	0.775	Decade Total	25.080	Decade Total	94.003	Decade Total	113.089
Decade Median	0.095	Decade Median	2.906	Decade Median	10.401	Decade Median	12.347

Year	Coal	Year	Coal	Year	Coal
1971	14.544	1981	20.081	1991	14.786
1972	15.015	1982	20.170	1992	16.364
1973	15.302	1983	20.476	1993	14.762
1974	15.495	1984	20.719	1994	13.647
1975	16.001	1985	21.278	1995	13.792
1976	17.554	1986	21.481	1996	13.196
1977	18.273	1987	21.732	1997	12.530
1978	19.846	1988	22.313	1998	11.362
1979	20.556	1989	20.141	1999	12.064
1980	19.872	1990	20.725	2000	12.390
Decade Total	152.586	Decade Total	188.391	Decade Total	122.503
Decade Median	16.001	Decade Median	20.719	Decade Median	13.647

Source: GARF, f. R-9407, op. 1, d. 48, l. 2; GARF, f. R-8361, op. 1, d. 89, l. 4; GARF, f. R-8361, op. 1, d. 326, l. 10; Davydov, ed., *Vorkutaugol'*, 164.

Notes

Oral History

This book makes use of interviews conducted with thirteen subjects, most of whom are former Gulag prisoners or members of their immediate families. Interviews were conducted by the author in Syktyvkar and Vorkuta, Komi Republic, Russian Federation, between 17 April 2003 and 31 July 2004. All interviews were conducted and recorded under the auspices of the University of Chicago Social and Behavioral Sciences Institutional Review Board Protocol 03–1008. In accordance with the protocol, the names of interview subjects have been changed for their protection.

Archives

Arkhiv NIPTs "Memorial"
Arkhiv upravlenii administratsii munitsipial'nogo obrazovaniia "Gorod Vorkuta" (AUAMOGV)
Arkhiv upravlenii ispolneniia nakazanii ministerstva iustitsii Rossiiskoi Federatsii po Respubliki Komi (AUIN MIu RF po RK)
Gosudarstvennyi arkhiv Rossiiskoi Federatsii (GARF)
Gosudarstvennoe uchrezhdenie Respubliki Komi Natsional'nyi Arkhiv Respubliki Komi fondokhranilishche no. 1 (GURK NARK 1)
Gosudarstvennoe uchrezhdenie Respubliki Komi Natsional'nyi Arkhiv Respubliki Komi fondokhranilishche no. 2 (GURK NARK 2)

Rossiiskii gosudarstvennyi arkhiv ekonomiki (RGAE)
Rossiiskii gosudarstvennyi arkhiv sotsial'no-politicheskoi istorii (RGASPI)
The National Archives Public Record Office (TNA PRO)
Vorkutinskii muzeino-vystavochyni tsentr (VMVTs)

Introduction

1. "Istoriia stroiki," *Zapoliar'e*, 26 June 2001. Kirov had been assassinated in 1934. For a discussion of the assassination and the debate surrounding it, see Matthew E. Lenoe, *The Kirov Murder and Soviet History*, Annals of Communism Series (New Haven: Yale University Press, 2010).

2. On the "secret speech" of 1956 and the renewal of criticism at the Twenty-second Party Congress, see Miriam Dobson, *Khrushchev's Cold Summer: Gulag Returnees, Crime, and the Fate of Reform after Stalin* (Ithaca: Cornell University Press, 2009), chaps. 3, 7.

3. Ibid.

4. For an overview of the Gulag as an institution, see Steven A. Barnes, *Death and Redemption: The Gulag and the Shaping of Soviet Society* (Princeton: Princeton University Press, 2011), 16–27.

5. This estimate is based on official mortality statistics for 1942–47 and 1949–54. See Appendix A, tables A.6.1 and A.6.2.

6. See Appendix B, table B.1.

7. See Appendix C, table C.1.

8. Viacheslav Davydov, ed. *Vorkutaugol'* (Syktyvkar: OAO Komi Respublikanskaia Tipografiia, 2001), 16. V. Griner, *Poslednie dni bab'ego leta* (Syktyvkar: Komi knizhnoe izdatel'stvo, 1975).

9. Mikhail Pavlovich Roshchevskii, ed. *Respublika Komi: Entsiklopediia* (Syktyvkar: Komi knizhnoe izd-vo, 1997), 1: 318–20, 324–25.

10. Work on the Gulag in European north tends to follow this model as well, treating the system of camps and colonies as a separate entity. See, e.g., N. A. Morozov, *Gulag v Komi krae, 1929–1956* (Syktyvkar: Syktyvkarskii gosudarstvennyi universitet, 1997); N. A. Morozov, *Osobye lageria MVD SSSR v Komi ASSR: 1948–1954 gody* (Syktyvkar: Syktyvkarskii gosudarstvennyi universitet, 1998); N. V. Upadyshev, *GULAG na evropeiskom severe Rossii: Genezis, evoliutsiia, raspad* (Arkhangel'sk: Pomorskii gos. universitet, 2007).

11. On the Gulag as a project of internal colonization, see Lynne Viola, *The Unknown Gulag: The Lost World of Stalin's Special Settlements* (New York: Oxford University Press, 2007), 4, 185–88; Lynne Viola, "Die Selbstkolonisierung der Sowjetunion und der Gulag der 1930er Jahre," *Transit-Europaeische Revue* 38 (2009): 34–56; Lynne Viola, "Stalin's Empire: The Gulag and Police Colonization in the Soviet Union in the 1930s," in *Stalinism and Europe: Terror, War, Domination, 1937–1947*, ed. Tim Snyder (New York: Oxford University Press, forthcoming); Den Khili [Dan Healey], "Nasledie Gulaga: Prinuditel'nyi trud sovetskoi epokhi kak vnutrenniaia kolonizatsiia," in *Tam, vnutri: Praktiki vnutrennei kolonizatsii v kul'turnoi istorii Rossii*, ed. Aleksandr Etkind, Dirk Uffelmann, and Il'ia Kukulin

(Moscow: Novoe literaturnoe obozrenie, 2012), 684–728. Relatedly, geographer Judith Pallot writes about a "geography of penality" that developed in the Stalin era and has had longstanding consequences even in the post-Soviet era. Judith Pallot, "Forced Labour for Forestry: the Twentieth-Century History of Colonisation and Settlement in the North of Perm' Oblast'," *Europe-Asia Studies* 54, no. 7 (2002): 1055–84.

12. Stephen Kotkin, *Magnetic Mountain: Stalinism as a Civilization* (Berkeley: University of California Press, 1995); Kate Brown, *A Biography of No Place: From Ethnic Borderland to Soviet Heartland* (Cambridge: Harvard University Press, 2004).

13. On the "small peoples" of the north and their relations with the Russian and Soviet empires, see Yuri Slezkine, *Arctic Mirrors: Russia and the Small Peoples of the North* (Ithaca: Cornell University Press, 1994). The relationship between the spread of the Gulag and the Soviet Union's native peoples has not yet been properly studied.

14. Aleksandr Isaevich Solzhenitsyn, *The Gulag Archipelago, 1918–1956*, 3 vols. (New York: Harper & Row, 1974), 1: 4.

15. See, e.g., Anne Applebaum, *Gulag: A History* (New York: Doubleday, 2003); Robert Conquest, *The Great Terror: A Reassessment* (New York: Oxford University Press, 1990).

16. J. Arch Getty, Gabor T. Rittersporn, and Viktor N. Zemskov, "Victims of the Soviet Penal System in the Pre-War Years: A First Approach on the Basis of Archival Evidence," *American Historical Review* 98, no. 4 (1993): 1017–49.

17. Golfo Alexopoulos, "Amnesty 1945: The Revolving Door of Stalin's Gulag," *Slavic Review* 64, no. 2 (2005): 274–306.

18. Viola, *Unknown Gulag*.

19. Barnes, *Death and Redemption*.

20. Alan Barenberg, "Prisoners without Borders: Zazonniki and the Transformation of Vorkuta after Stalin," *Jahrbücher für Geschichte Osteuropas* 57, no. 4 (2009): 513–34; Wilson T. Bell, "Was the Gulag an Archipelago? De-Convoyed Prisoners and Porous Borders in the Camps of Western Siberia," *Russian Review* 72, no. 1 (2013): 116–41.

21. In using the term "zone" I follow the convention in official Soviet documents and Gulag memoirs. Jacques Rossi, *The Gulag Handbook*, trans. William A. Burhans (New York: Paragon House, 1989), 137–38.

22. For another example of how spatial approaches have been applied to regions in Soviet Russia, see Nick Baron, *Soviet Karelia: Politics, Planning and Terror in Stalin's Russia, 1920–1939* (New York: Routledge, 2007).

23. V. I. Il'in, "Gorod-kontslager': Sotsial'naia stratifikatsiia gulagovskoi vorkuty (1930–50-e gody)," in *Stratifikatsiia v Rossii: Istoriia i sovremennost'*, ed. Iu. M. Rapaport (Syktyvkar: izd-vo SyktGU, 1999), 44–70.

24. Sheila Fitzpatrick, *Tear off the Masks!: Identity and Imposture in Twentieth-century Russia* (Princeton: Princeton University Press, 2005), chap. 4.

25. My approach to identity and space is similar to that proposed by Kate Brown. Kate Brown, "Out of Solitary Confinement: The History of the Gulag," *Kritika: Explorations in Russian and Eurasian History* 8, no. 1 (2007): 78.

26. Sheila Fitzpatrick, "War and Society in Soviet Context: Soviet Labor before, during, and after World War II," *International Labor and Working-Class History* 35 (1989): 41–47; Donald Filtzer, "From Mobilized to Free Labour: De-Stalinization and the Changing Legal Status of Workers," in *The Dilemmas of De-Stalinization: Negotiating Cultural and Social Change in the Khrushchev Era*, ed. Polly Jones (London: Routledge, 2006), 158; Donald Filtzer, *Soviet Workers and Late Stalinism: Labour and the Restoration of the Stalinist System after World War II* (Cambridge: Cambridge University Press, 2002), 39–40. In a similar vein, Richard Hellie argued that this was part of the "third service class revolution" launched by Stalin. Richard Hellie, "The Structure of Modern Russian History: Toward a Dynamic Model," *Russian History* 4, no. 1 (1977): 1–22. Thanks to Emma Gilligan for bringing this issue to my attention.

27. On the comparison between Soviet and American company towns, see Kate Brown, "Gridded Lives: Why Kazakhstan and Montana Are Nearly the Same Place," *The American Historical Review* 106, no. 1 (2001): 17–48; Kate Brown, "The Closed Nuclear City and Big Brother®: Made in America," *Ab Imperio* 2 (2011): 159–87.

28. Stephen Kotkin's works on Magnitogorsk comprise the most detailed study of a Soviet company town. Kotkin, *Magnetic Mountain*. For a recent study that emphasizes the connections between industrialization and militarization, see Lennart Samuelson, *Tankograd: The Formation of a Soviet Company Town: Cheliabinsk, 1900s–1950s* (New York: Palgrave Macmillan, 2011).

29. William Taubman, *Governing Soviet Cities: Bureaucratic Politics and Urban Development in the USSR* (New York: Praeger, 1973), chap. 7.

30. Pavel Grebeniuk, *Kolymskii led: Sistema upravleniia na severo-vostoke Rossii, 1953–1964* (Moscow: ROSSPEN, 2007).

31. Nanci Adler, *The Gulag Survivor: Beyond the Soviet System* (New Brunswick, NJ: Transaction Publishers, 2002); Marc Elie, "Les politiques à l'égard des libérés du Goulag," *Cahiers du Monde Russe* 47, nos. 1–2 (2006): 327–48; Marc Elie, "Les anciens détenus du Goulag: Libérations massives, réinsertion et réhabilitation dans l'URSS poststalinienne, 1953–1964" (PhD, EHESS, 2007); Marc Elie, "Ce que réhabiliter veut dire," *Vingtième Siècle. Revue d'Histoire*, no. 107 (2010): 101–13.

32. Dobson, *Khrushchev's Cold Summer*, chap. 4. Quotation from 111.

Chapter 1. From the Margins to the Home Front

1. G. A. Chernov, *Iz istorii otkrytiia Pechorskogo ugol'nogo basseina*, 2nd ed. (Syktyvkar: Komi knizhnoe izd-vo, 1989), 86–90; A. A. Chernov, *Poleznye iskopaemye Pechorskogo kraia s pai-khoem, vaigachem i iuznoi ostrovom novoi zemli* (Arkhangel'sk: Kraiplan, 1935), 21.

2. Chernov, *Iz istorii otkrytiia*, 94.

3. GURK NARK 1, f. R-1668, op. 1, d. 77, l. 73.

4. Antipov, "O gornykh izsledovaniiakh v Pechorskom kraie, proizvdennykh v 1857 godu," *Gornyi zhurnal* 4 (1858): 1–37; N. N. Mamadyshskii, *Ussinskii krai podvorno-ekonomicheskoe izsliedovanie poselenii r. Ussy Pechorskago uiezda v 1909 g.* (Arkhangel'sk: Gub. tip., 1910); S. V. Martynov, *Pechorskii krai* (S.-Peterburg: Tip. M. M. Stasiulevicha, 1905); Chernov, *Iz istorii otkrytiia*, 10–11.

5. Chernov, *Iz istorii otkrytiia*, 13–14.

6. Ibid., 18.

7. A. A. Chernov, *Geologicheskie stroenie i vazhneishchie poleznye iskopaemye Komi oblasti* (Viatka: GSNKh, 1926), 7; Chernov, *Iz istorii otkrytiia*, 19–25.

8. For more on the discovery of coal in Vorkuta, see Alan Barenberg, "'Discovering' Vorkuta: Science and Colonization in the Early Gulag," *Gulag Studies* 4 (2011): 21–40.

9. On the connections between the first five-year plan and the creation of the Gulag, see Lynne Viola, "Stalin's Empire: The Gulag and Police Colonization in the Soviet Union in the 1930s," in *Stalinism and Europe: Terror, War, Domination, 1937–1947*, ed. Tim Snyder (New York: Oxford University Press, forthcoming); Den Khili [Dan Healey], "Nasledie Gulaga: Prinuditel'nyi trud sovetskoi epokhi kak vnutrenniaia kolonizatsiia," in *Tam, vnutri: Praktiki vnutrennei kolonizatsii v kul'turnoi istorii Rossii*, ed. Aleksandr Etkind, Dirk Uffelmann, and Il'ia Kukulin (Moscow: Novoe literaturnoe obozrenie, 2012), 684–728; Nick Baron, "Conflict and Complicity: The Expansion of the Karelian Gulag, 1923–1933," *Cahiers du Monde Russe* 42, no. 2/4 (2001): 615–47; James R. Harris, "The Growth of the Gulag: Forced Labor in the Urals Region, 1929–31," *Russian Review* 56, no. 2 (1997): 265–80.

10. Iurii Nikolaevich Afanas'ev and V. P. Kozlov, eds., *Istoriia stalinskogo Gulaga: Konets 1920-kh–pervaia polovina 1950-kh godov*, 7 vols. (Moscow: ROSSPEN, 2004), 2: 58–59.

11. O. V. Khlevniuk, *The History of the Gulag: From Collectivization to the Great Terror* (New Haven: Yale University Press, 2004), 23–24; Afanas'ev and Kozlov, eds., *Istoriia stalinskogo Gulaga*, 2: 80–81; Lynne Viola, *The Unknown Gulag: The Lost World of Stalin's Special Settlements* (New York: Oxford University Press, 2007), chap. 3.

12. RGASPI f. 17, op. 3, d. 817, l. 17.

13. RGASPI f. 17, op. 3, d. 821, l. 3.

14. Chernov, *Iz istorii otkrytiia*, 94.

15. GURK NARK 1, f. R-1668, op. 1, d. 77, ll. 28ob., 73.

16. Further scientific study included a visit by botanist B. N. Gorodkov in the summer of 1931. His research claimed that the soil, which was permafrost deeper than 30 meters, would be advantageous to mine construction. B. N. Gorodkov, *Vechnaia merzlota v severnom krae* (Leningrad: AN SSSR, 1932), 8–9, 102–3. The study of soil conditions continued in 1932. G. F. Pisarev and N. G. Datskii, *Vechnaia merzlota i usloviia stroitel'stva v Usinskoi lesotundre* (Leningrad: AN SSSR, 1934).

17. GURK NARK 1, f. R-1668, op. 1, d. 86, l. 45.

18. Chernov, *Iz istorii otkrytiia*, 110–11.

19. Viola, *Unknown Gulag*, 9–10, 188–90.

20. RGASPI f. 17, op. 3, d. 875, l. 6.

21. V. G. Nevskii, ed. *Pokaianie: Komi respublikanskii martirolog zhertv massovykh politicheskikh repressii*, 9 vols. (Syktyvkar: Komi knizhnoe izd-vo, 1998–2009), 8, pt. 3: 128–29, 131, 147.

22. Ibid., 8, pt. 3: 132–33, 140–41.

23. Ibid., 8, pt. 3: 141.

24. Maksim Gorky, Leopold Leonidovich Averbakh, and Semen Georgievich Firin, eds., *Belomorsko-Baltiiskii kanal imeni tov. Stalina* (Moscow: Belomostroi, 1933).

25. Steven A. Barnes, *Death and Redemption: The Gulag and the Shaping of Soviet Society* (Princeton: Princeton University Press, 2011), 36–38.

26. A. N. Kaneva, "Ukhtpechlag: Stranitsy istorii," in Nevskii, ed., *Pokaianie*, 8, pt. 1: 93.

27. Nevskii, ed., *Pokaianie*, 8, pt. 3: 147, 149.

28. Kaneva, "Ukhtpechlag," 95.

29. Nevskii, ed., *Pokaianie*, 8, pt. 3: 149.

30. GURK NARK 1, f. R-1668, op. 1, d. 77, ll. 28ob, 73.

31. Nevskii, ed., *Pokaianie*, 8, pt. 3: 147, 149.

32. VMVTs, f. OF, d. 1057/10, l. 2. K. Plastinina, a non-prisoner who made the journey in 1936, recalled that it took two months in total. VMVTs, f. OF, d. 1057/12, l. 1.

33. VMVTs, f. OF, d. 1066, ll. 1–13. In some winters, like that of 1939–40, not a single train was able to pass between Rudnik and the supply depot at Vorkuta-Vom because it was impossible to clear the railroad of snow. VMVTs, f. OF, d. 1057/14, l. 4.

34. Fyodor Vasilevich Mochulsky, *Gulag Boss: A Soviet Memoir*, trans. Deborah A. Kaple (New York: Oxford University Press, 2011), chap. 4.

35. Such projects include, for example, the Kuibyshev hydroelectric complex, begun in 1937 and abandoned in 1940. Khlevniuk, *History of the Gulag*, 336.

36. M. Baital'skii, *Notebooks for the Grandchildren: Recollections of a Trotskyist Who Survived the Stalin Terror* (Atlantic Highlands, NJ: Humanities Press, 1995), 97.

37. Ibid., 136–41.

38. Ibid., 176–98.

39. Ibid., 198–208.

40. A. B. Roginskii, M. B. Smirnov, and N. G. Okhotin, *Sistema ispravitel'no-trudovykh lagerei v SSSR, 1923–1960: Spravochnik* (Moscow: "Zven'ia", 1998), 498.

41. J. Arch Getty and Oleg V. Naumov, *The Road to Terror: Stalin and the Self-Destruction of the Bolsheviks, 1932–1939* (New Haven: Yale University Press, 1999), chap. 7.

42. Afanas'ev and Kozlov, eds., *Istoriia stalinskogo Gulaga*, 4: 69–70.

43. Nevskii, ed., *Pokaianie*, 8, pt. 1: 187; J. Arch Getty, Gabor T. Rittersporn, and Viktor N. Zemskov, "Victims of the Soviet Penal System in the Pre-War Years: A First Approach on the Basis of Archival Evidence," *American Historical Review* 98, no. 4 (1993): 1048.

44. Barnes, *Death and Redemption*, 84.

45. Nevskii, ed., *Pokaianie*, 7: 100. Quotation from 107.

46. Ibid., 7: 107–11.

47. On the regime for "politicals" in imperial and early Soviet prisons, see G. M. Ivanova, *Gulag v sisteme totalitarnogo gosudarstva* (Moscow: Moskovskii

obshchestvennyi nauchnyi fond, 1997), chap. 1; Michael Jakobson, *Origins of the Gulag: The Soviet Prison Camp System, 1917–1934* (Lexington: University Press of Kentucky, 1993), 114–17.

48. Historian Mikhail Rogachev, who had access to the Komi police archives, managed to compile a list of 191 confirmed participants, based largely on files compiled in 1937–38 during the "mass operations" of the Great Terror. Nevskii, ed., *Pokaianie*, 7: 121–35. On the organized nature of the hunger strike, see witness testimony from the Komi FSB archives in ibid., 7: 113–15.

49. Ibid., 7: 102.

50. Ibid., 7: 115.

51. Ibid., 7: 104.

52. Ibid., 7: 118.

53. This is what Mikhail Rogachev, the leading historian of the strike, concludes. Ibid., 7: 104–5.

54. For example, camp guards broke up a meeting in a barracks in Rudnik on 20 May 1937 where prisoners discussed the poor conditions in the camp and decided to elect their own "elder." In response, two alleged ringleaders were confined to the internal camp prison for fifteen days each. Ibid., 7: 118–19.

55. M. Iunge, Bernd Bonwetsch, and Rolf Binner, eds., *Stalinizm v sovetskoi provintsii, 1937–1938 gg.: Massovaia operatsiia na osnove prikaza 00447* (Moskva: ROSSPEN, 2009), 44.

56. David R. Shearer, *Policing Stalin's Socialism: Repression and Social Order in the Soviet Union, 1924–1953* (New Haven: Yale University Press; Stanford: Hoover Institution, Stanford University, 2009), chap. 10.

57. Khlevniuk, *History of the Gulag*, 165.

58. Getty, Rittersporn, and Zemskov, "Victims of the Soviet Penal System," 1048.

59. GURK NARK 1, f. R-1668, op. 1, d. 485, l. 4 ob.; GURK NARK 1, f. R-1668, op. 1, d. 416, l. 112.

60. GARF, f. R-9414, op. 1 ch. 2, d. 360, l. 289ob.

61. One historian has even gone so far as to describe the Gulag camps of this time as functionally equivalent to "extermination" camps. Khlevniuk, *History of the Gulag*, 170–81. Quotation from 170.

62. Ibid., 175–76.

63. Ibid., 170.

64. Nevskii, ed., *Pokaianie*, 7: 187.

65. Ibid., 7: 188.

66. It is difficult to determine with precision exactly how many prisoners were arrested and executed under this operation, because of sloppy recordkeeping and procedures during the operation. For example, some prisoners were found to have been convicted two or three times by the "troika," and some of those convicted had been released, transferred, or had already died. Some prisoners were mistakenly shot, whereas the names of four prisoners appear twice in the list of those executed. Ibid., 7: 192–95.

67. Ibid., 7: 194.

68. Ibid., 7: 190.

69. This appears to be consistent with how operational order no. 00447 was implemented across the Soviet Union, where it was often used by regional and local authorities to eliminate potentially problematic populations that might be difficult to get rid of using standard procedures. Iunge, Bonwetsch, and Binner, eds., *Stalinizm v sovetskoi provintsii*, 46.

70. Nevskii, ed., *Pokaianie*, 7: 196; Baital'skii, *Notebooks for the Grandchildren*, 218–26.

71. Nevskii, ed., *Pokaianie*, 7: 203.

72. Ibid., 7: 204. Kashketin's name is closely associated with the executions. He was soon promoted and allegedly planned a second, much larger round of executions in Ukhtpechlag. However, Kashketin was arrested after the fall of Nikolai Ezhov in November 1938. He was executed on 9 March 1940. Ibid., 7: 209.

73. Ibid., 7: 204.

74. V. M. Poleshchikov, *Za sem'iu pechatiami: Iz arkhiva KGB* (Syktyvkar: Komi knizhnoe izd-vo, 1995), 13–15.

75. Nevskii, ed., *Pokaianie*, 7: 205.

76. Ibid., 7: 201–3.

77. Kaneva, "Ukhtpechlag," 141, 143. Signs that the director was in trouble emerged as early as May 1937, when he was removed from membership in the Obkom, surely an ominous sign.

78. GARF, f. R-9401, op. 1a, d. 15, ll. 106–106ob.; Kaneva, "Ukhtpechlag," 142.

79. GARF, f. R-9401, op. 1a, d. 22, ll. 67–67ob.

80. Khlevniuk, *History of the Gulag*, 119–22, 175–77.

81. Kaneva, "Ukhtpechlag," 144.

82. For example, Eduard Berzin, the longtime head of *Dal'stroi* in Kolyma, was arrested in December 1937. Roginskii, Smirnov, and Okhotin, *Sistema ispravitel'no-trudovykh lagerei v SSSR*, 120. According to Pavel Grebeniuk, Berzin's fall may have been connected to Stalin's dislike for his long-term plans for Kolyma. Such plans called for the construction of a rail link from Kolyma to the "mainland" and the complete transition of Dal'stroi to a non-prisoner labor force by 1947. Pavel Grebeniuk, *Kolymskii led: Sistema upravleniia na severo-vostoke Rossii, 1953–1964* (Moscow: ROSSPEN, 2007), 29–30.

83. VMVTs, f. OF, d. 1057/14, l. 3.

84. In fact, until 23 October 1940 Vorkuta was technically part of the Nenets autonomous district of Arkhangel'sk oblast', rather than Komi ASSR. RGASPI, f. 17, op. 116, d. 60, l. 12.

85. GURK NARK 1, f. R-1668, op. 1, d. 416, l. 112. For instance, Rudnik was 480 kilometers from the central Ukhtpechlag administration in Chib'iu, and they communicated solely by radio. On long-distance communication between camp sections, see Mochulsky, *Gulag Boss*, 29.

86. Vladimir Vasil'evich Zubchaninov, *Uvidennoe i perezhitoe* (Moscow: RAN In-t mirovoi ekonomiki i mezhdunar. otnoshenii, 1995), 92.

87. See the 2 August 1939 "Temporary instruction on the imprisonment regime for prisoners in NKVD ITLs," in Aleksandr Kokurin and N. V. Petrov, eds.,

GULAG (Glavnoe upravlenie lagerei), 1917–1960 (Moscow: "Demokratiia", 2000), 457.

88. Ivan Gronskii, *Iz proshlogo* (Moscow: Izvestiia, 1991), 175.

89. V. I. Il'in, "Gorod-kontslager': Sotsial'naia stratifikatsiia gulagovskoi vorkuty (1930–50-e gody)," in *Stratifikatsiia v Rossii: Istoriia i sovremennost'*, ed. Iu. M. Rapaport (Syktyvkar: izd-vo SyktGU, 1999), 51.

90. Mikhail Baital'skii stated in his memoirs that there were delays in introducing barbed wire because a barge full of it sank on its way to Vorkuta, therefore delaying its introduction for a year. Baital'skii, *Notebooks for the Grandchildren*, 232.

91. Vorkutstroi contrasts sharply with Dal'stroi, an organization that had sole authority over the vast territory of Kolyma in the far northeast, including multiple camps, enterprises, and towns. Grebeniuk, *Kolymskii led*, 17–45; David J. Nordlander, "Origins of a Gulag Capital: Magadan and Stalinist Control in the Early 1930s," *Slavic Review* 57, no. 4 (1998): 791–812; David J. Nordlander, "Magadan and the Economic History of Dalstroi in the 1930s," in *The Economics of Forced Labor*, ed. Paul R. Gregory and V. V. Lazarev (Stanford: Hoover Institution Press, 2003), 105–26.

92. Zubchaninov, *Uvidennoe i perezhitoe*, 96.

93. RGASPI, f. 17, op. 3, d. 1023, ll. 7, 67–72; RGASPI, f. 17, op. 3, d. 1025, ll. 5–6. Drafts of the 10 May resolution with editing by Lavrentii Beriia can be found in GARF R-5446, op. 24a, d. 22, ll. 47–44.

94. See Appendix C, table C.1; *Narodnoe khoziaistvo SSSR v 1956 godu* (Moscow: Gos. stat. izd-vo, 1957), 72.

95. Khlevniuk, *History of the Gulag*, 242–43; Roginskii, Smirnov, and Okhotin, *Sistema ispravitel'no-trudovykh lagerei v SSSR*, 46.

96. Roginskii, Smirnov, and Okhotin, *Sistema ispravitel'no-trudovykh lagerei v SSSR*, 108–9.

97. Ibid., 387.

98. GARF, f. R-9401, op. 1a, d. 93, ll. 147–47ob.

99. VMVTs, f. NVF, d. 3766/087, l. 1.

100. RGASPI, f. 17, op. 116, d. 60, l. 12.

101. Detailed planning and construction of the railroad was initiated by Sovnarkom resolution no. 1952–343, dated 28 October 1937. For a description of the resolution and accompanying report, see Raisa Glushchenko, ed. *Pechorstroi: Istoriia sozdaniia, 1940–2000* (Pechora: Pechorskoe vremia, 2000), 11–13. The rail line, it should be noted, was intended to link the growing camp centers of Vorkuta, Inta, Pechora, and Ukhta to points southwest, not to the Komi capital Syktyvkar. In fact, Syktyvkar was not linked by rail to the Northern Pechora main line until the early 1960s.

102. On Frenkel's career, see Aleksandr Isaevich Solzhenitsyn, *The Gulag Archipelago, 1918–1956*, 3 vols. (New York: Harper & Row, 1974), 2: 75–80; Ivanova, *Gulag v sisteme totalitarnogo gosudarstva*, 91–92; Thomas Lahusen, *How Life Writes the Book: Real Socialism and Socialist Realism in Stalin's Russia* (Ithaca: Cornell University Press, 1997), 50–51; Khlevniuk, *History of the Gulag*, 35.

According to Solzhenitsyn, Frenkel formulated the scheme by which prisoners were classified according to physical capabilities, and also devised the system of graduated rations, whereby the amount prisoners were fed depended on their economic performance.

103. GARF, f. R-9401, op. 1a, d. 0056, ll. 197–200.

104. For a fascinating, if one-sided account of Sevpechlag during the construction of the rail line, see Mochulsky, *Gulag Boss.*

105. Roginskii, Smirnov, and Okhotin, *Sistema ispravitel'no-trudovykh lagerei v SSSR*, 192.

106. A list of Poles imprisoned in camps of the Pechora coal basin can be found in Agnieszka Knyt, ed. *Wiezniowie lagrów w rejonie Workuty*, 2 vols. (Wilno: "Memorial", 1999–2001), 1: 57–439.

107. V. P. Iampol'skii, ed. *Organy gosudarstvennoi bezopasnosti SSSR v Velikoi Otechestvennoi voine: Sbornik dokumentov*, 2 vols. (Moscow: Rus', 2000), 2, book 2: 404. On the amnesty, see ibid., 2, book 1: 477.

108. See Appendix A, table A.2.1; Getty, Rittersporn, and Zemskov, "Victims of the Soviet Penal System," 1048.

109. See Appendix A, table A.3.1.

110. See Appendix A, table A.4.1; J. Otto Pohl, *The Stalinist Penal System: A Statistical History of Soviet Repression and Terror, 1930–1953* (Jefferson, NC: McFarland, 1997), 36–37.

111. GURK NARK 1, f. R-605, op. 3, d. 69, l. 61ob.

112. Once the war began, guards were recruited from those declared unfit for combat within Komi ASSR, and so a large proportion of them were disabled in some way. Il'in, "Gorod-kontslager'," 56–57.

113. Vladimir Il'in writes that of 2,530 non-prisoners "working in construction in 1942," 1,412 (or 56 percent) were former prisoners. Ibid., 55.

114. Zubchaninov, *Uvidennoe i perezhitoe*, 46, 51.

115. Ibid., 90.

116. Ibid., 158.

117. VMVTs, f. OF, d. 1702, 3 February 1968, l. 1.

118. VMVTs, f. OF, d. 1702, 16 May 1968, l. 1.

119. VMVTs, f. OF, d. 1702, 27 May 1968, ll. 2–3.

120. Mikhail Baital'skii was released in early 1941 and made his way to Kirov before war broke out, where he lived until his second arrest in 1950. Baital'skii, *Notebooks for the Grandchildren*, 239–40, 264.

121. VMVTs, f. NVF, d. 3766–098, l. 1.

122. GURK NARK 2, f. 392, op. 2, d. 72, l. 2.

123. GURK NARK 2, f. 392, op. 2, d. 72, l. 8. The 1942 total population figure comes from GARF, f. R-9414, op. 1 ch. 2, d. 370.

124. Jacques Rossi gives the following definition: "*propusknik*, 'pass-holder,' unescorted prisoner (with a pass; see *beskonvoinyi*)." Jacques Rossi, *The Gulag Handbook*, trans. William A. Burhans (New York: Paragon House, 1989), 343–44. Synonyms given by Rossi include *raskonvoirovannyi* ("not transported under convoy"), *bezkonvoinyi* ("without a convoy"), and *vol'nokhozhdenets* ("free mover"). In using the term "de-convoyed" I follow Wilson T. Bell, "Was the Gulag an Ar-

chipelago? De-Convoyed Prisoners and Porous Borders in the Camps of Western Siberia," *Russian Review* 72, no. 1 (2013): 116–41.

125. The singular form of this term, *zazonnik*, translates literally, but awkwardly, as "one who lives outside the zone." Describing prisoners in the 1940s as de-zoned is probably anachronistic, as it appears to have come into use only in the 1950s. However, it is useful to apply the term to prisoners living outside the zone in the 1940s in order to draw the reader's attention to the continuity of practices throughout the life of the Soviet prison-camp system.

126. Kokurin and Petrov, eds., *GULAG, 1917–1960*, 458, 462–64.

127. GURK NARK 2, f. 392, op. 2, d. 72, l. 7.

128. GURK NARK 2, f. 1875, op. 1, d. 48, l. 59.

129. Kokurin and Petrov, eds., *GULAG, 1917–1960*, 458.

130. For instance, one non-prisoner named Skorokhod was criticized in June 1940 in a speech by A. I. Zakhlamin, the head of the Vorkutlag politotdel, for having a particularly close relationship with a prisoner. The charge leveled was that the orderly that worked for Skorokhod remained with the family in their apartment when Skorokhod was away on vacation. GURK NARK 2, f. 1875, op. 1, d. 18, l. 31.

131. AUIN MIu RF po RK, f. 1, op. 3, d. 7059, l. 35.

132. GURK NARK 2, f. 392, op. 2, d. 72, l. 3.

133. GURK NARK 2, f. 1875, op. 1, d. 24, l. 4.

134. VMVTs, f. OF, op. 2985, d. 1–4, l. 60.

135. *Narodnoe khoziaistvo SSSR v 1956 godu*, 74.

136. John Barber and Mark Harrison, *The Soviet Home Front, 1941–1945: A Social and Economic History of the USSR in World War II* (New York: Longman, 1991), 185.

137. Mochulsky, *Gulag Boss*, 77.

138. See Appendix A, table A.6.1.

139. GARF, f. R-8361, op. 1, d. 45, l. 19.

140. GARF, f. R-9414, op. 1 ch. 2, d. 382, ll. 1–1ob.

141. GARF, f. R-9414, op. 1, d. 1227, l. 158.

142. GARF, f. R-9414, op. 1, d. 1227, ll. 159–60.

143. GARF, f. R-9414, op. 1, d. 328, l. 6.

144. GARF, f. R-9414, op. 1 ch. 2, d. 428, l. 14.

145. GARF, f. R-9414, op. 1, d. 328, l. 48.

146. Afanas'ev and Kozlov, eds., *Istoriia stalinskogo Gulaga*, 4: 102–3.

147. GURK NARK 2, f. 392, op. 2, d. 72, l. 60.

148. M. B. Rogachev, "Usinskaia tragediia: Ianvar' 1942 goda," *Rodniki parmy* 4 (1996): 212, 216; Poleshchikov, *Za sem'iu pechatiami*, 40; Nevskii, ed., *Pokaianie*, 7: 176; Zubchaninov, *Uvidennoe i perezhitoe*, 122.

149. Aleksandr Solzhenitsyn refers to the uprising briefly in *Gulag Archipelago* as the "Retyunin affair of January 1942." Although he is short on details, he does point out the remarkable fact that Retiunin was a non-prisoner. Solzhenitsyn, *Gulag Archipelago*, 3: 228–29. Short accounts also appear in Steven A. Barnes, "All for the Front, All for Victory! The Mobilization of Forced Labor in the Soviet Union during World War Two," *International Labor and Working-Class History*

58 (2000): 249–50; Ivanova, *Gulag v sisteme totalitarnogo gosudarstva*, 54. An account of the uprising that includes long quotations from the official verdict in the case against the rebels (without any archival citations) can be found in Irina Osipova, "Otriad osobogo naznacheniia no. 41," in *Soprotivlenie v GULAGe*, ed. Semen Samuilovich Vilenskii (Moscow: Vozvrashchenie, 1992), 132–44. V. M. Poleshchikov, a former KGB officer, wrote an account of the uprising based on a variety of archival sources, including the reports of camp informers. His publication is very useful in that it reprints some of these reports verbatim, albeit without archival citations. Poleshchikov, *Za sem'iu pechatiami*, 37–65. The most complete published secondary source on the rebellion is Rogachev, "Usinskaia tragediia," 210–22. Rogachev also published a collection of documents (with commentary) on the rebellion in Nevskii, ed., *Pokaianie*, 7: 165–209.

150. Nevskii, ed., *Pokaianie*, 7: 176.

151. Ibid., 7: 171.

152. Ibid., 7: 178.

153. Ibid., 7: 209. Murmillo was later shot for his role in aiding the rebels.

154. Ibid., 7: 179.

155. Ibid., 7: 179–80.

156. Rogachev, "Usinskaia tragediia," 218.

157. According to Rogachev, this was after "getting fairly drunk." Ibid., 218–19.

158. GARF, f. R-9414, op. 1, d. 45, ll. 102–3; GURK NARK 2, f. 392, op. 2, d. 72, l. 56.

159. Rogachev, "Usinskaia tragediia," 219. GURK NARK 2, f. 392, op. 2, d. 72, l. 64.

160. GURK NARK 2, f. 392, op. 2, d. 72, l. 64.

161. Nevskii, ed., *Pokaianie*, 7: 181.

162. Ibid., 7: 166–74.

163. Ibid., 7: 181–82.

164. Rogachev, "Usinskaia tragediia," 212; Zubchaninov, *Uvidennoe i perezhitoe*, 93.

165. GURK NARK 2, f. 1875, op. 1, d. 48, l. 43. This was also the case in other camps at this time. Mochulsky, *Gulag Boss*, 46.

166. As Zubchaninov remembered, "I met the head of the [Leso]*reid* Retiunin. . . . He served his sentence in the Vorkuta mines, where he headed one of the best mining brigades. After he was released he was made the chief first of a small lumber operation and now of the Ust'-Usa reid. His gait was reminiscent of a bear, his head, covered with shaggy red hair, inclined forward slightly, and his eyes stared like those of a bear. But he was a romantic. In his hut, which stood on top of tall piles, lay a volume of Shakespeare [which he could recite from memory]." Zubchaninov, *Uvidennoe i perezhitoe*, 93.

167. Tarkhanov's comments were reported to Kabakov, the Narkom NKVD Komi ASSR from his deputy Kornilov in February 1942. According to Kornilov, Tarkhanov described Retiunin in such a fashion on 30 January, nearly a week after the rebellion began. GURK NARK 2, f. 392, op. 2, d. 72, l. 17.

168. Nevskii, ed., *Pokaianie*, 2: 783; Rogachev, "Usinskaia tragediia," 212.

169. GURK NARK 2, f. 392, op. 2, d. 72, l. 58; Rogachev, "Usinskaia tragediia," 212–13.

170. Poleshchikov, *Za sem'iu pechatiami*, 43.

171. GURK NARK 2, f. 392, op. 2, d. 72, l. 58; A. L. Voitolovskaia, *Po sledam sud'by moego pokoleniia* (Syktyvkar: Komi knizhnoe izd-vo, 1991), 98–99; Poleshchikov, *Za sem'iu pechatiami*, 43; Nevskii, ed., *Pokaianie*, 7: 181–82.

172. Excerpts from this confession can be found in Poleshchikov, *Za sem'iu pechatiami*, 59–60.

173. Nevskii, ed., *Pokaianie*, 7: 204–6.

174. Mochulsky, *Gulag Boss*, chap. 19; A. F. Anufriev and V. D. Zakharov, "Vrazheskii desant na Pechore," in *Kniga pamiati Respubliki Komi: Imena voinov, ubitykh v boiakh, umershikh ot ran v gospitaliakh, propavshikh bez vesti v gody Velikoi Otechestvennoi voiny (1941–1945 gg.), zemliakov Komi i prizvannykh voenkomatami respubliki*, ed. Valentin Mikhailovich Kotel'nikov and Antonina Makarovna Kalimova (Syktyvkar: Komi respublikanskaia tip., 1996), 379–85.

175. L. Gorodin, "Odnoetapniki," *Chistye Prudy* 4 (1990): 297.

176. Cited in Nevskii, ed., *Pokaianie*, 7: 198.

177. In his memoirs, Zubchaninov described Retiunin as a "romantic," suggesting that he viewed Retiunin as a righteous, if misguided, bandit. Zubchaninov, *Uvidennoe i perezhitoe*, 93. Such views of the rebels seem consistent with Eric Hobsbawm's observations about bandits and how they are remembered. E. J. Hobsbawm, *Bandits* (New York: New Press, 2000), chap. 10.

178. GURK NARK 2, f. 392, op. 2, d. 72, l. 15.

179. Aleksandr Nikolaevich Panov, a prisoner in Lesoreid who did not participate in the uprising but was subsequently executed anyway, gave written testimony on 11 July 1942 that Retiunin warned him that new executions were imminent. Poleshchikov, *Za sem'iu pechatiami*, 49. An NKVD informant told the investigators that a former prisoner in Lesoreid had related being told by Retiunin of anticipated executions. GURK NARK 2, f. 392, op. 2, d. 72, ll. 22–23. Such testimony is corroborated by Zubchaninov, *Uvidennoe i perezhitoe*, 120–22.

180. Hobsbawm, *Bandits*, chap. 1.

181. GARF, f. R-9414, op. 1, d. 45, ll. 102–5.

182. Nevskii, ed., *Pokaianie*, 7: 204–9.

183. Ibid., 7: 200–2.

184. Ibid.

185. In 1942, Vorkutlag produced 706,000 tons of coal. The plan target was 750,000 tons of coal. GARF, f. R-8361, op. 1, d. 45, l. 2.

186. GURK NARK 1, f. R-605, op. 4, d. 48, ll. 1–23.

187. V. Velichko, "Siianie severa," *Pravda*, 26, 27, 30, 31 May 1946.

188. On *Belomor* and its composition, see Cynthia Ann Ruder, *Making History for Stalin: The Story of the Belomor Canal* (Gainesville: University Press of Florida, 1998).

189. Terry Martin, *The Affirmative Action Empire: Nations and Nationalism in the Soviet Union, 1923–1939* (Ithaca: Cornell University Press, 2001), chap. 1.

190. See, e.g., Vladimir Iakovlevich Kantorovich, *Bol'shaia Pechora* (Moscow: Molodaia gvardiia, 1934).

Chapter 2. Saving Leningrad, Defining Vorkuta

1. V. D. Zakharov, ed. *Ugol'naia sokrovishchnitsa severa: Sbornik dokumentov i materialov* (Syktyvkar: Komi kn. izd-vo, 1984), 75–76.

2. The German blockade of the city was partially lifted after Operation Spark in February 1943. David M. Glantz, *The Battle for Leningrad: 1941–1944* (Lawrence: University Press of Kansas, 2002), 286.

3. On the symbolic importance of gifts in Soviet public culture, see Jeffrey Brooks, *Thank You, Comrade Stalin!: Soviet Public Culture from Revolution to Cold War* (Princeton: Princeton University Press, 2000).

4. Karen Petrone, *Life Has Become More Joyous, Comrades: Celebrations in the Time of Stalin*, Indiana-Michigan Series in Russian and East European Studies (Bloomington: Indiana University Press, 2000).

5. *Pravda*, 18 August 1943. Note that the city of Vorkuta was not referred to by name, and the Pechora coal basin was called the Arctic coal basin.

6. Sheila Fitzpatrick, "Postwar Soviet Society: The 'Return to Normalcy,' 1945–1953," in *The Impact of World War II on the Soviet Union*, ed. Susan J. Linz (Totowa, NJ: Rowman & Allanheld, 1985), 129–56.

7. Edward Buca, *Vorkuta* (London: Constable, 1976), 49.

8. Vorkutlag and the other camps belonging to the Fuel Section of the GULZhDS (Main Administration of Railroad Construction Camps) were transferred to the GULGMP by Beriia's order on 5 October 1943. GARF R-9401, op. 1a, d. 142, l. 163.

9. GARF, f. R-9401, op. 1a, d. 142, ll. 207–11; GURK NARK 2, f. 1, op. 3, d. 1062, l. 1.

10. GARF, f. R-8361, op. 1, d. 121, ll. 7–7ob.

11. Appendix C, table C.1.

12. M. Mal'tsev, "Ogon' iz vechnoi merzloty," in *Grani otvagi i stoikosti*, ed. A. I. Usov (Syktyvkar: Komi knizhnoe izd-vo, 1978), 171. The Leningrad Gorkom stated that coal from the Pechora basin made up over 60 percent of the city's supply in 1944. GURK NARK 2, f. 1875, op. 1, d. 62, l. 85.

13. Appendix C, table C.1; *Narodnoe khoziaistvo SSSR v 1956 godu* (Moscow: Gos. stat. izd-vo, 1957), 72.

14. On changes in the Gulag population after the war, see Steven A. Barnes, *Death and Redemption: The Gulag and the Shaping of Soviet Society* (Princeton: Princeton University Press, 2011), chap. 5. On national resistance and Soviet counterinsurgency efforts in the western borderlands, see Alexander Statiev, *The Soviet Counterinsurgency in the Western Borderlands* (New York: Cambridge University Press, 2010), chaps. 4–9; David Wolff and Gaël Moullec, *Le KGB et les pays baltes: 1939–1991* (Paris: Belin, 2005), chap. 2.

15. Appendix A, table A.2.1.

16. Appendix A, table A.1.1.

17. GARF, f. R-8361, op. 1, d. 72, ll. 6ob.–7, 16.

18. Appendix A, table A.4.1. In fact, nearly half of all Lithuanian prisoners held in Gulag camps as of 1 January 1946 were held in Vorkuta. J. Otto Pohl, *The Stalinist Penal System: A Statistical History of Soviet Repression and Terror, 1930–1953* (Jefferson, NC: McFarland, 1997), 36–37.

19. This influx of prisoners changed the proportion of counterrevolutionary prisoners in the population. Whereas at the beginning of 1943 just over half of all prisoners in Vorkutlag had been convicted of such crimes, by the beginning of 1948 the proportion had risen to 70 percent. Appendix A, table A.2.1. This 1948 figure was nearly twice the average for Gulag camps across the Soviet Union, which was 38 percent. Pohl, *Stalinist Penal System*, 31.

20. Appendix A, table A.3.1.

21. Leonid Agranovich, *Stop-kadr: Meierkhol'd, Vorkuta i drugoe kino* (Moscow: Sovpadenie, 2004), 124.

22. Appendix A, table A.6.1.

23. Buca, *Vorkuta*, 70–72.

24. The rapid increase in the prison population resulted in widespread clothing shortages. For example, the camp had only 32 percent of the padded jackets required for the prisoners according to Gulag regulations. This was an essential piece of cold-weather gear for prisoners. GARF, f. R-8361, op. 1, d. 72, l. 19.

25. E. V. Markova, *Vorkutinskie zametki katorzhanki "E-105"* (Syktyvkar: Pokaianie, 2005), 49.

26. John Barber and Mark Harrison, *The Soviet Home Front, 1941–1945: A Social and Economic History of the USSR in World War II* (New York: Longman, 1991).

27. Two and a half times as many fresh vegetables arrived in the camp in 1943 as in 1942. GARF, f. R-8361, op. 1, d. 52, l. 19.

28. GARF, f. R-8361, op. 1, d. 72, l. 17.

29. Markova, *Vorkutinskie zametki*, 47.

30. According to Mal'tsev's own memoirs, he was able to increase the amount of food that Vorkuta received in 1944–1945. After an audience with Mikoian (who was in charge of domestic trade during the war) and his deputy in 1944, Vorkuta received two rail cars of glass in order to build greenhouses and was allowed to set up "decentralized purchasing of fruits and vegetables" in Tashkent, Kirov, and Gor'kii. Mal'tsev, "Ogon' iz vechnoi merzloty," 169–70.

31. Barber and Harrison, *Soviet Home Front*, 83.

32. GARF, f. R-8361, op. 1, d. 52, l. 20. The increase in local food production was possible thanks to a relatively warm summer in 1943.

33. Appendix A, table A.1.1.

34. Markova, *Vorkutinskie zametki*, 61–64. Markova was saved when a nonprisoner blaster, shocked to learn that a woman had been assigned such a job, intervened on her behalf.

35. On the treatment of women in the camps, including the risk of rape and sexual assault, see Barnes, *Death and Redemption*, 97–105.

36. E. A. Zaitsev, ed. *Sbornik zakonodatel'nykh i normativnikh aktov o repressiakh i reabilitatsii zhertv politicheskikh repressii* (Moscow: Izd-vo "Respublika", 1993), 43.

37. Iurii Nikolaevich Afanas'ev and V. P. Kozlov, eds., *Istoriia stalinskogo Gulaga: Konets 1920-kh–pervaia polovina 1950-kh godov*, 7 vols. (Moscow: ROSSPEN, 2004), 2: 220–21.

38. Andrew Armand Gentes, *Exile to Siberia, 1590–1822: Corporeal Commodification and Administrative Systematization in Russia* (New York: Palgrave Macmillan, 2008).

39. Barnes, *Death and Redemption*, 143.

40. Afanas'ev and Kozlov, eds., *Istoriia stalinskogo Gulaga*, 2: 220. GARF, f. R-9414, op. 1 ch. 2, d. 446, l. 6; GARF, f. R-9414, op. 1 ch. 2, d. 459, l. 9; GARF, f. R-9414, op. 1 ch. 2, d. 478, ll. 12–13.

41. Agnieszka Knyt, ed. *Wiezniowie lagrów w rejonie Workuty*, 2 vols. (Wilno: "Memorial", 1999–2001), 1: 455.

42. Markova, *Vorkutinskie zametki*, 51.

43. Aleksandr Kokurin and N. V. Petrov, eds., *GULAG (Glavnoe upravlenie lagerei), 1917–1960* (Moscow: "Demokratiia", 2000), 132–33. This was written to Beriia in response to a suggestion from Nikita Khrushchev that the use of katorga punishments and longer prison terms be increased.

44. Mal'tsev, who lived from 1908–1982, is often mischaracterized as coming to Vorkuta from a military background. Both his official autobiography and most secondary sources describe him as a career army officer before he became the director of Vorkutstroi and Vorkutlag in 1943. Mal'tsev, "Ogon' iz vechnoi merzloty," 161–62. Although he served in the military during the first two years of the war, he in fact spent the majority of his career working for the NKVD and later the MVD. A. B. Roginskii, M. B. Smirnov, and N. G. Okhotin, *Sistema ispravitel'no-trudovykh lagerei v SSSR, 1923–1960: Spravochnik* (Moscow: "Zven'ia", 1998), 251–52; Mal'tsev, "Ogon' iz vechnoi merzloty," 162.

45. The name of the organization was changed by Beriia's order on 9 March 1944, and it remains the name of the entity responsible for coal mining in Vorkuta today. GARF, f. R-9401, op. 1a, d. 158, l. 100b.

46. VMVTs, f. NVF, d. 3766/102.

47. AUIN MIu RF po RK, f. 1, op. 3, d. 7060, l. 81.

48. Vladimir Vasil'evich Zubchaninov, *Uvidennoe i perezhitoe* (Moscow: RAN In-t mirovoi ekonomiki i mezhdunar. otnoshenii, 1995), 132.

49. For an example of awards, see AUIN MIu RF po RK, f. 1, op. 3, d. 7062, l. 48. For punishments, see AUIN MIu RF po RK, f. 1, op. 3, d. 7063, l. 93.

50. Later, Kapler would become one of the most famous film critics in the Soviet Union, hosting the television program *Kinopanorama*. Thanks to Michael Khodarkovsky for setting me on the paper trail that led to Kapler.

51. Svetlana Allilueva, *Dvadtsat' pisem k drugu* (Moscow: "Izvestiia", 1990), 163–71.

52. Kapler's situation was similar to that of Boris Tseitlin, a filmmaker who worked as the photographer of Sevpechlag in nearby Abez'. Fyodor Vasilevich Mochulsky, *Gulag Boss: A Soviet Memoir*, trans. Deborah A. Kaple (New York: Oxford University Press, 2011), chap. 25.

53. *Vorkuta during the Great Patriotic War*, a pictorial representation of Vorkuta's achievements during the Second World War that was prepared for top NKVD officials, was presumably a product of Kapler's handiwork. The book can be found in GARF, f. R-9414, op. 6, d. 9. The order from 18 October 1943 to compose the book can be found in AUIN MIu RF po RK, f. 1, op. 3, d. 7060, l. 165.

54. E. Kotliar, "'Faust' v ITL," in *Teatr GULAGa*, ed. M. M. Korallova (Moscow: Memorial, 1995), 46.

55. GURK NARK 1, f. R-0605, op. 1, d. 1314, l. 53; Aleksandr Klein and A. A. Popov, "Zapoliarnaia drama . . . ," in *Pokaianie*, ed. M. B. Rogachev (Syktyvkar: Pokaianie, 1999), 2: 223.

56. Ukhtizhemlag, nearby in Ukhta, had been home to some kind of theater company since at least 1933. A. N. Kaneva, *Gulagovskii teatr Ukhty* (Syktyvkar: Komi knizhnoe izd-vo, 2001), 25. Magadan had its own theater company since 1933. A. G. Kozlov, *Teatr na severnoi zemle: Ocherki po istorii magadanskogo muzykal'no-dramaticheskogo teatra im. M. Gor'kogo (1933–1953 gg.)* (Magadan: Magadanskaia oblastnaia universal'naia nauchnaia biblioteka im. A. S. Pushkina, 1992), 13.

57. Both Fitzpatrick and Bauman emphasize the fact that patron-client relationships often develop in societies where uncertainty is a structural feature of life. Zygmunt Bauman, "Comment on Eastern Europe," *Studies in Comparative Communism* 12, nos. 2–3 (1979): 184; Sheila Fitzpatrick, *Tear off the Masks!: Identity and Imposture in Twentieth-century Russia* (Princeton: Princeton University Press, 2005), chap. 10.

58. The importance of these privileges to survival is underscored by Kapler's experience. During his second five-year term of imprisonment, he was sent to a nearby camp in Inta and barely survived years of manual labor. Agranovich, *Stop-kadr*, 134.

59. For instance, architect Vsevolod Lunev was rewarded 1,500 rubles upon the completion of one of his buildings. VMVTs, f. NVF, d. 3027/067.

60. VMVTs, f. NVF, d. 3027/44.

61. Klein and Popov, "Zapoliarnaia drama . . . ," 223.

62. By 1946, separate barracks had been set aside for the theater company. Within these barracks, the most privileged occupied corners separated by curtains, giving them a significant measure of privacy. E. B. Galinskaia, "Teatr za poliarnym krugom," *Rodniki parmy* 90 (1990): 145–46.

63. Fitzpatrick emphasizes this point as well. Fitzpatrick, *Tear off the Masks!*, 185.

64. On the connection between the Gulag, "internal colonization," and the Soviet "civilizing mission," see Den Khili [Dan Healey], "Nasledie Gulaga: Prinuditel'nyi trud sovetskoi epokhi kak vnutrenniaia kolonizatsiia," in *Tam, vnutri: Praktiki vnutrennei kolonizatsii v kul'turnoi istorii Rossii*, ed. Aleksandr Etkind, Dirk Uffelmann, and Il'ia Kukulin (Moscow: Novoe literaturnoe obozrenie, 2012), 684–728.

65. Fitzpatrick, *Tear off the Masks!*, 200. By that same token, Kapler and Mordvinov were acting much like members of the artistic intelligentsia did outside the camps. Both likely had significant previous experience participating in patronage activities that proved invaluable in navigating patron-client relationships in a new context.

66. Aleksandr Isaevich Solzhenitsyn, *The Gulag Archipelago, 1918–1956*, 3 vols. (New York: Harper & Row, 1974), 2: 552.

67. GURK NARK 2, f. 1875, op. 1, d. 82, l. 40.

68. GURK NARK 1, f. R-642, op. 1, d. 875, l. 10.

69. The fact that Ukhta, the center of Ukhtizhemlag (and one-time capital of the sprawling Ukhtpechlag, from which Vorkutpechlag was subdivided in 1938), became a city only a week before Vorkuta, on 20 November 1943, seems to suggest that the decision was not entirely his own. Mikhail Pavlovich Roshchevskii, ed. *Respublika Komi: Entsiklopediia* (Syktyvkar: Komi knizhnoe izd-vo, 1997), 3:

221. Even if he was not following direct orders, there were plenty of precedents for him to follow in creating a city alongside Vorkutlag. The capital of Dal'stroi, Magadan, was given city status in 1939. Pavel Grebeniuk, *Kolymskii led: Sistema upravleniia na severo-vostoke Rossii, 1953–1964* (Moscow: ROSSPEN, 2007), 34.

70. VMVTs, f. NVF, d. 3027/111, ll. 1–2.

71. GURK NARK 1, f. R-642, op. 1, d. 875, l. 1. The order creating the city was published in *Vedomosti Verkhovnogo Soveta SSSR*, no. 53 (24 December 1943): 4.

72. VMVTs, f. OF, d. 1702/l, 31 May 1963, l. 3.

73. VMVTs, f. OF, d. 2996/1, l. 3.

74. Ibid., l. 3. Additional details drawn from photographs of the boulevard dated 1946 published in Viacheslav Davydov, ed. *Vorkutaugol'* (Syktyvkar: OAO Komi Respublikanskaia Tipografiia, 2001), 12–15.

75. Such albums can be found in GARF, f. R-9414, op. 6.

76. AUIN MIu RF po RK, f. 1, op. 3, d. 7067, l. 321; GURK NARK 1, f. R-605, op. 1, d. 1029, l. 292; GURK NARK 1, f. R-1515, op. 1, d. 4, l. 65; GURK NARK 1, f. R-1515, op. 1, d. 5, ll. 74, 85, 96.

77. VMVTs, f. OF, d. 2996/1, ll. 2–3.

78. Ibid., l. 5.

79. Galinskaia, "Teatr za poliarnym krugom," 149.

80. AUIN MIu RF po RK, f. 1, op. 3, d. 7069, l. 16.

81. Iurii Tregubov, a prisoner in Rechlag from 1950 to 1952 who worked in a brigade that renovated barracks, commented that the barracks for ordinary nonprisoners were much worse than those for prisoners. Iurii A. Tregubov, *Vosem' let vo vlasti Lubianki*, 2nd ed.(Frankfurt am Main: Posev, 2001), 193–94.

82. See Appendix B, table B.1.

83. The first group of three hundred arrived in May 1943. GARF, f. R-9479, op. 1, d. 128, l. 34.

84. The first of these orders came from the State Defense Committee on 10 January 1942 and affected all men of German nationality between the ages of seventeen and fifty who had been exiled to the Novosibirsk, Omsk, Krasnoiarsk, and Altai regions, as well as to Kazakhstan. Nikolai Fedorovich Bugai, *"Mobilizovat' nemtsev v rabochie kolonny—I. Stalin": Sbornik dokumentov (1940-e gody)* (Moscow: Gotika, 1998), 39–40. It was followed by several other orders over the next two years. The text of many of these orders can be found in ibid., pt. 1. For a summary of the labor conscription of ethnic Germans, see Barnes, *Death and Redemption*, 148–51.

85. GARF, f. R-8361, op. 1, d. 72, l. 16.

86. Afanas'ev and Kozlov, eds., *Istoriia stalinskogo Gulaga*, 5: 471. The official order to move the "mobilized" Germans out of the zone did not arrive until March 1946, however. GARF, f. R-9479, op. 1, d. 154, l. 83.

87. GARF, f. R-9479, op. 1, d. 217, l. 285.

88. GARF, f. R-8361, op. 1, d. 52, l. 6. Afanas'ev and Kozlov, eds., *Istoriia stalinskogo Gulaga*, 2: 242.

89. AUIN MIu RF po RK, f. 1, op. 3, d. 7066, l. 195.

90. Afanas'ev and Kozlov, eds., *Istoriia stalinskogo Gulaga*, 2: 250.

91. By July 1945, 10,695 "repatriates" had been sent to Vorkuta. Of these, 2,219 had already been sentenced to exile. GARF, f. R-9414, op. 1, d. 1248, l. 54.

92. GARF, f. R-9414, op. 1, d. 1265, l. 11.

93. GARF, f. R-8361, op. 1, d. 110, l. 36.

94. Afanas'ev and Kozlov, eds., *Istoriia stalinskogo Gulaga*, 2: 250.

95. This concept was introduced by Golfo Alexopoulos. Golfo Alexopoulos, "Amnesty 1945: The Revolving Door of Stalin's Gulag," *Slavic Review* 64, no. 2 (2005): 275.

96. An authoritative analysis of the amnesty and its implications can be found in ibid., 274–306. For the text of the amnesty, see I. T. Goliakov, *Sbornik dokumentov po istorii ugolovnogo zakonodatel'stva SSSR i RSFSR, 1917–1952 gg.* (Moscow: Gos. izd-vo iurid. lit-ry, 1953), 426–27. In Vorkuta, 10,900 prisoners were released under the amnesty. GARF, f. R-9414, op. 1, d. 1246, l. 2.

97. On releases and categorization, see Golfo Alexopoulos, "Exiting the Gulag after the War: Women, Invalids, and the Family," *Jahrbücher für Geschichte Osteuropas* 57, no. 4 (2009): 563–79.

98. GARF, f. R-9401, op. 1a, d. 158, l. 100b.

99. Skakovskaia refers to her mother as a *peresidchitsa*, literally one who has overstayed her term. I. Skakovskaia, "O Vorkute i vorkutianiakh," *Volia* 8–9 (2002): 58. Jacques Rossi refers to a *peresidchik* as a "prisoner not released upon sentence expiration." Jacques Rossi, *The Gulag Handbook*, trans. William A. Burhans (New York: Paragon House, 1989), 301. On prisoners not released during the war, see chapter 1.

100. Skakovskaia, "O Vorkute i vorkutianiakh," 60.

101. Ibid., 59.

102. In 1947 alone the company performed nearly six hundred times. GURK NARK 1, f. R-0605, op. 1, d. 1314, l. 53. The company prepared as many as thirteen new productions per year. Galinskaia, "Teatr za poliarnym krugom," 143.

103. One historian has suggested that, at certain times at least, it became the custom for audiences *not* to applaud the performances. Galinskaia, "Teatr za poliarnym krugom," 146.

104. Kotliar, "'Faust' v ITL," 50. This remarkable conversation raises another dimension of patron-client relationships: to what degree did participation in a system of privileges corrupt prisoners?

105. B. L. Afanas'ev, ed., *Pechorskii ugol'nyi bassein* (Leningrad: Lenizdat, 1959), 51.

106. While I was working at the Vorkuta municipal archives in July 2004, the archivists put together a small exhibition on the city's contribution to the Second World War. Although it paid tribute at length to camp director Mal'tsev, it failed to mention the existence of a prison camp at all.

107. See, e.g., Amir Weiner, *Making Sense of War: The Second World War and the Fate of the Bolshevik Revolution* (Princeton: Princeton University Press, 2001).

108. V. Velichko, "Siianie severa," *Pravda*, 26, 27, 30, 31 May 1946.

109. V. Evgrafov, "Gorod za poliarnym krugom," *Ogonëk* 45 (1947).

CHAPTER 3. IN SEARCH OF "NORMALCY"

1. The indoor pool was built nearby on Lenin Street and completed in 1957. "Plavatel'nyi bassein v zapoliar'e," *Zapoliar'e*, 22 June 1957.

2. VMVTs, f. OF, d. 3111, l. 1.

3. VMVTs, f. OF, d. 2996/2, ll. 21, 27; GURK NARK 2, f. 2216, op. 1, d. 1, l. 44.

4. This figure is a composite of data gleaned from GURK NARK 1, f. R-1941, op. 1, d. 22, ll. 17, 20, 32, 44, 52, 58, 64; GURK NARK 1, f. R-1941, op. 1, d. 31, ll. 4–40; GURK NARK 1, f. R-1941, op. 1, d. 40, l. 9; GURK NARK 1, f. R-1941, op. 1, d. 53, ll. 1–2; GURK NARK 1, f. R-1941, op. 1, d. 64, ll. 3–4, 57.

5. On demobilization, see Mark Edele, *Soviet Veterans of the Second World War: A Popular Movement in an Authoritarian Society, 1941–1991* (New York: Oxford University Press, 2008), chaps. 1–3. On the famine see V. F. Zima, *Golod v SSSR, 1946–1947 godov: Proiskhozhdeniie i posledstviia* (Moscow: Institut Rossiiskoi Istorii RAN, 1996); Elena Zubkova, *Russia after the War: Hopes, Illusions, and Disappointments, 1945–1957* (Armonk, NY: M. E. Sharpe, 1998), chap. 4; Donald Filtzer, *Soviet Workers and Late Stalinism: Labour and the Restoration of the Stalinist System after World War II* (Cambridge: Cambridge University Press, 2002), chap. 2. On the end of rationing, see ibid., chap. 3. On the restoration of industry see Yoram Gorlizki and O. V. Khlevniuk, *Cold Peace: Stalin and the Soviet Ruling Circle, 1945–1953* (New York: Oxford University Press, 2004), 52–58, 69.

6. Zubkova calls this "the crisis of postwar expectations." Zubkova, *Russia after the War*, chap. 10.

7. Sheila Fitzpatrick, "Postwar Soviet Society: The 'Return to Normalcy,' 1945–1953," in *The Impact of World War II on the Soviet Union*, ed. Susan J. Linz (Totowa, NJ: Rowman & Allanheld, 1985), 129–56.

8. M. Baital'skii, *Notebooks for the Grandchildren: Recollections of a Trotskyist Who Survived the Stalin Terror* (Atlantic Highlands, NJ: Humanities Press, 1995), 350. Evgeniia Ginzburg expressed similar sentiments about the city of Magadan when she returned there as an exile in 1947. Evgeniia Semenovna Ginzburg, *Within the Whirlwind* (New York: Harcourt Brace Jovanovich, 1981), 207.

9. GARF, f. R-9414, op. 1 ch. 2, d. 478.

10. GARF, f. R-8361, op. 1, d. 326, ll. 6–7, 10.

11. GURK NARK 1, f. R-1675, op. 1, d. 2225, l. 3. This plan was largely in response to a May 1948 Sovmin resolution that set ambitious targets for the extraction of coking coal in Vorkuta in order to supply a new steel plant being built in Cherepovets. GURK NARK 2, f. 1, op. 4, d. 344, ll. 2–5.

12. In 1947, coal production in the Soviet Union as a whole surpassed its prewar levels. *Narodnoe khoziaistvo SSSR v 1956 godu* (Moscow: Gos. stat. izd-vo, 1957), 72. As Oleg Khlevniuk and others have pointed out, after the Second World War MVD officials became increasingly concerned with the low productivity of prisoner labor and economic inefficiency of the camps. Oleg Khlevniuk, "The Economy of the OGPU, NKVD, and MVD of the USSR, 1930–1953," in *The Economics of Forced Labor: The Soviet Gulag*, ed. Paul R. Gregory and V. V. Lazarev (Stanford: Hoover Institution Press, 2003), 54–58.

13. Steven A. Barnes, *Death and Redemption: The Gulag and the Shaping of Soviet Society* (Princeton: Princeton University Press, 2011), 113–16.

14. J. Arch Getty, Gabor T. Rittersporn, and Viktor N. Zemskov, "Victims of the Soviet Penal System in the Pre-War Years: A First Approach on the Basis of Archival Evidence," *American Historical Review* 98, no. 4 (1993): 1048–49; Iurii Nikolaevich Afanas'ev and V. P. Kozlov, eds., *Istoriia stalinskogo Gulaga: Konets 1920-kh–pervaia polovina 1950-kh godov*, 7 vols. (Moscow: ROSSPEN, 2004), 4: 55.

15. Appendix A, tables A.6.1, A.6.2.

16. For example, there was a shortage of 65 tons of sugar in 1948 and 131 tons of milk in 1950. GARF, f. R-8361, op. 1, d. 0155, l. 23; GARF, f. R-8361, op. 1, d. 0273, l. 177.

17. GARF, f. R-8361, op. 1, d. 155, l. 23.

18. Leonid Borodkin and Simon Ertz, "Forced Labour and the Need for Motivation: Wages and Bonuses in the Stalinist Camp System," *Comparative Economic Studies* 47, no. 2 (2005): 425.

19. GARF, f. R-8361, op. 1, d. 209, l. 45.

20. V. P. Popov, *Ekonomicheskaia politika sovetskogo gosudarstva, 1946–1953 gg*. (Tambov: Tambovskii gos. tekhn. universitet, 2000), 65.

21. GARF, f. R-9414, op. 1 ch. 2, d. 150, l. 141. Wage distribution in the Gulag followed the system of wage differentiation by geography and sector that operated in the civilian economy. Borodkin and Ertz, "Forced Labour and the Need for Motivation," 434–35.

22. GARF, f. R-9414, op. 1, d. 151, ll. 71–74. Camp directors and Gulag officials appear to have shared a positive view of the reform. Borodkin and Ertz, "Forced Labour and the Need for Motivation," 435.

23. On the use of lapa in camp jargon, see Jacques Rossi, *The Gulag Handbook*, trans. William A. Burhans (New York: Paragon House, 1989), 198.

24. Aleksandr Klein, *Ulybki nevoli: Nevydumannaia zhizn', ulybki, sud'by, sluchai* (Syktyvkar: Prolog, 1997), 62–63.

25. GARF, f. R-9414, op. 1, d. 510, l. 40; Afanas'ev and Kozlov, eds., *Istoriia stalinskogo Gulaga*, 4: 314–15. In addition, "special camp" prisoners were not allowed to be given cash, a regulation that greatly complicated the implementation of wage reforms in special camps.

26. Joseph Scholmer, *Vorkuta* (New York: Holt, 1955), 231. Other former prisoners made similar observations. Baital'skii, *Notebooks for the Grandchildren*, 357; Armand Maloumian, *Les fils du Goulag* (Paris: Presses de la Cité, 1976), 156–57. Camp authorities confirmed that many of the goods that prisoners actually wanted to purchase were virtually unavailable, especially tobacco. GARF, f. R-9414, op. 1 ch. 2, d. 151, l. 74.

27. Scholmer, *Vorkuta*, 231.

28. GARF, f. R-9414, op. 1 ch. 2, d. 519, l. 185; GARF, f. R-8361, op. 1, d. 273, l. 165. On the history of the workday credit system, see Simon Ertz, "Trading Effort for Freedom: Workday Credits in the Stalinist Camp System," *Comparative Economic Studies* 47, no. 2 (2005): 476–91.

29. GARF, f. R-8361, op. 1, d. 273, l. 165.

30. See Appendix A, table A.5.1.

31. A. A. Ugrimov and T. A. Ugrimova, *Iz Moskvy v Moskvu cherez Parizh i Vorkutu* (Moscow: Izd-vo "RA", 2004), 240.

32. Baital'skii, *Notebooks for the Grandchildren*, 350.

33. A. B. Roginskii, M. B. Smirnov, and N. G. Okhotin, *Sistema ispravitel'no-trudovykh lagerei v SSSR, 1923–1960: Spravochnik* (Moscow: "Zven'ia", 1998), 291–92.

34. Afanas'ev and Kozlov, eds., *Istoriia stalinskogo Gulaga*, 2: 326–30 (quotation from 326). On the special camp reform see Barnes, *Death and Redemption*, 165–72; G. M. Ivanova, *Gulag v sisteme totalitarnogo gosudarstva* (Moscow: Moskovskii obshchestvennyi nauchnyi fond, 1997), 63–66.

35. Afanas'ev and Kozlov, eds., *Istoriia stalinskogo Gulaga*, 2: 370–71.

36. Ibid., 4: 125.

37. Barnes, *Death and Redemption*, 168; E. V. Markova, *Vorkutinskie zametki katorzhanki "E-105"* (Syktyvkar: Pokaianie, 2005), 112–13.

38. Aleksandr Kokurin and N. V. Petrov, eds., *GULAG (Glavnoe upravlenie lagerei), 1917–1960* (Moscow: "Demokratiia", 2000), 555–67.

39. GARF, f. R-9401, op. 1a, d. 234, l. 35. Thanks to Wilson Bell for generously sharing this document with me.

40. GARF, f. R-9414, op. 1, d. 554.

41. Afanas'ev and Kozlov, eds., *Istoriia stalinskogo Gulaga*, 2: 336–40.

42. N. A. Morozov, "Istrebitel'no-trudovye gody," in *Pokaianie : Komi respublikanskii martirolog zhertv massovykh politicheskikh repressii*, ed. V. G. Nevskii (Syktyvkar: Komi knizhnoe izd-vo, 1998), 1: 100.

43. GARF, f. R-8361, op. 1, d. 140, ll. 5, 10.

44. GURK NARK 2, f. 1875, op. 13, d. 1, ll. 1ob.–2.

45. Ibid., l. 2ob.

46. N. A. Morozov, *Osobye lageria MVD SSSR v Komi ASSR: 1948–1954 gody* (Syktyvkar: Syktyvkarskii gosudarstvennyi universitet, 1998), 9.

47. Markova, *Vorkutinskie zametki*, 123–24.

48. Kokurin and Petrov, eds., *GULAG, 1917–1960*, 555. GARF, f. R-8361, op. 1, d. 326, ll. 33, 100.

49. GARF, f. R-9414, op. 1 ch. 2, d. 478.

50. Golfo Alexopoulos, "Exiting the Gulag after the War: Women, Invalids, and the Family," *Jahrbücher für Geschichte Osteuropas* 57, no. 4 (2009): 563–79.

51. "V bessrochnuiu ssylku," *Istochnik* 2 (1994): 92–93.

52. GARF, f. R-9479, op. 1, d. 900, l. 216. This change had been requested as early as August 1948. GARF f. R-9479, op. 1, d. 373, ll. 84–85.

53. Appendix A, table A.6.2.

54. GARF, f. R-9414, op. 1 ch. 2, d. 478.

55. Ibid.

56. Ibid.

57. On German POWs in the Soviet Union, see Andreas Hilger, *Deutsche Kriegsgefangene in der Sowjetunion, 1941–1956 : Kriegsgefangenenpolitik, Lageralltag und Erinnerung* (Essen: Klartext, 2000); S. Karner, *Arkhipelag GUPVI: Plen i internirovanie v Sovetskom Soiuze, 1941–1956* (Moscow: RGGU, 2002); Ralf

Stettner, *Archipel GULag: Stalins Zwangslager-Terrorinstrument und Wirtschaftsgigant: Entstehung, Organisation und Funktion des sowjetischen Lagersystems, 1928–1956* (Paderborn: Schöningh, 1996).

58. Karner, *Arkhipelag GUPVI*, 232–36.

59. GARF, f. R-9414, op. 1, d. 1363, l. 1.

60. GARF, f. R-9414, op. 1, d. 575, ll. 25–26, 66–67.

61. Markova, *Vorkutinskie zametki*, 83–85.

62. Scholmer, *Vorkuta*, 133, 179.

63. Ibid., 97–98, 181.

64. Ibid., 73–74, 180–81.

65. Ibid., 94–95.

66. Ibid., 189.

67. On the insurgent movements against the (re)establishment of Soviet power in the western borderlands and the Soviet counterinsurgency against them, see Alexander Statiev, *The Soviet Counterinsurgency in the Western Borderlands* (New York: Cambridge University Press, 2010).

68. Barnes, *Death and Redemption*, 185–91; V. A. Kozlov, *Massovye besporiadki v SSSR pri Khrushcheve i Brezhneve (1953–nachalo 1980-kh gg.)* (Moscow: ROSSPEN, 2010), 46–58.

69. GARF, f. R-9414, op. 1 ch. 2, d. 151, ll. 238–43.

70. Numerous examples of open resistance can be found in Afanas'ev and Kozlov, eds., *Istoriia stalinskogo Gulaga*, 6: 209–313; Kozlov, *Massovye besporiadki v SSSR*, 51–58.

71. Gorlizki and Khlevniuk, *Cold Peace*, 124.

72. VMVTs, f. OF, d. 2996/1, ll. 8–9.

73. GURK NARK 1, f. R-0605, op. 1, d. 1391, ll. 1–7.

74. VMVTs, f. OF, op. 2996, d. 1, l. 9.

75. VMVTs, f. OF, d. 2996/2, ll. 47–52.

76. GURK NARK 2, f. 2216, op. 1, d. 1, ll. 1, 10–11.

77. William Taubman, *Governing Soviet Cities; Bureaucratic Politics and Urban Development in the USSR* (New York: Praeger, 1973), chap. 6.

78. GURK NARK 2, f. 2216, op. 1, d. 1, ll. 1, 10–11.

79. V. D. Zakharov, ed. *Ugol'naia sokrovishchnitsa severa: Sbornik dokumentov i materialov* (Syktyvkar: Komi kn. izd-vo, 1984), 119.

80. On the Gulag press, see A. I. U. Gorcheva, *Pressa Gulaga, 1918–1955* (Moscow: Izd-vo Moskovskogo univ., 1996).

81. GURK NARK 2, f. 2216, op. 1, d. 27, l. 75.

82. Other institutional changes included the transfer of responsibility for the distribution of food and goods in the city from the camp complex to the USSR Ministry of Trade in 1951. Shops, warehouses, and cafeterias, along with the employees who worked there, were no longer part of the camp system. GARF, f. R-9401, op. 1a, d. 384, ll. 89–90. The MVD attempted to transfer other institutions to the city and trade union in 1952, including all cultural, sports, medical, and children's facilities. However, both the Gorispolkom and the trade union refused to accept responsibility for them because of a lack of funds and expertise to run them. GARF, f. R-5446, op. 87, d. 1229, ll. 34–41.

83. GURK NARK 1, f. R-1941, op. 1, d. 22, ll. 6–7; GURK NARK 1, f. R-1941, op. 1, d. 64, ll. 28–33, 42.

84. Golfo Alexopoulos, "Amnesty 1945: The Revolving Door of Stalin's Gulag," *Slavic Review* 64, no. 2 (2005): 274–306; Alexopoulos, "Exiting the Gulag," 563–79.

85. Appendix A, table A.5.3.

86. Viacheslav Davydov, ed. *Vorkutaugol'* (Syktyvkar: OAO Komi Respublikanskaia Tipografiia, 2001), 22–23. The tekhnikum was created on 8 February 1944. M. Mal'tsev, "Ogon' iz vechnoi merzloty," in *Grani otvagi i stoikosti*, ed. A. I. Usov (Syktyvkar: Komi knizhnoe izd-vo, 1978), 167.

87. GURK NARK 2, f. 1, op. 4, d. 979, l. 80.

88. In April 1952 Sovmin assented to the MVD's longstanding request to extend wage bonuses to help recruit non-prisoners to MVD enterprises considered to be of paramount economic importance, such as Vorkuta. According to Oleg Khlevniuk, twenty-three thousand former prisoners were recruited in such a manner in 1952 by various MVD enterprises. Afanas'ev and Kozlov, eds., *Istoriia stalinskogo Gulaga*, 3: 567.

89. GURK NARK 2, f. 1875, op. 1, d. 90, l. 16.

90. GURK NARK 2, f. 1, op. 5, d. 5, l. 166. See also the case of the Korotenko family. Ibid., l. 167.

91. I. Skakovskaia, "O Vorkute i vorkutianiakh," *Volia* 8–9 (2002): 80.

92. On the postwar village, see Zubkova, *Russia after the War*, chap. 6; Jean Lévesque, "Foremen in the Field: Collective Farm Chairmen and the Fate of Labour Discipline after Collectivization, 1932–1953," in *A Dream Deferred: New Studies in Russian and Soviet Labour History*, ed. Donald A. Filtzer and Wendy Z. Goldman (New York: Peter Lang, 2008).

93. GARF, f. R-5446, op. 80, d. 2487, l. 1.

94. Afanas'ev and Kozlov, eds., *Istoriia stalinskogo Gulaga*, 3: 320.

95. GARF, f. R-9401, op. 1a, d. 384, ll. 86–95.

96. GURK NARK 2, f. 1, op. 4, d. 979, ll. 80–82.

97. Khlevniuk, "Economy," 56.

98. Cathy A. Frierson and Semen Samuilovich Vilenskii, eds., *Children of the Gulag* (New Haven: Yale University Press, 2010), 345.

99. GURK NARK 1, f. R-1941, op. 1, d. 22, ll. 17, 20, 32, 44, 52, 58, 64; GURK NARK 1, f. R-1941, op. 1, d. 31, ll. 4–40; GURK NARK 1, f. R-1941, op. 1, d. 40, l. 9; GURK NARK 1, f. R-1941, op. 1, d. 53, ll. 1–2; GURK NARK 1, f. R-1941, op. 1, d. 64, ll. 3–4, 57.

100. Iurii Aleksandrovich Poliakov, *Naselenie Rossii v xx veke: Istoricheskie ocherki*, vol. 2, *1940–1959* (Moscow: ROSSPEN, 2001), 240.

101. See note 99 above.

102. Markova, *Vorkutinskie zametki*, 49–50.

103. Ugrimov and Ugrimova, *Iz Moskvy v Moskvu cherez Parizh i Vorkutu*, 248.

104. Evfrosiniia Kersnovskaia, a prisoner working in the mines of Noril'sk, made similar observations about the importance of cooperation between prisoners and non-prisoners. Evfrosiniia Kersnovskaia, *Skol'ko stoit chelovek* (Moskva: ROSSPEN, 2006), 523–24.

105. Scholmer, *Vorkuta*, 88–89.
106. Ibid., 91.
107. GURK NARK 2, f. 1875, op. 13, d. 1, ll. 5, 13, 15.
108. GURK NARK 2, f. 1875, op. 13, d. 11, l. 81.
109. See, e.g., ibid., l. 1.
110. Scholmer, *Vorkuta*, 170.
111. GURK NARK 2, f. 1, op. 5, d. 5, l. 10.
112. Scholmer, *Vorkuta*, 168.
113. GURK NARK 2, f. 1875, op. 1, d. 140, l. 69.
114. GARF, f. R-8361, op. 1, d. 350, l. 45.
115. In 1950, the number of prisoners working as guards in Vorkutlag increased to 1,891, or 37 percent of the total. GARF, f. R-8361, op. 1, d. 273, l. 168.
116. GARF, f. R-8131, op. 32, d. 1815, l. 123.
117. Ibid., l. 165. According to the same report, on 6 September 1951, another guard-prisoner raped a five-year-old boy outside the camp zone.
118. Ibid., l. 101.
119. GURK NARK 2, f. 2216, op. 1, d. 7, l. 85.
120. Ibid., l. 107.
121. Ibid., l. 110.
122. Ibid., l. 111.
123. GURK NARK 2, f. 1, op. 5, d. 2, l. 65; GURK NARK 2, f. 2216, op. 1, d. 7, l. 111.
124. GURK NARK 2, f. 2216, op. 1, d. 31, l. 17; GURK NARK 2, f. 1, op. 5, d. 2, l. 66.

Chapter 4. Vorkuta in Crisis

1. GARF, f. R-9492, op. 5, d. 199, ll. 67–68.
2. V. M. Zubok, *Zhivago's Children: The Last Russian Intelligentsia* (Cambridge: Belknap Press of Harvard University Press, 2009), 44–46.
3. Miriam Dobson, *Khrushchev's Cold Summer: Gulag Returnees, Crime, and the Fate of Reform after Stalin* (Ithaca: Cornell University Press, 2009), 26.
4. Moshe Lewin pointed out that such bureaucratic reshuffling became systemic. "Incessant tinkering" resulted in a "bureaucratic neurosis" where reorganization was a substitute for genuine reform. Moshe Lewin, *The Soviet Century* (New York: Verso, 2005), 342. Thanks to Auri Berg for bringing this argument to my attention.
5. The camp newspaper, *Zapoliarnaia kochegarka*, first announced Stalin's illness in its 5 March issue, and announced his death in its 7 March issue. "Pravitel'stvennoe soobshchenie o bolezni . . . ," *Zapoliarnaia kochegarka*, 5 March 1953; "Ot Tsetranl'nogo Komiteta Kommunisticheskoi Partii . . . ," *Zapoliarnaia kochegarka*, 7 March 1953.
6. *Zapoliarnaia kochegarka*, 11 March 1953.
7. Edward Buca, *Vorkuta* (London: Constable, 1976), 229.
8. Joseph Scholmer, *Vorkuta* (New York: Holt, 1955), 212–13.
9. Aleksandr Kokurin and A. I. Pozharov, "Novyi kurs L. P. Berii," *Istoricheskii arkhiv* 4 (1996): 137–39; Oleg Khlevniuk, "The Economy of the OGPU, NKVD,

and MVD of the USSR, 1930–1953," in *The Economics of Forced Labor: The Soviet Gulag*, ed. Paul R. Gregory and V. V. Lazarev (Stanford: Hoover Institution Press, 2003), 54.

10. Kokurin and Pozharov, "Novyi kurs L. P. Berii," 140–43; Khlevniuk, "Economy," 54.

11. *Pravda*, 28 March 1953. Correspondence regarding the amnesty and guidelines for its implementation can be found in Kokurin and Pozharov, "Novyi kurs L. P. Berii," 143–48.

12. Ibid., 148–50.

13. Ibid., 132–64; Khlevniuk, "Economy," 54–55.

14. Yoram Gorlizki and O. V. Khlevniuk, *Cold Peace: Stalin and the Soviet Ruling Circle, 1945–1953* (New York: Oxford University Press, 2004), 124–33.

15. This amnesty was frequently associated with Voroshilov, especially among prisoners, because, as chairman of the Council of Ministers, his name appeared below the declaration in *Pravda*. *Pravda*, 28 March 1953.

16. On Stalin-era amnesties and categories of released prisoners, see Golfo Alexopoulos, "Amnesty 1945: The Revolving Door of Stalin's Gulag," *Slavic Review* 64, no. 2 (2005): 274–306; Golfo Alexopoulos, "Exiting the Gulag after the War: Women, Invalids, and the Family," *Jahrbücher für Geschichte Osteuropas* 57, no. 4 (2009): 563–79; Steven A. Barnes, *Death and Redemption: The Gulag and the Shaping of Soviet Society* (Princeton: Princeton University Press, 2011), 157–60.

17. GARF, f. R-9414, op. 1 ch. 2, d. 519, ll. 124, 177.

18. GARF, f. R-9414, op. 1 ch. 2, d. 519, l. 2.

19. GURK NARK 2, f. 1875, op. 1, d. 160, l. 69.

20. V. A. Kozlov, *Massovye besporiadki v SSSR pri Khrushcheve i Brezhneve (1953–nachalo 1980-kh gg.)* (Moscow: ROSSPEN, 2010), 57–58.

21. Iurii Nikolaevich Afanas'ev and V. P. Kozlov, eds., *Istoriia stalinskogo Gulaga: Konets 1920-kh–pervaia polovina 1950-kh godov*, 7 vols. (Moscow: ROSSPEN, 2004), 6: 465.

22. GARF, f. R-8131, op. 32, d. 3032, ll. 176–77. Similar problems were noted throughout the Gulag. Afanas'ev and Kozlov, eds., *Istoriia stalinskogo Gulaga*, 2: 430–31.

23. GARF, f. R-8131, op. 32, d. 3031, l. 62.

24. According to Miriam Dobson, rumors of violence caused by the amnesty, combined with overall anxiety about the new course of affairs after Stalin, converged to create an atmosphere of panic in many parts of the Soviet Union. Dobson, *Khrushchev's Cold Summer*, 40.

25. AUIN MIu RF po RK, f. 1, op. 3, d. 7150, l. 1.

26. GURK NARK 2, f. 2216, op. 6, d. 57, ll. 37–41; GURK NARK 2, f. 2216, op. 6, d. 62, ll. 10–11; GURK NARK 2, f. 2216, op. 6, d. 54, l. 158.

27. According to Marc Elie this misperception was widespread. Marc Elie, "Les anciens détenus du Goulag: Libérations massives, réinsertion et réhabilitation dans l'URSS poststalinienne, 1953–1964" (PhD, EHESS, 2007), 38.

28. On the "chief administrations" and their eventual abolition, see A. B. Roginskii, M. B. Smirnov, and N. G. Okhotin, *Sistema ispravitel'no-trudovykh lagerei v SSSR, 1923–1960: Spravochnik* (Moscow: "Zven'ia", 1998), 58–59; Simon Ertz,

"Lagernaia sistema v 1930-e–1950-e gg.: Evoliutsiia struktury i printsipov upravleniia," in *Gulag: Ekonomika prinuditel'nogo truda*, ed. L. I. Borodkin, Paul R. Gregory, and O. V. Khlevniuk (Moskva: ROSSPEN, 2005), 106–10; Kokurin and Pozharov, "Novyi kurs L. P. Berii," 138–39.

29. On the principle of edinonachal'e in the Gulag, see David J. Nordlander, "Origins of a Gulag Capital: Magadan and Stalinist Control in the Early 1930s," *Slavic Review* 57, no. 4 (1998): 806–7.

30. Roginskii, Smirnov, and Okhotin, *Sistema ispravitel'no-trudovykh lagerei v SSSR*, 192, 368.

31. Such a separation of functions between the Gulag and civilian ministries was not without precedent. As scholars such as Paul Gregory and Valery Lazarev have pointed out, in the 1940s and early 1950s hundreds of thousands of Gulag prisoners were provided under contract to civilian ministries. Paul R. Gregory, "An Introduction to the Economics of the Gulag," in Gregory and Lazarev, eds., *Economics of Forced Labor*, 12–18; V. V. Lazarev, "Conclusions," in Gregory and Lazarev, eds., *Economics of Forced Labor*, 195.

32. Ertz, "Lagernaia sistema v 1930-e–1950-e gg.," 117.

33. GARF, f. R-9414, op. 1, d. 2613, ll. 4–7.

34. RGAE, f. 8225, op. 27, d. 444, ll. 128, 138.

35. GARF, f. R-9492, op. 5, d. 199, ll. 34–36. The proposal was subsequently repeated at least twice. GARF, f. R-9492, op. 5, d. 200, ll. 73–76, 120–25.

36. GARF, f. R-9492, op. 5, d. 199, ll. 37–40.

37. Amy W. Knight, *Beria, Stalin's First Lieutenant* (Princeton: Princeton University Press, 1993), 194–224; William Taubman, *Khrushchev: The Man and His Era* (New York: W. W. Norton, 2003), 249–57.

38. Kozlov, *Massovye besporiadki v SSSR*, 59–60.

39. GARF, f. R-9413, op. 1, d. 160, l. 62. Much of the archival material on the Rechlag strike, including most of the above file, has been reprinted in Afanas'ev and Kozlov, eds., *Istoriia stalinskogo Gulaga*, 6: 434–576. For purposes of brevity I will refer to the original archival sources except in the cases where the published documents were consulted instead of the archival originals.

40. Marta Craveri and Oleg Khlevniuk, "Krizis ekonomiki MVD (konets 1940-kh–1950-kh godov)," *Cahiers du Monde Russe* 36, nos. 1–2 (1995): 179–90; Khlevniuk, "Economy," 51–58.

41. Marta Craveri, "Krizis Gulaga: Kengirskoe Vosstanie 1954 goda v dokumentakh MVD," *Cahiers du Monde Russe* 36, no. 3 (1995): 319–44; Marta Craveri, "The Strikes in Norilsk and Vorkuta Camps, and Their Role in the Breakdown of the Stalinist Forced Labour System," in *Free and Unfree Labour: The Debate Continues*, ed. Tom Brass and Marcel van der Linden (New York: Peter Lang, 1997), 364–78; Marta Craveri, *Resistenza nel gulag: Un capitolo inedito della destalinizzazione in Unione Sovietica* (Soveria Mannelli (Catanzaro): Rubbettino, 2003); Kozlov, *Massovye besporiadki v SSSR*, chap. 1; Barnes, *Death and Redemption*, 212–13.

42. Barnes, *Death and Redemption*, 213.

43. GARF, f. R-9414, op. 1, d. 2613, ll. 12–15. Vladimir Kozlov has noted that prisoners transferred from Peschanlag provided the spark for the Gorlag strike as well. Kozlov, *Massovye besporiadki v SSSR*, 69.

44. Although Derevianko had been serving as the official chief of Rechlag since only 16 June 1953, for the previous two years he had served as the deputy director of KVU in charge of Rechlag. Before this he had been director of SVITL, the primary camp of Dal'stroi, from 1948 to 1951. Roginskii, Smirnov, and Okhotin, *Sistema ispravitel'no-trudovykh lagerei v SSSR*, 382–84.

45. On the Gorlag uprising, see Andrea Graziosi, "The Great Strikes of 1953 in Soviet Labor Camps in the Accounts of Their Participants: A Review," *Cahiers du Monde Russe et Sovietique* 33, no. 4 (1992): 419–46; Craveri, *Resistenza nel gulag*, chap. 8; Kozlov, *Massovye besporiadki v SSSR*, chap. 1; Afanas'ev and Kozlov, eds., *Istoriia stalinskogo Gulaga*, 6: 320–413.

46. Just days earlier, he had responded to acts of resistance in other parts of Rechlag, such as the savage beating of a duty officer and the distribution of leaflets urging prisoners to, among other things, "Demand an immediate review of your cases and complete release." The alleged ringleaders had been rounded up and held in the isolation prison, thus ending the unrest. Afanas'ev and Kozlov, eds., *Istoriia stalinskogo Gulaga*, 6: 434–35.

47. Ibid., 6: 466–67.

48. A. A. Ugrimov and T. A. Ugrimova, *Iz Moskvy v Moskvu cherez Parizh i Vorkutu* (Moscow: Izd-vo "RA", 2004), 287–88, 291.

49. GARF, f. R-9413, op. 1, d. 160, l. 64.

50. GARF, f. R-9492, op. 5, d. 199, l. 69.

51. GARF, f. R-9413, op. 1, d. 160, ll. 227–38.

52. Such concessions had also been offered to the prisoners in Gorlag in June, and had been successful in convincing some of the prisoners to return to work. Afanas'ev and Kozlov, eds., *Istoriia stalinskogo Gulaga*, 6: 386–98.

53. GARF, f. R-9413, op. 1, d. 160, ll. 65, 69. Scholmer, *Vorkuta*, 236–37, 244, 246.

54. GARF, f. R-9413, op. 1, d. 160, l. 4.

55. A draft Sovmin resolution, the accompanying letter from Zasiad'ko, and the response from MinIust can be found in GARF, f. R-9492, op. 5, d. 200, ll. 73–113.

56. GARF, f. R-9492, op. 5, d. 199, ll. 67–72.

57. Kozlov, *Massovye besporiadki v SSSR*, 80. Although changes in the special camp regime were drafted in August 1953, the Presidium put off any definitive decisions about the future of the special camps until 1954. Andrei Artizov and others, eds., *Reabilitatsiia: Kak eto bylo*, 3 vols. (Moscow: "Demokratiia", 2000–2004), 2: 65–66. See also ibid., 2: 386, n. 11; and Afanas'ev and Kozlov, eds., *Istoriia stalinskogo Gulaga*, 6: 676, n. 219.

58. Ugrimov and Ugrimova, *Iz Moskvy v Moskvu cherez Parizh i Vorkutu*, 290.

59. Afanas'ev and Kozlov, eds., *Istoriia stalinskogo Gulaga*, 6: 549; Buca, *Vorkuta*, 243–44. Camp section 6, however, was an exception, as the prisoner ventilation brigade refused to work throughout the strike. Scholmer, *Vorkuta*, 249–50.

60. Ugrimov and Ugrimova, *Iz Moskvy v Moskvu cherez Parizh i Vorkutu*, 290.

61. GARF, f. R-9413, op. 1, d. 160, ll. 35–36.

62. On the debate surrounding the use of such sources, see Sarah Davies, *Popular Opinion in Stalin's Russia: Terror, Propaganda and Dissent, 1934–1941* (New York:

Cambridge University Press, 1997); Jochen Hellbeck, "Speaking Out: Languages of Affirmation and Dissent in Stalinist Russia," *Kritika: Explorations in Russian and Eurasian History* 1, no. 1 (2000): 71–96; Sarah Davies, "To the Editors," *Kritika: Explorations in Russian and Eurasian History* 1, no. 2 (2000): 437–40.

63. GARF, f. R-9413, op. 1, d. 160, ll. 145–46.

64. GARF, f. R-9413, op. 1, d. 160, ll. 143–44.

65. GURK NARK 2, f. 2216, op. 1, d. 57, ll. 93–94.

66. GARF, f. R-9413, op. 1, d. 160, ll. 9, 33.

67. GARF, f. R-9413, op. 1, d. 160, l. 67.

68. GARF, f. R-9413, op. 1, d. 160, ll. 143–44.

69. Scholmer, *Vorkuta*, 234–35.

70. Ugrimov and Ugrimova, *Iz Moskvy v Moskvu cherez Parizh i Vorkutu*, 291.

71. Ibid., 288.

72. Buca, *Vorkuta*, 249–50. Having "outed" himself as a leader of the strike, it is no surprise that Buca was clearly identified by camp director Derevianko as the leader of the "sabotage" in camp section 10. GARF, f. R-9413, op. 1, d. 160, l. 136.

73. Afanas'ev and Kozlov, eds., *Istoriia stalinskogo Gulaga*, 6: 546–50; Kozlov, *Massovye besporiadki v SSSR*, 73. He later claimed in testimony that he used his new position of authority to maintain order in the zone and steer the strike in a peaceful direction. As a result of this testimony, Kolesnikov's conviction for his role in the strike was overturned less than a year later.

74. Kozlov, *Massovye besporiadki v SSSR*, 71–74.

75. Aleksandr Kokurin and N. V. Petrov, eds., *GULAG (Glavnoe upravlenie lagerei), 1917–1960* (Moscow: "Demokratiia", 2000), 579, 587. On the career of Maslennikov, see Aleksandr Kokurin, N. V. Petrov, and R. G. Pikhoia, eds., *Lubianka: VChK-OGPU-NKVD-NKGB-MGB-MVD-KGB, 1917–1960: Spravochnik* (Moscow: "Demokratiia", 1997), 22–23, 30, 41, 36, 57, 85, 150.

76. GARF, f. R-9413, op. 1, d. 160, ll. 151–52 ; *Soviet "Justice": "Showplace" Prisons vs. Real Slave Labor Camps: Consultation with Mr. Adam Joseph Galinski* (Washington, DC: U.S. G.P.O., 1960), 15–16; Ugrimov and Ugrimova, *Iz Moskvy v Moskvu cherez Parizh i Vorkutu*, 292.

77. Ugrimov described his tone as "benevolent." Ugrimov and Ugrimova, *Iz Moskvy v Moskvu cherez Parizh i Vorkutu*, 292.

78. GARF, f. R-9413, op. 1, d. 160, ll. 257–58.

79. GARF, f. R-9413, op. 1, d. 160, ll. 240–48. Kniazev's allegations were subsequently investigated by the Komi ASSR Procuracy. Afanas'ev and Kozlov, eds., *Istoriia stalinskogo Gulaga*, 6: 553–56, 680 n. 270.

80. GARF, f. R-9413, op. 1, d. 160, l. 258.

81. GARF, f. R-9413, op. 1, d. 160, ll. 251–53.

82. Daniel Field, *Rebels in the Name of the Tsar* (Boston: Houghton Mifflin, 1976).

83. GARF, f. R-9413, op. 1, d. 160, l. 240.

84. GARF, f. R-9413, op. 1, d. 160, l. 247.

85. Dobson, *Khrushchev's Cold Summer*, 33–37.

86. Stephen Kotkin, *Magnetic Mountain: Stalinism as a Civilization* (Berkeley: University of California Press, 1995), chap. 5.

87. Thus, "speaking Bolshevik" would entail "thinking Bolshevik." On the latter concept see Hellbeck, "Speaking Out," 71–96.

88. Aleksandr Isaevich Solzhenitsyn, *The Gulag Archipelago, 1918–1956*, 3 vols.(New York: Harper & Row, 1974), 302–3.

89. Barnes, *Death and Redemption*, 211.

90. Ibid., 231–32.

91. GARF, f. R-9413, op. 1, d. 160, ll. 1–2.

92. Kokurin and Petrov, eds., *GULAG, 1917–1960*, 582.

93. Ugrimov and Ugrimova, *Iz Moskvy v Moskvu cherez Parizh i Vorkutu*, 295–96.

94. Kokurin and Petrov, eds., *GULAG, 1917–1960*, 582.

95. Scholmer, *Vorkuta*, 266–67.

96. GARF, f. R-9413, op. 1, d. 160, l. 135.

97. Kokurin and Petrov, eds., *GULAG, 1917–1960*, 582.

98. Ibid., 583. Arkhiv NIPTs "Memorial" f. 2, op. 3, d. 66, l. 137.

99. Buca, *Vorkuta*, 271. Kokurin and Petrov, eds., *GULAG, 1917–1960*, 583.

100. Of the 135 wounded, 83 sustained minor injuries. Kokurin and Petrov, eds., *GULAG, 1917–1960*, 584.

101. Of those killed, the majority were Ukrainians (56.6 percent), Lithuanians (18.9 percent), and Estonians (7.5 percent), all percentages that were higher than the respective weight of each nationality in the general population of Rechlag. GARF, f. R-9413, op. 1, d. 160, ll. 185–87.

102. Afanas'ev and Kozlov, eds., *Istoriia stalinskogo Gulaga*, 6: 544. Later reports suggest that as few as 22 prisoners were actually investigated as organizers. GARF, f. R-9414, op. 1, d. 2613, l. 137.

103. Afanas'ev and Kozlov, eds., *Istoriia stalinskogo Gulaga*, 6: 546–50, 57–59; Buca, *Vorkuta*, 280–313.

104. Afanas'ev and Kozlov, eds., *Istoriia stalinskogo Gulaga*, 6: 544. GARF, f. R-9414, op. 1, d. 2613, l. 137.

105. Afanas'ev and Kozlov, eds., *Istoriia stalinskogo Gulaga*, 6: 539–46.

106. Ibid., 6: 590–91.

107. GARF, f. R-9492, op. 5, d. 200, l. 120; GARF, f. R-9414, op. 1, d. 772, ll. 154–57.

108. GARF, f. R-9414, op. 1, d. 772, l. 118. These accusations were echoed by officials from other camps that had received prisoners transferred from Rechlag. Ibid., l. 113.

109. Afanas'ev and Kozlov, eds., *Istoriia stalinskogo Gulaga*, 2: 466–67.

110. GARF, f. R-9401, op. 1a, d. 526, ll. 165–66.

111. Roginskii, Smirnov, and Okhotin, *Sistema ispravitel'no-trudovykh lagerei v SSSR*, 59. Marc Elie, "Khrushchev's Gulag," in *The Thaw: Soviet Society and Culture in the 1950s and 1960s*, ed. Denis Kozlov and Eleonory Gilburd (Toronto: University of Toronto Press, 2013), 114.

112. Curiously, in April 1954 MUP minister Zasiad'ko actually requested that responsibility for Vorkuta's mines be transferred back to the MVD. GARF, f. R-5446,

op. 88, d. 74, l. 100. While it is possible that he had simply given up on his earlier efforts for MUP to gain greater control over Vorkuta, this could also have been a way of expressing his frustration. In any case, his request was denied.

113. Elie, "Khrushchev's Gulag," 115; Barnes, *Death and Redemption*, 232–33.

114. Kokurin and Petrov, eds., *GULAG, 1917–1960*, 151–63.

115. On the existing regulations, which had been in place since 1947, see GARF, f. R-9401, op. 1a, d. 234, ll. 32ob., 42ob.–43ob. This was part of a postwar attempt to tighten security in Gulag camps.

116. Kokurin and Petrov, eds., *GULAG, 1917–1960*, 154–56, 158.

117. On the shortage of prisoners working in the mines, see RGAE, f. 8225, op. 27, d. 497, l. 238.

118. GURK NARK 2, f. 1875, op. 1, d. 176, l. 56.

119. Oleg Borovskii, *Rentgen strogogo rezhima* (Moscow: Vremia, 2009), 202.

120. Ibid., 220.

121. GURK NARK 2, f. 1875, op. 1, d. 176, l. 57.

122. AUIN MIu RF po RK, f. 1, op. 3, d. 7154, l. 158.

123. GURK NARK 2, f. 1875, op. 1, d. 176, l. 57.

124. AUIN MIu RF po RK, f. 1, op. 3, d. 7161, ll. 276–89.

125. AUIN MIu RF po RK, f. 1, op. 3, d. 7154, ll. 277–78.

126. See, e.g., AUIN MIu RF po RK, f. 1, op. 3, d. 7154, ll. 237–42.

127. GURK NARK 1, f. R-1307, op. 1, d. 520, l. 44.

128. For a contrasting interpretation of the granting of de-zoned status, see Barnes, *Death and Redemption*, 233–34.

129. GURK NARK 1, f. R-1307, op. 1, d. 531, ll. 3–4, 40–47; GURK NARK 1, f. R-1307, op. 1, d. 75, l. 4; GURK NARK 1, f. R-1307, op. 1, d. 520, l. 2.

130. GURK NARK 1, f. R-1307, op. 1, d. 75, l. 5.

131. GURK NARK 1, f. R-1307, op. 1, d. 75, l. 4.

132. For example, in January–February 1956, only 44 prisoners were transferred back into the zone for committing various crimes. GURK NARK 1, f. R-1307, op. 1, d. 520, l. 2. Over that same period of time 1,471 prisoners were granted the right to live outside the zone.

133. AUIN MIu RF po RK, f. 1, op. 3, d. 7158, l. 32.

134. M. Baital'skii, *Notebooks for the Grandchildren: Recollections of a Trotskyist Who Survived the Stalin Terror* (Atlantic Highlands, NJ: Humanities Press, 1995), 391. Edward Buca also noted the seeming randomness with which passes were granted. Buca, *Vorkuta*, 318.

135. GARF, f. R-9401, op. 2, d. 465, l. 3; Arkhiv NIPTs "Memorial" f. 2, op. 3, d. 66, ll. 184–85; Heinrich Koerner and Bernhard Roeder, "Slaves into Serfs," *The Observer*, 8 June 1956, 6–7; Pavel Negretov, *Vse dorogi vedut na Vorkutu* (Benson, VT: Chalidze Publication, 1985), 8–9.

136. For instance, at the beginning of 1951 there were 296,100 square meters of living space for approximately 92,200 prisoners and non-prisoners working for KVU. This translates into just over 3.2 square meters per person. GARF, f. R-8361, op. 1, d. 326, ll. 8, 16. By the beginning of 1952 KVU's non-prisoner employees occupied an average of 4.57 square meters per person. GARF, f. R-8361, op. 1, d. 326, l. 90.

137. GURK NARK 1, f. R-1307, op. 1, d. 520, l. 44; Baital'skii, *Notebooks for the Grandchildren*, 392.

138. AUIN MIu RF po RK, f. 1, op. 3, d. 7156, l. 111.

139. AUIN MIu RF po RK, f. 1, op. 3, d. 7158, l. 257.

140. Ibid, ll. 25–26.

141. GURK NARK 1, f. R-1307, op. 1, d. 520, l. 44.

142. AUIN MIu RF po RK, f. 1, op. 3, d. 7160, l. 71. This led to some improbable scenarios, such as the case of a prisoner who was granted a fifteen-day leave to visit his mother and get married in a village in Kiev oblast', who subsequently returned to Vorkutlag nine days late. GARF, f. R-9401, op. 2, d. 491, ll. 89–91. For more on this case, see Alan Barenberg, "Prisoners without Borders: Zazonniki and the Transformation of Vorkuta after Stalin," *Jahrbücher für Geschichte Osteuropas* 57, no. 4 (2009): 530.

143. Koerner and Roeder, "Slaves into Serfs," 6–7; Khlevniuk, "Economy," 57. Others have cautioned about using such comparisons to the Gulag. Jeffrey S. Hardy, "Re-Assessing the Archipelago: The Soviet Penal System in Comparative and Transnational Context" (Paper presented at the annual meeting of the Association for Slavic, East European, and Eurasian Studies, New Orleans, LA, 17 November 2012).

Chapter 5. The "Second Birth" of Vorkuta

1. "Po prizyvu partii i pravitel'stva," *Zapoliar'e*, 10 June 1956.

2. Similar anxieties were expressed across the Soviet Union. Miriam Dobson, *Khrushchev's Cold Summer: Gulag Returnees, Crime, and the Fate of Reform after Stalin* (Ithaca: Cornell University Press, 2009).

3. Sovmin resolution no. 1579, 26 August 1953, "O merakh neotlozhnoi pomoshchi pechorskomu ugol'nomu basseinu." Thanks to Nikolai Mastrakov for sharing the document with me.

4. RGAE, f. 8225, op. 27, d. 497, l. 238.

5. Donald Filtzer, *Soviet Workers and Late Stalinism: Labour and the Restoration of the Stalinist System after World War II* (Cambridge: Cambridge University Press, 2002), 29–34.

6. Sheila Fitzpatrick has noted that it was ironically anything but "organized." Sheila Fitzpatrick, *Stalin's Peasants: Resistance and Survival in the Russian Village after Collectivization* (New York: Oxford University Press, 1994), 97–99.

7. GURK NARK 1, f. R-605, op. 3, d. 259, l. 297.

8. Ibid., l. 301ob.

9. GURK NARK 2, f. 2216, op. 7, d. 30, l. 28.

10. RGAE, f. 8225, op. 27, d. 506, ll. 67–69.

11. GURK NARK 1, f. R-1675, op. 1, d. 2281, l. 22ob.

12. For correspondence surrounding the effectiveness of orgnabor and its replacement with other recruitment policies, see GARF, f. R-5446, op. 90, d. 1039, ll. 202–201 (descending page order); GARF, f. R-5446, op. 90, d. 1038, ll. 210–195.

13. "Sokrashchenie vooruzhennykh sil SSSR v seredine 50-x godov," *Voennye arkhivy Rossii* 1 (1993): 273, 290–91, 295–96; William Taubman, *Khrushchev: The Man and His Era* (New York: W.W. Norton, 2003), 379–80.

14. NARK, f. R-1675, op. 1, d. 2281, ll. 14–15, 19–21, 22ob; "Put' k sozdaniiu postoiannykh kadrov," *Zapoliar'e*, 3 December 1957.

15. GARF, f. R-5446, op. 90, d. 1039, l. 206. See also Donald A. Filtzer, *Soviet Workers and De-Stalinization: The Consolidation of the Modern System of Soviet Production Relations, 1953–1964* (Cambridge: Cambridge University Press, 1992), 71–72; Allen Kassof, *The Soviet Youth Program: Regimentation and Rebellion* (Cambridge: Harvard University Press, 1965), 116. For a detailed account of recruitment to the Virgin lands, see Michaela Pohl, "The Virgin Lands between Memory and Forgetting: People and Transformation in the Soviet Union, 1954–1960" (PhD, Indiana University, 1999), chap. 5.

16. *Pravda*, 19 May 1956.

17. GARF, f. R-5446, op. 90, d. 1039, l. 206.

18. *Zapoliar'e*, 10 June 1956.

19. As Dan Healey has pointed out, some personnel were sent to Gulag camps via raspredelenie, most notably doctors. Dan Healey, "Doctors within the Zone: Staffing the Gulag's Medical Service" (Paper presented at the annual meeting of the Association for Slavic, East European, and Eurasian Studies, New Orleans, LA, 17 November 2012).

20. Figures calculated from NARK, f. R-1941, op. 1, d. 22, ll. 4–5; GURK NARK 1, f. R-1941, op. 1, d. 40, ll. 30–30ob.; GURK NARK 1, f. R-1941, op. 1, d. 43, ll. 18–19; GURK NARK 1, f. R-1941, op. 1, d. 53, ll. 6–7; GURK NARK 1, f. R-1941, op. 1, d. 64, l. 12; GURK NARK 1, f. R-1941, op. 1, d. 75, ll. 17–18, 21.

21. GURK NARK 1, f. R-1941, op. 1, d. 224, l. 20.

22. Melanie Ilic, *Women Workers in the Soviet Interwar Economy: From 'Protection' to 'Equality'* (New York: St. Martin's Press, 1999), chap. 10.

23. VMVTS, f. OF, d. 1057/12, l. 1; Al'bert Efimovich Bernshtein, *Aiach-Iaga—izobil'naia reka vremeni* (Syktyvkar: Komi knizhnoe izd-vo, 2006), 56–66.

24. GARF, f. R-7416, op. 7, d. 2903, ll. 180–90; RGAE, f. 8225, op. 27, d. 497, l. 238.

25. *Zapoliar'e*, 28 August 1955.

26. Irina Mikhailovna Sakharova and Dmitrii Stepanovich Karev, eds., *Sbornik zakonodatel'nykh aktov o trude* (Moskva, 1960), 400–402. This was part of an overall attempt by the Khrushchev regime to strengthen legislation to protect women's health, even as efforts were made to mobilize more women into the workforce. Melanie Ilic, "What Did Women Want? Khrushchev and the Revivial of the *Zhensovety*," in *Soviet State and Society under Nikita Khrushchev*, ed. Melanie Ilic and Jeremy Smith (New York: Routledge, 2009), 104–21; Filtzer, *Soviet Workers and De-Stalinization*, 62–70, chap. 7.

27. GARF, f. R-5446, op. 90, d. 880, ll. 175–74.

28. GURK NARK 1, f. R-1688, op. 1, d. 266, ll. 103–4.

29. GARF, f. A-259, op. 42, d. 2969, ll. 1–2, 4; GARF, f. A-259, op. 45, d. 2813, l. 80; GARF, f. A-259, op. 45, d. 2814, ll. 13, 15; GARF, f. A-259, op. 45, d. 2942, ll. 24–25.

30. Ibid., 27; GARF R-7416, op. 7, d. 3799, ll. 55–57. Melanie Ilic suggests that women in the pre-Second World War era also sought to circumvent laws that prevented them from working underground in mines. Ilic, *Women Workers in the Soviet Interwar Economy*, 172.

31. *Pravda*, 8 October 1959.

32. Filtzer, *Soviet Workers and De-Stalinization*, 68.

33. *Sbornik zakonodatel'nykh aktov o trude* (Moscow: Iurid. lit., 1974), 680–87. *Vedomosti Verkhovnogo Soveta SSSR* no. 7 (18 February 1960): 70–72.

34. L. Ia. Gintsberg and N. M. Smirnova, *L'goty rabotaiushchim na Krainem Severe* (Moscow: Iurid. lit-ra, 1975), 35–36.

35. Elena Zubkova, *Russia after the War: Hopes, Illusions, and Disappointments, 1945–1957* (Armonk, NY: M. E. Sharpe, 1998), chaps. 4, 6.

36. Al'bert Efimovich Bernshtein, *Na rubezhe vekov* (Syktyvkar: Miian Kyv, 2002), 120.

37. *Itogi vsesoiuznoi perepisi naseleniia 1959 goda*, 16 vols. (Moscow: Gosstatizdat, 1962), 1: 12.

38. Ibid., 1: 25.

39. Such bonuses had been offered since 1932, with the exception of the period from 1942 to 1945. "Polozhenie o l'gotakh dlia lits, rabotaiushchikh v raionakh Krainego Severa RSFSR" (10 May 1932). *Sovetskii Sever*, no. 3 (1932): 151–53; *Sbornik zakonov SSSR i ukazov Prezidiuma Verkhovnogo Soveta SSSR: 1938–1975* (Moscow: Izvestiia Sovetov deputatov trudiashchikhsia SSSR, 1975), 1: 431; I. Dvornikov, ed. *Sbornik vazhneishikh zakonov i postanovlenii o trude* (Moscow: Profizdat, 1958), 114–15. Vorkuta was specifically included in the bonus zone from 12 August 1946. GURK NARK 2, f. 1, op. 4, d. 9, l. 81.

40. V. D. Zakharov, ed. *Ugol'naia sokrovishchnitsa severa: Sbornik dokumentov i materialov* (Syktyvkar: Komi kn. izd-vo, 1984), 135.

41. Gintsberg and Smirnova, *L'goty rabotaiushchim na Krainem Severe*, 36.

42. *Sbornik zakonov SSSR i ukazov Prezidiuma Verkhovnogo Soveta SSSR: 1938–1975*, 3: 71–72.

43. GARF, f. R-5446, op. 1, d. 486, ll. 17–22; GARF, f. R-5446, op. 1, d. 664, l. 86.

44. Kotkin observed a similar phenomenon in Magnitogorsk in the 1930s. Stephen Kotkin, *Magnetic Mountain: Stalinism as a Civilization* (Berkeley: University of California Press, 1995), 79.

45. *Za ugol'*, 30 April 1958.

46. *Pravda*, 19 May 1956. The irony of this, of course, was that Komsomol'sk-na-Amure had been built primarily using prisoner labor after the failure of recruiting through the Komsomol. Jonathan A. Bone, "À la recherche d'un Komsomol perdu: Who Really Built Komsomol'sk-na-Amure, and Why," *Revue des études slaves* LXXI, no. 1 (1999): 59–92. Seen in this light, the process that took place in Vorkuta in the 1950s is the mirror image of the one that took place in Komsomol'sk-na-Amure in the 1930s.

47. *Zapoliar'e*, 8 July 1956.

48. Mikhail T., interview by author, digital recording, Syktyvkar, Russia, 31 October 2003.

49. On the shortcomings of labor recruitment in the 1930s, see Kotkin, *Magnetic Mountain*, 78–80.

50. A typical example of such writing about the city can be found in "Za 67-i parallel'iu," *Pravda*, 6 March 1960.

51. See, e.g., "Gorod za poliarnym krugom," *Ogonëk*, no. 45 (1947): (between 8–9).

52. Victor Zaslavsky, *The Neo-Stalinist State: Class, Ethnicity, and Consensus in Soviet Society*, rev. ed. (Armonk, NY: M. E. Sharpe, 1994), 139.
53. Ibid., 140–43.
54. GURK NARK 2, f. 2216, op. 7, d. 57, ll. 117–18.
55. *Zapoliar'e*, 22 June 1956.
56. Ibid.
57. Bernshtein, *Na rubezhe vekov*, 126.
58. Ibid., 169.
59. *Zapoliar'e*, 19 October 1956.
60. *Zapoliar'e*, 10 October 1956.
61. GURK NARK 2, f. 1791, op. 1, d. 108, l. 59.
62. GURK NARK 2, f. 2216, op. 14, d. 56, l. 11.
63. GURK NARK 2, f. 70, op. 3, d. 6, l. 28.
64. See, e.g., *Za ugol'*, 30 April 1958.
65. GURK NARK 2, f. 2216, op. 7, d. 102, ll. 10–11.
66. GURK NARK 2, f. 1791, op. 1, d. 108, l. 81.
67. RGASPI, f. M-1, op. 8, d. 773, ll. 40–41.
68. *Zapoliar'e*, 23 November 1956.
69. This is estimated from ten-month figures in GURK NARK 2, f. 2216, op. 7, d. 103, l. 77.
70. GURK NARK 1, f. R-1675, op. 1, d. 1716, l. 152.
71. This is estimated from half-year totals found in GURK NARK 2, f. 2216, op. 15, d. 9, ll. 74–75.
72. GURK NARK 1, f. R-1675, op. 1, d. 1713, ll. 151–52.
73. GURK NARK 2, f. 2216, op. 14, d. 19, l. 66.
74. GURK NARK 2, f. 2216, op. 14, d. 56, l. 27.
75. GURK NARK 2, f. 2216, op. 14, d. 19a, l. 49.
76. Ibid., l. 67.
77. GURK NARK 2, f. 2216, op. 14, d. 22, ll. 48–49.
78. GURK NARK 2, f. 2216, op. 15, d. 44, l. 9.
79. *Zapoliar'e*, 10 June 1956.
80. *Zapoliar'e*, 10 August 1957.
81. *Zapoliar'e*, 16 February 1957.
82. Bernshtein, *Na rubezhe vekov*, 120.
83. GURK NARK 2, f. 2216, op. 7, d. 100a, ll. 96–98.
84. GURK NARK 1, f. R-1688, op. 1, d. 559, l. 6.
85. GURK NARK 2, f. 2216, op. 7, d. 32a, l. 219.
86. Mine no. 1, for example, built some 13,000 square meters of housing from 1955 to 1958, yet as of May 1959, 311 workers and their families (out of approximately 5,000 mine workers) still lived in private apartments or in dormitories. GURK NARK 1, f. R-1688, op. 1, d. 529, ll. 12, 72.
87. GURK NARK 2, f. 2216, op. 14, d. 22a, ll. 135–36.
88. On the campaign's formulation and launch, see Mark B. Smith, *Property of Communists: The Urban Housing Program from Stalin to Khrushchev* (DeKalb: Northern Illinois University Press, 2010), chap. 10.
89. Steven E. Harris, "'I Know All the Secrets of My Neighbors': The Quest for Privacy in the Era of the Separate Apartment," in *Borders of Socialism: Private*

Spheres of Soviet Russia, ed. Lewis H. Siegelbaum (Gordonsville, VA: Palgrave Macmillan, 2006), 171–89.

90. GARF, f. A-259, op. 1, d. 1186, ll. 338–48.

91. "Zavod domostroieniia," *Zapoliar'e*, 3 August 1960.

92. "Bar'er nado oboiti," *Zapoliar'e,* 4 March 1961. The problems described echo those encountered during the construction of Akademgorodok. Paul R. Josephson, *New Atlantis Revisited: Akademgorodok, the Siberian City of Science* (Princeton: Princeton University Press, 1997), 16–17.

93. B. Orlovskii, "Planirovka novykh mikroraionov Vorkuty," *Arkhitektura SSSR* 6 (1962).

94. RGAE, f. 14, op. 1, d. 2259/30, l. 1.

95. See, e.g., "Timan," a neighborhood begun in 1976 that was intended to house sixteen thousand people. "Mikroraion Timan," *Zapoliar'e*, 23 February 1980.

96. GURK NARK 1, f. R-1307, op. 1, d. 543, l. 58.

97. RGAE, f. 8225, op. 27, d. 497, l. 238.

98. GURK NARK 1, f. R-1307, op. 1, d. 393, l. 58.

99. Donald A. Filtzer, *Soviet Workers and Stalinist Industrialization: The Formation of Modern Soviet Production Relations, 1928–1941* (Armonk, NY: M. E. Sharpe, 1986), 52–53; R. W. Davies, *The Soviet Economy in Turmoil, 1929–1930* (Cambridge: Harvard University Press, 1989), 531; R. W. Davies, *Crisis and Progress in the Soviet Economy, 1931–1933* (London: Macmillan, 1996), 543.

100. The proportion of women in the local population (camp and city included) had risen from approximately 27 percent in 1954 to 42 percent in 1960. Figures calculated from sources for Appendix A, table A.1.2, Appendix B, table B.2, and GURK NARK 1, f. R-1941, op. 1, d. 224, l. 20.

101. In 1958, nearly half of all workers had skipped work at least once. However, by 1965 the rate of absenteeism had fallen to just 15 percent. GURK NARK 1, f. R-1675, op. 1, d. 2281, l. 23; GURK NARK 1, f. R-1675, op. 1, d. 2346, l. 2.

102. GURK NARK 1, f. R-1675, op. 1, d. 1746, l. 6.

103. GURK NARK 1, f. R-1675, op. 1, d. 1747, ll. 81, 83–84.

104. GARF, f. A-259, op. 1, d. 1186, ll. 338–48.

105. V. Griner, *Poslednie dni bab'ego leta* (Syktyvkar: Komi knizhnoe izdatel'stvo, 1975), 6.

106. "Ko vtoromu rozhdeniiu basseina," *Zapoliar'e*, 6 February 1960.

107. "Ugol' zapoliar'ia—metallurgii Urala," *Sovetskaia Rossiia*, 6 August 1959.

108. Viacheslav Davydov, ed. *Vorkutaugol'* (Syktyvkar: OAO Komi Respublikanskaia Tipografiia, 2001), 164.

109. Some high-quality coking coal was even sent abroad, with Italy importing 1.25 million tons of coal from Vorkuta in 1969. RGAE, f. 14, op. 1, d. 2260/2, l 4. Coal from Vorkuta was also shipped to several other foreign countries in the 1980s and early 1990s, including Finland, Sweden, Britain, Denmark, Germany, Spain, Hungary, Czechoslovakia, Romania, and Turkey. Davydov, ed., *Vorkutaugol'*, 164.

110. Mikhail T., interview by author, 31 October 2004.

111. GURK NARK 1, f. R-1941, op. 1, d. 224, l. 20; GURK NARK 1 f. R-1941, op. 1, d. 22, ll. 4–5.

112. V. I. Il'in, *Vlast' i ugol': Shakhterskoe dvizhenie Vorkuty (1989–1998 gody)* (Syktyvkar: Syktyvkarskii gos. universitet, 1998), 269.

113. V. M. Piskov, ed. *Sotsial'noe obespechenie i strakhovanie v SSSR; Sbornik ofitsial'nykh dokumentov* (Moskva: Iuridicheskaia literatura, 1964), 127–40.

114. In the 1980s KVU organized and financed the construction of cooperative apartment buildings in other regions of the country for retiring workers. Il'in, *Vlast' i ugol'*, 193–94.

Chapter 6. From Prisoners to Citizens?

1. Leonid Pavlovich Markizov, *Do i posle 1945* (Syktyvkar: KOGUP, 2003), 145–55. Quotation from 155.

2. GURK NARK 2, f. 2216, op. 14, d.56, l. 27.

3. Nanci Adler, *The Gulag Survivor: Beyond the Soviet System* (New Brunswick, NJ: Transaction Publishers, 2002); Stephen F. Cohen, *The Victims Return* (Exeter, NH: Pub.Works, 2010); Miriam Dobson, *Khrushchev's Cold Summer: Gulag Returnees, Crime, and the Fate of Reform after Stalin* (Ithaca: Cornell University Press, 2009); Marc Elie, "Les politiques à l'égard des libérés du Goulag," *Cahiers du Monde Russe* 47, nos. 1–2 (2006): 327–48; Marc Elie, "Les anciens détenus du Goulag: Libérations massives, réinsertion et réhabilitation dans l'URSS poststalinienne, 1953–1964" (PhD, EHESS, 2007); Marc Elie, "Ce que réhabiliter veut dire," *Vingtième Siècle. Revue d'Histoire*, no. 107 (2010): 101–13; Amir Weiner, "The Empires Pay a Visit: Gulag Returnees, East European Rebellions, and Soviet Frontier Politics," *Journal of Modern History* 78, no. 2 (2006): 333–76.

4. GARF, f. R-9414, op. 1 ch. 2, d. 519, ll. 124–28.

5. J. Arch Getty, Gabor T. Rittersporn, and Viktor N. Zemskov, "Victims of the Soviet Penal System in the Pre-War Years: A First Approach on the Basis of Archival Evidence," *American Historical Review* 98, no. 4 (1993): 1017–49.

6. Golfo Alexopoulos, "Amnesty 1945: The Revolving Door of Stalin's Gulag," *Slavic Review* 64, no. 2 (2005): 274–306.

7. Dobson, *Khrushchev's Cold Summer*, 109.

8. GARF, f. R-9414, op. 1 ch. 2, d. 519, l. 2.

9. *Vedomosti Verkhovnogo Soveta SSSR* no. 17 (4 October 1955): 467–68; GURK NARK 2, f. 2216, op. 6, d. 57, l. 89. This was more than 10 percent of all the prisoners throughout the Gulag who were freed under the amnesty. GARF, f. R-9414, op. 1, d. 323, l. 12.

10. *Vedomosti Verkhovnogo Soveta SSSR* no. 17 (4 October 1955): 472; *Vedomosti Verkhovnogo Soveta SSSR* no. 24 (21 December 1956): 615.

11. *Vedomosti Verkhovnogo Soveta SSSR* no. 24 (6 November 1957): 692–93; N. D. Zakharov and V. P. Malkov, eds., *Sbornik dokumentov po istorii ugolovnogo zakonodatel'stva SSSR i RSFSR, 1953–1991 gg.*, 3 vols. (Kazan': Izd-vo Kazanskogo universiteta, 1992–1995), 1: 26–27.

12. Andrei Artizov and others, eds., *Reabilitatsiia: Kak eto bylo*, 3 vols. (Moscow: "Demokratiia", 2000–2004), 1: 116–17; Adler, *Gulag Survivor*, 86; Elie, "Les anciens détenus du Goulag," chap. 4.

13. E. A. Zaitsev, ed. *Sbornik zakonodatel'nykh i normativnikh aktov o repressiiakh i reabilitatsii zhertv politicheskikh repressii* (Moscow: Izd-vo "Respublika", 1993), 78–80.

14. GARF, f. R-9414, op. 1 ch. 2, d. 513, l. 34.

15. Artizov and others, eds., *Reabilitatsiia*, 2: 29–33.

16. GARF, f. R-9414, op. 1 ch. 2, d. 516, ll. 78, 82, 91, 97.

17. Zakharov and Malkov, eds., *Sbornik dokumentov*, 1: 23. On parole's elimination, see O. V. Khlevniuk, *The History of the Gulag: From Collectivization to the Great Terror* (New Haven: Yale University Press, 2004), 206–7; J. Arch Getty and Oleg V. Naumov, *The Road to Terror: Stalin and the Self-destruction of the Bolsheviks, 1932–1939* (New Haven: Yale University Press, 1999), 549–50.

18. AUIN MIu RF po RK, f. 1, op. 3, d. 7156, ll. 94–95; AUIN MIu RF po RK, f. 1, op. 3, d. 7159, ll. 97–102; GURK NARK 2, f. 1875, op. 1, d. 176, l. 61. In the beginning, cases had to be considered by the Supreme Court of Komi ASSR. By the end of 1954, however, they were being decided locally in Vorkuta.

19. GURK NARK 2, f. 1875, op. 1, d. 176, l. 61; GARF, f. R-9414, op. 1 ch. 2, d. 513, l. 34; GARF, f. R-9414, op. 1 ch. 2, d. 519, l. 125; GARF, f. R-9414, op. 1 ch. 2, d. 517, l. 24; GARF, f. R-9414, op. 1 ch. 2, d. 524, l. 19.

20. GURK NARK 2, f. 1875, op. 1, d. 176, l. 61; GARF, f. R-9414, op. 1 ch. 2, d. 513, l. 34. This was done under the auspices of article 457 of the Criminal-Procedural Code of the RSFSR. *Ugolovno-protsessual'nyi kodeks RSFSR* (Moscow: Gosudarstvennoe izdatel'stvo sovetskoe zakonodatel'stvo, 1934), 103. See also Elie, "Les anciens détenus du Goulag," 73–76.

21. Zakharov and Malkov, eds., *Sbornik dokumentov*, 1: 22; Elie, "Les anciens détenus du Goulag," 67–73.

22. GURK NARK 2, f. 1875, op. 1, d. 176, l. 60; GARF, f. R-9414, op. 1 ch. 2, d. 513, l. 34.

23. GARF, f. R-9414, op. 1 ch. 2, d. 519, l. 2.

24. R. Kh. Gizatulin, *Nas bylo mnogo na chelne: Dokumental'noe povestvovanie* (Moscow: 1993), 7, 120; E. I. Cherneta-Gizatulina, *I zamiraet dusha v razdum'iakh* (Moscow: P-Tsentr, 2000), 17, 23, 76.

25. Oleg Borovskii, *Rentgen strogogo rezhima* (Moscow: Vremia, 2009), 220.

26. Steven A. Barnes, *Death and Redemption: The Gulag and the Shaping of Soviet Society* (Princeton: Princeton University Press, 2011), 237–45.

27. GARF, f. R-9479, op. 1, d. 896, l. 151.

28. Artizov and others, eds., *Reabilitatsiia*, 1: 289.

29. Viktor N. Zemskov, "Massovoe osvobozhenie spetsposelentsev i ssyl'nykh (1954–1960 gg.)," *Sotsiologicheskie issledovaniia* 1 (1991): 20.

30. RGAE, f. 8225, op. 27, d. 506, l. 184.

31. Artizov and others, eds., *Reabilitatsiia*, 1: 216, 259–60, 286–87.

32. GARF, f. R-9414, op. 1 ch. 2, d. 512; GARF, f. R-9414, op. 1 ch. 2, d. 514; GARF, f. R-9414, op. 1 ch. 2, d. 518.

33. For instance, on 1 February 1966 there were 2,737 prisoners organized into three camp points. GURK NARK 1, f. R-1307, op. 1, d. 393, l. 51.

34. Judith Pallot, "Forced Labour for Forestry: The Twentieth Century History of Colonisation and Settlement in the North of Perm' Oblast'." *Europe-Asia Stud-*

ies 54, no. 7 (2002): 1068–69; Judith Pallot, "Russia's Penal Peripheries: Space, Place, and Penalty in Soviet and Post-Soviet Russia," *Transactions of the Institute of British Geographers* 30, no. 1 (2005): 98–112; Judith Pallot, Laura Piacentini, and Dominique Moran, "Patriotic Discourses in Russia's Penal Peripheries: Remembering the Mordovan Gulag," *Europe-Asia Studies* 62, no. 1 (2010): 1–33.

35. GURK NARK 1, f. R-1307, op. 1, d. 393, l. 58.

36. Marc Elie, "Khrushchev's Gulag," in *The Thaw: Soviet Society and Culture in the 1950s and 1960s*, ed. Denis Kozlov and Eleonory Gilburd (Toronto: University of Toronto Press, 2013), 109–42; Jeffrey S. Hardy, "Gulag Tourism: Khrushchev's "Show" Prisons in the Cold War Context, 1954–59," *The Russian Review* 71, no. 1 (2012): 49–78; Jeffrey S. Hardy, "'The Camp Is Not a Resort': The Campaign against Privileges in the Soviet Gulag, 1957–61," *Kritika: Explorations in Russian and Eurasian History* 13, no. 1 (2012): 89–122.

37. One of the most moving descriptions of this feeling was written by Evgeniia Ginzburg. Evgeniia Semenovna Ginzburg, *Within the Whirlwind* (New York: Harcourt Brace Jovanovich, 1981), 173.

38. Aleksandr Klein, *Moi nomer "2P-904": Avtobiograficheskie stikhi i poema* (Syktyvkar: 1992), 60.

39. Ibid.

40. Of the many stories explaining the remarkable power of the shared prisoner experience, one of the most remarkable is Jacques Rossi, "Dva rasskaza," *Volia* 8–9 (2002): 143.

41. Joseph Scholmer, *Vorkuta* (New York: Holt, 1955), chap. 6 ; Barnes, *Death and Redemption*, 185–97.

42. Federico Varese, "The Society of the *vory-v-zakone*, 1930s–1950s," *Cahiers du Monde russe* 39, no. 4 (1998): 515–38.

43. GURK NARK 2, f. 2216, op. 6, d. 63, ll. 37–41; GURK NARK 2, f. 2216, op. 6, d. 62, ll. 10–11; GURK NARK 2, f. 2216, op. 6, d. 54, l. 158.

44. On these news features throughout the USSR, see Dobson, *Khrushchev's Cold Summer*, 44–48.

45. *Zapoliar'e*, 21 October 1956.

46. GURK NARK 2, f. 2216, op. 14, d. 108a, l. 154.

47. VMVTs, f. OF, d. 3094/1–2, l. 336.

48. William Taubman, *Khrushchev: The Man and His Era* (New York: W. W. Norton, 2003), 294–99.

49. Artizov and others, eds., *Reabilitatsiia*, 2: 208–14. Quotation from 213.

50. GURK NARK 2, f. 2216, op. 7, d. 92, l. 43.

51. GURK NARK 2, f. 2216, op. 6, d. 27, ll. 51–55.

52. GURK NARK 2, f. 2216, op. 14, d. 17a, l. 53.

53. GURK NARK 2, f. 2216, op. 6, d. 27, ll. 45–46.

54. GURK NARK 2, f. 1791, op. 1, d. 27, ll. 24–25.

55. GURK NARK 2, f. 2216, op. 14, d. 19a, l. 49; GURK NARK 2, f. 2216, op. 14, d. 19, l. 94; GURK NARK 2, f. 2216, op. 14, d. 17a, l. 56.

56. Weiner, "Empires Pay a Visit," 360–71.

57. GURK NARK 2, f. 2216, d. 92, l. 106.

58. GARF, f. R-8131, op. 32, d. 4851; Weiner, "Empires Pay a Visit," 333–76.

59. GURK NARK 2, f. 2216, op. 14, d. 17a, l. 53.

60. Irina Paert, "Demistifying the Heavens: Women, Religion, and Khrushchev's Anti-religious Campaign, 1954–64," in *Women in the Khrushchev Era*, ed. Melanie Ilic, Susan E. Reid, and Lynne Attwood (New York: Palgrave Macmillan, 2004), 203–21; Elena Zhidkova, "The Antireligious Campaign in Kuibyshev Oblast' during the Thaw," *Russian Studies in History* 50, no. 1 (2011): 3–18.

61. GURK NARK 2, f. 2216, op. 6, d. 27, ll. 48–51. Quotation from 48.

62. "Krivchuk obviniaet," *Zapoliar'e*, 21–22 March 1959.

63. GURK NARK 2, f. 2216, op. 15, d. 13, l. 20.

64. Pavel Negretov, *Vse dorogi vedut na Vorkutu* (Benson, VT: Chalidze Publication, 1985), 142–45.

65. Elie, "Ce que réhabiliter veut dire," 101–13.

66. Adler, *Gulag Survivor*, 28; Elie, "Les anciens détenus du Goulag," 249–50.

67. Artizov and others, eds., *Reabilitatsiia*, 1: 257–59.

68. Ibid., 2: 120.

69. According to Marc Elie, the 1954 commissions rehabilitated only 4 percent of the cases that they reviewed, whereas the 1956 commissions rehabilitated only 6.5 percent. Elie, "Ce que réhabiliter veut dire," 104.

70. Dobson, *Khrushchev's Cold Summer*, 53.

71. Adler, *Gulag Survivor*, chaps. 3, 5; Dobson, *Khrushchev's Cold Summer*, chap. 2.

72. Markizov, *Do i posle 1945*, 155.

73. Aleksandr Klein, *Ulybki nevoli: Nevydumannaia zhizn', ulybki, sud'by, sluchai* (Syktyvkar: Prolog, 1997), 286.

74. Iurii P., interview by author, digital recording, Vorkuta, Russia, 1 June 2003; Galina S., interview by author, digital recording, Vorkuta, Russia, 14 May 2003; Negretov, *Vse dorogi vedut na Vorkutu*.

75. Dobson, *Khrushchev's Cold Summer*, 54.

76. Elie, "Ce que réhabiliter veut dire," 105, 108.

77. Elie, "Les anciens détenus du Goulag," 250.

78. Galina S., interview by author, 14 May 2003.

79. GARF, f. R-9414, op. 1 ch. 2, d. 492.

80. Scholmer, *Vorkuta*, chap. 12.

81. See, e.g., GARF, f. R-9479, op. 1, d. 910, ll. 216–17.

82. GARF, f. R-9479, op. 1, d. 920, l. 313–14.

83. Ironically, the Gorkom explicitly stated that discrimination was not to have a "campaign character" (*kampaneiskii kharakter*). GURK NARK 2, f. 2216, op. 15, d. 18a, l. 71.

84. On the 1950–1951 campaign, see GURK NARK 2, f. 1, op. 4, d. 979, ll. 25–27.

85. GURK NARK 2, f. 2216, op. 14, d. 54, l. 59.

86. Ibid., ll. 59–61.

87. Ibid., ll. 62–63, 101.

88. Ibid., ll. 122–26.

89. GURK NARK 2, f. 2216, op. 14, d. 65, ll. 4–6.

90. GURK NARK 2, f. 2216, op. 15, d. 17, ll. 107–8.

91. GURK NARK 2, f. 2216, op. 15, d. 18a, ll. 68–71.
92. GURK NARK 1, f. R-1675, op. 1, d. 1746, l. 95.
93. GURK NARK 1, f. R-1675, op. 1, d. 1745, l. 183.
94. GURK NARK 1, f. R-1688, op. 1, d. 274, ll. 16–19.
95. GURK NARK 2, f. 2216, op. 14, d. 68, ll. 97–98.
96. GURK NARK 1, f. R-1675, op. 1, d. 1711, ll. 13–14.
97. Mikhail T., interview by author, digital recording, Syktyvkar, Russia, 31 October 2004.
98. V. Frid, *58 1/2: Zapiski lagernogo pridurka* (Moscow: Izd. dom Rusanova, 1996), 363, 368–70. Quotation from 363.
99. Adler, *Gulag Survivor*, 109.
100. Orlando Figes, *The Whisperers: Private Life in Stalin's Russia* (New York: Metropolitan Books, 2007), 566.
101. Galina S., interview by author, 14 May 2003.
102. Negretov, *Vse dorogi vedut na Vorkutu*, 37–39. Quotation from 37.
103. Ibid., 140–41.
104. GURK NARK 1, f. R-1675, op. 1, d. 1707, l. 91. Similar allegations were made that former prisoners only hired other former prisoners of their nationality. GURK NARK 2, f. 2216, op. 14, d. 17a, l. 52.
105. GURK NARK 2, f. 2216, op. 14, d. 54, l. 110.
106. GURK NARK 2, f. 70, op. 3, d. 6, l. 28.
107. RGAE, f. 8225, op. 27, d. 490, l. 104.
108. RGAE, f. 8225, op. 27, d. 506, ll. 184–88; RGAE, f. 8225, op. 27, d. 509, ll. 37–39; RGAE, f. 8225, op. 27, d. 504, l.14.
109. See, e.g., Markizov, *Do i posle 1945*, 155.
110. Elie, "Ce que réhabiliter veut dire," 106.
111. Al'bert Efimovich Bernshtein, *Na rubezhe vekov* (Syktyvkar: Miian Kyv, 2002), 115–17.
112. GURK NARK 1, f. R-1688, op. 1, d. 273, ll. 226–27.
113. GURK NARK 1, f. R-1941, op. 1, d. 128, l. 11.
114. GURK NARK 1, f. R-1675, op. 1, d. 2281, l. 21.
115. Ibid., ll. 14–15.
116. Iurii P., interview by author, 1 June 2003.
117. *Zapoliar'e*, 7 December 1960.
118. Galina S., interview by author, 14 May 2003.
119. Pavel Negretov, "How Vorkuta Began," *Soviet Studies* 29, no. 4 (1977): 565–75; Negretov, *Vse dorogi vedut na Vorkutu*.
120. Adler, *Gulag Survivor*, 42, 109. Miriam Dobson, on the other hand, concludes, "Of the millions who came back from the camps, many no doubt *did* return home and find work, but stories of successful reintegration leave little trace in the archives." Dobson, *Khrushchev's Cold Summer*, 112.
121. Negretov, *Vse dorogi vedut na Vorkutu*, 13–14. An example of one of Negretov's published letters can be found in "Pora navesti most," *Zapoliar'e*, 1 July 1956.
122. V. I. Il'in, *Vlast' i ugol': Shakhterskoe dvizhenie Vorkuty (1989–1998 gody)* (Syktyvkar: Syktyvkarskii gos. universitet, 1998), 269.

EPILOGUE

1. V. Griner, *Poslednie dni bab'ego leta* (Syktyvkar: Komi knizhnoe izdatel'stvo, 1975), 150–51.

2. GURK NARK 2, f. 2216, op. 15, d. 44, ll. 35–56.

3. GARF, f. R-5446, op. 1, d. 789, ll. 119–31.

4. Griner, *Poslednie dni bab'ego leta*, 8.

5. Appendix C, table C.1.

6. Appendix B, table B.1; "1989 USSR population census" (Minneapolis, MN: East View Publications, 1996).

7. "Mikroraion Timan," *Zapoliar'e*, 23 Februrary 1980.

8. Archie Brown, *Seven Years That Changed the World: Perestroika in Perspective* (New York: Oxford University Press, 2007), 5, 11–17. Quotation from 5.

9. V. I. Il'in, *Vlast' i ugol': Shakhterskoe dvizhenie Vorkuty (1989–1998 gody)* (Syktyvkar: Syktyvkarskii gos. universitet, 1998), 15–30. Il'in described this as "miner's liberalism," a desire for both greater autonomy for the mines and increased state subsidies for miners (153).

10. Ibid., 29, 33. The miners and their leaders apparently concluded that the strike was an effective means of accomplishing economic and political goals. Thus, further strikes would follow periodically in the 1990s and early twenty-first century.

11. Ibid., 112–24.

12. Ibid., chap. 6.

13. *Statisticheskii ezhegodnik Respubliki Komi* (Syktyvkar: Goskomstat Respubliki Komi, 2011), 290.

14. Il'in, *Vlast' i ugol'*, 189–90.

15. Igor Artemiev and Michael Haney, "The Privatization of the Russian Coal Industry: Policies and Processes in the Transformation of a Major Industry," (2002), http://elibrary.worldbank.org/content/workingpaper/10.1596/1813-9450-2820.

16. British economist Paul Hare, who was sent to Vorkuta by the World Bank in 1993, predicted that mining-related employment in Vorkuta would fall by half, and perhaps as much as three-quarters, by the end of the 1990s. Paul G. Hare, "Coal in Vorkuta: Subsidies and the Social Safety Net," in *Privatization, Enterprise Development, and Economic Reform: Experiences of Developing and Transitional Economies*, ed. Paul Cook, C. H. Kirkpatrick, and F. I. Nixson (Northampton, MA: Edward Elgar Publishers, 1998), 291–93.

17. Il'in, *Vlast' i ugol'*, 184, 212.

18. Ibid., 148.

19. Ibid., 144–47.

20. Ibid., 197–201.

21. On the development of the Russian Mafia, see Federico Varese, *The Russian Mafia: Private Protection in a New Market Economy* (New York: Oxford University Press, 2001); Vadim Volkov, *Violent Entrepreneurs: The Use of Force in the Making of Russian Capitalism* (Ithaca: Cornell University Press, 2002).

22. Il'in, *Vlast' i ugol'*, 118, 124.

23. *Statisticheskii ezhegodnik Respubliki Komi*, 205.

24. Hilary Pilkington, "No Longer 'On Parade': Style and the Performance of Skinhead in the Russian Far North," *Russian Review* 69, no. 2 (2010): 187–209.

25. Hilary Pilkington, "Beyond 'Peer Pressure': Rethinking Drug Use and 'Youth Culture'," *International Journal of Drug Policy* 18, no. 3 (2007): 213–24.

26. Il'in, *Vlast' i ugol'*, 213.

27. *Statisticheskii ezhegodnik Respubliki Komi*, 45.

28. "Navechno zamorozhennye," *Izvestiia*, 27 May 1998.

29. Such comments betrayed an astonishing lack of sensitivity toward the struggles of Vorkuta's citizenry (and in particular its ex-prisoner population) in difficult economic times. Further, the article failed to even pose the question of why, given its ugliness and troubled past, Vorkuta became a place where hundreds of thousands of people, ex-prisoners among them, had chosen to settle over the previous five decades. Anne Applebaum, "The Great Error," *The Spectator*, 28 July 2001, 18–19.

30. As of March 2012 Mordashov was reported to be worth $15.3 billion, making him the forty-fifth richest person in the world. Forbes, "Alexei Mordashov," http://www.forbes.com/profile/alexei-mordashov/ (accessed 13 March 2012).

31. Severstal, "Vorkutaugol," http://www.severstal.com/eng/businesses/resources/coal_mining/vorkutaugol/ (accessed 13 March 2012).

32. Severstal, "Severstal' vygrala konkurs na pravo osvoeniia ugol'nogo uchastka no 1 Usinskogo mestorozhdeniia v Komi," http://vorkutaugol.severstal.com/rus/press_center/news/document1466.phtml (accessed 13 March 2012).

33. ITAR-TASS, "Vorkutaugol to launch new coalmine with 4 mln t capacity in 2020," www.lexisnexis.com/hottopics/lnacademic (accessed 23 April 2012).

34. Severstal, "Vorkutaugol' v 2011 godu napravila na sotsial'nye proekty v regione prisutstviia svyshe 40 millionov rublei," http://vorkutaugol.severstal.com/rus/press_center/news/document1503.phtml (accessed 12 March 2012).

35. *Statisticheskii ezhegodnik Respubliki Komi*, 45.

36. Vorkutaugol, "O kompanii," http://www.vorkutaugol.ru/rus/about/index.phtml (accessed 12 March 2012).

37. GURK NARK 1, f. R-1675, op. 1, d. 2281, l. 21.

38. "Implementation Completion and Results Report (IBRD-46110) on a Loan in the Amount of US$80 Million to the Russian Federation for a Northern Restructuring Project" (World Bank, 2010), 12, ICR1343.

39. *Statisticheskii ezhegodnik Respubliki Komi*, 99.

40. Ibid., 205.

41. Ibid., 115.

42. Komiinform, "Poselek Komsomol'skii 'pereedet' v Vorgashor," http://www.komiinform.ru/news/81654/ (accessed 13 March 2012).

43. On the so-called *vakhtoviki* and their strategies and coping methods, see Gertrude Eilmsteiner-Saxinger, "Commuting to the Siberian Far North—When Extreme Becomes Normality," *TRANS-Internet-Zeitschrift für Kulturwissenschaften*, no. 17 (2010), http://www.inst.at/trans/17Nr/4–5/4–5_eilmsteiner-saxinger.htm (accessed 22 February 2012).

44. Andrei Sakharov Museum, "Pamiatnik zhertvam politicheskikh repressii," http://www.sakharov-center.ru/asfcd/pam/pam_carddc45.html?id=276 (accessed 4 May 2012).

45. For example, memorial volumes appeared in 1959, 1964, and 1984, marking the twenty-fifth, thirtieth, and fiftieth anniversaries of the extraction of coal from Vorkuta's first mine. B. L. Afanas'ev, ed. *Pechorskii ugol'nyi bassein* (Leningrad:

Lenizdat, 1959); N. Ushpik, *Vorkuta* (Syktyvkar: Komi knizhnoe izd-vo, 1964); V. D. Zakharov, ed. *Ugol'naia sokrovishchnitsa severa: Sbornik dokumentov i materialov* (Syktyvkar: Komi kn. izd-vo, 1984).

46. See, e.g., V. Griner, *Vyshe poliarnogo kruga: Povest', ocherki* (Syktyvkar: Komi knizhnoe izd-vo, 1980), 100–115.

47. V. M. Zubok, *Zhivago's Children: The Last Russian Intelligentsia* (Cambridge: Belknap Press of Harvard University Press, 2009), 342–43.

48. See, e.g., "Zharkoe leto 53-ogo," *Zapoliar'e*, 9 July 1989; "Naideno mesto kashketinskikh rasstrelov," *Zapoliar'e*, 15 September 1995.

49. On the history of the Memorial movement, see Nanci Adler, *Victims of Soviet Terror: The Story of the Memorial Movement* (Westport, CT: Praeger, 1993); Kathleen E. Smith, *Remembering Stalin's Victims: Popular Memory and the End of the USSR* (Ithaca: Cornell University Press, 1996).

50. Albert Leong, *Centaur: The Life and Art of Ernst Neizvestny* (Lanham: Rowman & Littlefield, 2002), 218–24.

51. Andrei Sakharov Museum, "Pamiatnik repressirovannym grazhdanam Pol'shi i drugikh stran," http://www.sakharov-center.ru/asfcd/pam/pam_card1ff6.html?id=281 (accessed 24 April 2012); Andrei Sakharov Museum, "Pamiatnyi krest zhertvam kommunisticheskogo terrora," http://www.sakharov-center.ru/asfcd/pam/pam_card12dd.html?id=280 (accessed 24 April 2012); Andrei Sakharov Museum, "Pamiatnyi krest zhertvam politicheskikh repressii," http://www.sakharov-center.ru/asfcd/pam/pam_cardb567.html?id=279 (accessed 24 April 2012); Andrei Sakharov Museum, "Chasovnia pamiati Litovskikh zakliuchennykh, pogibshikh pri podavlenii vosstaniia 1 avgusta 1953 g.," http://www.sakharov-center.ru/asfcd/pam/pam_card4bb2.html?id=277 (accessed 24 April 2012); Andrei Sakharov Museum, "Pamiatnik zhertvam voiny i politicheskikh repressii," http://www.sakharov-center.ru/asfcd/pam/pam_cardd5b4–2.html?id=278 (accessed 24 April 2012).

52. Steven Lee Myers, "Above the Arctic Circle, a Gulag Nightmare for Tourists?" *New York Times*, 6 June 2005. Several years later, Shpektor remained publicly committed to the idea. Prava cheloveka v Rossii, "V Komi razrabotaiut kontseptsiiu memorial'nogo kompleksa GULAG," http://www.hro.org/node/13388 (accessed 7 May 2012).

53. Biznes-novosti Respubliki Komi, "V Den' VDV v Vorkute otkryli pamiatnik voinam-internationalistam," http://www.bnkomi.ru/data/news/5422 (accessed 24 April 2012).

54. Dan Healey has also emphasized the difficulty of coming to terms with the coexistence of these first two narratives in former Gulag towns. Den Khili [Dan Healey], "Nasledie Gulaga: Prinuditel'nyi trud sovetskoi epokhi kak vnutrenniaia kolonizatsiia," in *Tam, vnutri: Praktiki vnutrennei kolonizatsii v kul'turnoi istorii Rossii*, ed. Aleksandr Etkind, Dirk Uffelmann, and Il'ia Kukulin (Moscow: Novoe literaturnoe obozrenie, 2012), 684–728.

55. Applebaum, "Great Error," 18–19.

Index